AF487282

THE DAYS ARE LONG BUT THE YEARS ARE SHORTER

THE DAYS ARE LONG BUT THE YEARS ARE SHORTER

ANGEL BALESTIER

atmosphere press

Published by Atmosphere Press

Cover design by Kevin Stone

Atmospherepress.com

In family life, love is the oil that eases friction, the cement that binds closer together, and the music that brings harmony.

—Friedrich Nietzsche

This book is dedicated in loving memory to:
Mrs. Evelyn "Cookie" Richardson Balestier

TABLE OF CONTENTS

MY MUSIC CAREER STARTS

I got up early on one of the coldest Monday mornings in Red Hook, Brooklyn. I needed a job. I had decided that hanging with the guys wasn't cutting it; there was no future in it, at least not for me. I could become a wise guy, but the thought of it wasn't something I wanted. I had already been involved in gangs, and that was not as glamorous as is portrayed in the movies, so I was here walking up 9th Street towards the train station, where I took the D train to Chambers Street Station. When I arrived, I went up the stairs and walked down West Broadway to Warren Street. It was very windy and cold, and I was near the waterfront as I walked into the first employment office. I just stared at all the listings, and I picked one: a shipping clerk position for $75 a week. The clerk set up an interview for me the very next day at National Recording Studios. They were located in mid-town Manhattan on the west side at 730 Fifth Avenue across from Tiffany's, the famous Jewelry store between 56th and 57th Streets.

The very next morning, I was dressed in a suit and tie. It was really cold as I walked down to the subway station. I was shaking, but it wasn't only from the cold; I was a nervous wreck. I had to land this job at any cost. I arrived at the 48th Street stop at Rockefeller Center in Manhattan at 8:00 a.m.

I had arrived very early, so I walked to the Automat on 57th Street and had some coffee. Looking at my watch, I did not want to be late, and with the cold wind blowing in my face, I walked leisurely up 57th Street to 5th Avenue. I made it alright and walked into the building's warm lobby, which felt good, but it was still early, 9:30 a.m. It was a busy lobby; I noticed elevator operators and a big concession stand that sold newspapers, magazines, candy, and coffee; everything possible was available, and to my amazement, as I looked straight ahead, there sat Ed Sullivan, who was getting his shoes shined, so I decided to get my shoes shined too – why not? I needed to look good and kill some time. I figured this was a good spot, so there we sat on a two-chair shoe shine stand in the lobby of this building parlor, getting our shoes cleaned from all the rain stains.

Meanwhile, Ed Sullivan was talking to the elevator operator's captain, so I waited for their conversation to end, and I asked the captain if he knew where National Recording was located. He said it was on the sixth floor. I was blown away when Ed Sullivan pointed and said, "You take that car over there." So as soon as my shoeshine was finished, I got up, thanked him, and off I went. I got in the elevator and gave the operator my floor number. When we reached the sixth floor, the doors opened, and I made a slight left, and there it was to my right. I walked through the double doors and introduced myself to the receptionist. She was very attractive and pleasant. She asked me to wait just a few minutes.

I had arrived early, and I was very nervous all the time, thinking, "What if they don't like me?" A few minutes passed, and a young, tall, dark-haired guy with an Israeli accent greeted me and invited me inside; his name was Akiba Katz. He proceeded to show me around—a nice guy, well-dressed in a black blazer and thin tie. I was glad I had put on a tie that morning.

We talked for some time, and he said he was looking for

someone to take over his position. What a break! He asked where I lived, and I said Red Hook, Brooklyn. He mentioned he was also from Brooklyn; I think he said Canarsie. My interview went better than I expected, and I was hired right then and there as the new shipping clerk that very same day.

Here I was in this very small room that faced the main lobby, studios A and B in front of me, and master control to my right—just about every room accessible within minutes. The studios were owned by Carl Lustic, Hal Lustic, and Irv Kauffman. The Lustic brothers had their father, Max Lustic, working for them. Max knew where everything was, but you had to be careful; he liked to go under the control room at their Brian Park Studio on 42nd Street, where they stored their tapes. If you didn't wear a hard hat, you could get cut from spikes that came through the concrete. If Max got hurt, Hal would give you a hard time, maybe even fire you.

I started to learn a great deal from my immediate supervisor, Akiba Katz. Little did I know, but he was on his way to becoming a full-fledged recording sound engineer. He began by showing me around the main office—who to talk to and where to get postage and order supplies. Akiba introduced me to their traffic manager, Susan Plainer; Marie Del Santie, their bookkeeper; and their engineers: Jack Shats, Tom Shee, Mack Anderson, Freddie Weinberg, Dick Mack, Dave Sanders, Arthur Carlton, Bob Marton, Larry Faine, and Joe Jorgensen, along with many other employees. He was great, and I found him informative. He showed me how to set up the different rooms, which was not as complex as today.

They had seven rooms, and they, for the most part, were all equipped for voice-over work, except for Studio A, or their larger room called Brian Park on 42nd Street. It was located on the second floor of the Woolworth Building, where the majority of large orchestras were recorded with live musicians. I was in a trance and loved every minute of it. I was amazed; I had never seen anything like this before. I was hooked; there was no way I would lose this job.

Time passed quickly; a few weeks later, I was sent to Brian Park. We were going to be doing a commercial with "Elsie the Cow" for Nestle. I felt sorry for the cow they brought to the studio; she was slipping all over the place because of the polished tiles in the lobby. It was a real cow that they brought down from a farm in upstate New York. National Studios did lots of Commercials; it was their staple, but there were a few music sessions now and then.

This was the very first time I attended a session with none other than Sammy Davis Jr. I was excited; he was going to be singing "Mack the Knife" for the "Three Penny Opera." I was in a trance; I had seen some of his movies, and I knew at the time that he was appearing on Broadway doing Golden Boy. And here I was, face to face with him—the one and only Sammy Davis, Jr. I was blown away. Then, I noticed Elizabeth Taylor and a few other guests arriving. It was a party; they were serving champagne, just having a great time. I wondered; is this the way it is?

I'd never been near anything like this. Sammy Davis was very friendly when he greeted me. I will never forget this day. The band continued rehearsing for a while and then gave Tom Shee the signal that they were ready for a take. I had no idea what that meant; it was all new and strange to me, but when the conductor counted it off, Sammy came in singing, "Oh, the Shark has pretty Teeth, Dear." Wow, I knew I wasn't leaving. I was hooked for life. The term "take" was ingrained in my head. These were really good times for me, and I felt that, for once in my life, I had gotten into something good.

During the day at the studios at 730 Fifth Avenue, I would be in the hall, and I would hear a singer doing vocal overdubs. I was fascinated hearing them singing, and I knew that this was what I wanted to do: be involved in music. Time passed, and I learned very quickly what was required in all the rooms, never missing a cue. One day I was in the hall, and there was a group singing in studio C. Every time they came to the solo spot in the tune when the singer stepped up to the mike to do his part in Italian, he would just break up laughing. This is great I thought, what a treat. I wasn't aware that I had spent too much time in the hall and that Hal Lustic had been looking for me; when he found me, we got into an argument, and he fired me. I was heartbroken, and I thought to myself, "How could I be so stupid?" I didn't say a word to anyone at all, but the next day, when I didn't show up and Max found out what happened, he went straight to Hal and made him hire me back. Max was the most honest and lovable guy you ever set your eyes on; he had a heart of gold. The following day when I showed up, I explained to Max what had happened. I told him how grateful I was and thanked him for sticking up for me. Max, to me, was a saint.

Rich Mays, one of the house engineers, knew anytime he needed something, all he had to do was come to the shipping room; we had his back. There were times when he'd come and say, "Hey, I'm doing a radio spot, I need some football players hitting pads, off we'd go into the studio. This was only because the sound effects guy was not available. There were two in town that carried a lot of items in small shopping carts, and they mostly did all the effects in town but sometimes a situation would come up where they were unavailable.

National Studios B Thru G on Fifth Avenue was always very busy with very popular announcers. The studio music was normally recorded and mixed either in Studio A or at their larger facility, Bryant Park. Once mixed, you would take your music master quarter-inch mono tape and record your announcer live to another quarter-inch mono machine for your final master. Sometimes, it was straight to a quarter-inch mono in most cases, like for Bayer Aspirin or Pall Mall cigarette commercials, since there was no music. I found that this was a great place to see movie stars. I remember the likes of Joseph Cotton, who was doing a voice-over for Buffering. It was all different for me, a kid from the streets of Brooklyn, but I was sucking it all in and enjoying every moment possible. In the mornings, my duties were very easy and not complicated at all. I would clean the counters in the rooms, load the two Ampex quarter-inch machines (thread them with tape) with a 2500' pancake roll of 3M – 331 low noise tape, sharpen pencils, and provide writing pads with our logo, set up a Neumann U47 microphone and music stand with a light in case they wanted the lights off, two clean ashtrays (in those days everybody smoked) depending on the product, that's what you did, you ate, drank or smoked whatever product we were working on to keep the clients happy.

We had our master control room, which had three lathes, and that's where we made acetate 12-inch disc masters (also known as transcriptions disc) of all of Macy's, Saks Fifth Avenue, and Orbach's department store radio commercials for all their Thursday sales. We had messengers that delivered the transcriptions to the radio stations, especially all the ones in the surrounding area of Rockefeller Center. Whenever we had a large duplication order of radio spots, we would send them out on 5-inch plastic reels with label copy. We had a process that worked well and would always be done during the evening hours when we would pull all the mono machines from all the rooms. We would line them up in front of our master control room and assemble the master tape, which was recorded at a lower speed of 7.5 ips. We would then play it back tails (backward) on our playback machine at 15 ips and also set our recorder at 15 ips with our 5-inch plastic reel as our take-up reel, making sure that the number 2 stamped on the reels was facing up. We would then press play and record on the machines. When we finished recording, we'd cut the tape and reload another plastic reel. We turned the recorded plastic reel over, showing the number 1, and it was now ready to be spot-checked, which was done randomly. Now our next step was to put a strip of red tape on it, indicating it was headed out (forward). Now you had your 7-1/2 ips radio spot ready to go in a 5-inch box labeled with the agency's logo, the title of the spot or spots, and their lengths.

All envelopes were carefully packed and separated per region, each one ready for the Post office or the American Express truck or hand-delivered by messenger. I worked hard and in less than a year, maybe not even six months, I filled the position of shipping clerk full-time. I became in charge of their department thanks to the help and training of Akiba Katz, who was very talented and well-liked by everyone at National. The fact that he was a Yeshiva Student was a plus, and Irv Kauffman liked him a lot, so it was obvious he would soon become an engineer, and in time, he did become a sound engineer with a great following. National Studios was a great place to work; we did commercials with six studios booked all day long, normally from 9 a.m. to 6 p.m.

The money was really good. I learned to thread a 35mm projector in the room where they did most of their voiceovers straight to film. For me, it was a great learning experience, and I was taking advantage of it as much as possible. I just fell into this, and I realized it was a great opportunity; there was no stopping me. If anything was offered and I was available, I was there no matter what time, night or day. I was the biggest sponge around; you couldn't stop me.

We did a lot of work for "Westinghouse" at that time; they were doing special packages based on the Vietnam War, priceless items that were like what "National Geographic" is today, and that provided us with a great deal of work. I was doing very well at National Studios, and I got along with everyone. I had also met Larry Fain, a young Cuban who was also one of the engineers at National. He was aware that I was looking for a place to live, so he asked me if I wanted to share an apartment. He had a girlfriend in Brooklyn and was not there most of the time. I immediately took him up on the offer. It was a residential hotel, "The Bryant Hotel," which was located on

West 57th Street in Manhattan. This was going to work for me as I didn't have to depend on the subway; it was within walking distance, and it was adjacent to the Ed Sullivan Theater, where years later, The David Letterman Show would eventually do their taping. It was furnished, and we had a hot plate. There were Chinese and Spanish restaurants downstairs, which was very good on cold nights; you could always hang out at the bar.

The Carnegie Deli, great for anything quick, was within walking distance. Right down the street, there was Victor, the Cuban restaurant, not to mention the famous Automat "Horn & Hardart," which was located on 6th Ave (Avenue of The Americas) and 57th Street. I had a lot of friends who worked at these places, so as you can imagine, my expenses were very low. I had a really good job, and we would work as much overtime as they would offer. The surroundings at National were very corporate. You were required to wear a coat and tie at all times, and the only time when you were allowed not to wear them would be in the evenings when there were no clients present.

When both Akiba and I moved up in the ranks, I saw an opportunity open up for me to help a very dear friend, and I took advantage of it. My friend, Manny Figueroa, and his wife, Anna, were now living in my old neighborhood on the top floor next to a funeral home in Williamsburg, Brooklyn. I loved this couple, and I felt I could help them out. We went back quite a way. Manny was doing time in Leavenworth for going AWOL from the army. He was one of many hundreds who protested the war and did not want to go to Vietnam and possibly die; they had a child on the way. While he was in prison, Anna was living in the rear of my building at 18 Stagg Street, in a small dingy, dark apartment.

Money was very tight in those days and things were very rough for everyone. When she needed my help, I would not hesitate to assist her. I would often drive her to the commissary to buy groceries. They were both my very dear friends and had always been there for me. When we first met, we were just punk kids in the Red Hook projects, hanging out in the streets, and, in those days, Anna would walk home from the subway down the middle of the projects, but mostly Manny would throw snowballs at her. I had met Manny a few years earlier; a tall, husky, muscular guy who hung around with a black guy by the name of Godfrey. They would always stay near Centre Mall in front of the buildings where they lived. Manny was always well-dressed, wearing a fedora hat and carrying his Wolensak tape machine, playing all the Latin all-stars or the Alan Freed shows he would tape every evening.

We lived down the street and they were notorious for launching these big snowballs at you as you passed by. I, like everyone else, found Manny very intimidating, but as we started to hang out, we became the best of friends and had nothing but great times together. We were always playing pranks on everyone in Red Hook. We had no money, and the majority of us had no fathers at home; some of us were under the sole authority of a stepfather who, for the most part, had no interest in us. We were mischievous kids, to say the least, who would later find different paths in life. Some of us just drifted apart; I have no idea what happened to Benny, Godfrey, or Raul. I hope and pray that they found peace and comfort wherever they may be, for they, at the time, were dear friends.

Manny had been pardoned by President Kennedy for going AWOL; he was now out and looking for work, which wasn't easy. I found out about it and finally was able to recruit him. I felt really good because he was now working with me at National Recording.

I would run into Ed Sullivan all the time, and I would always comment on the artist who appeared on his show on Sunday; he would say, "Glad you enjoyed it." Ed Sullivan, as I remember, always walked Fifth Avenue in a very cheerful mood; he would always wave at you and say hi! New York

City was a great place in those days; people were friendlier, and you would see Fifth Avenue dotted with Schrafft's delivery guys all dressed in their white outfits, with their coffee carts heading to different buildings with all their deliveries. Celebrities shopped at all the great stores; it was great. You could walk from 60th Street passed Saint Patrick's Cathedral and the skating ring on Rockefeller Center. It was wonderful, down to 42nd Street; eighteen blocks and you wouldn't feel it at all.

During the holidays, you were able to find anything you wanted during your walk. I had finally become adjusted to mid-town, which I thought I would never be able to do; but this part of the city had changed me. I was scared of the thought of socializing or being around other people; time changes people and I started dating and going out at night and weekends with friends. While I was working at National, I met a Japanese guy by the name of Peter, who showed me a lot of things I found interesting.

The next thing I know I'm reading Siddhartha and lots of Asian things. Peter and I became really good friends. Whenever possible, we would get together and just roam the town, which kept me from hanging out in Brooklyn for some time. We just went to every place together. I was introduced to Sushi and many other Japanese things that I'd heard about but had not yet experienced. Peter was a great guy to know; he was very influential and knew a lot of people, as well as many other things. He was educated at Columbia University. His family had a lot of money, but he enjoyed hanging out with guys from the street. I guess that's why he chose me from a party I attended on Avenue E, where we all got stoned one day. He called me because he wanted me to meet someone interested in me. I questioned him like no tomorrow. "Who is it?" But he wouldn't tell me. I was very surprised and nervous at first. I didn't know who he was talking about or what I was getting into, but eventually, I did give in. He arranged a dinner meeting at Toots Shor's Restaurant in Manhattan; a very beautiful and expensive restaurant, but he was always very generous, so money was not an issue.

Her name was Tangy Yamamoto, and she was from Osaka, Japan. I had no idea this was where he was going. Peter was always full of surprises; what a beauty. She had long black hair, stood about five feet tall, was very beautiful, and spoke perfect English. She did not like to dance, which was another attraction as far as I was concerned, since I wasn't a great dancer myself and never cared for it. We hit it off right away and that whole summer we went out just about every day. My life was changing for the better. We went out to dinner just about every other night, so I was enjoying different types of cuisines. We became regular customers at the Benihana restaurant, which was on 56th Street. I was pleased because National Studios was just up the street on Fifth Avenue and had a side door on 56th Street, which made it very convenient for us. I do think of her often and wish it had turned out a lot better. I considered Tangy another big loss in my life, but I was obsessed with becoming a sound engineer in the music industry, and here was my chance. I had to go for it. I loved her, but my interest was in music.

I had nothing to offer her. My sole devotion was aimed toward an industry that I dearly loved, and I would pursue everything possible that I could. There was no stopping me. I decided one day, while I was working at National's Brian Park Studio, to take time out as I had promised and booked and paid for her flight to Japan. I have never heard from her ever again. I was saddened by the breakup, but that's life. I wished, and often have, that it had turned out differently, and as for my dear friend Peter, the last time I saw him was in 1965. I didn't ask any questions, and he didn't either, and I have not seen or heard from him since. The music business kept me busy; I was enjoying the process of recording, and all the different people I was meeting. I was learning an awful lot, and my career was growing.

I was finally making something of my life, and the money was good. I stayed away from the hustling crowd. Time passed and I stayed pretty much to myself, absorbing as much as I could. There was a lot I wanted to learn, and I wasn't going to sit back and not put any time into it. I became a workaholic. One morning, Jack Shatts, one of the staff engineers at National, said to me, "I'd like to talk to you when you have a minute."

I said, "Once I finish my work here, I have a few other things I have to deal with; but I'll be there soon."

When I was finished, I went to see him, and he said, "Listen, Angel, yesterday when you were setting up the band for the Grammys at Bryant Park..." That's all I heard. I asked Jack what I had done wrong?

Jack said, "No, wait a minute, it's not bad news. Phil Ramone saw you; he would like you to call him when you have a chance. He wants to meet you."

I asked Jack who Phil Ramone was, and he told me that Phil was a very nice and influential man in the music industry and that he was the owner of a studio on West 48th Street called A&R Recording. "I think it would be worth your time to speak with him," and he handed me Phil Ramone's business card.

I didn't think much about it or what it involved. I had no idea who Phil Ramone was or why he wanted to talk to me. The next day, when I called Phil and introduced myself, he invited me to meet him at his studio for an interview.

I decided to take the day off so, bright and early the very next morning, I went to see him. I was very nervous about the whole thing and, nonetheless, at the same time more curious than anything. I never really asked Jack anything about this and I should've, but here I was, very excited. This was my second encounter with someone setting up an appointment to see me.

I arrived at my subway stop on 50th Street, got off, and

went upstairs. As I approached the corner on West 48th Street and Avenue of the Americas on this bright and chilly morning, I noticed that there was a "Chuck Full of Nuts" on the corner. Then I saw it, Jim & Andy's, the musician's hangout that everyone always talked about; the place was a walk down. I had never seen it or been inside. It was closed as it was too early, but in a few hours, they would open and would be serving lunch. I could see it was a small bar and grill. I had never felt this way before, and I wondered what was happening. I felt so at ease but at the same time, I was very nervous as I approached 112 West 48th Street. I could feel a sigh of relief, and right away I wondered what it would be like to work here. There was an aura about this place that was kitty-corner to Radio City. I just felt at home, it was a feeling that still to this day I find very hard to describe.

I was clueless, but at the same time, for some reason, I knew that this would be where music could become my world. I was excited and nervous at the same time; I had butterflies in my stomach. I pressed the elevator buzzer and a tall black gentleman in blue coveralls opened the door. He was holding a bible; it was as if God had led me here. I asked him where I could find Phil Ramone and he asked me to get in the elevator and he would show me. He took me up to the second floor. The elevator door opened, and I saw an open door in front of me and to my right. As I looked through the open sliding glass counter, a tall blonde and a brunette were talking to a tall gentleman in a white shirt and red tie who was holding a cigarette holder in his right hand. I introduced myself to them and I was escorted by the tall blonde into a private office with a large conference table I noticed several cases of Dewar's White Label Scotch lying on the floor.

I recognized Phil Ramone right away, and I introduced myself. I was very nervous. I couldn't stop from shaking and Phil said to relax. He introduced me to Art Ward, who extended his hand. The guy in the white shirt, Norman Jensen,

Don Frye, the blonde, Janet, and Roberta, the brunette. I was still very nervous about the whole thing, but they were at ease and very well-dressed. These guys were all in suits and ties, including Phil Ramone. We talked for quite a while about my background and what they expected from their personnel, and the studio in general, and it finally hit me; yes, there's a job offer here.

Norman Jensen said they had two studios on the 4th floor, studios A and B, a small mastering room, and the mix-down room here on the second floor. He decided to show me around, which took about an hour; he was very thorough. We later returned to the second floor, and all this time, Norman had his cigarette holder in his right hand and was pleasant at all times. He asked what my duties were at National Recording, so I described what a normal day was like there, and what I did, but I gathered he already knew from Jack. We talked for a while and after answering a few questions with everyone else still present, Phil Ramone asked me if I would be willing to come to work at A & R Recording. I was blown away, and needless to say surprised. It was that cut and dry; how could I not say yes? My eyes were red, but I was ready. I accepted their offer, and we all shook hands. This was 1962 and I would become an A&R Recording employee.

Phil walked me out and I rang the bell for the elevator. We stood there talking and, as the door opened, I turned around and asked him, "By the way, we didn't discuss money. How much does the job pay?"

Phil replied, "Whatever you're getting, we'll double." Over time I would be making double, what a change! That was really good money.

Going down in the elevator, my eyes were all red. I was very excited, and the elevator operator said, "Welcome aboard kid."

I answered, "Are you here all the time?"

"All the time," he answered.

I asked him what they were like to work for, and he replied, "They are good people. They'll treat you well. There's a lot of good music made here, you'll like it."

I had never been so excited in my whole life. "I was moving up in the world," I thought. Wow! What a break. I would be making more money, and I would be learning an awful lot of new things and meeting new people. The elevator was operated by this towering, tall black man, the Rev: Bob Bleilock. He was a real preacher.

I went back to work at National Studios the next day. I could not thank Jack Shatts enough. He said, "Don't worry, you stand on your own. I'm happy for you; it's a new start." He was right. I informed Carl Lustic that I was leaving; I was giving him my two weeks' notice. He didn't care. I knew the only thing I would miss would be none other than Max Lustic, who always stood up for me against both of his sons. It worked out well for my old friend Manny, who also deserved a break, so the position was there for him since he was next in line and by far the best candidate for it. I, on the other hand, wanted more insight into the music end; since I had been at National Studios, the only music experience that I witnessed was "The Three Penny Opera" with Sammy Davis Jr. I wanted more to do with music and I knew A & R Recording was the place for me; it just felt so natural.

I loved the location. The whole area around A&R Recording had a special feel to it: Rockefeller Center, Manny's Music Store, and the Metropole down the street; the whole area had a musical vibe about it. I felt a whole different world existed for me at A&R. I remember that at National, Joe Jorgensen was always playing, "The Girl from Ipanema" with Stan Getz and Astro Gilberto, which was recorded at A&R. The studio and staff had a great reputation, and I was joining them. I had not come down from that; it would take me some time. I loved the place. I later learned that the record they kept playing was a B side that was played in error by the Disc Jockey at the radio station, and the rest was history.

Monday morning, I reported for work at A&R Recording Studios; a new beginning. I was assigned to do setups with Don Hahn who, at the time, happened to be Phil Ramone's roommate. He had worked at a radio station in Canada, so he had audio experience. Don started by showing me the ropes, where setup sheets were placed; and finding out who was assigned to the session, the instrumentation and the layout of the room, microphones and where to get tape from, and which type of tape to use. I was learning an awful lot about the studio, and fast. I remember one day we had a setup to do and the setup sheet called for Piano, Bass, Drums, Rhythm guitar, Lead guitar, and a twelve (12) string guitar; well, I thought it meant twelve guitars.

I had never dealt with a twelve-string before, so I took it to mean twelve (12) guitars, and that's what I set up for; all with matching microphones. When Don saw this, he just started laughing and proceeded to explain to me what it meant; he was really good about it and didn't make it an issue. I don't think to this day he even remembers. Don was a great instructor, and I enjoyed the time I spent working with him; I learned an awful lot from him. There was a lot to learn here, and sometimes it came in various forms. I'm glad I was put to the test because that is how you learn. Sol Gubin, who was one of the top drummers in New York City, a friend and prankster, would take grains of rice and place them on his snare drum. Well, once we were in the control room and checking microphones you started hearing this static; your first reaction was to change the microphone. I was never sure what I would encounter or whom I would meet; things were always different. One day I called for the elevator, and who came in right behind me was the most beautiful woman you would ever want to see, with the greatest smile in the world. She was draped in a great-looking fur coat. She leaned against the wall and asked, "Where are you fellas going?"

I said, "Fourth-floor Studio A."

She replied, "Well, so am I." She said to me, "What a lovely day."

I responded, "Yes, it is."

She asked me, "What do you do?" I told her I was a setup guy. She was just adorable and very nice, but little did I know that I was speaking with none other than the great Lena Horne.

When we got off the elevator, she told Phil Ramone that I was the most courteous and respectful guy at A&R. I was blown away. She didn't have to do that; and Phil's response was, "I have nothing but the best." That's a true story. The session started and I was in heaven for the whole evening. This was something I would never forget. On May 29, 1962, I was instructed to fall in with Don Hahn. I was not aware at the time that it was a remote for the 4th Annual Grammy Awards, which were being held at one of New York's Finest Hotels, "The Astor Hotel." This event was also being held simultaneously in Chicago and Los Angeles and they were recognizing accomplishments by musicians from the year 1961. The nominees were: Record of the Year, Henry Mancini for "Moon River;" Album of the Year (other than classical), Judy Garland for Judy at Carnegie Hall; Song of the Year, Henry Mancini & Johnny Mercer (songwriters), for "Moon River" performed by Henry Mancini; Best New Artist, Peter Nero. I had no idea I would be there; it was, for me, a great opportunity.

We were entertaining the teamsters; A&R had set up a table for them on the balcony right next to us, all the food and drinks it could hold was a way to appease them to let our crew work the floor, as well as the sound in the room, with no problems at all. We needed a very flexible, amicable, and friendly situation beneficial to all at this very important event, so we entertained and took care of their whole crew. We had a fantastic crew that was very creative and capable and knew how to handle anything that would come up, and they consisted of very strong Individuals. A&R was led by none other than Phil Ramone, one of the most memorable sound engineers. Only the best worked at A&R Recording: Don Frye, Ami Hadani, Tom Hidley, Don Hahn, Chuck Irwin, Jim Shearer, Bob Bostwick, and now I was added to the list. Who could forget that evening, although it was a lot of work? I found it enjoyable, and I loved every minute of it. I enjoyed being around the crowd of celebrities in attendance, and for me, what a treat! We were under the supervision of none other than Phil Ramone and his friend and innovator Tommy Dowd from Atlantic Records. Val Valentine and Jesse Kaye from MGM Records, who were founding members of the Grammys, were also in attendance, and they had also decided to drop by for a short visit.

This would be my very first-time meeting Val Valentine, who would play a big part in my recording career. There were many other executives of major record labels who came by. It was a black-tie affair, and everyone looked very elegant. This show was not televised because, from 1959 to 1970, it was considered the non-televised era, so the Grammy Award Ceremonies were not aired live on television. I have been on many remotes in my life, but this one was the one that to this day has stayed with me throughout my years in the music business; I wished it would've gone on forever. What a cast. There was so much talent in that room it was unreal. Back then the Grammy Awards were just getting started.

Dinner was served at a round table that held 10 to 12 people. It was very intimate. Don Hahn and I were on the balcony, where we had a good view of the stage as well as all the performers. We were using a small Altec Console, and we had set up the stage using just a few microphones for the band, being very careful to dress all the cables very neatly; we were aware that after the show we would be responsible for packing and striking all the equipment, we were responsible for everything.

Tommy Dowd came by and asked, "Did you guys hear that?" He thought he had heard feedback, which we didn't hear; we had checked everything, and things seemed to be working to everyone's satisfaction. He listened for a while, then said, "OK," and left.

At this point, I'm looking down from the balcony and who do I see? None other than Carl Lustic, who was surprised to see me. He walked over to talk to me and so did Phil Ramone, who said to him, "Look, Cuffs, don't hold up my crew." Carl always wore a suit and tie, and his pants were always cuffed; he was very straight. We, on the other hand, were a little more hip, shall we say, so at that point, he just left and I never saw or spoke to him again. I never did ask my friend Manny if he ever mentioned it at all. I doubt he did. The years that followed marked the most memorable and wonderful times in my career, both personally and professionally. Things went well; I had not felt any better in years.

A&R always had the most spectacular Christmas parties in town, with some of the best-talented players and singers performing during the evening. The parties were held at "Toots Shor's," located on the westside at 51 West 51st Street. This place was famous and had a great history going back to the 40s and 50s. They had this enormous oversized circular bar that was a New York landmark. What a place and what a party. I enjoyed this place like no one else, and in the back of my mind I kept thinking this is where Tangy and I were first introduced; boy how life has its changes. A&R gave us all cash bonuses, which I never had or heard of; it was all new to me. While I was at A&R, we worked with some of the greatest artists in the music industry. One of them was Bobby Scott, who was with Mercury Records. Many nights during his sessions he'd be tooting his bottle of scotch. That guy was always really nice to me, and his sessions were the best. They were great nights; this wasn't work. One of his compositions included "He Ain't Heavy, He's My Brother," which became a hit for Neil Diamond (in 1970).

I was always working alongside Phil Ramone as his assistant on many of his sessions, and I learned so much. I knew I had finally found something I could put my finger on. I liked what I was doing, and the people I came in contact with were extremely talented and always treated me as one of their own. One evening we were overdubbing Bill Henderson, a great singer, very friendly and very sincere; and Creed Taylor producing a real layback session when we rolled tape and Bill Henderson started singing. It was another world for me. I couldn't believe what I was hearing when he started singing, "When My Dreamboat Comes Home." I was completely blown away by the sound, which was captured by my boss, Phil Ramone, and here I was in the same room and I was part of it. Bill was a little apprehensive about his vocal sound. He was troubled by a little tickle in his throat, but both Creed Taylor and Phil reassured him he sounded great.

Phil said, "You sound like the man," meaning Ray Charles. I just nodded my head in approval and we continued.

Phil turned around and said, "You got the machine?"

I said, "Yes."

I had been watching him, but not well enough. I noticed every time the 3-track machine would roll only one of the lights would go on. I would stop it and roll back to the top of the tune. This went on a few times. Phil finally turned around and said, "What's wrong? Why are you stopping the machine?"

I said, "Those other lights were off on the electronics."

He said, "No man, were doing a sel-sync." I was embarrassed and he said, "Don't worry man, I'll show you later." Which he did; he went on to explain it very thoroughly, which he was good at. Phil explained that we were doing Selective Synchronous Recording, or Sel-Sync, as it is known to most of us today; this is the process of selectively using the record heads as playback heads so that new signals can be recorded on other tracks in perfect sync with the existing tracks. Sel-sync recording dramatically changed the recording process, allowing overdubbing of individual recorded tracks. Phil was very kind to me; from my first day at A&R, he took me under his wing.

I remember having dinner with both him and his mother, a very pleasant lady. It was always great to be around her, not to mention the sessions that I assisted Phil on were always the best sessions in town. To me it was an experience that I would never forget. I loved every minute of it. I was not just setting up or seconding but involved, and I was always kept informed. I was being trained by the very best in the business. I considered this a great adventure for me as well as a great opportunity, and a very promising career. I was learning so much from Phil Ramone. I met so many people through him. I was on cloud nine every evening. There were times when the likes of Mickey Mantle, who was a friend of his, would just drop by; there is nothing more astonishing than when you're in a control room, and all of a sudden, the door opens and there you are face to face with famous Basketball, Baseball and Football players, dropping by to say hello. For a kid from the other side, there are no other perks. It was a great treat. There were other people that I had the privilege of meeting that would work at A&R, such distinguished personalities as Morris Levy from Roulette Records, Teddy Reig, a young Quincy Jones, who, at the time was the head of Mercury Records. Don Costa of United Artists, Mitch Miller who, believe it or not, I listened to when I was just a kid among many others. I never knew who I would run into. This place was used by the very best in the music business. We had a small cutting room behind Studio A so that after a session we could cut a transcription (Reference Dub) for the clients to take with them at the end of the session; in those days we didn't have cassettes, so it was either a dub or a reel-to-reel copy. A&R also had a company called Admins Ltd: that was run and operated by Jim Shearer, who was mainly the catalyst for all their remotes, be it at the White House or various club dates in town, and then there was Paul Ford, who was a friend and close consultant to Tom Hidley, who worked at Harvey Radio on 6th Avenue, which was within walking distance of where A&R bought all of their audio supplies; especially all their vacuum tubes. The studio was in high demand back then. It just seemed like just about everyone in New York City recorded there; every Agency, film, and record label was aware of us and used the facility frequently.

We would record agency dates during the day and record dates in the evenings, or just straight music sessions; it all depended on their bookings. We were one of the busiest studios in town. Things were changing for me, and I enjoyed every moment of it. I had fallen into the right spot at the right time and place. I was now being teamed up with Ami Hadani a tall Israeli who, to me, was the nicest man on the planet, to say the least, and was always very relaxed. He showed me a few things.

My very first session with Ami was assisting him on The Joe Cuba Sextet session; that evening we recorded "Bang Bang," and "El Pito (I'll Never Go Back to Georgia) with Teddy Reig producing for Roulette Records. Teddy was a very big man, and the most pleasant person you'd ever want to meet. He would arrive early at the session, hang his coat and hat up and he always brought Cuban cigars which he would put in a mug full of brandy. As they absorbed the brandy, they would just get enormous; I had never seen anything like this before. He would save them and then, during the session, he would smoke them, always offering you one. I couldn't, I knew they would knock me on my ass. He would also bring large bags of pistachios and pumpkin seeds that he would ask me to put on top of the Ampex machine's electronics so that the vacuum tubes would keep them warm. Teddy came to relax and to do his session in style and never made you feel you were not part of the team. He was a jolly man, never to be forgotten; a real Teddy bear. We did a lot of recording dates for Roulette Records, we were recording the maestro, Tito Puente with La Lupe, who was a Cuban singer of boleros, and guarachas and was well known for her energetic performances. She was the most acclaimed Latin singer in New York City due to her partnership with Tito Puente. Those were very wild sessions, you can't imagine the performances in this studio, they were, for me, memorable sessions that always made you feel you were at a concert; it was pure magic. We also had Celia Cruz recording with a large orchestra; Ami Hadani on the board and me as his second engineer, now that was a treat for me because, as much as I loved working with Phil Ramone, whose sessions were always great, Ami had become another one of my mentors, and there wasn't a session we worked on that I didn't learn something new.

We worked as a team and did a lot of the Latin dates together. Roulette Records was a regular client, and their Latin sessions were always very exciting with large rhythm sections. We were recording everything at once to half-inch 3-tracks with echo live, a different perspective that you do not get in today's sessions. It's different today, I'll hear a song that I was involved with, and I hear a guitar or percussion part that's been added and sounds wrong, the original balance was what that producer heard at the time, so why mess with it; there was a reason for it being that way. I assisted Phil Ramone on some of the best, if not the greatest, sessions, with none other than Burt Bacharach and Dionne Warwick. We recorded some of the most amazing tunes such as "Alfie," "Do You Know the Way to San Jose," "Don't Make Me Over," and many others.

I remember the very first time I met Dionne Warwick. She came into the studio wearing a beautiful brown jacket with flowers and matching pants, which was the style in the 60s; she looked great, what a lady. I escorted her to the vocal booth. It was very warm in the booth, so I asked her if she wanted me to hang her jacket up in the control room. She said yes and thanked me. I took her jacket and headed for the control room and, as I entered the control room, Rudy, one of the other second engineers, gave me a strange look thinking I had her pants, till he finally realized it was her jacket, which happened to match her pants. Everyone broke out in laughter; these guys were something else, some of the most wonderful characters to be around, a staff that was out of this world, this was family and great to be around. I was in a trance watching from the control room as Burt Bacharach rehearsed the band, he ran the rhythm section till all the changes and entrances to the tune were exactly what he wanted. He would run down the rest of the orchestra with Dionne and the background vocals, I had found my niche, and I loved it. These rehearsals were great for us because they gave us a chance to get a balance of the band, and also the opportunity to change or adjust any microphones. Burt was always at the piano with Dionne and finally ready to record to quarter-inch mono and half-inch 3-tracks. We were always ready to go once we had a band balance and changed anything that was either faulty or just needed changing for the good of the recording; this is how we were trained.

We were just waiting for the word and finally, here it came, the count-off: ah 1, ah 2, ah 3 and downbeat of music, we were now recording, and after recording a few takes Burt clapped his hands and gave the band a five-minute break. Burt walked into the control room to listen to a playback and, after a few playbacks, he selected the master take which I must say was a great experience. When the band was dismissed, we hung out a bit and I remember Burt saying to Phil that he was going to the West Coast because his wife at the time, Angie Dickerson, wanted to have their baby there. Another one of my most memorable moments was in Studio A with Bert Berns producing and in walked Neil Diamond, who greeted me and went inside the studio. In about a half hour, we were recording "Solitary Man," and "Sherry Sherry." I remember that we needed lots of handclaps so we all just jumped in and started clapping with lots of energy, this was a great session. I remember after the session Phil Ramone said to Bert Berns, I think Sherry Sherry is the side. It was amazing to hear a discussion like that, and then hearing the record on the radio, what a charge; it was something that to me was unimaginable.

Bert brought in a group that he loved to work with, they were called "The Exciters," who held a special place in the Bert Berns repertoire – as well as his heart. They were the only group to work with him from the very beginning of his career to the very end. The Exciters' classic "Tell Him," Marked Bert Bern's arrival as one of the greatest songwriters of the era, and it was the beginning of an important relationship with another duo of writers, Jerry Leiber and Mike Stoller (who produced the track). He loved the quartet so much that they were the only group to record for both his Bang and Shout record labels, where he made some of his best records with the Exciters in those final days. There was always some excitement in this four-story building going on. One day who comes in but none other than Louie Armstrong for a Schaeffer Beer commercial. I had come in at 8:00 a.m. to set up the room. I checked all microphones and by 9:00 a.m. we were ready to roll tape, a typical recording date at A&R Recording. It was so cool to see this man just go up to the microphone and, as we say, just nail it. Louie was a very nice person, and all he did was wait for you, he was always ready.

He was a humorous man, but all business; we were here to work. I remember him coming in early on the morning of a session that was scheduled for 10:00 a.m. We recorded three radio spots as they were called, and we were done by 1:00 p.m. a three-hour session. We were recording some of the best artists in the music industry who were at the top of the charts: Peter Paul & Mary, Leslie Gore, Neil Diamond, the Thad Jones and Mel Lewis Big Band, Eddie Fischer, Bill Henderson,

The Johnny Mann Singers, and many more amazing artists. To me it seemed like we never stopped recording, if you did not pay attention, it was on you because things moved very fast; but how could you not pay attention to something that was given to you, on top of that we were getting paid.

I considered myself very fortunate for being at the right place at the right time because this was the 60s, it was music,

music, music, non-stop. I was absorbing and learning a craft that I loved and deep inside I felt this would take me a very long way, there was no question about it. Friday nights, if there weren't any sessions booked, we had the Mel Lewis and Thad Jones big band and everyone took a shot at it with always a different setup, with the brass on risers or in a circle, which was a great experience for everyone, and it was sanctioned by the union as long as it was recorded at 7½ ips and a tone every 60 seconds which we never did. I remember one day Phil asking Bernie Glow, who specialized in jazz and commercial lead trumpet from the 1940s to 1970s, about my session the previous weekend, and he remarked nice but had too much drums. Phil responded with, "Well he's Latin." We all laughed. Bernie was very cool, a great player.

The next recording engineer I was teamed up with was an Italian guy from New Jersey, who was very friendly and extremely talented; and I quickly found out that anything I wanted to know, all I had to do was ask; we hit it off right away. I was very fortunate to be working with none other than my dear friend Roy Cicala. One evening I was assisting Roy on his very first session, which was an R&B session for Bang Records. We recorded a tune that took us all by surprise, We had no idea what was to come from the title I Spy for the F B I which became very controversial in the music scene.

The tune received so much attention in the trades and lots of press. I remember Roy being interviewed by Billboard Magazine, and all he kept saying was, "I loved it." There were so many hit records coming out of A&R that people traveled from all over the world just to record there. This was where I first met Jimmy Bowen and Keely Smith, who at the time were married. Jimmy Bowen had been very successful producing the likes of Frank Sinatra, Dean Martin, Sammy Davis Jr. and, now on this particular evening, he was producing Morgana King, who you might remember; she played Carmela Corleone, Michael's mother, in The Godfather. Jimmy Bowen was well-mannered and very easy going, a great producer to be around; he knew what he wanted, and when he'd gotten what he was after, as an artist, he was very complimentary and a real pro.

We were experiencing problems in our echo chambers, getting some very light clicks, and the fact that Morgana's voice was so light you could hear everything. There were no drums to mask it, what we had was a very light string session. I assisted Roy and we started troubleshooting. We spent a good hour during Jimmy's session, with his permission, unplugging the vending machines. After putting a few dollars in change in the hot chocolate machine, we found that it was this machine that was triggering the clicks. We talked to Jimmy about it, and he was more than happy that we found the culprit. What a guy; I liked Jimmy very much and little did I know that we would meet again years later. A&R did a lot of commercials for both radio and TV, lots of them with none other than George Romanis, the king of agency commercials that were heard worldwide, either on Radio or TV. A great deal of the commercials that we recorded were for Schaefer Beer, Ford Cobra, Dodge, Colgate Toothpaste, Camel Cigarettes, Ballantine Beer, Newport Cigarettes, 7UP, Winston Cigarettes, Chevron Gasoline, Fresca, Noxzema Shave Cream, Coca-Cola, just to mention a few. We did the first BOLA Wine commercials Spots with Vaughn Meader, who was an American comedian and impersonator achieving fame with The First Family album, spoofing our new President, John F. Kennedy.

I doubt that there was a commercial that was not recorded at A&R. We did a very big male ensemble for The William Esty Agency "SUNOCO" gasoline campaign (People on the Go, People in the Know) and many, many other commercials; we were always doing some recording.

Our booking department should've gotten an award for being able to fit so many sessions in two rooms. There were times when things did not go exactly as planned, like the time when we were doing a Pepsi Cola Spot called "On the Beach," with Quincy Jones Orchestra. We were going upstate New York, everything was packed. Very early the next morning, we headed out; traffic was a mess and, after a while, we realized time was getting the best of us, but we were sure we'd make it on time. Assumption is always a big mistake, and Upstate New York can be very tricky if you're not careful or familiar with the area. After traveling for a while, we were not aware that we had mistakenly passed the home where we were supposed to be. We noticed that a car suddenly came out of nowhere and came after us; we thought the driver wanted to race, so we sped away as fast as we could on this narrow road. Finally, after much horn honking, the driver was able to wave us down.

What cell phones could've solved back then. Finally, we followed him to the location and, as soon as we arrived, I started setting up the band in the backyard of this beautiful home that overlooked the vast forest of Upstate New York. I started with the drums. Grady Tate, the drummer, said to me, "Careful, I don't want to fall off this cliff." I was setting his drum kit between two rocks, along with the rest of the band, on a hill for a 60-second spot called "On the Beach." The agency, Honcho, wanted to hear the sound of the wind and the leaves from the trees. This happened to be his residence, a fantastic place with a great view, as well as lots of trees. We started to unpack the truck when I noticed the machines that were being taken off the truck were quarter-inch machines and, unfortunately, they had packed half-inch tape; this immediately spelled trouble. I headed the other way and kept working on the band's setup. Jim Shearer, who had also noticed our predicament, ran and headed for a house down the hill, and fortunately for us, they had a Wolensak tape machine in the house.

Jim was able to buy a reel of tape from their kid for $20.00, but nevertheless, it was too late; none of us were able to escape the wrath of Phil Ramone, who lined us all up next to the truck and read us our rights, a lesson well learned.

Phil let us know right then and there that, in his crew, there was no room for mistakes. There was no pointing of fingers; not one word was said. We would never discuss that incident again, even among ourselves. We started recording; everything worked just fine; it had been a lucky day for us. After a few hours, we wrapped all our equipment and headed back to town again. There was no discussion of the incident, which could've cost us a lot, but I must say Phil did handle it well. All in all, they were fun times, and we made the best of it.

We were accustomed to spending a lot of quality time downstairs at our most loved and frequent hangout known throughout the city, "Jim and Andy's," which was a musician hang-out. Whenever we had a session, if we needed a certain musician, we could use our intercom, which had been installed right next to their cash register, to see if anyone was around and available, be it a guitar, bass or trombone, or multiple players, depending on the situation. On many occasions, this allowed some musicians to become a side man on some of the best sessions in town.

I would often have dinner with Ami Hadani at Jim and Andy's. We would talk for hours about California, and he'd show me pictures of a mastering room that he once had on the West Coast. We had developed a friendship that would take us a long way, and although I worked with many other engineers, I, for the most part, became his second engineer. There wasn't anything he wouldn't do for me. I was a young Puerto Rican kid from the streets, and he understood that; he never put me down. If anything, he encouraged me every step of the way. I loved all the sessions we were doing, especially the Latin sessions. What Ami brought to those sessions was special, and they respected him for it. He taught me an awful lot; from him, I learned etiquette in the studio and how to handle the artist, which is very important. It was as if he were present during their first rehearsals.

Tito Puente and La Lupe loved Ami, and I was paying really close attention. I realized that I could learn an awful lot from him when it came to recording. I was able to ask him anything. He was very genuine and would take the time. Every morning, when we would order coffee from the Sixth Avenue Deli, he'd say no, try something different; he was my Webster dictionary, my mentor, an experienced and trusted advisor. I had no idea what he and Tom Hidley were planning or how my life would change because of them. I would tell him how I had lived in San Francisco for a very short time and that I didn't care for it. The town was too cold for my liking, not to mention I had no direction from anyone.

He asked me if I had ever been to L.A. I said no, I had wanted to, but I didn't know anyone there. He said that Los Angeles was different, the weather was warmer, and that if I saw the Sunset Strip, I would like it. It was always sunny and people were really friendly. He would always tell me stories of many artists who lived in Los Angeles and the restaurants that he thought were good. We would talk about how he felt about real wood, veneers, and Formica, that it was worth saving your money and buying something that would last you a lifetime. I learned an awful lot from him, which has stuck with me to this day. He had many talents, and I feel extremely fortunate to have spent the years I did under his wing. He would also tell me stories about Los Angeles, all of them very positive. I was intrigued, and I pictured the possibility of someday visiting. I liked this man. He was always very nice to me, and I respected him. Here was someone I looked up to, and it seemed that we talked the same language. The music scene was now changing. There was a large exodus, and many of us New Yorkers would eventually be heading to the West Coast.

I was now living in Williamsburg, Brooklyn, where the mornings were always very cold; I would always allow myself enough time if it was snowing just in case the trains started running late.

I didn't want to take any chances, but luckily, I didn't live that far from the train station. My stop would be at Rockefeller Plaza and Avenue of America (6th Avenue), which was always cleared of any snow. When I would arrive, I would take the elevator to the 4th floor and head straight to the board to grab the setup sheet posted for my session. I would go ahead and start my setup. I always made sure I had plenty of time so I wouldn't be in any rush. The day was going fine, a little cold, but that was life in New York City. time passed, and in the afternoon during the setup, Ami came into the studio to check things out. He had no changes, which made me very happy. I was getting to know his setups well. On this particular day, he told me that Tom Hidley was leaving A&R; he had decided to move back to California. I was taken by surprise, and I also felt sad.

Tom and I had also become good friends. He was a very likable guy and always very business-like and savvy; he'd spend time with me. I liked Tom very much. He would often show me an awful lot of things that I had never seen or dealt with. He was a good man. He would also show me pictures of a windmill where he lived in upstate New York, and we would just talk for hours. I couldn't wait to see and speak with Tom personally. When we finally did, he said things were changing Balestier; that's what he always called me. We talked for a while, and I had to agree that times were changing. He told me that if I was ever interested in going out west again, to let him know and to stay in touch. He would help me get a job. I was touched. I said that it had been a pleasure for me to work with him and that I would certainly stay in touch with him. He told me Ami would know how to reach him, but little did I know at the time that many things were already in place in California. TTG had already been formed, and he and Ami were partners.

When my session with Ami started that evening in Studio A, I started to think about Tom and working in California, which became challenging for me; I felt at a complete loss knowing Tom was leaving. I was going to miss him; there was no denying that at all. We proceeded with the Joe Cuba session, and that evening, we recorded what became a big all-time hit for them.

The romantic "To Be with You" with the vocals of Cheo Feliciano and Jimmy Sabater Sr... This band, at that time, had an enormous following in the New York City Latin community. The lyrics to Cuba's music used a mixture of Spanish and English, also known as Spanglish; they were great sessions, and the room was always packed with many visitors from all over. In 1965, we recorded their first crossover hit with the Latin and soul fusion feeling. It was such a great tune that was called "El Pito (I'll Never Go Back to Georgia). Jimmy Sabater said that none of us had ever been to Georgia, which was hilarious. He asked everyone in the room if they had Puerto Ricans there. We always had a great time with these guys. They were always happy and great storytellers who loved to joke around with you. All the guys in the band were big womanizers, so it was very common for them to bring their girlfriends and wives to all their recording sessions.

The control room was always full of pretty women. I remember one day being asked by one of the band members if I would do him a favor; he said, "Look, my cousin is bringing my son over, so please say that this girl here is with you, OK?" I agreed. Why not? She was beautiful. I remember during the session, Ami leaning over and saying to me to be careful and don't fall for her. The Joe Cuba Sextet was very popular in the Latin scene, and the sound we got if you listen to those albums, you can't duplicate it. We would set up bongos, timbales, and cowbell players in a circle in between packing blankets held up by six music stands so they could hear themselves with no headphones; man, you could feel the energy that came from that circle.

I remember many things in that session, but one, in particular, was Ami asking for a level from the cowbell player;

he hit it hard, and one of the musicians yelled don't hit that hard, and Ami responded over the talkback, "No let him play like he wants."

Joe Cuba responded really loud from the other end of the room Now!! that's an Ingeniero Musical.

We did the same thing with Joe and his congas. We put the lead singer, Jimmy Sabater, in one booth, the background singers in another booth, and we started recording straight to our Ampex half-inch 3-track tape machine. What a memorable evening, but while everyone was enjoying themselves, in the back of my mind, all I could think of was Tom Hidley leaving. The fact that no one else said a word baffled me, but I didn't push it. Tom left for California two weeks later. There were no parties. It was kept very quiet. Hidley, as I called him, was very pleasant and knew his stuff. I missed going to the shop and just talking with him, but, yes sir; as he said to me earlier, the times they were a changing, and we definitely would have to face it sooner or later because they were changing fast. Roy Cicala had taken Tom Hidley's place as chief tech while the studio found another tech in the interim. Roy and I became very close friends in a very short period. We would stay in touch till his end in 2014. I remember him always saying to everyone how impressed he was with the way I kept the studio.

Roy would always comment about my saying that all the microphone booms had to be lined up like soldiers. He'd share information with me, which I always considered an act of respect. He was not one to have secrets either. If something came up, he would say, "Look at this. Isn't that wild? Let me show you how it works." The man was very innovative but not secretive at all; he always shared. There were times when he would try different ways of setting the room, particularly in some of "The Young Rascals" sessions. He would try different setups in the room with the band, but no one questioned it. This was a great time to be in the studio because all sorts of recording applications were being taught by Roy.

If you had any interest, it was right there for you, no secrets at all; you couldn't buy what was being taught. I felt great because Roy was now requesting me on all of his sessions, especially the ones with his wife Lorrie Burton and her partner Pam Sawyer, who were songwriters. You couldn't ask for anything better, and time just moved on; I felt very fortunate.

The evenings were always a busy time for all of us. The studio was doing really good business; it was the most popular place in Manhattan. We were very close to everything in town. This was one of the most popular places in the music industry. A&R was the place to be, and it showed with all the different clientele, all the artists and producers who loved the place. We would often have dinner at the Chinese restaurant that was located across the street next to the Kinney parking structure, which was where Roy would often hold court, he had many projects, and it seemed like I was his first call.

Winter had arrived. It was a very cold night in New York City, and on this very evening, we were headed to the East Side in mid-town to a very exclusive restaurant called "The Jamaican Arms." The restaurant had been chosen by two agency executives who wanted to do a demo. They were promoting a yellow airplane, and they wanted the lyrics to be authentic with that Jamaican accent. This remote was something that, for years, Roy and I would often reminisce about. It became our private greeting. Whenever it came up within a crowd, which it often did, particularly in the studio, we would start describing that particular evening, and everyone would just fall about laughing. The theme that particular night was all Jamaican "Yellow Bird from Out in the Eastern Sky," which was an ad for Eastern Airlines.

Roy had asked me if I would be available in the evening, and I said yes; the next thing I knew, we were packing a portable Nagra machine. I managed to find a spot right in front. I got our equipment out of the car as fast as I could and started to do my setup on stage while Roy handled other business. We went over the script with the agency producers as well as the trio and what the client wanted; I made sure that our machine was ready, as well as our microphone. During the evening, the client kept buying us drinks. They were excited about what was happening and how Roy and I were handling the trio. We were very comfortable and everything was going well.

We did a few versions per the agency guys' instructions. We didn't have a console, just the portable quarter-inch mono Nagra machine to fade. What I did was when the trio would go into the vamp of the tune, I would slowly bring the microphone into my left armpit slow, and that became our master fader. We knew there would be a bump, but it would work (we could edit or cut it out later; ah, the era of the razor blade). This went on for some time. The client was very generous. They had bought and paid for whatever we and the band wanted. Needless to say, we were all really hammered. When we were finally done recording the group, the client was very excited. Everything had gone better than they had expected. They thanked us and, typically by New York City tradition in those days, we were handsomely tipped, and they gave us their punch list of instructions for the presentation the following day.

We started to pack our gear and went outside. By now, the snow was coming down fast, with large flakes of snow all over; it was hard to see, and my car was completely covered in snow. It wasn't cold; that would come later when it would stop, and the wind would be unbearable. It was a big storm, and traffic was not very visible in any direction. Roy and I had gotten smashed, so we decided to play it safe; we took a different route back to the studio: 55th Street down to Fifth Avenue. This way we would be able to turn right on 5th Avenue and head to 57th Street. It wasn't as crowded, and it was also safer and a faster way, and the best place to safely make a left turn. On our way there, Roy and I had a slight petty spat about the direction we were going, and he reached over, pulled the keys from my ignition, and threw them out the window in front of Saint Patrick's Church. There was no panic; we were so smashed we just started laughing, and to our amazement, we were able to find the key chain really fast. Boy, how lucky can you be? The snow kept coming down thick. We made a left-on 57th Street and slowly headed down to 7th Avenue where we made a left turn; we reached 48th Street, and I made another left by the Metropole, which was located right on the corner.

We had decided on this route because it made it a lot easier for us to park my car at the Kinney Parking Garage across the street from the studio; I could not drive to Brooklyn that evening, and what an evening and a memorable one; we laughed, back to the studio. We always had great times; it was always great. Roy was my mentor and friend, and we respected each other. all I can say about Roy is that he was a great friend and teacher. All we ever did was just laugh all the time while taking care of business. Those were great days filled with lots of great memories that would last us a lifetime. We were always there, and thanks to Roy, if there was work to be done, I was there. Here's another thing: in the early days, radio stations and commercial recording studios bought all their tape in bulk. We were using half-inch 201 or 206 and quarter-inch 111 or 131 tape that came in what was called pancake style in boxes of 10 reels per case, separated by sheets of foam on plastic hubs, or you could get it on 12-inch metal reels in boxes depending on your situation. We always built our reels for the masters, so reels were purchased separately.

Now, once the case of tape was used, we normally discarded the box and foam; there was no need to store it, it was a fire hazard, and we didn't have the room.

I would take all the foam that came with our tape, and I would have a seamstress I knew in the neighborhood sew small pillows. I would sell them all over town, especially in my neighborhood in Red Hook, Brooklyn. It became a popular item during the summer months for guys with convertibles or anyone who could afford to spend $3.00 a pair. They were very cool, in different colors, and very stylish, and it seemed like everyone wanted them.

I also kept all the quarter-inch tape ends and would wind them onto 7-inch plastic reels. Phil Ramone didn't want to see the ends around. He'd say to me, "Throw them away." They bugged him, and they took up a lot of room on the counter above the machines. I had asked Phil if I could keep them, and he said yes, just get rid of them; he didn't want to see them around. At the time, audio cassettes were not in vogue yet, the only medium available to play your recordings away from the studio after your session was either an acetate or tape copy. Acetates took longer, and they scratched easily. It was more convenient and faster to make a reel-to-reel copy. Everyone was buying portable tape machines, so in a very short time, I became their tape supplier, which in turn allowed me to save more money. I was very happy with everything that was going on I was making money and things were going just fine. I'm in my comfort zone. Time goes by, and then one morning, as I'm setting up the room, Ami informs me that he is also leaving for California. I was shocked, saddened, and surprised. We had become close friends, and he, like Roy, had shown me an awful lot of things that, as long as I live, I will never forget. I would miss our coffee in the mornings from the 6th Avenue Deli. Those mornings were something; it was a ritual for me. I looked forward to them and oh! How we joked and teased Louie, the delivery guy, working on the Latin sessions with Ami had been one of my best experiences. The fact that he was now leaving to me was a big loss.

He said he was opening a studio in Los Angeles, and he gave me the name of the studio and address. He said that Tom and he were partners and that if I ever went out to California, I would have a job, no questions asked. I was in a daze about the whole thing. It was not what I expected to hear. I felt lonely; I was losing someone that I had become very fond of and always looked forward to working with. I knew he understood me. I was sworn to secrecy by Ami. I was prepared for all the questions the rest of the staff would be asking. There was no doubt Ami and I, in the short time that we had known each other, had become very good friends.

My very first reaction was to follow as quickly as possible, and that evening as I went down to the subway station in Rockefeller Center, all I could think about was all the changes that would take place; that's all I thought about on that long train ride home to Brooklyn which felt like the longest ride I had ever taken. I had lots of friends, but now I was losing a close one. It was on this long ride home that I finally decided I would make the move.

A new lifestyle for the family, the weather was another factor for me to consider. I didn't like the snow, and after dealing with it for so many years, I was ready for the change. I had the chance of a lifetime waiting for me in California. In my heart that evening, I knew that I needed to make the move; it was the right decision. Ami and Tom were offering me a new start in life, and I knew deep inside it was the chance of a lifetime. We had become good friends, and I trusted them. I was looking for a new life for me and my family. This was it; there were no other offers. I had grown tired of New York City, and I kept thinking over and over what Tom had said to me before he left that times were changing; I had to take the chance. That evening I told my girl about my plans. It was a big move, but it was also the chance of a lifetime. We knew California would be a big change, and that this was a great opportunity for me. I could not pass it up. I knew for a fact that if I stayed in New York City, there was nothing for me. I would just be following the same routine as everyone else, but I wanted to grow and change my life completely and leave some kind of signature for my children so they could be proud of their father for giving them a better and safer life.

Brooklyn at that time was not the safest place to bring up a kid, not those days, and I had two in mind that I wanted to raise in California. They didn't have to live in such a dangerous city; it wasn't fair on them. The next day I informed Ami that I had thought about it on my way home, and all night, that was all I could think about, that I would be leaving for Los Angeles in the summer of 1966. He put his arms around me and said he was happy about my decision. He knew I would be happier in Los Angeles and he looked forward to seeing me there and assured me that Tom felt the same way. I thought it out very carefully. I had heard stories of people driving cross country and getting stuck in the middle of the desert because of car problems, but I would not have any problems in the desert. I was very fortunate since earlier on, not knowing I had purchased an air-cool car, and now I was spending my time driving as much as possible in my 1960 Corvair.

I was constantly searching for information regarding which routes to take cross country. I was asking everyone I knew questions, making sure that I was well prepared for this road trip to California. I remember asking another engineer, Dave Sanders, who was familiar with the road, and he commented that Route 66 was the way to go and that it would take us to California.

January 1966, a 12-day strike took everyone by surprise; it ended all service on the subways and buses in the city, affecting millions of commuters. Fortunately, I had a car, so at times, four of us would all hop in my car and head to Manhattan across the Williamsburg Bridge. The traffic and crowds of people on foot were enormous, but by now I was accustomed to parking across the street from the studio at Kinney's garage, and in the evenings my girl would meet me at Jim & Andy's for dinner, and then we'd go back home to Brooklyn. In April 1966, I gave my notice to Norman Jensen. He was not surprised at all and wished me the best. Norman asked me if I was going to work with Ami, and I said no, and he said he understood. I knew Norman understood my reluctance to admit where I was going. I hated lying to him; he was another one that I would miss, but I had already told everyone who asked that I was going to California to manage a drive-in. I didn't know if there would be any retaliation but there wasn't. These were the nicest people you would ever want to work for, and like everyone else, I was also more than saddened that I was leaving A&R. Although New York City was my home at that time, it didn't offer me much as they say Puerto Ricans at that time were not the flavor of the month. I felt very strongly that California was the chance of a lifetime both for me and my family; I could not and would not lose sight of that. For me, it was a no-brainer. I was excited and felt good about my move.

A&R Recording, for me, was a great place to work, and in addition, I learned and was taught many things by some of the best sound engineers in the business while meeting and making numerous friends. They had a great reputation so that once you became an employee, people in the music business treated you with respect because of the people you were associated with.

They knew you were capable of handling any recording session. When word got out that I was leaving for California, everyone in town made it a point to wish me the best; some even said they would see me there soon. They had nothing negative to say about Los Angeles; they praised it. I would miss everyone and would always remember the good times and how wonderful everyone had been to me. Don Hahn would often say, "I know you're going with Ami," and I would just say, "No." I hated to keep it from him. I had learned a great deal from Don, but I was sworn to keep it a secret. Roy Cicala and I had become very close friends. He was very persistent, and he wanted me to stay. He told me that I was crazy to leave New York City. There were a lot of changes going on in the music industry; who knew that Roy Cicala would become the new owner of one of New York City's most popular recording studios, The Record Plant? The former owners,

Chris Stone and Gary Kellgren, would eventually head west to Los Angeles. Brooks Arthur, who had a great reputation for recording and producing a lot of hit records with such artists as Bobby Darin and Janis Ian, had also tried to convince me to stay, but he also had a secret of his own; he would eventually be making a big move from Mirror Sound. I didn't know he was going to work at A&R – who knew? I was already working in L.A. when I found out about it.

I had started making final arrangements for the move out west when Phil and his wife Ann had decided to hold a small wedding reception at the Studio. I was asked by Norman Jensen, our studio manager if I would dress it, and I was more than happy to do it. I put a lot of time and effort into decorating the room. I was happy for them; after all, they had both been good to me from the very first day, and they had made me feel like part of the family. Ann and I had hit it off, and she remained the same, always greeting me with a genuine smile. What a lady. Whenever she visited, I enjoyed her presence, and while Phil was out in the studio, we would just gossip to no end. Those were certainly good times in the studio. She at the time was working for Pat Williams as his secretary. He was an arranger and composer, the friendliest guy you would ever want to meet.

Pat and I would meet again in Hollywood at TTG Studios during The Mary Tyler Moore Show recordings.

Phil Ramone, what can I say? The man was the nicest person I had ever encountered as a boss, but not in that sense; he treated me like family and with the utmost kindness and respect. If it had not been for him, I would not have had the experience as well as all the challenges, encounters, and endorsements throughout my recording career. Phil took me into A&R Studios and never questioned me about anything. He just cut me loose. I found it strange; here was a man who didn't know me from Adam and had just given another engineer, Jack Schatz, his business card at a Grammy meeting and asked to meet me. He was the one who found me and gave me a great calling card. To this day I'm more than grateful. I knew I was going to miss him very much, as well as his memorable recording sessions and lessons.

I was still working at A&R, so before hitting the road for California, I helped Roy Cicala with the installation of the 4th channel to our console in Studio A. For years, A&R had a small Ampex outboard mixer to the left of the console underneath in a small cabinet. This was where the existing 3rd channel Ampex mixer was located, and we would put either percussion or strings through here to gain more positions on the board. The console had only twelve positions (they were rotary Pots,). We were accustomed to recording to our Ampex half-inch 3-track safety and mono simultaneously, and now by just adding another pot to our Ampex sub mixer, it would give us the ability to record on an extra channel and the ability to record on a 4-track machine. A&R would eventually have 4-track capabilities. This was our goal, and I spent a lot of time just tidying things up. I was leaving, and I didn't want anyone to ever say what a mess that guy left. Corny as it may sound, I was proud of this place and its people.

A & R Recording was an innovative place to work, and by now I had worked with Phil on many sessions, including Harry Belafonte's album, where all the arrangements had a brass section, which sounded fantastic. I don't know what happened to those recordings, but I enjoyed every hour of those dates, especially meeting Harry Belafonte and his baby daughter Sherrie. I loved all the sessions not only because of the notoriety but because it also gave you great credentials. We always took great pride and care in all the recordings, and we were also ready to try anything and experimented as much as time would allow. There were no stupid questions here, just questions to be answered, and they were always confirmed and answered.

The next day, I told Roy I was sure glad I wouldn't have

to deal with 4-tracks in California. He turned around in his chair and said, "I thought you said you weren't going to work in a studio?"

I quickly responded with, "Well, if by chance I do..."

He quickly reached inside a box and showed me a 1-inch metal hub for 8-tracks and said this is what's coming next and then double that to 2-inch multi-track 16/24-tracks and more. I did not believe him, but at the same time, I did because if you knew Roy, you would understand; he was very talented and innovative and he was always tinkering with many different things and always coming up with something new. I knew deep inside I would miss my friend as well as all our sessions together. There was something to be said because they were always an adventure and always very enjoyable; you never knew what new experience you would draw from his sessions. I remember years later, as I sat in my office in Hollywood reading Billboard when I came across an article about how Roy was coming to California to build studios in Malibu that would be shaped like the Pyramids.

I was very excited, and I imagined possibly working with my old friend again. I even imagined moving to the beach if it came to pass, which, unfortunately, never did. The city council vetoed the whole idea. I remember mentioning the article to Lee Decarlo, another great engineer who had worked at A&R who often said if you don't hear from Roy, he's either making a deal someplace or recording someone very influential, and there was a lot of truth to that statement. He was always involved in various things. I have no idea how he found the time, but he did. I kept working, and although I was really busy, I kept asking all sorts of questions regarding my trip out west. I had decided earlier on to travel during the summer months and avoid rain or snow. I had also decided that traveling would only be in the daylight hours; it was now May 1966. It was time to go, so we started packing and reviewing maps for the long trip out west. I loaded all our clothes in my 1960

Corvair and placed all my records and anything that would help create a bed in the back seat of the car. In a few days, we would be bound for California. We were all excited about the trip to Sunny California, not knowing what obstacles faced us except for the fact that my comfort zone was that I was assured of a job.

I had never done this before, and I had a very long distance to cover. I was carrying a lot of responsibilities on my shoulders and was a bit nervous, but I could not show it. I knew deep inside that come rain or shine, I would make it to California, not to prove a point but for a better life, I just knew it. I had all the maps I needed. I knew that if I stayed on Route 66 as my friend and fellow sound engineer Dave Sanders said, we would be OK. I remember going over the routes with him, and he as well as others assured me that Route 66 was the way out west. The night before our departure, friends and family came by to see us. I had tried to keep it quiet, but it was impossible, lots of folks had come by to pay their respects and say their goodbyes. It was something that no one in our family had ever done for me. It was a task that I had taken on, and I was determined to complete it.

Deep inside I knew that it would work. I was looking forward to California; that was all I thought about. I had been ready mentally since the day I told Ami I would be there, and as I said earlier, the fact that I had a job waiting for me and whom I would be working with was part of the excitement. I could not turn back now. What was the point? Everything was set; the car had been serviced, and we were packed. That night, after everyone left, I sat down at the kitchen table and, as I had many times before, I went over the route we were going to take. I made a list of various numbers just in case I had to reach anyone in an emergency; it was getting late, and I was so wound up it became impossible for me to sleep. I had to relax. I knew that I had to be in shape; we had a long ride ahead of us, and everyone was counting on me.

We were California-bound, covering a great deal of ground.

This was serious business; I had to be on my toes from day one, but at the same time, it was a vacation that had to last me a long time. I had spoken with Ami and Tom several times, and I said it would probably take me a month. Tom said it would probably be shorter than that, but I wanted to allow for some room just in case. I didn't want to feel rushed at all. I had heard stories of hazards on the road and felt that the majority were cars overheating crossing Texas. Well, I had already addressed that, so I was very confident, but when you're on the road, you never know what can come up. I had taken every precaution possible. I had accounted for the weather; that's why I had decided to travel during the summer. There was no way I would've tried this trip during winter and gotten stuck in a snowstorm or, say, a tornado. I had also decided that we would travel only during the day; no need if it came to pass to be stuck someplace in the middle of the night; that made no sense at all. I had been given a great portable bar, the kind you carry with a top handle; that's where I kept some of our cash, maps as well, and my .38, which was loaded and ready at all times, and I was serious about it. I stocked the car with a bunch of drinks and munchies and some over-the-counter medicines, just in case. I had also gotten a bunch of coins; you have to remember this was pre-cellphone days. It was all landlines all the way. It was the 60s, phone booths at all the gas stations, plus I had promised that we would stay in touch as much as possible. I couldn't take the chance of worrying anyone, so I always stayed in touch. I didn't want anyone to think we'd been kidnapped or had an accident out in the desert.

I wanted to make this a fun trip as much as I could. I had to keep my promise and get to California safe and sound. That was my goal, and I was going to try my best come hell or high water. I talked to many folks who had made this trip before many times, so I had made it my business to pay close attention to their advice about diners, the roads, different cities, and the possible weather we could encounter, but it was all good like

I said we would be traveling during the summer. I would not make a trip like this during the winter; that would've been not only dangerous but a big mistake. I had always felt it would be or would become a great vacation that had to last me a very long time, and besides I personally wanted to see the great outdoors that I had dreamed and read so much about, and for me here finally was the opportunity of a lifetime. I had saved enough money, enough to last me for this trip I had no debt at all so come hell or high water I was indeed ready for anything that came our way. I had after all this time with very careful planning put my plan into action there was no stopping now. The fact that I had a job waiting for me made it I would say a lot easier I was in a great comfort zone since I was not going to pursue employment for once in my life, I was very fortunate. The drive out west would be a great experience for me and there would be many things to learn along the way it was my dream leaving New York City was not a problem I would miss all my friends and co-workers but the opportunity weighed everything else nothing could compete with this; I had dreamed many times even when I was a little boy of leaving New York City the winters had gotten to me I still remember my mother asking me what do you want in life? And my answer which always infuriated her was to leave New York City. I could not do what everyone else did work at a factory raise a family in an apartment and wait for the big payoff whatever that was and if it ever came. I had a career to pursue, and I was proud of what I was doing the people around me were just full of great encouragement. I had come a long way the ball was in my corner now and I had to run with it, and I could not and would not look back. There was no need I knew deep inside I was on the right path and now I had to make it real once I was comfortable with my decision.

I knew that I was certainly ready; that evening we had a great dinner and said our goodbyes to friends. Everyone gave us their blessings, and all I could think of was California, here we come.

HEADING WEST

We got up early the next day, Monday, May 16; it was my birthday. I had turned 22 years of age, we said our goodbyes to the family, and on that bright sunny day in Williamsburg, Brooklyn, I headed to Manhattan and connected with the Holland Tunnel. I drove nonstop through the classic New Jersey Turnpike and made a few stops in Philadelphia, Ohio, and Indiana, only stopping for gas. Our first overnight stop was in a small town in Illinois, right outside of Chicago, called Mattoon, to see my girl's uncle and his wife, whom I had met earlier that year. They were both teachers, and they knew it would be a remarkable trip going west for us. He was happy for his niece, and they had asked us to stop by on our way to the West Coast. It would be my first time in Chicago. My girl had a lot of family in that part of the country, and it would be a shame not to visit and take advantage of their hospitality. It would also provide us with the rest we needed, and as it turned out, we did have a great time visiting with them. They loved showing us the sights. They were aware that we were hungry and tired after leaving Brooklyn and being on the road for such a long time, so they stepped it up and went out of their way to spare no expense and fed us well.

They cooked their specialties, the best Puerto Rican food we had enjoyed in some time. I felt at home; it was unforgettable. I must say it was a great decision and time well spent.

The stop in Mattoon was a welcomed sight, and seeing the Chicago sights was great, not to mention that we were able to get some well-needed rest. We were staying in the country in a very large house with room to spare. It was great. The car was functioning well, so we had no worries. The weather was fantastic, so the short visit turned into a few days. I decided to make a few calls to New York City as well as Los Angeles to let everyone know we were doing well.

Time to go, so off we went back on Route 66, heading west. I kept driving during the day and when it would start to get dark, I'd search for a motel. Everything was going very well; we continued enjoying all the sights. Then, Texas, our biggest state. This was something; it was hot and dry, and it felt like we were spending our entire life going through the desert and seeing motorists stranded, in some cases not too pretty. I was thankful I had bought a car that did not depend on the water. My 1960 Corvair air-cooled did not depend on a radiator. I remember seeing some poor souls on the side of the road with their hoods up and smoke just coming out; lots of white smoke; you could certainly see the despair and frustration on people's faces. Our car was so small that we really could not stop to give anyone a ride. It was very apparent to anyone who saw us, but whenever we arrived at any gas station or any place where there was life, we would inform them that there was someone in need of road assistance. The heat was out of this world. We had no air conditioning, but I guess being a fan of hot weather helped. Whenever or wherever we stopped, people were very cordial, and they loved our accents, which was something that always came up, especially with the waitresses at all the different diners. They hadn't heard a Puerto Rican with a Brooklyn accent; heck, I had never heard a Texan accent before, so we were even. The diners we stopped at were fascinating. I had seen them on the East Coast, but these were bigger and roomier ones. The service was always great, and we were treated well at every stop. Our next stop was New Mexico. We were in the middle of the desert, and my car started to make a strange noise. My heart started beating as the red light came on the fan belt, so I pulled over to the side of the road. I had been warned about this. Corvair's were notorious for breaking fan belts, so I had come well prepared. I had bought plenty of spares. I stopped, got out, and changed the fan belt, but every time I turned the starter, the fan belt light came on. Something was wrong; it was getting late, and I feared we might get stuck on the side of the road in the dark.

A couple of guys in a pickup saw us and stopped. They said there was a place in town owned by Jerry Unser right over the hill that could fix the problem; they would be more than happy to tow us. They said that they could put a chain under my front bumper and tow us over the hill; all I had to do was keep the chain extended nice and tight. I said OK, I'll try my best.

We hooked the chain to my car and got inside. Things were going as planned; I must admit I was a bit nervous because I had never done anything like this before. We were now going slowly uphill, and I was really nervous, completely white knuckles, hoping we would make it over the hill. I was very scared; I was trying to keep my eyes on the road at all times and hoping this would not take too long. We were all wide-eyed. I was trying not to look scared, but in reality, I was terrified. I had no idea what was going on.

We were now going downhill; the wind was blowing, it was very hot in the car, and we were gaining speed. Our car was moving fast. I was trying not to rear-end the pickup truck, and as much as I was trying, I couldn't control the speed; things were happening fast. I didn't dare apply the brakes too fast for fear that the chain in front would snap. I was told to keep the chain tight, but now and then it would develop a slight loop that I couldn't control at all. I decided to apply the brakes lightly as I was told earlier to keep the chain tight, but that wasn't helping at all; everything was happening so fast that all I could think about was our safety. The speed was increasing quickly. Suddenly the chain hit the ground, and I saw sparks. It split in two and broke away from the pickup. I quickly applied the brakes, but the chain whipped right up and it came towards me like a massive snake. It quickly went under the car and took the wheel right out of my hands. I felt all four wheels slide. My body quickly turned to the right as the car spun around. Everyone was screaming; it all happened so quickly that the car rapidly turned over and went over the embankment on the side of the road, but as fate would have it, we landed in a sand dune completely safe. We were upside down, and everyone was in shock, crying and screaming their hearts out. I stepped out of the car as fast as I could to make sure we were all OK, and we were all in a state of shock. I reached over and took the chain off. I don't know where I found the strength, but I turned the car back over on its wheels. I quickly ran and checked to make sure that everyone was safe. I couldn't lose my cool; I had to remain strong for everyone.

We still had a long way to go. We finally managed to get the car to the garage to be serviced. We went to a local motel, washed up, had some food, and got some rest.

The next day, bright and early, off we went again. The car had been repaired; everyone was cheerful and in a good mood the worst had passed. When you're on the road, the unexpected creeps up on you. We had just managed to escape the worst of all, or so I thought we had, but there's always the unexpected. I drove for a few miles, but by the time we got to Santa Rosa, my car died again, again I opened the hood to check the fan belt, but it was all busted. The same problem, so here we were again on the side of the road, not knowing what to do, with no cars in sight, but as luck would have it, a colorful psychedelic school bus with two hippies came along, who stopped and offered to help us. They were delivering the bus to San Francisco and were really helpful and took the family to a nearby motel while I waited for a tow truck from town.

I returned with the tow truck, and my car was taken to a mechanic in town who said he would have the car ready the very next day. The hippies hung around. They offered us a ride to Los Angeles, but our car would be fixed with no problems.

In the morning, we said our goodbyes and took off on the road again. People at that time were very helpful and friendly. It was the 60s and the love generation was on our side. We arrived in Arizona and we were so happy because we knew that California would be coming up soon and our new home, wherever that was, waited for us. The weather had also been on our side. We didn't experience any rain or storms; we were very fortunate and thankful for what we were seeing, and enjoying it. life was good; it didn't get any better than that, so I thanked our lucky stars. The trip so far, except for a couple of mishaps, was going well. I never once felt like giving up at all; nothing was going to stop me. I was not going back. When I had decided to come out west, it was for good, so here we were. I could sense that we were not that far from Sunny California. I called Ami at the studio, which I did periodically to let him know we were still good and on our way, and reassure him everything was on schedule. Traveling through the desert was an experience. We enjoyed the trip and all the different people and places. We had been traveling mostly by day, usually starting at daybreak till sundown. We were having a great time and didn't want for anything so far. We had gotten this far safe and sound.

The people who helped us along the way were generous, helpful, and sincere. I thanked our lucky stars that so far our trip had gone so well and that our journey very soon would be coming to an end. We kept going; our next stop would be Kingman, Arizona. When we arrived, we stopped at a Holiday Inn. The staff went out of their way to accommodate us. It was hot and dry with a light wind blowing, but to us, it felt fantastic. The sky was bright blue and clear. We made really good use of their swimming pool; we enjoyed it to the fullest. We just ate and rested really well; we would be leaving for

California in a few days. I knew in my heart that we were safe we'd been on the road now for well over a month, enjoying ourselves. Monday morning came, and our short vacation in Kingman was over. We didn't have the time, or we would've stayed there a few more days. We drove through Las Vegas; we had never seen anything like this before. What a sight! The lights on every hotel looked great: The Golden Nugget, The Sands, The Tropicana, The Flamingo, and The Dunes; all their marquees had names that I recognized, even some that I knew that had recorded at A&R. What a feeling. We were now experiencing the bright lights on the marquees, still on during the daytime, and I wondered what it would look like in the evenings. Unfortunately, we couldn't stay to see it. The sights were unreal, but I was in a rush to get to California. We were in Nevada and I had to keep moving. I knew that if I kept moving, it would be a matter of time before we approached the San Bernardino Mountains in California.

It was a holiday, and I realized everything would be closed. The traffic was unbearable but not a factor to me. I had already been driving through a considerable amount of traffic. What difference was a little more going to make? At this point, it didn't matter to me.

California, from a distance, looked fantastic. The green landscapes had a hypnotic effect on me. I was excited I had finally arrived. Before leaving New York City, Ami had written the name and address of the studio for me on a small piece of paper. This was my first time in Los Angeles and I was being very careful. I wanted to find the studio, which was located at 1441 North McCadden Place in Hollywood. Unfortunately, I had gotten off someplace in Glendale, and as I drove thru the hills, making all sorts of turns, I realized I was lost, and then it hit me.

I remember my conversations with Ami, where he said to me that the studio was not far from the Sunset Strip. I stopped at a gas station and asked where Highland and Sunset Blvd were. I was told I was a long way off; it was getting dark, so I had to hurry and get as close as I could to our destination. I got in my car, headed for the Freeway and got off by the Forest Lawn exit. I could see the Forest Lawn cemetery on my left as well as the Warner Brothers lot to my right. I kept on driving, and as I approached the corner on Barham Blvd, I noticed the Universal Studios lot in front of us. I made a quick left, went over Barham Boulevard, made a quick left onto the Cahuenga Pass, and went down alongside the freeway past the Hollywood Bowl. I was so excited and pumped going down Highland heading south. I saw Hollywood High on my right. When we reached the corner, the sign read Sunset Blvd and the Texaco gas station was on my left and Stan's Drive-in facing us. I was excited and immediately turned left. I knew we were in the right area; there was no question about it. I headed east looking for McCadden Place, but I passed it and I didn't even know that I was right there. I saw the Cinerama Dome. the next corner was Vine Street. I made a quick right soon after I passed Delongpre Street, and finally, I made a right on the next corner on Fountain Avenue and headed west. We were all exhausted, hungry, and tired. I kept driving desperately looking for a motel for the night. I knew there had to be one around there someplace. I kept driving, and to our surprise, there it was; McCadden Place. I made a right, and to my left, I saw a big white building with big Roman gilded gold letters that read TTG. This was it: 1441 North McCadden Place. The building was closed, so we had to find a place to stay quickly. It was getting dark out, and everyone was getting restless. Traffic was unbearable as it was a holiday weekend. I made a left turn onto Sunset Boulevard as we traveled west, I saw a Travelodge Inn on our right. There were lots of bright lights up ahead, and as we approached the motel, I noticed there was a restaurant called Carolina Pines, which took up the whole corner on La Brea Avenue, Sunset Boulevard and Tiny Naylor's, another car-hop restaurant across the street.

We checked into the motel where we were reminded again how lucky we were because of the holiday weekend, which I had completely forgotten about; I had not planned for any holidays at all. We were sure lucky. As soon as we checked in, I called Ami and left word with his answering service, "Your Girl," that we had just arrived in town. I waited to hear from him. After a few minutes, he called. He sounded very excited and happy to hear from me. I told him where we were staying, and he told me not to worry; everything was going to be alright. Just eat something and get some rest, he advised.

We arranged to meet at the studio on Tuesday morning. He asked if everyone was Ok and if we needed anything. I said we were okay and that if we did, I would call him. I was relieved. I had never felt so much reassurance. We had traveled a long way, and for me, it was great hearing a familiar voice.

That night, I spent a great deal of time just looking out the window. I kept wondering what would come next. I was a long way from home. But a question I was constantly asking myself was, where was home? In New York City I just wondered around, staying busy and always in a new apartment. And that had to change. I needed to form some new roots, I knew deep inside that home is where you make it, and I knew that come hell or high water, Los Angeles would become my home. There would not be any turning back or getting homesick.

I was home, and I felt it in my bones. I felt that for once I had a purpose in life. It was now Monday, July 4, 1966. The town was hopping with lots of traffic, hippies, and beautiful girls wearing colorful dresses. Go Go Dancers at some of the clubs, which unfortunately at the time, we could not go in. But I could just imagine what the crowds were like. We decided to take a walk and see what the Sunset Strip was really like. It was fantastic, and the people were wonderful. We went to IHOP, located on the corner of Orange and Sunset Blvd, and had something to eat. Back to the motel for some rest. We were exhausted after all the walking. We'd been out for hours, but were too excited to sleep.

On Tuesday, we walked to McCadden Place, which was only two and a half blocks away, right across from the one and only Hollywood High School, which, to us, was quite a complex with a lot of charm, WOW! Hollywood, we're here! We crossed Highland Avenue again, staring at the girls on roller skates serving food at "Stan's Drive-In." This place was right out of the movies. It was exciting. The crowds were just amazing with all the laughter. I knew it was early, but we were so full of energy, so we decide to go further down Sunset Boulevard. On the corner of Vine Street and Sunset Blvd, there it was, the famous record store Wallach's Music City. This was where everyone could preview their 45s or LPs (vinyl records). They had about six booths, and you could go in to make sure your records were in good shape and didn't skip before you purchased them.

I had decided we would have to have dinner at Stan's Drive-In, no question about it. They took great care of their customers and their kids. Little did I know that "Stan's Drive-In" was one of the studios favorites. The fact that it was located right there on the corner was a great asset. We walked into the studio, and I asked to see Ami. To my surprise, his nephew David, who was taking care of the front desk at the time, replied, "He's been waiting for you." Ami came out of his office, put his arms around me, and welcomed us to California.

Tom Hidley came downstairs from his shop to pay his respects and greeted me by saying, "Balestier, you finally made it." We talked for a bit, telling road stories. They wanted me to see the studio, so they arranged for their assistant, Fred Borkgren, to show us around. We proceeded to the second floor, which had a long, enormous stairway leading to the top. The building consisted of three floors, but the third floor had not been developed. In later years, it would become a projection room when TTG would start doing music scoring sessions for Motion Pictures and TV Series.

Fred was great; he said that he had heard so much about me—that was all Ami and Tom talked about. They were pleased I was moving to California. Fred, a native Californian, knew the town well and offered to help. He told us that if he could be of any assistance, to let him know; he'd be glad to lead us in the right direction.

We were in Studio A on the second floor. You could fit a very large orchestra here with two vocal booths—one that was completely isolated, and another that was portable for background vocals. The room had real wood floors that were clean, not cement like A&R, and 20 feet thick sound insulated walls all along the back, covered in burlap, which hid about a third of the back section of the room.

The place was an enormous room, great for recording big shows, which was the main goal. The control room was also very large; the console was elevated. There was room for three production people plus an engineer. The monitors were JBL, which Tom had suspended. They were (L C R), and right behind the console were large racks that housed the amps and patch bays.

The very spacious control room had a separate station for the second engineer. In this section, you had complete control of Three Ampex Machines. One was a half-inch 4-track, 2 quarter-inch 2-track machines, and a quarter-inch mono full track machine with a 3-track machine behind the control room door for tape slap echo. Directly behind the racks was the entrance to Tom's Maintenance shop, with a second door that led to the coffee room with a large window that looked out into McCadden Place. Four burners keeping coffee ready at all times, and soda and cigarette machines were adjacent to the men's restroom. The lady's room was on the other side at the top of the stairs.

On the wall, messages on the bulletin board with an assortment of phones in different colors for all the different answering services, which were available 24/7 for all the artists, contractors, and musicians. This room looked like The New York

Stock Exchange—very loud, Smokey; everyone smoked. It was very crowded during the breaks with a lot of commotion. Here's where musicians would normally take their calls for other sessions, it was a standard for someone to say, "Call your service, 'NINA,' 'YOUR GIRL' or 'ARLYN'S," which were the most popular ones in town in those days.

They had an office on the third floor that was occupied by a gray-haired gentleman, Julie Losch, who was doing sales for the studio. He was a record promotion man who had, in the early days, broken Jimmy Rogers' hit record "Honey Comb" A nice man and always great to talk with; he and I would later become very good friends. I would learn an awful lot from Julie Losch. The man had a lot of experience and knew a lot of people in the music business.

Two studios on the first floor were not open yet, as well as bathrooms for men and women. The tape library was opposite the main reception area near Ami's office. The building had a large elevator, and that helped whenever the cartage companies delivered all the musicians' instruments going up to the second floor, especially Emil Richards whenever he was on a date. That elevator was full; he had an enormous collection of percussion instruments that would just fill the back of the studio as well as the halls.

There were only a few cartage companies back then—Modern Van and Storage and Old Men King, who delivered all the percussion instruments. A few years later, Al Rodriguez, who worked for him, would form his own company called Musicians Transfer, and a few others would follow. Drummers, for the most part, had a lot of equipment, the likes of Hal Blaine or Louie Bellson who had their guys.

My tour was over, so I sat down with Ami and Tom. We were trying to see when I would be available to start work. I said first I have to find an apartment, and it's got to be close by. They both agreed and recommended I take my time looking around, and they suggested Hollywood. Tom said, "You don't want to deal with the freeway, at least not now." He suggested that I should get used to traveling around and see what we liked before making any decisions.

We talked at length about the studio and what my duties would be, but they both seemed very confident and said I would know what to do, and they would not get in my way. I was grateful and impressed; this was not what I was expecting from Ami and Tom. I had no idea I had earned so much confidence and trust.

I had come to work, and they knew I would not abuse any of it. They also said to be very careful; this was not New York City. Tom said, "If you get a ticket, do not try to bribe the cops." I said I would be very careful; I wasn't planning on doing too much driving or speeding in town. I was excited about the whole setup of the studio.

I was getting ready to leave, and to my surprise, they handed me the keys to the building. They both told me to keep them posted, and make sure and let them know if we needed anything. They were very helpful. Aside from Phil Ramone at A&R, this had never happened to me. I felt welcomed; what a sigh of relief. I had my job, and here we were at last in California.

I had no idea where to start; it was a new city; a different world from where we had come, but I felt very lucky and privileged.

I wanted to start looking for an apartment as soon as possible. Getting settled was going to be a big task for us, yet it seemed like we were being watched by someone above, and I still believe that to this day. We didn't know Hollywood that well at all; we had just arrived here from New York City, and that was very noticeable. I started reading the Green Sheet, the local newspaper; all the addresses were foreign to us. Try pronouncing Cahuenga and Sepulveda just arriving from New York City.

We started looking all over town; some places looked good,

but kids were not accepted, so we kept looking. We stopped in Echo Park way up in the hills where some Asian family wanted to rent out half of their second floor, but that was not going to work at all, not with a jealous girlfriend. We kept on searching and asking Fred Borkgren questions and getting directions to various parts of the city. We ended up looking all over the city for an apartment; it wasn't easy. I drove as far as Watts, not realizing where we were. It was becoming really hard, spending all day looking for the right apartment. We were not locals, and our credentials read New York City. We had two kids, which is always a big stumbling block, but we kept at it; something had to turn up, but it wasn't easy.

We were spending a lot of time looking around Hollywood again, avoiding the valley. The motel was getting too crowded and expensive. I was exhausted looking for an apartment within the neighborhood area. One day, we started early, drove down Fountain Avenue, made a right on Bronson, and a left on Mattila, just hoping to see a for rent sign. I made a left turn on Van Ness Avenue, and there it was—a sign that read, "Furnished Apartment for Rent," right on the corner.

This was 1278 Van Ness Avenue; it was exactly what we had been looking for. It was a pure blessing—how lucky can you be?

We needed a furnished apartment, which had become a handicap; we had no furniture, and I couldn't afford to furnish one right away. We were very fortunate because they allowed kids, which was another plus, and the school was not far; it was only two blocks down the street on Santa Monica Blvd and Van Ness Avenue, across from Paramount Pictures.

We rented the apartment, drove down to Santa Monica to Sears, and purchased all the needed linens and some essentials. The kids were registered in school the very next day. Finally, I would be able to start work full-time and bring home a paycheck. I knew it would not be easy because that meant that with one car, everyone had to wait on me. But everyone was very patient; we would make do, and in time, we would have an additional car. It was just a matter of time.

We started to enjoy life in Hollywood. Things here where different; people were nicer, and the weather, well, there was no question—you couldn't beat it. Not have to walk up any stairs to get to your apartment or have drunks just hanging in front of your building—that was a plus. We felt comfortable; California surprised us. I was more than grateful to have made the move out west. Things were falling into place little by little. Any free time we had, we'd walk and just check things out; they were good times. The neighborhoods were safe; no fences or gates, and people were friendly. Back then, Hollywood was way different. I was very excited because I didn't have to be looking over my shoulder. I knew my family was safe.

The supermarkets fascinated us; they sold everything in one location. We'd never seen anything like it. They sold beer, wine, and hard booze in the supermarkets, which back then was unheard of in New York City. We had started a new life in a new state, and with it came a new set of rules, as Tom Hidley had said to me back east; the times were changing. There was no way of mistaking these changes; there was no way around it.

I went to the DMV on Cole Place in Hollywood and took my driving test, and finally, I had my California Driver's license and my I.D. This helped; there would be no more disappointment at the Hollywood Ranch Market. Many times, we would have to forgo many things and wait through the weekend to get what we needed because of not having proper local I.D. But now we were in a better spot, and things were finally falling into place. We had erased some obstacles that had stood in our way for some time. Unfortunately, no one could help us; we had to do it ourselves, and it was OK because it was a great learning process. I was comfortable; everyone was in great health; the school was very close to the apartment.

This worked for us, and I had a great job to boot. That was all I could ask for. I was not far from work; I could just walk.

Being new in town it was easy for me. How lucky can you be? Now I had to get ready because once you get going in the studio environment, at least back then, you have no idea when you're going to be home especially working at TTG.

It was the analog age, and things were very different. We had a distinctive sound, and everyone wanted to cash in on it. The exodus of musicians and producers from New York City was massive. Just walking down Sunset Blvd, every time I turned around, I would run into people from back east. Every time they would ask me, "Where are you working?" When I would tell them, they would either say they were booked that week or the following. It was very exciting. Times had changed, as Tom had said, but it was for the better, and I was excited.

This indeed was a different city, and it offered us just about all we wanted. like I've said, people were nicer here, and the safety factor was a plus. How long all this would last who knew? One never does, but we were really happy here from day one. I love that we had made the move. The evenings were great; you could walk anywhere, and it was great for us since it was all brand new to us.

The mornings were also great; we didn't have all the traffic to deal with. The majority of the time, we would walk just to see what it was like. We enjoyed the parks, especially Griffith Park, Echo Park, MacArthur Park, and Chinatown. We were new tourists in a town that was now our new home. I loved it; there was always a new place to see, and it was always very convenient to get anywhere. I knew that in time, we would not be able to go around town; work was just around the corner, it was best to try and do as much as possible now while time was on our side.

We made friends with a few people who were from Tennessee, and they were also in the same situation. We would get together and just walk Hollywood Blvd. It was all new to us, and we enjoyed every minute of it because there was always something to do, and many places to see, in a very short time, you could be at the beach, the mountains, or the desert. Monday morning was right around the corner I had a 10:00 a.m. session booked. It would be my first since I've arrived, and I'm excited about it.

TTG EARLY DAYS

I had been spending a considerable amount of time looking for an apartment, and now that it was finally over, I was excited, along with everyone else, it was time to get serious about work. We had been spending way too much time just seeing the town. It was my very first day at work, July 25, 1966. The first session I'm working on is for a commercial for Marcal Towels with Chico Hamilton, whom I had met earlier at A&R in New York City. It was not a big session, just Chico on drums, and another musician from his group, Jimmy Cheatam, who remembered me from A&R, welcomed me. It was a very comfortable session for me, like a welcome home party.

If you were from New York City and had been on the staff at A&R, clients confided in you. They expected the very best from you. I as a second engineer, stayed on top of everything when it came to client's needs and their documentation, which was a full detail of everything that went on in the studio. The majority of clients that came to TTG during that time had worked at A&R, so they recognized me and were happy to see me. There were many clients, including several musicians that I knew on a first-name basis, so it made my transition in California very easy.

The more recording sessions that I worked on, the more I became accustomed to the room, I loved this place. It was very big, and it had a certain aura about it. Musicians loved to play in this room, and, I might add, very famous ones who now lived in Los Angeles because this was where the music scene was happening. We were all over the airwaves. Everyone treated each other as family. They were eager to help, and we talked and greeted each other with such affection, honesty, respect, and warmth, which impressed me from day one.

Fred Borgkren, who was TTG first assistant engineer, the only one at the studio who had experience working with Tom Hidley in the early days and had many stories to tell. He would tell me stories about how Tom had been a milkman in Orange County, and how they did remotes out of Tom's Chevy convertible. Later, they went to work for Wally Heider who was a lawyer turned studio entrepreneur who now owned a studio on Cahuenga Blvd and Selma in Hollywood, which he just called Wally Heider Recording. Fred and I started working together daily. We had hit it off from day one, and we were in charge of aligning and calibrating all the machines in the studio. This meant setting records and playback levels, cleaning and demagnetizing the heads on all the Ampex tape machines. We were changing tubes, when necessary. If tubes needed to be changed, then they were all changed; not just one but all of them. Can you believe we even had our own tube test machine? Tom Hidley was a believer that if one was bad, then the others would follow in a very short time. So, we would start with a completely new batch, and it worked. We never had any downtime. We didn't have the reputation of holding up any recording session for any reason. We knew our equipment and knew how to maintain it. We were proud of what we had.

The information that was being passed on to us by Tom Hidley was priceless. The man was very meticulous, and it has instilled confidence and trust in all of us. This was something not taught in any school in the world. You couldn't buy it. You rarely get that kind of training. We were being trained by one of the best. Tom Hidley made sure that we knew and understood every piece of gear in our control room. He made it a point to teach both Fred and me everything, which made us an asset to the studio and, in the long run, would help our careers in years to come. We were both well aware that we were fortunate to have this training. For Fred and me, this became another feather in our caps. We did all the setups, and back then, they were all big sessions. We had a running joke. There were lots of times we would say, "Yeah, Ami, you can always fit the biggest band on the smallest piece of paper." But I must say, to his credit, it always worked. And he'd laugh and say, "See, I told you guys." Another great session had just taken place at TTG, and as usual, we were a big part of it. Our typical recording sessions in those days in the mid-60s consisted of some of the best artists and musicians in the world. There were always lots of stars at the studio. L. A. had become the music capital, with droves of people always visiting Southern California. You never knew who would show up for any given session, but normally our roster consisted of the best in town with such players as:

Keyboard, Piano, Celeste, B-3 Hammond Organ: Al DeLory, Larry Knechtel, Mike Melvoin, Don Randi, Mac Rebennack (aka: Dr. John), Mike (Michel) Rubini, Leon Russell

Bass, both Acoustic and Electric: Max Bennett, Chuck Berghofer, Jimmy Bond, Red Callendar, Jim Hughart, Carol Kaye, Larry Knechtel, Joe Osborn, Bill Pittman, Ray Pohlman, Lyle Ritz.

Guitars, Acoustic and Electric: James Burton, Glen Campbell, Al Casey, Jerry Cole, Mike Deasy, John Goldthwaite, Rene Hall, Carol Kaye, Barney Kessel, Don Peake, Bill Pittman, Ray Pohlman, Howard Roberts, Irv Rubins, Louie Shelton, Billy Strange, Tommy Tedesco, Al Vescovo, P.F. Sloan, Lou Murrell.

Drums: Hal Blaine, John Clauder, Jim Gordon, Jim Keltner, Earl Palmer, Jeff Pocaro, Frankie Capp, Louie

Bellson, Paul Humpherie, John Raines, Ed Greene, Irv Cotler.

Percussion, two to three players: Frank Capp, Gary L. Coleman, Julius Wechter, Joe Pocaro, Emil Richards, Ken Wild, Larry Bunker, Gene Estes.

Woodwinds: Gene Cipriano, Steve Douglas, Jim Horn, Plas Johnson, Jay Migliori, Nino Tempo. Trumpets: Bud Brisbois, Roy Caton, Chuck Findley, Ollie Mitchell, Tony Terran, Pete & Conti Candoli

Trombones: Lou Blackburn, Richard "Slyde" Hyde, Lew McCreary.

String Section: usually, Sid Sharp as concertmaster

Background Singers: John Bahler, Tom Bahler, Ron Hicklin, Stan Farber, Sally Stevens, Jackie Ward, and many others that would change depending on the artist or product.

We were often recording variety shows like The Hollywood Palace, which we did every week.

The Lineup of stars always varied depending on availability. Every hour, we were told to take a five-minute break in later years changed to Ten-minute, it applied to the musicians. My place was to remain in the control room for playbacks. After a few playbacks, maybe a possible edit, then I would also take a break. These sessions were exciting, everyone came to play excited and in a great mood. We were making music that was being heard all over the airwaves, they were exciting times.

I would often find myself standing outside with many of the musicians for the duration of our break. I would just hang out and talk with none other than Elvis Presley's guitar player, James Burton, who was always dressed impeccably. We often talked about my move from New York City, and how Ronnie Tutt the drummer, and the rest of the band were doing record dates in town while the King was chilling out. James was a musician that you would often see on many sessions at TTG, and again what a great individual. I felt at ease, and I would always just ask questions about Elvis Presley, which he would always be more than happy to answer; they were fun times.

Johnny Fresco, for the most part. was the producer/contractor on these dates they were long days but with what we were doing time seemed to pass quickly. While I was working at TTG, I was very fortunate to meet and be befriended by my dear friend, Marshall Leib, a tall ex-marine who worked for Liberty Records. He had been a member of the legendary vocal group "The Teddy Bears" with the legendary producer Phil Spector. Marshall and I would be like two old ladies, always exchanging stories and I was fascinated by many of them; we would always have a great time.

I remember Marshall often telling me stories that, after graduating from Fairfax High in Los Angeles, his friend Phil Spector had become obsessed with the song "To Know Him Is to Love Him," a song that he had written for their group. They had auditioned for ERA Records and financed the record with Phil Spector, Marshall Leib, Harvey Goldstein (who left the group early on), lead singer Annette Kleinbard, with last minute recruit, drummer Sandy Nelson. They recorded the song at Gold Star Studios on Vine Street for $75, it was released on ERA's Dore label in August 1958. Marshall said that it took about two months before "To Know Him Is to Love Him" began to get airplay.

I was so curious, Marshall's stories were always really interesting, and at times he would have me just busting at the seams with laughter. I miss my old friend, I just wanted to know more and as always Marshall just told me; or rather answered any questions I asked.

Marshall would often volunteer a lot of information; I loved the guy. That's why, in later years, I made sure that anything he wanted in the studio was available to him. He said the record stayed in the Billboard Hot 100 for 23 weeks, in the Top Ten for 11 of those weeks, and commanded the #1 chart position for three weeks. They had other releases on the Imperial label that were well-recorded soft pop; unfortunately, they didn't do as well, and within a year of their debut, Phil Spector disbanded the group. Spector was not the only Teddy Bear who went on to a different career after the group broke up. Harvey Goldstein became a certified public accountant, and Annette Kleinbard continued to write and record songs and changed her name to Carol Connors. Among her credits are the Rip Chord hit "Hey Little Cobra," and among many others, the Academy Awards nominated Rocky theme song "Gonna Fly Now." I remember when she was doing the demo for Rocky right there at TTG.

Marshall continued to work for Liberty Records, being good friends with the Everly Brothers, all three had been in the Marines. Marshall said and I quote, "When we were in the service, we did nothing." I worked with Phil and Don earlier on with Lenny Worneker producing when they were signed to Warner Bros. Marshall had a lot of projects, he was responsible for, recording Deacon Jones, which I considered a great session. I was proud that he always requested me as an engineer, which would continue during my days at MGM Records.

While at TTG, we had long sessions. Sometimes we would start at say ten in the morning which meant we had to be at the studio at six in the morning to set up the orchestra as well as the control room (unless we were lucky enough to do it the night before). But we still had to be there early enough for the cartage companies; it was something that was ingrained in all of us from Tom and Ami. I mean all of us. We made sure that all legends had, who was producing, the label, the name of the artist or project, and the length of the tune, including any false starts. We made sure that our piano was always in tune with Paul Loften, who was our primary tuner. Paul was a preacher and a fine tuner. Once he'd finish, he would play you something on the piano and quote you a verse from the bible always very timely. Another great tuner Keith Albright, who tuned by ear he does most of the studios in town and still rides his bike to every session. The man could tell you who had which piano in town, what type, the year it was made, and the model. Then there was Joe Spencer who traveled with a little dog, but Joe's main thing was harpsichords, and I believe he owned a few of them that he rented out. Clyde Reasinger, who was from New York City, moved to California and became the staff tuner at NBC in Burbank and remained there for 26 years. We would talk all the time about his move from New York City, where he was first trumpet and first call. But with his move out west, he wasn't getting the work he was used to getting back east, so he started tuning in addition to playing a nice man who knew his job very well. All the tuners that I have mentioned all tuned by ear, no machine, which has always been my preference at A & R, we had Willie Lannin, who was the brother of the big orchestra leader Lester Lannin. Every time Willie came to tune the piano, he would set his machine up and get his hammer and start tuning. We would just mess with him to no end. We would send a 10k-tone thru the headsets, and his machine would pick it up. It would just drive him crazy. We would always cop to it, and he'd say to us in a very friendly manner, You son-of-a-bitches.

We did many large agency dates that were under the direction of none other than George Romanis, who had decided to move his whole operation to Los Angeles. The agencies followed him; he was the king of commercials always big national campaigns for well-known products, and his sessions were always big with lots of percussion, with acoustic and electric bass players. George was a big guy over 6-feet tall and a wonderful person. He always treated me as part of the family and rely on my notes, and he was always very complimentary. I remember he would always say Ami, when are you going to give the kid a chance? He would say "For Christ's sake let him record something," and he meant it, but I understood it wasn't time yet. George liked that I always marked all the legends with his comments in regards to the take. I was very detailed on all track sheets. I felt that it was very important. He would say things like, It's a mother, or That's the one don't lose it. I was having the time of my life. I have always been a believer that you can't have enough documentation. You have no idea what you can use as a reference. if you have an incomplete take, how long is it? Maybe you can use the front of it or a verse, does it have a good front? Did we listen to it? and that's why the markings of (C) for complete, (PB) for playback, (LFS) for a long false start, (INC) for incomplete, (M) for master were and have always been extremely important. Not to mention any comments that you can pick up at the time. Dates are really important.

Whenever you're in a control room as an assistant, listen to what is being said. Your engineer has enough to do. You cannot ever have enough documentation that is why you're the assistant. You must know your position.

I remember in the early days although not asked, we were involved in all session setups until the session was on its way. We shared information. It felt good to see a session take off without a hitch. We were very proud of what we were doing, and we treated everything like there was no tomorrow. Anyone who worked at TTG during the 60s, 70s will tell you that it had one of the best staffs in the west coast. There was always some action going on the place never rested, everything that we were working on had a great deal of notoriety. It was very special we had a strong sense of loyalty to our studio first and foremost to our clientele who came from all over the world to record with us in Hollywood. TTG in its early days was very busy. We had a great share of the business in town. We were doing great, but we had only one room, something that we knew had to be addressed down the line. We were doing large advertising agency campaigns, one that came to mind was for

ZEE Paper Towels. The agency wanted to emphasize an exotic tropical feel, and they brought in none other than the master of all, Martin Denny. Many of you might not remember, but Martin was born in New York City, and he had a fascination with Latin rhythms. He had collected a large number of ethnic instruments from all over the world, which he used to spice up his stage performances and were a sight to see. His original combo back then consisted of Augie Colon on percussion and birdcalls, Arthur Lyman on vibes, John Kramer on string bass, and Denny on piano; he was the father of exotica. The agency hired him for a big commercial campaign that consisted of various spots in lengths (10, 20, 30, 60-second radio spots) with different disclaimers depending on the region or state. I had to ship all these spots all over the country at the time, not an easy task. I ended up after the session all by myself, carefully placing labels in the correct order, packing hundreds of packages and delivering them in my 1960 Corvair to the local post office station on Santa Monica and Wilcox Avenue. Boy what a task but I did it.

We were always busy doing various commercial campaigns that were very profitable and kept everyone busy. B B D & O another advertising agency from New York City, had hired a very close friend and very funny, talented composer and producer, Tommy Oliver. Whenever Tommy booked a session, we would have a great time; there was never a dull moment. I remember one evening he and I ran out of cigarettes. We went into the coffee room, and the machine had taken our money. It was very late; we looked at each other and decided to turn the machine upside down. After that, whenever you wanted a pack of cigarettes, you just pulled the lever a couple of times, and out came whatever brand you chose.

Tommy arranged and produced albums for various artists, such as Doris Day, Edie Adams, Wayne Newton, Charles Boyer, Frankie Avalon, Joey Heatherton, Pat Boone, Kenny Rogers, John Denver, Joanie Sommers, Denny Provisor (later with The

Grass Roots), and The Jefferson Airplane. Also, in the 1970s and 1980s, he would serve as musical producer and bandleader for such game shows as "Name That Tune" and "Face the Music." His credits also included work on such popular shows Donnie and Marie, Playboy After Dark, the revival of the well-known 1979 show Laugh-In, and The John Denver Special.

The agencies often used TTG because they were familiar with all of us. We had done many other commercials for them, including all of their Chevron Gasoline campaigns, which were big. They liked the way we operated. Yes, you want the business, but is important that you're sincere about it, because if not, it would show. When you have producers and writers from out of town that you are dealing with, comfort and respect will play a big part.

We always had a big crowd, and since Hollywood was very attractive and the music scene was in Los Angeles, they loved to come and record at our studio. A big part of it was also word of mouth. We extended a great deal of respect to anyone who recorded here, especially from back east, and they always raved about it.

BBD&O, at the time, was one of our biggest clients and one of the biggest agencies by far. They would spend a lot of time here and paid us very well. There was never any quibbling as far as rates went. Our studio was near everything, which was a big plus for us. We had maintained a great relationship with this agency from day one. We knew the staff back in New York City, so they were very well at ease with our studio and staff. They would always send their commercials our way, knowing full well that we understood what they wanted, and they respected us for it.

When agencies have staff people traveling between the East and West Coast, it's important that they have a home base. I believe that they felt they had a home at TTG, and we worked our tails off to ensure their return time and time again. We had the track record to prove it, and we were consistent. We never shorted them on anything and always treated them with the utmost respect at all times.

BBD&O was now doing a big campaign for FORD with Tommy Oliver as a composer and musical director. Again, this would require many hours of recording time, not to mention duplicating and putting together various masters. This was a very big campaign. We were certainly going to be very busy, no question about it, but the fact that it was Tommy Oliver made it more exciting.

First thing Monday morning, I started setting up and going over various things with Ami for any possible changes. I was checking everything. I would be the second engineer on this date, so I made sure that any information went through me, and that included any label copies regarding the spots and the sequence of the presentation, a very important detail.

The brothers John and Tom Bahler, along with a few other singers, were hired for this special presentation, which would be going by the title of "Ford is the Going Thing." These were promotional campaigns that consisted of a large orchestra with a vocal group that Tommy earlier had produced here at TTG for Liberty Records called "The Love Generation." The group was very pleasant, which made the sessions go by pretty fast; they were pros at it. The agency staff enjoyed themselves throughout all the live recording, and when we finished recording the band, we went into vocal overdub mode. When we were done, we took our lunch break; everything had gone as planned.

I hung out with the agency producer and Tommy while Ami went to his office to conduct other business. I remember the agency producer asking me, "Angel how's California treating you so far? Do you think you'll ever go back to New York City?" Before I could answer, Tommy said, "He's not going anywhere; we're keeping him here." The room just broke out in laughter. That's how Tommy treated me, and he was always very kind and sincere about it. I miss the guy; they didn't come any better. I was the luckiest guy on earth; he always made me feel that way. There was no way I was going to leave all this behind; I knew I had finally found my home.

I was appreciated very often and complimented by everyone who recorded here. How could I not like it here? It was great being in California, every day I was reassured I had made the right choice. Tommy always kept a certain humor and spirit going throughout this whole process, which is a gift. We had started with the orchestra in the morning, with a 10:00 a.m. downbeat. Lunch from 1:00 p.m. to 2:00 p.m. and we would break for dinner at 6:00 p.m. Vocal overdubs would start at about 8:00 p.m. or earlier, depending on our dinner break. We would then continue recording vocals and mixing, and right after that, I would assemble the master tape. Sometimes, if it was possible, I would try to assemble a master reel on the go as we were mixing.

While I was making a copy (a safety) of the master, I would play it over the studio speakers to check the sequence and strike our session or set up the next day's recording session. This was the usual for either Fred or myself; we were the assistant engineers, and these were our duties and responsibilities. There was no room for mistakes at all. Then I would proceed to make tape copies Mono Full Track-7.5 ips of all the radio spots 10; 20; 30; 60 second spots. Some sets were split; some others would get all four spots, and I had to do them two at a time. We only had two mono machines. They were normally run to a 5-inch plastic reel, and depending on the amount of tape, 502 – 2-inch hubs meaning it held 600 feet of audio tape, and 503 – 3-inch hubs held 300 feet of audio tape.

I would always ask before this took place, "Are you providing label copy, or are we?" I would make all sorts of copies per their regions. There needed to be no room for error. All the boxes had the studio's logo name address and phone number, along with the name of the spots and timings of each spot. We packaged and shipped each copy either by air, messenger, or local post office, whichever was fastest for their given destination.

I was busy using a 2-track machine, taking the output of one channel, usually channel two, bringing it up through the board to get an accurate level; this would not change, and after carefully monitoring, and setting the recording levels, I would now turn the master over for I would be recording the spots (Tails) backwards. The same process we used when I worked at National Recording in New York City this; process always worked, it was not hit or miss and the speed was a great factor. We had to get these spots out as quickly as possible.

I would then start making copies, and after each set, I would cut off the reel, add a new plastic take-up reel on the machines, and start recording again. I would then spot-check each copy and put a piece of red tape to hold the tape over the reel, red indicating it was headed out. We didn't have audio Cassettes or CDs back then; quality control was very important. You needed to listen and pay attention to your product at all times. The sequence had to be correct because when it left your hands it went to the disc jockeys at the radio stations, and they would transfer your tape and have it ready to play on the air. If it was wrong you would lose your client.

This process took place at least twice a year and your day would end usually around 10:00 or 11:00 a.m. the following day. We were well known for our speed and were considered the first stop for various agencies. Time passed very quickly and now, through Tom Hidley, TTG had entered into a deal with a copyist by the name of Bob Ross, who had a small recording studio, Harmony Recording, formerly on Melrose Avenue and had since moved to Delongpre Avenue off Vine Street.

The time had finally arrived, we would now have Studio 2 on the first floor operational. Bob Ross would bring in his console as well as his engineer, Roy Durkee, who was a very popular recording engineer with a big following when it came to R&B sessions; it was a win-win situation. We now could do more small record recording sessions and have the flexibility to do our vocal overdubs downstairs in Studio 2. We didn't have to tie up our large room and we could accept more bookings; this gave us the competitive edge that we needed for such a long time. We could now free Studio A for more live recording sessions and we were now able to accommodate their clients as well. It seemed like a good deal since the first floor had been dark for some time.

We needed to expand; there was no need for us to occupy a large studio to do small sessions or vocal overdubs. It all made perfect sense. The opening of Studio 2 became a plus for us and a very welcomed sight for everyone concerned since we had a great relationship with many record labels. Liberty Records, for one, gave us the ability to work with such artists as The Ventures, Bobby Vee, Timi Yuro, Mel Carter, Vikki Carr, Trombones Unlimited, Jackie DeShannon, and many more from their roster of artists. We were very busy with The Ventures, a group that was formed in 1958 in Tacoma, Washington, and in later years would be inducted into the Rock N Roll Hall of Fame. They were fans of the studio as well as their producer Joe Saraceno. The first time they came in to record we tried to record them like you would any other band, but we were losing that live sound which was a big part of their sound, so finally Ami decided that it would be best if we recorded them live all against the wall to the right on the north side of the Studio with no baffles (partitions). As soon as we made the change, everyone was happy, and the session continued.

Many things happened in Studio A, one of the most memorable ones that I have never forgotten. We had just finished a session, the room had been cleared, and we were setting up risers for The Buddy Rich Band. I had never met Buddy Rich before in my life. I knew very little about him. I knew that he was the drummer who had played for Tommy Dorsey, Harry James, Count Basie, and Frank Sinatra, among many others. I would find out many other things later on from my very dear friend Louie Bellson. I was hanging out with Louie, so I asked him if it was true. He said, "Ange," as he would always call me.

I said, "You know, I've heard lots of stories about Buddy Rich. Is he cool?"

He said, "Oh yeah, very cool." And then he started to tell me that Buddy began playing drums at an early age in vaudeville when he was 8 years old and billed as "Traps the Drum Wonder." I was blown away. I was amazed, and I wasn't aware of any of this.

I said, "Are you for real?"

Louie said, "Look, Ange, listen to me. At the peak of his childhood career, Buddy was also the second-highest-paid child entertainer in the world." Who knew? I certainly didn't. We kept talking, and he went on to tell me that at the age of 11, he was also performing as a bandleader. So now here I was on this day, I'm in Studio A with none other than Dick Bock producing for Imperial Records. I'm setting up the band with their recording engineer, Lanky Linstrote, moving big booms for the microphones as well as all the risers which had just arrived.

What happened next, I will never forget. It so happened that one of the band members asked the road manager if he could have $20.00? He very quickly replied in a very annoyed response. "What happened to the $20.00 I gave you yesterday?"

Well, I guess he went back and told Buddy Rich who called for the band to sit down as he proceeded to lecture them about the fact that they were going to Japan; and I quote: "If you're caught with any shit (drugs), you will experience a lot of problems and possibly end up in jail. Japan is not a country where you can just play around and ignore their laws."

Those were his very words, and he kept on scolding the guys in the band. I didn't want to stay in the room; not only because I had other things to do, but it was none of my business. I felt it was their business, so I would allow them their privacy. Buddy was screaming at the top of his lungs, and as he saw me trying to get past him, he yelled, "Sit down. No one is leaving this room." I sat down and listened as he lectured all his musicians. After all was said and done, we started to get a balance of the band. Buddy Rich did his count off: a one, two, three, downbeat; we started recording. We continued as if nothing had ever happened, and all in all, it was a great session and an experience watching the man Buddy Rich play drums with such ease.

I appreciated everything Louie told me about Buddy Rich more than anything; after that I was able to appreciate his sessions a lot more. The session went very well. The engineer was a well-seasoned mixer, and very fast at the controls, so we wasted no time recording. I had never met his producer, Dick Bock, who was a wonderful and talented man in and out of the studio. He would always take a crack at doing an edit of a pickup; he loved editing audio tapes, and it was a sight to see; what I was witnessing was quite an experience. Dick would come down from the console past all the machines and controls as everyone watched him make his mark on the tape, he was very fast but he would just cover the playback head with the white grease pencil so badly that you had to clean the heads on the machine to avoid dropouts when you played back the tune. We had some sessions with Ravi Shankar who had befriended Dick, who was the founder of World Pacific Records, a subsidiary of Liberty Records. Ravi Shankar recorded most of his albums for Bock's label. Those were great sessions; the studio would be set up by Ravi with his back to the west side of the studio facing east towards the control room and everyone else around him. We had an enormous number of flowers that were brought in by some of his followers, candles, and incense that were lit and placed around the players in the studio and control room.

The Byrds, who were recording at the same studio and had heard Shankar's music, would later on incorporate some of its elements in theirs. This was also followed by many other groups as well as Eric Burton and the Animals on the tune "San Franciscan Nights;" the Sitar had become very popular. The Byrds, as it was told to me by David Crosby during a session in Studio 2, would introduce the genre to their friend, none other than George Harrison. I can't say enough to describe all these sessions; they were the most memorable sessions, and not to mention they were very historical.

We stayed very active at TTG, doing work for Dunhill Records, UNI Records, Capitol Records, and through a long friendship of Tom Hidley's, with MGM Records out of New York City, which was headed by none other than Val Valentine, who years earlier had worked for Capitol Records. Val had done a lot of recordings with Frank Sinatra; Val's title was director of engineering and boy did he use that title. When any album was recorded for MGM Records and released, the only credit that was given would read "Director of Engineering, Val Valentine." A lot of the acts didn't know our real names because we weren't getting any sound engineering credits on any of the albums, we were often asked by many group members, "Who is that guy?"

Then there was Jesse Kaye on the West Coast who was head of A&R for MGM Records. He was the one who made all the rounds to all the studios in town whenever MGM had one of their artists in-house. He would always come by to see a session in progress, introduce himself, and often hand you a piece of candy; a very nice man. One day while I was recording a session in Studio 2, Jesse dropped by just to say hello. He asked me if there was a turntable around. He wanted to listen to a dub from a Righteous Brothers session, "Peace Brother Peace" He said, "Listen to this Angel, it's a very expensive session. Phil Spector used 6 pianos. We don't know how it will do but it's a big one." Unfortunately, the record didn't do that well but the experience of being around Jesse was worth more than anything else. He was full of information, and if you listened to him closely, you would gain a lot of insight into the music industry, he was good friends with none other than Lou Costello (of Abbott & Costello fame). Jesse was full of surprises and what a wonderful person. I'm glad I had the privilege of working with him; and with all the work we were doing for MGM Records, how could you not deal with such a lovely man? We were a busy studio, the busiest studio on the West Coast. Now, with all this activity, it became obvious to everyone at TTG that we needed someone to run our front office. We were very busy; I could no longer do it.

In the early days, I would book all the sessions and do all the billing. I did our billing with books I would buy at "Pick'n Save," a thrift store on Sunset Blvd. The books came with white, pink, and yellow receipts, all numbered with no logos. I would just put our rubber stamp with the name and address of the studio, everything else was handwritten in black ink per Ami's request. I answered all the phone calls and made coffee. I remember when we had no money, I would take paper towels and cut circles to create a filter for the coffee machine, and file all the tapes in our makeshift library next to Ami's office. I would handle all the mail and buy all the supplies that were needed for the office, pick up all our tapes, would drive my 1960 Corvair down to 636 North LaBrea Avenue, where 3M had a small office. I would be greeted by Ruth and Gordon Menard, who was our local rep for Minnesota Mining (3M). I would often make my usual stops at Pinks to get a hot dog or Foster Freeze where I learned and had my first burrito in California.

Ami and Tom became well aware of what needed to be done; times were changing, I could no longer be chief, cook, and bottle washer. I had come into my own; I was a recording engineer and on demand. So, they started making inquiries to hire someone else with knowledge of recording studios to cover the front office. Ami finally made some calls, and, in the end, he hired Stephanie Murray, who had worked for Lester Sills at Col-Gems; she lived not far from the studio on

Beachwood Drive in the Hollywood hills. She was a lovely lady and more than capable for the job. A wonderful person, she knew the industry and its players extremely well. Stephanie became our introduction to Lester Sills, who brought in a new group they were grooming for a TV Series. They were an American Pop Rock Group assembled in Los Angeles in 1966 for the new American television series called "The Monkees" that would air from 1966 to 1968. The quartet was composed of Mickey Dolenz, Michael Nesmith, Peter Tork, and none other than Englishman Davy Jones. I knew it was a chance for us to move up even further in the music industry. It was obvious we needed to be recording more groups that had notoriety, especially for TV. The band's music was being supervised by Don Kirshner. Before that everyone had been doing numerous jobs. It was a new studio, we were operating with one room and it was a smaller staff, but everything was now changing very fast at TTG.

I noticed that Tom was getting angry way too often. It had come to his attention that all Fred Borkgren wanted to do was mix, he was not interested in making coffee in the mornings. I didn't care but Fred expected Stephanie to make it, since she was now our office girl. I always took it as a rule of thumb; the first one in makes the first pot of coffee. Tom would say, "Borkgren, when I come up the block, I want to smell that coffee brewing," and being the prankster that I am, one day I waited for him as he was coming up the block. I threw a cup of coffee at him which nearly missed. He just laughed it off. I loved it. Tom Hidley had a great sense of humor and he was good to me; I had no complaints, we knew at that time Fred's days were number at TTG, and his wife wanted him to bring home more money. They had two boys, and it wasn't easy for them. He was getting a lot of pressure at home which I understood, so it made it hard for him to concentrate.

I, on the other hand, was the new kid in town, and frankly, it didn't matter to me, and although things were getting tense daily, both Fred and I still found time to enjoy our weekends. Fred and I would never talk shop outside the studio, and I for one did sympathize with his feelings. I had met a construction worker while getting quotes to have the roof fixed and in passing, he said he had a son who lived in San Diego who was a member of a band, and invited me to go and see them play. So I decided I would go listen to them, and if I felt there was something there, I'd bring them into the studio and record them; it would give me something to do. There was plenty of downtime at the studio, both Ami and Tom had no objections. I approached Fred, but he never really participated in the recordings; his mind was someplace else. He wasn't really into it; whenever possible he would tag along with me on weekends to San Diego. After toying around with this group for some time, I decided to bring them to Hollywood and record them. I wanted to see how they would do in the studio, which is a lot different than at a club. It wasn't very promising, so I decided to start going down and hold some rehearsals with the band, to see if there was any chance for improvement. I would hold rehearsals, and if they had a club date I'd be there for moral support. One weekend, while we were there, Fred suggested we go to Tijuana. I was very green and knew nothing about Mexico or their food. I was a Brooklyn knight at heart, so we went all over the place. We just hung out in bars till the early morning hours. Fred loved showing me things that I was not familiar with; so, whenever I would ask him something, he would just go out of his way to explain things to me. By now we had become good friends.

Things kept changing and by now many other things were coming into play. I guess it was a godsend for Fred, the duet of Ike & Tina Turner an African-American Rock & Roll and Soul duo who had a career spanning sixteen years together as a recording group. The duo's repertoire included Rock & Roll, Soul, Blues and Funk. They were known for their wild and entertaining dance shows, especially for their scintillating cover of a song which I spent a few hours overdubbing horns, "Proud Mary," for which they won a Grammy Award.

Ike Turner had just opened his studio, which he named after Tina's real name (Anna Mae Bullock): Bullock Sound. He was now in desperate need of a sound engineer, and the situation became a saving grace for all. Ike had turned to Ami for advice. He told him he could not find a sound engineer he could trust. Ami spoke with Fred at length and, as it turned out, Fred didn't live that far from there, so Ami suggested him. Fred jumped at the opportunity right away. I was saddened by his departure from TTG, but things sometimes work out for the best.

If there was one thing you could say about Ike Turner was, he always had the best coke in town and always paid you really good money. Fred needed that, he had two growing boys, and I knew they wanted to buy a house. Times were changing and if he needed to make a move it was now. I have always said that we have no personal life in the music industry. We rarely see friends, and whatever free time we get we try to spend with our family, and sometimes, if at all possible, with friends. Unfortunately, time went by fast, as it happens in this business. Fred and I didn't see much of each other, because when you work at different studios, it's very hard because of schedules, and they will change, and you do not have a social life at all. As time went by, we just drifted apart. I will always remember our sessions not to mention our trips to San Diego.

I would not see Fred again for about another maybe 20 years. I have a lot of great fond memories of Borgkren, as Tom called him. He would always call us by our last names. I will never forget him, he was there when I needed help, I was new in California and needed to know the town and he went out of his way for me, showed me lots of things, and we hung out together. Those were great times. I miss the sessions both of us worked on as second engineers, the days when we would drive, fly or take the train down to San Diego. The father of our lead singer was in the Real Estate business on several occasions. Whenever we visited, he would loan us the family station wagon. Both parents were fascinated by the music industry to no end, so they treated us well. I had several meetings with the group, but that whole scene would end very soon. They were very young and one of the parents wouldn't let one of the members enter into a contract, which in the end put a dent in the group's career.

We're still in touch today and remain friends. Fred Heath, the lead guitar player, still plays in various clubs in San Diego; Randy Davis who has a great eye, does an awful lot of bike restoration as well as photography; and their drummer, Bob Moore, after serving in Vietnam, has had a great career in law enforcement and now lives in Atlanta. During the mid-60s TTG was one of the busiest studios in Hollywood. There is no denying that at all. I was twenty-two years old, a hustler from Brooklyn with a heavy accent, but very eager to succeed. I still think of all of us during those early days together at TTG. A few years went by and Julie Losch, being the promoter that he was, and I always talked. I said to him, "You know, Julie. I saw Aretha Franklin coming down those stairs. She looked fantastic but the carpet and stairs were so torn up it was embarrassing.

I didn't take a picture for fear the trades might get a hold of it and we wouldn't look good. He really took it so seriously that the very next day he had Ami install new carpet and paint the place to spruce it up. We now had a great looking red carpet with a beautiful pattern from the first floor straight up to the second floor; the place was painted. It looked great but, as faith would have it, didn't last long. The very first session we had after all the renovations was with Ike and Tina. Fred was not the engineer, he was busy recording someone else at Bullock, so I did the session; a long one. That's when we did "Rolling on The River" and it went all night. The next morning when Julie Losch came in, he noticed that they had burn holes in the carpet. He was furious. The sink in the ladies' room on the first floor was broken; it seemed there was chaos, but we were upstairs, I didn't hear a thing. There were a lot of other things that happened that evening, but why go into them.

When the movie Ike and Tina Turner was released, I found it amazing that Fred was not portrayed in any way shape, or form. What a pity. Unfortunately for us this happens way too often, but as Fred would tell me later; Ike had nothing to do with it—which makes sense. The British Invasion had an impact on popular music. It made everything change; everyone seemed to be recording more and more.

We had such fantastic players, as I mentioned earlier, that would be coined as the wrecking crew. These musicians were the best and extremely creative guys that would later come into their own; but during that time, they were the busy Kats in town. They were the world's best musicians, at the top of their game, performing on just about every record. Major motion picture or TV show, everyone was coming to the West Coast and making music. Artists, dancers, engineers, musicians, producers, singers, and writers were all making music history in the studios. I was very fortunate to have played a part in working on a great deal of recording sessions. We were part of music history, and we were extremely busy with our number one love. We ate and breathed Music.

There was a lot of excitement going on at TTG; ABC TV had booked our studio to record a big TV special that would be filmed live. They were covering Psychedelic music, which was at its peak, and they had decided to record none other than one of the best, Frank Zappa and The Mothers of Invention. They had recorded at TTG before I came out to California. I was really excited and looking forward to this TV Special, their band setup and sound would not be that hard to duplicate. Tom Hidley had already mixed some of their earlier tunes so we knew exactly what to expect.

The band, which was active from 1964 to 1969, and again from 1970 to 1975, performed works by their composer and guitarist, Frank Zappa. Their first release in 1966 was a double album (LP) which said it all, titled "Freak Out" on the MGM label.

There were certain rules we had to abide by during the taping of this TV Special; it came from the very top. Everyone needed to wear a mask that would be handed out at the front door to anyone in attendance. CYA (cover that butt), no different than anyone today. That evening the studio was filled within the hour. There were lots of groupies in attendance and a lot of curious groups, not to mention lots of press from the trades.

We set the band up so that the film crew members could have easy access to them. We also made room for the crew that was doing the light show, and projected it on the walls of the room. It was cool stuff; one of the best psychedelics shows I've ever seen in town, with smoke machines. Man, what a great sight to see.

When our first break came, I immediately went outside to clear my head. It was a warm Hollywood night. I walked across the street, and leaning against a tree I looked up past Stan's Drive-In towards Sunset Blvd. I lit a cigarette, and as I looked up and stared at the opened windows of the coffee room, the building looked like it was on fire from all the smoke that was coming out through the windows; clouds, and clouds of smoke.

I stood there mesmerized. That feeling hit me again that my coming to Hollywood was indeed a good move. It was changing me. I was involved in everything that happened at this studio. For once, I was asked for my opinion. Ami and Tom did not lie to me when they said that I would participate in everything, I had the feeling of finally belonging to something and all the creativity that came with it.

I remember that night working with Ami who had worked on the band's first album with Tom Hidley, and being introduced to Frank Zappa and other members of the band. I had never been on a TV Special before, except for the Grammys, but this was different. I felt very proud to be involved in this project.

"The Mothers of Invention" TV Special was Live from Hollywood. It was a trip and, by all means, very exciting and enjoyable. The evening ended well; everyone was pleased. Afterward, we hung out, just shooting the breeze for a few hours. Frank Zappa was a real Genius. I remember right after the special, he had written some string charts for his session; and as the parts were handed out to the string session, they always looked very skeptical and snobbish, because here was this strange-looking guy, a hippie with long hair, and a big mustache, writing for strings. They ran the parts down and boy were they surprised when they were done recording. They all stood up and applauded.

A few days passed, and one morning when I arrived, I was informed that I was booked with Ami, and we were going to be recording an album for MGM Records with none other than "Eric Burton and The Animals." This was another music group of the 1960s that was formed in Newcastle during the early part of that decade, and had relocated to London. They were known for their gritty, Bluesy sound and their deep-voiced frontman, Eric Burton; they had already recorded their number one signature song "The House of the Rising Sun." The band balanced tough rock-edged pop singles against Rhythm and Blues-oriented album material, and when I heard these tunes for the very first time, there was no question in my mind that they were great hits.

Being in the studio with these guys; well, what else is there to say. They were part of the British Invasion. They had a few personnel changes since they had suffered from poor business management and were now under the name, "Eric Burton and The Animals." They strived to achieve commercial success as a Rock band. Things were very well thought out way before the start. The group set their gear up with the help of their roadies as well as ours, microphones were chosen by us, the players did not get technical at all when they came to play; unlike today where someone would say use such and such mike, and if the studio doesn't have one they're the bad guys; which is unfair but this was not the case here... baffles or blankets were placed where we thought would work best. Everything was live. We put out headphones for the band to hear Eric's vocals since he was in a completely isolated vocal booth.

There was no rush. After very careful microphone placements and sound checks, we would run through the tune several times with Eric Burton live in the booth, and sometimes either Ami or I would run out into the studio to possibly turn an electrical plug around because of a hum in one of the amps. We turned off the main lights in the studio to make it comfortable and also avoid the hum from the fluorescents. We were selective as to who would be allowed in the control room, but as always it became very crowded; this was, after all, "The Animals." They were a hot act but all in all, it was a nice pace and it helped with the recordings. We were never rushed, but it was important to have everything in place so that when we started recording things would move quickly and efficiently. This was always our approach for all of our sessions.

We would move a mike on the drums or place or replace a pad on a guitar amp that was going directly through the console. In those early days we used alligator clips tied directly to the speakers, not like today where you just take a direct output from the amp into a direct box and have the flexibility to reverse the phase. We are as ready as one can be; everyone is pumped up and we're getting ready to start rehearsing.

We started running down San Franciscan Nights, Sky Pilot, down in Monterey and Painted Black would follow with everybody there in the same room: Berry Jenkins on drums, John Weider on electric violin, Danny McCullough on bass, and Vic Briggs on Guitar. When we start recording it will be straight to our Ampex 300 3-track tape machine. We had all the lights in the control room as well as the studio turned down low. It was one of the most memorable sessions that to this day still sticks in my mind. The outside world didn't matter to us, we had everything we needed right there in the studio: food, candles, and incense burning, with the scent of Blue Nun Wine, Cigarettes, Coffee, and some marijuana. The control room was full of groupies who were transfixed just listening to the music. I kept an eye on our slap echo machine, which was right behind the door, just in case I needed to rewind it during playback. Curious visitors, especially young hippies that were just hanging out, wanted to know what the machine was being used for. I would teach them how to rewind the machine for me while I attended to a playback; they loved it. For them it was an experience you couldn't buy, and they had the feeling of being part of the team.

We took great care listening and paying attention to this band that was creating history in this very studio—all live in this room: Vocals, guitars, Hammond B-3 Organ, and Drums. When we recorded "Sky Pilot," Eric Burton asked Tom Wilson if it was possible to get some bagpipe players. Tom, a man of action, made a call the very next day, and we had them. Eric wanted to tape them coming up the stairs and walking across into the back of the studio. We tried Eric's suggestion a couple of times and on the third try we nailed it.

Eric Burton was always right on the money, and the players, especially Vic Briggs, who was a major contributor, was amazing. These were great sessions. The hippie era; the summer of love and believe me when I say that there were girls all over the place. Tom Wilson what a great producer. You couldn't ask for anything better; he knew his band, their needs, knew how to deal with all studio matters, and was always very laid back. We committed to a sound. We didn't have multi-track machines, they would come at a later time, echo was applied live; right on the recording day. All instruments or vocal overdubs, flanging, and effects were done right then and there without wasting any time, and when finished we moved on to the next tune. The phrase we'll fix it in the mix had not come into vogue yet. We would go from 3-tracks to 3-tracks to double any vocals or instruments, but for the most part, we always tried and got the sound live; and committed to it right then and there. Once the session was over, we had pretty much a finished product, we would make safeties of the masters and they would be ready to ship to New York City for their mastering. These sessions were memorable recording sessions. No one ever got out of order and everyone was well organized.

I learned later on that Eric Burton was a big fan of TTG, it was he who turned Jimi Hendrix on to us. Unfortunately, the only credit for recording engineer that appeared on those albums was Val Valentine as Director of Engineering. I was never happy at all, simply because Ami and I were the only engineers who worked on that album. We were the ones who spent all the hours with the group, but it was always that way when we would record any artist for MGM Records. This was a common practice that went on for many years, because back then it was not a common practice to put a recording engineer's name on any albums; we were a lost child.

I started to demand credit for my work. Years later I would have that conversation with Norman Granz, when he started his new label, Pablo Records. I said, "No one knows what we do, Norman. It's the only form of a resume that we have. We are being short-changed." Norman responded by giving us credit on all of his Pablo Records catalog; we were no longer being excluded. The hits just kept on coming. We were doing a great deal of recording and mixing on various projects; our workload had increased.

I remember on many sessions where I was the second engineer with Ami, when you heard loud static that came from any given fader on the board. This was upstairs in Studio A; this was an older board, the faders were exposed on the bottom, and they accumulated dust. Ami would take his index finger, rub his nose, and run it along the fader; this would stop the fader from making any more noise for the time being. It was a funny sight to see, but it always worked. This occurred very often during large sessions, and eventually there would be some modifications made, but they would come years later.

In 1967, a big surprise was unveiled which made us the most sought-after studio on the West Coast. Tom Hidley had been working very diligently in his shop; no one in the studio knew what he was doing, but he applied all his experience and surprised us all with the first 2"-16 Track Machine with recording heads from EMI, on an Ampex 300 deck, with MCI electronics. The machine and its capabilities took the town, as well as the music industry by surprise. We were now the busiest studio in town, booked months in advance. We needed to have a 2-inch editing block for the machine; it was something we knew was needed, although no one had ever cut 2-inch tape, the challenge would soon come into play, but the mystique of it all demanded an editing block; every recording machine had an editing block right on the deck, and we knew we had to have one. Tom called a machinist he knew on Cahuenga Blvd, who made us an editing block, but we could not get an editing block with a shallow groove across the middle to hold the tape in place.

All machines came with factory-installed editing blocks which was an industry standard on all quarter-inch, half-inch, and later 1-inch machines. Tom said that Ampex had a patent on it, so he wouldn't do the same thing because of the possibility of being sued for infringement. So, he settled for a very flat surface which did have some drawbacks. We were now faced with a block that, to do an edit, you had to be really careful. First you made your marks with your white grease pencil, pull the tape from the head assembly, place it on the block gently, lay the tape across the block to make your cut with your razor blade. Once you made your cut you would match both ends of your incoming and outgoing take; being very precise. You would now apply the half-inch editing tape on both ends to hold your edit tape in place, and apply your half-inch editing tape on your cut and rub your adhesive tape to smooth out any air bubbles. Now you would trim the editing tape on the top and bottom we had no 2" editing tape.

When you were done, you played your edited section back to make sure your cut was correct, and once done to the top play, the completed tune. Every time we did an edit you could hear the oohs and aahs from all the spectators in the control room. Believe me, whenever we did edit, the control was full with everyone in the session just gazing at us and the tape. This was new, they had never witness anyone cutting tape this big before, in fact, I still say, and I truly believe that on some sessions the only reason for a pickup, was to see us edit the tape. All the notes were correct, nothing was wrong at all, but the biggest cop out was the feel, yeah, the feel. I still have this editing block. It's a collector's item, with lots of memories. I've had some offers but I could not bring myself to sell it. I guess since it's from a time and a place that went down in history, I'm holding an item that I have no idea where it will end up, I'm the guy that can't erase any tape.

My collection is not a big one, but it's an impressive and memorable one, we had another issue with the pinch roller. We wanted to assemble masters on either one or two reels. It made it convenient, there was no need to carry a bunch of 2-inch reels around. They were heavy, so we wanted to assemble master reels or at least leader masters, head and tails with either plastic or paper leader, preferably plastic (less wear and tear on the head assembly). Paper leader was commonly used in the early days; years later we found out that it was very abrasive for the head stack. So slowly we turned to plastic. The pinch roller on this 2-inch multi-track machine had grooves unlike any other of our machines, which had a solid roller. But on this particular machine we could not use any kind of leader on the tape because the pinch roller would shred it; you had to make sure your editing tape had adhered on the cut or you stood the chance of losing the take. You also had to be careful with all splices. The machine tape path was not designed for any edits.

Also, the slightest grease pencil mark on the tape would cause dropouts, another flaw it had was whenever you punched in, because of the design, the red recording light on the deck would not stay on to indicate it was recording; it would only flick red once, which always scared me to no end. But we were assured by Tom that we were recording. You also had to keep the electronics on any given channel on input. When you punched in the record, you had to push that channel into output to hear the artist in sync with the track, because the electronics did not switch automatically. The most important thing you had to watch out for when you were doing an overdub session, be it vocals or instruments, but particularly vocals, was that as soon as you punched out you had to open the gate fast in order to avoid getting any pops. You had to have your act together on this machine it was all rhythm. We went ahead and did it anyway, till eventually all the bugs were worked out. The machine, from a technical standpoint, became a great attraction. It worked great, and from a business standpoint, was a great draw for the studio sought after by everyone. We were now the talk of the town, that was all the trades talked about; and we became a big hit in town. Our bookings grew at a pace that surprised all of us it was a great feeling.

The first artist to use our 16-track machine was none other than Wayne Newton. We took a picture of him by the machine and Julie Losch, who always promoted us, ran with it. Wayne Newton at the time was on the top of the Billboard charts with a number one hit "Daddy Don't You Run So Fast," so we used that to our benefit. TTG by now was busier than anyone had anticipated. We had gained so much notoriety because of this machine that groups and single artists, who would later come into their own, wanted to record here. Tom Hidley was busy in his new shop downstairs, as always, designing and brainstorming away. Tom had our in-house carpenter, Ron Ballmer, turn a closet near Studio 2 into an acoustic echo chamber. He had the walls shellacked, which took several coats; the walls needed to be hard to get the sound that we needed. I doubt that today very few would even attempt such a task, but we did, and it worked. I'm well aware of all the digital echo chambers on the market today, and I take my hat off to all the great manufacturers, there are some great ones; but the sound and setup of a real live echo chamber, although yes it does tie up a lot of gear and real estate, is by all means entirely different. We had been renting echo chambers from one of our best recording studios in Hollywood, United Western Studios, at 6000 Sunset Blvd, which was Bill Putnam's place. We were growing and needed more chambers and United needed their echo chamber back. We had the room and Tom Hidley as always put it to good use by adding this new echo chamber. We were very fortunate Ami's friend, Simon Waronker, a retired record executive whose son Lenny had become a very successful producer at Warner Records, was now using the studio on a very consistent basis. He was very happy with the place and had become a big fan of TTG; spending a lot of time at the studio. It was good for everyone, since Lenny had a stream of hits under his belt that alone created a great deal of notoriety for us. He was a very young and energetic guy, who would let you get things done and never rush you. His sessions were always very exciting with a lot of great artists. I loved working with the acts that Lenny Waronker was producing, there was no question that he had a good pool of acts.

Well, let me say I always had the feeling we were at a concert or just listening to the world's best stereo system. Lenny was producing such great acts as the Everly Brothers, and I had the pleasure of personally working on their album and, according to his secretary, Judy Betz, by mistake, I was not given any credit on their album, Van Dyke Parks, The Beau Brummels, Harpers Bizzare, Randy Newman, Ry Cooder, Arlo Guthrie, Maria Muldaur, Gordon Lightfoot, Rickie Lee Jones, James Taylor, and so many others. Lenny was a great producer who was responsible for building many acts at Reprise Records; as well as Warner Brothers. We were having great times in Studio 2, what a great addition to TTG. Everybody wanted to record here, it seemed like there was no letting down, the staff was the happiest it had ever been.

We were now recording and making great music with some of the best artists in the music industry. The times were surely changing, and we were entering a new phase. Bob Ross's deal with us had finally taken its course. We had removed his console, and we went dark for a very short time. Tom, with the help of Paul Ford (who by now had moved to the West Coast), started building a new console for Studio 2. The new custom-made console was a great attraction for the room, except for the fact that I could not see or be seen behind it. There were times when clients thought I was not in the control room, so I had to make it a practice to stand in order to be seen.

The board was an eight-buss console with sixteen positions, two pan pots, and to the left of the console, a six-foot rack that held eight Lang PEQ Equalizers, a matrix that had small gold pins eliminating the use of patch cords, and avoiding the possibility of patching something in the bay out of phase. Our new 2-inch 16 track had now set us apart from most studios in town. Our roster of record labels and artists just kept on growing. TTG at this point was the busiest it had ever been.

It was late 1968, I was upstairs in Studio A working with another great act, Lou Reed and The Velvet Underground, with Doug Yule, Sterling Morrison, and none other than their drummer Maureen "Mo" Tucker, who had for me a rather unusual drum setup. She generally played on tom-toms and an upturned bass drum, using mallets as often as drumsticks, and she rarely used cymbals. This was something very new for me, I hadn't dealt with a drummer with this kind of setup before, but I was determined to make the best out of it. After moving a few microphones around, I knew that it worked; after all, it was their sound. I kept working at it, and finally, Maureen was happy with the sound we had. Now, I spent some time working on guitar sounds, but we were at a stalemate. They had these Vox Amps, and I kept trying to figure out what kind of sound Lou Reed was looking for; we'd been at it for some time now.

Ami came into the room to see what was happening. He threw some suggestions around, but Lou was still standing on the side, not looking happy at all. We experimented a while longer. I took a Shure 545, placed it at the very top edge of the amp, and recorded some of the music. I asked Lou to come into the control room and listen. To my surprise, as well as everyone else in the room, it was the sound, he wanted. All he said after that was, "Don't lose that; it's a great sound." When we finally started recording, everyone was in a great mood. Ami tapped me on the back and headed downstairs. The session lasted two days.

We did continue doing record work as usual, we were also starting to do a great deal more TV Dramas and Variety shows. We found the pay was better and there was a consistency that you just couldn't ignore, especially if you wanted to survive as a recording studio. So, with the help of Jules Losch and many other clients, arrangers, and producers, we started doing a good deal of TV shows that kept us busy year-round. We became very successful at it. We started doing shows like "Laugh-In" with Dan Rowan and Dick Martin, "Police Woman" starring Angie Dickinson, "The Rookies" with George Stanford Brown, Sam Melville, Kate Jackson, Gerald S. O'Loughlin, "Charlie's Angels," "The Streets of San Francisco," "The Mod Squad," starring Michael Cole as Peter "Pete" Cochran, Peggy Lipton as Julie Barnes and Clarence Williams III as Lincoln "Linc" Hayes. We were also doing a considerable amount of pre-records for a lot of very popular variety specials. This was great, I was enjoying the weekly rush on such shows as "The Dean Martin Show" with "The Golddiggers," "The Flip Wilson Show," "The Smothers Brothers Show," "The Lennon Sisters," "Vietnam Live Shows with Dennis James and Pat Boone," "The Tim Conway Show," "The Carol Burnett Show," "Archie Bunker," "The John Wayne Specials," "The Andy Williams Christmas Specials," "Barney Miller," and Movies of the Week. It seemed like practically everyone had their shows recorded at TTG. I remember being so busy in Studio A, recording "Where's Papa" with Jack Elliott and Allyn Ferguerson, and spending a great deal of time with Charo working on her own TV Specials, and Variety shows never seemed to end. Once you were finished off you went to the next one.

Everywhere you turned a new show was ready to start the cycle all over again. We were still doing record sessions but more during the evenings in Studio A and Studio Two as a lockout. All in all, we still had a lot of unforgettable recording sessions. One that comes to mind is the Tony Martin session in Studio A what a night. We had none other than a man I held in high esteem, my very dear old friend, Richard Wess of Bobby Darin Fame-"Mack the Knife who was now on this very evening conducting. I was working with Ami the producer Gerry Granahan wanted to create a nightclub atmosphere, so he requested for us to make the room look smaller as, if we were in a night club.

We knew right away we could emulate the atmosphere of a nightclub. We set the studio up with lights on all music stands and large colored spotlights over Tony Martin, and we put him where he was very comfortable on the conductor's podium, which was elevated right in the middle of the room. The man was a performer and he loved every minute of it. We had set up a small bar we turned the lights down low the place looked fantastic. We, as well as the producer, were pleased. It was a memorable session; the reaction from everyone in the control room was fantastic, and visitors were pleasantly amazed. It was a great evening for everyone in attendance.

I remember during the session, while we were on a break, Cyde Charise asked Tony what he wanted for dinner. Did he want to go out? His reply was, I don't know should we order out? He was in a trance, really into what was going on at the time, and again she asked, "What do you want for dinner?" Again, he replied, I don't know order Chinese, Italian, whatever you want. We were busy recording, and food was not that important to anyone, including us at least not at the time.

When you have a formula that's working, it's best to take advantage of it, and we had it down. Tony Martin did not want to leave the studio. This formula worked, and that was pretty much what very often happened here no one was ever in a hurry to go home, and they would always return.

We had another icon on our hands: "The Dean Martin Show" came into play in 1967. We were now starting to do pre-records every week for Greg Garrison Productions, with none other than Van Alexander as musical director and Lee Hale producing. The show was a great one to work on; it was funny, and it went very fast. Dean Martin sang his signature song for the show "Everybody Loves, Somebody Sometime." I can still remember the first session, our new traffic manager Dick Paisage got on my case because we were eating pizza at the front entrance, and he figured that when Dean Martin showed up, it wouldn't look good. I felt different about it and didn't move. Dean would often come to the studio for some of the numbers to check tempo and a few minor things that never took much time. On this particular day when he pulled up, he saw us and said, "Hey! Pizza. How about a slice?" I handed him one and we went upstairs. needless to say, this pissed Dick off; but what could he possibly do or say about it. What a pleasure we were dealing with a pro, who for the most part did a lot of his numbers live. The friendships that developed during this show have been so memorable and dear to me.

Lee Hale, what a great producer and gentleman. He made the hours the most pleasant that I have ever spent in any recording studio. The show consisted of The Golddiggers and many other performers who were added as regulars. Dom DeLuise and Nipsey Russell doing sketches set in a barber shop; also, we had Kay Medford and Lou Jacobi in sketches set in a diner; and Medford also pretending to be the mother of Martin's pianist, Ken Lane. Leonard Barr, Guy Marks, Tom Bosley, Marian Mercer, Charles Nelson Reilly, and Rodney Dangerfield were also featured doing various sketches. The band leader for the taping was none other than Les Brown and his band Renown; everything was top-notch. This show kept us busy with the number of stars we had to deal with every week. You had to be on your toes; they all had special needs and requests, which at times presented a few challenges.

We had such a special entourage of guests every week that consisted of very well-known celebrities such as Ann-Margret, Walter Brennan, Sebastian Cabot, Gale Gordon, Rocky Graziano, Andy Griffith, Goldie Hawn, Artie Johnson, Marty Robbins, Dale Robertson, Forrest Tucker, Tommy Tune, Jennifer Warren, Nancy Wilson, Kenny Rogers & The First Edition, Jill St. John, The Temptations, Dionne Warwick, Dorsey Burnette, Doug Dillard, Donna Fargo, Tom T. Hall, William Holden, Ferlin Husky, Doug Kershaw, Gladys Knight & the Pips, Kris Kristofferson, Rita Coolidge, Loretta Lynn, Audrey Meadows, Ray Price, Charlie Rich, Jeannie C. Riley, The Statler Brothers, Crystal Gayle, Freddie Fender, and many other guests.

The Dean Martin show was one of the best shows I have worked on. It was, for me, a whole different world; impossible to ever duplicate or forget. I was working with people I never dreamed I would cross paths with, and I enjoyed every minute of it. I must say that to this day, I cannot forget the man who made our day in the studio. Van Alexander, being in the same room with him was priceless. Van Alexander was a great music man, we both stayed in touch till his death at the age of 100 on July 19, 2015.

We also had Jimmy Bowen. I was Phil Ramone's second back in New York City in the early 60s at A & R Studios, when I first met Jimmy. At the time he was producing Morgana King. Jimmy now had his own production company, Amos Productions, and now he had his engineers, Eddie Brackett and Chuck Britz, working for him as independent engineers. This was a new trend that I would also follow years later. We were very fortunate, Richard Wess loved the studio, and he made no bones about it and now we had Jimmy Bowen producing Sammy Davis Jr., and the first hit out of Studio A for this album, "I Gotta Be Me.

My dear friend Richard Wess arranged and conducted. We had Lola Falana and Keely Smith, who at the time was still married to Jimmy. They recorded their records with artists right in the middle of the room, with a full orchestra; which Richard had suggested and everyone loved the idea. Jimmy started to book Studio 2 regularly, and eventually, he just booked the room. He was producing a new artist, none other than Kenny Rogers & The First Edition. This is where we did "Ruby Don't Take Your Guns to Town." We also recorded Big Momma Torton for a feature called "Vanishing Point " One night as I looked out the control room, in walked Mac Davis, a country music singer, songwriter, and actor, who was from Lubbock, Texas. I proceeded to ask him about and he was nice enough to oblige me; a great guy. Mac, as I was told to address him, had already enjoyed much crossover success. He wrote for Elvis Presley and, produced "Memories," "In the Ghetto, and "A Little Less Conversation" He also had a great solo career in the 1970s; he had a huge hit with "Baby, Don't Get Hooked on Me," and for me, and I'm sure many others, one of the funniest records of all, "It's Hard to be Humble," making him a well-known name in pop music. Man, I sure enjoyed hanging and shooting the breeze with these guys, and whenever I was working upstairs, if I had a break, I would drop in on them to see who was recording. They would tease me since I was doing either a TV show or some rock band, but it was all in good taste, I could not call this work.

TTG was always full of surprises, at least for me. I remember as a kid my mother watching "The Eddie Fisher Show." She was no different from any other woman in America, she was in love with Eddie," Brought to You by Coke," "Coke Time," and later "Planter's Peanuts." Who could forget. at not me, and here I was now in the same room recording the man himself.

Freddy "Boom Boom" Cannon who had a big hit with a tune called "Palisades Park," booked studio time to record a remake of a classic. I walked into the control room in Studio A and looked at Cliff. who had a great smile on his face. I said, "What's up?" and with a big grin he showed me the music that was being passed around for the tune we were about to record: "Rock Around the Clock." I was thrilled to death that we spent a great deal of time on this record. Cliff Goldsmith was my assistant and I must say extremely helpful. I remember sometime later, Cliff and I were at a Thrifty Drug store down by Rodeo and La Brea Avenue, where they had these small jukeboxes at their coffee counter, and he asked if I had a quarter. While I was sitting there at the counter, he dropped the coin in the machine and there was the record, "Rock Around the Clock" by Freddy Cannon Boy: did we laugh? Cliff always showed me that music was very universal and that it was played everywhere, he showed me an awful lot during our days together, what a wise man. I was very saddened when we lost him at the age of 66 on June 22, 1991,He is truly missed by everyone who came in contact with him.

Time passed, and one day I was requested and booked with another band. I was recording a real high-energy tune that is still played today on the radio by a Real Native American Rock

Group. I had not heard of them till that very evening, but what I did hear when I rolled the tape was amazing-great stuff. The groupies that evening just stormed into Studio 2, which had become natural for that room with all the greats that recorded so many albums there. So, it seemed very natural for them. The group was called "REDBONE". The band consisted of two brothers, Pat and Lolly Vegas, Peter DePoe and Robert Anthony Avila, a Yaqui-Mexican American. We recorded all evening, getting the vocal tracks needed and getting the right sound. When the record company finally released the single, they reached the top 5 on the U.S. Billboard Hot 100 charts with their first million-selling gold-certified single, "Come and Get Your Love." Even today, it's a great feeling hearing that record on the air. I found myself going from one extreme to the other as far as recording music was concerned, because I never did the same thing twice, but what can you say? It was a great ride.

Here we go again; now I'm recording another great artist and a very visible TV star. During that time, most personalities were doing a lot of recording. If their show was a hit, the company would promote an album. So here, we were again with none other than Vince Edwards, aka: Doctor Ben Casey, for Buddah Records. He was a very conscientious artist and enjoyed himself in the studio. He loved to sing, and with the advent of multi-track, he was able to punch in lines with ease and attack any song gracefully, spending hours in the studio. Vince would always just put his heart into it. The sessions were always great ones; no pressure at all. He would always allow us sufficient breaks never in a rush. A real person, to say the least, very pleasant and respectful; no ego. If you were working with him, you were his guy. He also loved to order food from Martoni's. He'd ask, "who's hungry? Let's get some pasta and some Chianti for everybody." Vince loved the fact that we were both from Brooklyn; he was from Brownsville and I was from Red Hook. We would tease anyone who wasn't from the east coast. It was a wonderful time, a relaxed atmosphere for all of us.

We were so busy during that time that the only time we saw daylight was on our way home, bright and early the very next morning. And by the time evening came, you were getting ready to head back for a 6:00 or 8:00 p.m. downbeat. The sun would have to wait for us; in the interim, we just kept recording. TTG by now had been the toast of the town for quite some time. It was constantly booked: truth be told, the busiest studio in Hollywood. Producers, recording artists, and record labels had an obsession with TTG and its multitrack capabilities. They came from all over the globe, booking studio time. We were doing a lot of Rock'n Roll sessions with some of the greatest acts in music. I was working upstairs; I went into the coffee room, and there,to my surprise, was none other than Jimi Hendrix. He was working in Studio 2 with Jack Hunt, producing a group from Northern Ireland called "The Eire Apparent." I remember going down the stairs earlier, and I could hear their music coming down the hall. I had tried to look in the control room, but the lights were off; it was very dark in the room. So I went back upstairs and resumed my session. I was very busy in Studio A recording Ricky Nelson, with John Boylan producing and none other than Don Randi handling all the arrangements, and as usual, being very helpful. I was creating a few sound effects for Ricky Nelson's new project, which I did manually. I simulated a paddle on a canoe going downriver; everything was going well., I was enjoying working on this session with the producer, John Boylan, whom I had worked with many times before. It was great to work with him again; no egos to deal with, just straight ahead., John would be in the back as always, just swaying to the music. The man knew and loved his music. What a talented producer. I was enjoying this project. it was comfortable and all the players were first-class. The album was called "Perspective: Rick Nelson." His wife, Kristin Nelson, was an artist, her painting would become the back cover and, as always, even for this album no musicians or engineers received any credits.

The album was released on Decca Records. One of the songs that always stuck in my mind was Love Story written by Randy Newman and arranged by Jimmy Haskell. John Boylan and Don Randi also did some of the arrangements. This album was well thought out, and I enjoyed every minute of it, because John, being a seasoned producer who was well-liked and respected by everyone, helped us considerably. He knew his way around the studio. He was always aware of everything during the recording with Rick Nelson, nothing got past him.

We were trying various things because, as always, we were trying to come up with a hit record. the effects were John's idea. I enjoyed gathering all the various elements to accomplish what was needed, and there was a lot of excitement in the studio. I had heard a lot about Rick, and this was a chance for me to try and get to know him. I must say that when it was just the four of us in the control room, he was very open and the funniest man alive. The jokes between him and my second engineer, Cliff Goldsmith, kept us in stitches. So. instead of the usual recording session, it just became sort of a daily reunion.

We would talk about how he recorded his first single, when he debuted as a singer on the television sitcom and recorded his number one album "Ricky." He also went on to tell us stories about how in 1958 when he recorded his first number one single, "Poor Little Fool," he said it was a little scary but a great feeling to hear his record, which was a hit, played on the radio over and over again. I told him I liked the song and thought it sounded really good, and that I never imagined I'd be in the studio with him. He laughed; he was great a good guy.

We talked about his 1959 Golden Globe Nomination as Most Promising Male Newcomer after his role in the Western film "Rio Bravo," which I had seen numerous times. I asked him about John Wayne and Dean Martin, both of whom I had worked with. I a fan, no doubt about it. Rick Nelson had a lot of credits under his belt, and I needed to be on my feet; a lot was expected of me, but he never pushed his weight around; he was one of us.

We were ahead of schedule. I'm recording vocals, and a lot of things are going on. I'm making effects as we go, but at this point, I need a short cable to connect the organ speaker to a special box that I use on vocals through the Hammond B-3 Organ. I told John that I needed a few minutes. I went downstairs really fast, and as I approached the control room, I noticed the room was still very dark. I waited outside by the sound lock till I could adjust my eyes to the darkness. Finally, I managed to get Jack Hunt's attention. He turned down the monitors, and everyone's eyes were on me. I asked if I could go into the room and search for a cable I needed. "Anything you want, Balestier," was Jack's answer; he was high and in a good mood. I rushed inside the studio, found the cable, returned to the control room, and thanked everyone. I said sorry for the interruption and they kidded me a bit about my session, and the fact that I was solo. I said I didn't need a second engineer since I was just compiling effects. So, starting the machine and just walking up the two steps to the console, I'm OK with that. When I start the final mix, I will need a second engineer since I would be rolling at least three machines at that point, but Cliff will be my assistant; he's good and very quick.

Everyone was pumped up; after all they were "The Eire Apparent," being produced by Jimi Hendrix. As far as they were concerned, I was doing country and western music, which was far from it, but they just associated Rick Nelson with Country Music.

I said I liked working with Rick Nelson, he's real I was really into it. I said, "Look, I like all kinds of music." I told them you just have to listen to the message and enjoy all of it, because music speaks in different languages, and to me it's all heart and soul. As soon as I said that everyone started looking in my direction to listen. I, without knowing, was holding court. I had a captive audience. I was taken by surprise, because just then Jimi Hendrix turned around and asked me point blank, "Would you like to record my next album?" Wow!

I was taken by surprise I wasted no time and quickly responded, "Yes. I would love to record it." There was complete silence in the room, and you could hear a pin drop. I thought to myself, "Oh! no! What have I gotten myself into?" I was a little embarrassed, but at the same time mostly honored and surprised that Jimi would consider me for his next project. I had no idea he wanted a different engineer; I was under the impression Jack was his guy. This was a big surprise; the group and everyone else in the control room just stared at me.

I looked at Jack Hunt, who was sitting. I could feel his resentfulness, and how envious he was of me. He was not pleased, to say the least, but I had not solicited the album; it was Jimi's call and I had to say yes. I wanted to record his album; what else could I say? I was delighted; it was a great request and an honor, but Jack didn't think so; it was written all over his face. He couldn't and would not look me in the eye.

Jack had become very strange and defensive. As far as he was concerned, I had taken a session away from him, which was very far from the truth. I've described this scene many times just as it happened, word by word, but it didn't matter; it was indeed Jimi's request. In this case it was the artist who personally had asked me directly; it was his call. I could not and would not decline. I had said yes; it would be my pleasure and I looked forward to it. As soon as I answered, Jimi just ignored everyone else in the control room and continued talking to me.

He went on to tell me that he would be coming back to the West Coast. He wanted to book the whole month of October, and that we would discuss hours later. He asked me to inform our front office about it; Warner Brothers would confirm it and issue a purchase order. I didn't know what else to say but thank you. We'll see you then and we shook hands. What a big surprise. I was elated, and when I went back upstairs, I told John and Rick Nelson what had just happened. They just cheered me on; they were very supportive. I could not have asked for a better day. They were both fans and Rick said that it was great that I would be recording Jimi, and that he would just spread it around. I was so pleased; both he and John were nothing but the best.

Here I was working on his project, and he was excited and praising me for the fact that I would be recording another artist; what a guy. The sixties and into the early seventies around that period were marvelous times. Being in the studios with so many different acts in either studio, it seemed like no one ever went home; and if they did it was always for a short period. It was as if we never left the place; there was always something happening. We never knew what was coming next but, in the end, we were always happy.

We hung out a lot whenever we had time off; we would often throw parties that sometimes turned into a two to three-day major event. We had the most successful performers who either came to record or were visiting another artist working in either Studio A or Studio 2.

The sessions were always special to us. Just about everything we were working on was either seen in theaters, on TV, or being heard through the airwaves around the world.

Ami was now recording an album with Roger Williams, the pianist whose lush versions of familiar tunes like "Autumn Leaves" and "Born Free" became hit recordings. I remember that Roger would always bring two identical red striped shirts to work. He would work all morning and would change right after lunch and continue recording well into the evening. He wasn't very demanding at all; his recording dates were very pleasant as long as the piano was in tune, he was happy.

We were now starting to do a great deal of TV series and Variety Shows; just about all the notable ones were recorded here. Whenever there was a big special going on in town it was usually being done at TTG. We had a reputation for being fast, and everyone liked the sound; and in addition, we were now getting a lot of Rock groups who also wanted to record here. There was a certain mojo to this room, especially with our sound and multi-track capabilities. No one wanted to miss out.

I have said earlier on that there were a lot of incidents that happened in the studio. Well, here's another amusing one for you. I was booked to work with the Everly Brothers; their multi-tracks from Bradley's Barn in Nashville had arrived early that morning. Since Studio 2 was booked we were scheduled in Studio A for vocal overdubs. Lennie Waronker is producing, Cliff is my second engineer, which was Lennie's request, and he has already put up the first tune on the multi-track machine, "T for Texas, T for Tennessee."

The first thing we did was go over the track assignments. Phil told me to be careful not to go over track 8, we have a vocal track that we recorded on an RCA-77, we need to keep it. We started listening to other tunes to see what we had after playing back various tunes for about a half hour. We started again on the main tune, T for Texas, T-for Tennessee. We had been working on this tune now for less than an hour doing all kinds of vocal lines and all sorts of punch-ins. We were running out of tracks. We stopped to listen to the other vocal tracks we had recorded, and were told to go on to an open track. Cliff informed us that we had no more open tracks.

I looked at the track sheet and I told Lennie he's right; the only track we haven't gone on is track eight , and both Cliff and I say that's the track Phil said we save. In unison, everyone says, "Let's listen to it. Rewind." After a few playbacks it is determined that we should go over track eight . I looked at the guys and asked, "Are you sure? I thought we needed to save that track. That's the one Phil said we had to save. The one recorded on the RCA-77."

"No, it's OK to go over it."

I again asked, "Are you sure?"

Now we are hearing, "Yeah, go on eight, track eight. Record on track eight."

Cliff looks at me and I tell him, "OK, record on track eight."

After a few passes, both Don and Phil come into the control room for playback, and after listening to it a couple of times, Phil said, "Let's listen to that other track."

I said, "Which track? The other track? You mean track eight? The one you did at Bradley's Barn? We just recorded over that track."

"You didn't? I told you..."

At this point Lenny realizes what happened. Now no one is joking around anymore. He sits on the side of the console and starts punching himself in the stomach. We continued with the session. No one was blamed for anything, but we never spoke about it again; it was a sore subject. We did a few more sessions in Studio 2 and finally finished the album. I attended a party in Coldwater Canyon, and I received a copy of the LP. I looked at it and noticed quite a few engineer credits;

I was not one of them. Judy Betz, Lennie's secretary, later apologized to me. She said she completely forgot; but as always it was too late.

Jimi Hendrix and the Experience were entering the picture now. His group would be a milestone for the studio as well as for me. We have been recording a lot of Rock 'n Roll groups, playing it loud and everyone likes it. That's what we were selling that sound. They were coming from all over to record their music here at TTG in Hollywood, California, looking for that hit, not knowing when and if it would ever come, but you don't know unless you try.

We were having fun alright. It was October of 1968, and as

promised Jimi Hendrix returned, and we began recording his new album with the Experience. I would align and calibrate my machine for all my sessions daily and as early as possible. I did not want to waste any time. Back then, engineers, especially all of us on staff at TTG, did our tape machine alignments. That's how we were trained, and it did help everyone get a head start on any given project.

This album was very important to me. It required a lot of attention and detail to the artist, and there was a lot at stake here; not to mention my reputation. The sessions were not at all hard or stressful. I was left alone by Jimi to do whatever I wanted. Mitch Mitchell was very happy since I was spending a lot of time on his drum sound, and I would change microphones if the slightest thing didn't sound right.

I would record a section and bring him into the control room to listen, often changing the position of the microphones. We didn't have a large selection to choose from, so placement and EQ were important factors. I had to work with what I had. I was concentrating on the sound of Mitch's toms. I was very fortunate because Jimi was allowing me to do this, no questions asked, and never rushed me. These were very laid-back sessions, and a great school; because there was something

I could take advantage of without being rushed and sacrificing the sound that you wanted and needed to get for a project of this magnitude.

I kept recording various takes with Mitch, but I had noticed on my first playback that all my levels showed a real discrepancy; they were completely off. I asked Jimi if I could have a few more minutes to run some tones because I was not happy with the machine's response, he said, "Sure, go-ahead man. We have time." I quickly realigned the machine, but I knew right then and there that my machine had been messed with; I had been sabotaged.

The machine's playback and record settings were completely off; it was not how it should've been. The equalization switches had been tampered with. Some were set to N A B, and others to A M E, which is a different recording curve. The most commonly used in the USA is N A B. They were all off. Who could have possibly done this? I went directly to Tom; I was furious, but time was of the essence, I had a session and it needed to continue on time.

Ami, Tom, and I knew who had done it. Unfortunately we couldn't prove it. I couldn't for the life of me understand why anyone would do such a thing; there was nothing to gain by it because it wouldn't just hurt me. What about the studio's reputation? I kept asking the same question over and over. Why? I still couldn't deal with the fact of what happened, and I don't know why someone would do such a thing; it wasn't right because there was way too much at stake here. I never voiced any of this to anyone outside of Ami and Tom. There was no need to make a big issue of it but it could've been had I not caught it in time.

I wanted to keep it as quiet as possible. Tom told me from here on out align the machine, and make sure, from then on to lock the control room. which I found to be another unnecessary measure. I had to make sure that things went well. I felt really sad and angry that it had come to this, but what could I do. I continued with Mitch, and finally both he and I were pleased with the sound, and my machine was responding well. I was getting back what I was putting on tape, there was no mistaking all levels were correct. I was glad I had caught it before we started recording.

It was now time to deal with the bass placement, but that was not awkward at all just two amps stacked and a chair for Noel to be comfortable. Noel was Noel; he didn't speak that much when he first came into the studio. I introduced myself, asked if he was comfortable where I had placed him to Mitch's left side, facing west towards the control room, and he said it was cool. I had placed an AC strip for him to plug his amplifier into, and he was OK. I also gave him a pair of double headsets, and he stayed there in that very same position for all the sessions, never complained or requested anything at all.

I would usually be questioned by other players whether I was going direct, which I was, and also live, but he had no questions. I felt confident because, in addition to the sound and audio capabilities TTG had, what I believe to be one of the best crews in town talented guys so I had no reservations when it came to the crew. There was Mark Kaufman, our assistant tech right out of high school, who would eventually replace Tom Hidley. He was a witty, bright, energetic, intelligent, and gifted individual always thinking ahead. I remember, way before Jimi Hendrix returned, I went to Mark and said to him, I'm limited on this console. I need to record Drums in stereo two tracks, and I want to put the bass drum and snare on separate tracks in case I need more later on during the mix down. I have to be able to place that snare drum track in the middle or mid-right, but I only have two pan pots. I need to be able to do all this live. Panning was very tricky for us; We were very limited on this console. Consoles today have a pan pot on every fader, but that was not the case back then. Panning is the spread of your sound signal coming to your fader (either monaural or stereophonic pairs) into a new stereo or multi-channel sound field. A typical physical recording console has a pan pot control which is a knob with a pointer that can be placed from the 8 o'clock dial position fully left to the 4 o'clock position fully right.

That was what was needed; I desperately needed this flexibility for this session there was no way around this at all. The next thing I see is Mark coming down the hall with two patch cords and a small box. He had built me a panner which made it possible to record my drums in stereo, what a guy. Man he was a savior he had built a lot of things on the spur of the moment for me. He was responsible for building the box I used where I could go directly into a Leslie speaker of the Hammond B-3 with my vocals; an effect that I used on "Hair" with the Cowsills and, on most of my R&B sessions.

Mark always knew what you were talking about whenever you needed anything he was right there, and always came up with great results. I would be spending the whole month of October 1968 with "Jimi Hendrix and The Experience," so I needed to be on top of my game. I would find these sessions to be one of the most memorable ones that would stay with me for the rest of my life.

We had a few days where we would just spend time tuning up, getting sounds and positioning ourselves in the room, making sure that everyone was comfortable and could hear each other, and more importantly that the sounds we were looking for and hearing in the room were the same sounds that would be recorded to tape. Jimi and I often chatted about various things, The one thing that he was very curious about, and did bring up a few times, was the fact that here I was in Hollywood, California a Puerto Rican from Brooklyn, New York. He kept telling me that he had found it strange and had often wondered why? Since New York City had such a large population of Puerto Ricans, why there weren't that many of us recording or mixing, and why I, like many others, didn't stay there. He was curious and very serious about it. I had no idea how I was going to answer his questions. I had never been asked anything like that. No one cared or seemed that curious or concerned; Jimi was curious, and it was a very good question, but I certainly never thought much about it.

I said that I was very happy being here in my new home in sunny California. I remember one evening when the subject matter came up again, I said that being a Puerto Rican during that period did not present a lot of opportunities. I had to face a lot of prejudice in the early days in New York City, but I didn't let it get to me. When I started at A&R I began to experience all the freedom the music industry had to offer me, and I was hooked. They were great to me at A&R but when the opportunity presented itself for me to make the move to the West Coast, I took it. I had now started a new life here in California, and I was happy and enjoying all the freedom that it also presented me. I was here with two people who treated me as an equal. I loved the Sunshine State. I didn't miss the long walks to the subway on cold and rainy mornings, and I didn't miss the cold or snow at all, which was something I had wanted to escape for the longest time.

Now here in California, I was exposed to an awful lot of freedom, I enjoyed the people, the sunshine and just driving around town; being able to find parking wherever I went. Jimi said he understood how I felt about the change, and what I was saying. He said he had also gone through some changes. I didn't ask for any details, but we both knew what we were talking about. I found myself letting loose and expressing myself more than I ever had to anyone. I said funny Mary Travis asked me pretty much the same questions, and Jimi laugh and said I know she's a friend. I respected Jimi for who he was, and for trusting me with his album; so now it was my turn. I asked him why he had picked me to do this album, and he said he'd asked around and that I had a good reputation. Eric Burton, as well as his producer, Tom Wilson, had both recommended the studio and spoken very highly of me. I was floored. I never knew that they thought that much of me. It meant a lot to hear that, especially coming from Jimi. Whenever I was assigned to work on any of the Animal sessions, I was right there. If Tom Wilson, Eric Burton, and his group needed something they could rest assured I would provide it, so I guess in the long run I did something right and it had paid off. These conversations were out of this world for me. They were questions that I didn't even think about or ask myself; and frankly no one had ever asked me.

Jimi also said he had seen me behind the board upstairs in Studio A. He listened to what was being recorded and liked what he heard, and the way that I handled myself. He said he knew what I looked like; he recognized me the night I came into Studio B looking for a cable. We had many evenings like this. Just very similar conversations that would last for some time before any actual recording started. Jimi would hold court in the control room. To me it was fascinating. A friend of mine who was the leader of a group called "The Morticians," whom I had worked with for a short time and we had become good friends, was a fan, so I asked Jimi if it would be alright if he came to some of the sessions and Jimi said yes. That evening when my friend, Fred Heath, came into the studio, Jimi was great in welcoming him to his session.

Whenever we get together, we reminisce about his visit that evening. The fact that Jimi was very cordial to him, and how much he enjoyed those sessions. Jimi was always very curious and always made everyone feel comfortable and at ease. He knew what he wanted to know, and he knew how to ask you any question without being too intrusive. One night while we were sitting in the control room, Jimi brought the subject of New York City up again and asked me if I would ever consider moving back. I was hoping that the question would have nothing to do with a job, but I was very careful and curious at the same time as to why he would keep asking me how I felt about New York City. I said no, that I loved California and the people, the weather, and most of all the guys I was working with; we had worked in New York City at A & R Recording, and during that time we had built an indestructible friendship. Ami Hadani and Tom Hidley treated me with the utmost respect and had given me, as far as I was concerned, the chance of a lifetime. I would never move back to New York City; there was nothing there for me. I could not leave all that I had accomplished and earned behind. I was enjoying life, and although I had a great job in New York City, I knew that sooner or later I would've been passed by, and here I was my own man. Jimi told me that he loved people that were committed and said that he felt that I was at peace with myself.

I said yes that I was, and he never spoke about it again. Things from then on out just proceeded to get better, and we just kept on having a wonderful time, sessions started on time, and I asked Jimi for tune titles during playbacks. It was all good and going well. I remember an incident that occurred one evening while we were recording, we had a large crowd on this particular evening, both studios were working, and people were all over the place. To get to Studio 2, which was on the first floor, you had to walk down this long hall passed the restrooms on your left.

Tom's shop had been moved and was adjacent to the Studio's control room, which had a half door with glass to the engineer's right. This helped because it gave us a great view directly into the sound lock, the hall, and the vocal booth, which was directly behind us. Many times, we would make use of the sound lock if we had a large backup group, or a percussion player that we wanted to isolate; not to mention the vocal booth that was always set for any possible last-minute recording, be it guitar or upright bass at a moment's notice.

On this particular evening the band was jamming, which was something they often did just before they went into a tune. You could smell pot a mile away; it's the late 60s in Hollywood, where it had become pretty common and permissible for anyone to light up in the studio. The place was full of visitors and full of smoke; everyone was carrying drugs, and they were openly sharing. The smell of incense wafted throughout. We had a hash cake in front of the console sitting area, Kool-Aid laced with acid, lots of marijuana edibles, and Thai cigarettes. nothing was missing; you name it, we had it all right there in the room.

I was getting a balance when I just happened to look out the corner of my eye and, to my surprise, I saw a policeman standing in the hall. I immediately thought we were going to jail. He was in full uniform just bopping his head to the beat of the music and having the time of his life. Let me tell you, I was so frightened like I've never been before in my life. I was nervous, my hands were shaking seeing this policeman standing there, and it didn't seem like he was going away any time soon. What was scaring me to death was the fact that we had a lot of cocaine, to be exact, an 8 oz Styrofoam cup, which was full.

I reached over, being really careful not to spill any of it, and grabbed the cup. I placed it near the rack on my left, then I moved it. I was trying very hard to stuff the cup under the console, but it wouldn't fit in the hole because it was the bottom of one of the console's modules. I couldn't find a place where I could safely hide the cup. I'm also trying desperately not to panic. I have had many trying moments in my life, but this was a hell of a spot for me to be in; all I could think of was if for any reason the cop came into the control room it would all be over, we would end up in jail. I finally managed to push the cup up the hole and keep it snug with my left knee.

I calmly picked up the phone and called Tom in the shop, and I said, "We're all going to jail." I explained the situation. Tom came out of the shop and started talking to the policeman. To my freaked-out surprise, he walked him into the sound lock and started showing him around. I wouldn't look at them. Finally, he left; we never saw him again. I was relieved, but at the same time, mad as hell. I told Tom I insisted that the front desk pay more attention. They had to let me know when someone, anybody, was coming back to the studio. Whomever it was, they needed to check with me first. It was getting out of hand, and since it was Jimi Hendrix's fans who were coming from all over town to see him, I insisted they be stopped at the front desk. You never knew who to expect; they were coming from The Whiskey A-GO GO, The Troubadour, and from all over the strip just to see him.

Jimi would never say no to anyone; it was his session, so OK, sent them back. All the visitors were always very polite; that was never the problem. No one ever made any waves or started any trouble. If anything, sometimes they were really helpful, but we had to screen them. We couldn't be that loose about it. We also had a few who were clients who were either working upstairs or were scheduled to work in the same room at a later time; now that was the studio's problem. The room was always crowded with many friends, groupies, members of other bands, and equipment manufacturers who wanted to peddle their goods. A lot of musicians came to visit him, so in addition to recording I was doing traffic control in the Studio, which needed to be handled for the most part by the front desk; and sometimes with a lot of help from Terry Betz and the late Bob Porter.

When we were short of help, I would handle it all by myself. What I would do after my room was set, since I was left all alone, I would often find someone visiting who would volunteer. It was never a problem to help with either getting coffee or answering the phones. This usually would be a nice girl just because appearances did count.

I was fortunate because some visitors took pride in helping me out. They had the run of a studio and all the perks, especially groupies that would do anything just to be in the studio listening to Jimi Hendrix; but for the most part, I was on my own. I was OK with it as long as I had coverage at the front door. It became very important because of all the traffic, especially for this kind of artist. The only ones that were provided an assistant were outside engineers, to whom it would not be fair since they didn't know the room. I've been a guest engineer in many other studios, and it's not fair to be left alone. You don't know the patch bay, so any changes that need to be made cannot be done as quickly; you do need someone who knows the room and that warrants a second engineer. In the long run that helps everyone involved in the session.

Things were going very well in the studio. One day while Mitch and Noel were rehearsing, Jimi and I just happened to be in the control room, shooting the breeze and looking at all the multi-track tapes lying in front of the machine. Ami came into the control room in his friendly demeanor and said hello to Jimi. Then he asked if I would keep the monitors down. He said he was getting leakage and claimed it was going right up into Studio A: he said he was recording vocals. I said, "Sorry Ami, but they're just rehearsing out in the studio as you can tell. I have my monitors completely off." He looked around and just left, at which point Jimi looked at me, and we both just started laughing. We couldn't contain ourselves; it was amusing. I don't think anyone had ever heard us laugh so much; my side was just hurting from so much laughter, and we just couldn't stop. We found it hilarious, and it took us a while to contain ourselves.

Noel and Mitch were in the studio just jamming. I must admit it was pretty loud, but I couldn't just go and tell them to stop. To this day I have no idea how Ami solved it. I guess he did, I never heard anything more about it.

The band came here to play. They played with so much high energy, there was no mistaking these guys who were known for their sound. I had set the room with Jimi on two 500-watt amps stacked, Mitch with a large set of drums and his 28-inch tympani, and Noel Redding with his two 500-watt amps also stacked but a tight setup. I had our piano and Hammond B-3 ready to go just in case someone showed up to play, and some room mikes were always ready to record.

One evening I had Buddy Miles and about ten guitar players, and some of the most notable players in town. We had Dewey Martin from The Buffalo Springfield who sat in on drums as well as Steven Stills and Dave Crosby on guitar. All these guys had shown up just to jam with Jimi Hendrix and the Experience. Another great player, Lee Michaels, showed up. It was a good move to have the Hammond B-3 set, and these guys played their asses off.

We had no specific schedule; it was open end per Warner Brothers. The clock was Jimi's, if he wanted to keep going, we just kept on going. I would stop when he did. There was many a night when things were done on the spur of the moment; you never knew what would happen, but it was always constructive.

The sessions were well-run; nothing ever got out of hand. We were working on the album; no suits ever came by, and the only one in a jacket and no tie that came to our session was Chris Stone from the Record Plant in New York City. But that was an exception, a good one. There was so much curiosity from different artists, producers, and managers; you could not stop the visitors, and Jimi welcomed them all. He never turned anyone away. We had the likes of Vic Briggs from The Animals, and we had other guest artists I had worked with, such as Sonny Bono, Bill Cowsill of The Cowsills, Lou Reed, Jim Keltner, Jimmy Gordon, Leon Haywood, Bumps Blackwell, and Sam Cooke's manager, J.W. Alexander.

We had one session where Jimi wanted 13 chicks, so I called a few I knew, and they called a few. Before you knew it, we were in a studio full of groupies from all over town. I gave Jimi a hand-held mike for him to cruise around the room while he played his guitar. The band would play something, Jimi would do some riffs on the guitar stop, and he would ask a girl, "What's your sign?" She would answer something like I'm a Leo, and he would ask her, "Does that mean I can ball you?" When it first went down everyone seemed surprised, but then it became very natural, it seemed like the thing to do and it was a funny thing all around. The band continued playing and again Jimi would play another riff and stop, asking another girl, "What's your sign?" She'd answer I'm a Capricorn and again he would ask, "That means I'll take you Home?" The band again would play, and then he would move on to the next one. I don't know what ever happened to that track, but many have not been released. I think I slated that tune "All the Devil's Children."

What a scene with all the girls in the room; you just had to be there for this one, it was amazing. I must say all in all they were great sessions with good energy, and everyone was happy with lots of things going on all the time. The setup in the room was working well; there were no complaints at all. This was, if memory serves me right, the third day of recording and people were coming from all over town to listen and see Jimi Hendrix and The Experience record. Studio 2 was a small room, and it was packed. The control room held a sitting room in the front for maybe six people, and behind the console maybe four, tops; and that included me as the engineer. But some people sat on the sides and right behind me, and they always found room either standing or just lying on the floor. I kept an eagle eye on my machine as well as the numerous 2-inch multi-track audio tapes of previous recordings.

There was so much energy in the room with people all over the place; it was like a night club, but I must say everyone in attendance was very orderly. I was excited and felt fortunate to have such a great opportunity. I had never had this much fun back in New York City. That very same evening, while we were recording, I finally got a chance to meet two fellow New Yorkers, Chris Stone and Gary Kellgren, who were owners of the Record Plant in New York City.

Gary had done a few recordings with Jimi, and to me it was a great compliment when he said that I was getting a good sound. At this point he informed me that he had a new flanger for Jimi, who was excited and wanted to try it out. He handed it to him, and Jimi quickly left the control room, went out into the studio and started playing, which was unreal to hear, and see this man in action; just working this new piece of equipment. What a talent. And here I was witnessing and taking it all in. At one point a string broke and you hear Jimi say, "Did you see that?" The string did break, and it had wrapped around my Sony C-37 microphone.

Meanwhile, while Jimi was trying out the flanger in the studio, everybody else decided to take a much-needed break, and I was able to spend some time with both Chris and Gary. I enjoyed talking with them. I had heard a lot about the Record Plant, but I had never met either one of them before. The Record Plant was a very popular rock studio in New York City that opened in 1968, two years after I had left A&R for the West Coast. We started exchanging different views on all the different recordings we were doing at TTG. They were amazed about how we catered to a variety of different acts and TV shows that would change from day to day, and how we could just change to a different setup during the day to accommodate any type of music.

Gary said he liked the size of the room and that it looked and felt very comfortable. I commented that it was a great room for a rhythm section, and if set correctly it could hold about fifteen musicians. I told him that Herb Alpert's Tijuana band, the "Lonely Bull," had been recorded right here in this very room. We talked for some time while Jimi kept trying out the flanger; it was great. Gary said that Chris Stone was here to see Tom Hidley. I pointed him in that direction, which was right next to us. Little did I know at the time that The Record Plant was planning a move to the West Coast. These two guys were known for really plush studios with all the trimmings; carpet on the walls, very modern looking. Tom would be moving again, but at the time it was not that apparent; at least not to me. Gary hung around with me and we talked for a while about California while I kept an eye on Jimi, who was happy as a clam with his new toy, just playing away. After a while Chris came back into the control room and we said our goodbye's nice guys, but little did we know that Tom was planning to make a move to the Record Plant once they made their move to California. The Record Plant would open in 1969.

We had been recording nonstop all week, and when Friday came around Jimi told me that we needed to record on Saturday. I said, "OK. I was planning on going to San Diego, but your sessions come first. Canceling my plans is not a problem, your time in the studio is more important." We left to return on

Saturday at 1:00 p.m. I lived down the street from the studio, right on the corner of McCadden Place and Lexington. I was accustomed to walking to and from the studio daily, but on this particular day, I figured what the heck, I'll drive. I arrived early in my little 1960 Corvair. We had no maintenance engineers on weekends, so I knew this was going to be a hard day for me. I had no receptionist, so In addition, I had the phones to deal with, but fortunately that was the easy part. Sometimes we just wouldn't answer, but I was confident a volunteer would show up since it was a weekend.

I had to deal with the front door for starters, but I knew that eventually someone would come by and help me out, Typically some girl would just appear out of nowhere and she'd hang out, make us coffee, pickup lunch, and really help me out; and at the end would probably go home with one of us for the night.

This was a Saturday; we had not worked weekends at all. The sessions had all been scheduled for weekdays. I showed up early to carefully check everything, making sure I had enough tape, aligned the machine, and checked all the headphones and microphones. I had left the front door open just in case someone else showed up early. So, as soon as I was done, I walked back out to the front and headed towards my car to get my cigarettes, when in walks Jimi with two chicks' side by side and said, "I don't want to work today."

We just stood there in front of the building and I could tell he knew I was disappointed, but I couldn't blame him. We'd been putting in some very long hours, and we needed the break. After all, he was my boss; as far as I was concerned it was his call. What could I do? You just go with the flow, and after all, I was dealing with someone I liked and respected. I was working with an artist, a genius, and an icon. Jimi asked, "Do you have any plans for the day?"

I replied, "Well, I was going to San Diego and possibly spend the night, but I called it off since we decided to work the weekend."

Jimi turned around, looked at me and the chicks, and said, "What about one of these two?"

Without any hesitation at all, I reached over and grabbed the girl on his right, a brunette by the name of Anne. We went back to the studio, and I shut everything down.

We walked outside and Jimi had already left. I locked the front door to the building, and we both got in my car, went and got some food, and headed to my place. We continued with the album on Monday at 8:00 p.m. The music, as always, just sounded great and Jimi seemed very happy, he kept smiling during the session, and kept looking in my direction towards the control room, and I returned the look and smiled, what a guy. I knew we were in sync; everyone sounded great. They just played their asses off. A very productive night. We never mentioned the chicks at all. No kiss and tell, I hate it when guys do that. Jimi was great about it; we never mentioned anything at all.

Well, as the saying goes, all good things must come to an end, and as time would have it, so did these miraculous recording sessions that, for me, would last and last a lifetime. We had finished the album, and now it was time to wrap things up. Mitch packed his drums, and the roadies took them away. They packed Jimi's and Noel's amps and guitars, and away they went. The room hadn't been emptied for some time; now it seemed so enormous to me that I felt as if we had been recording for years.

Mitch put his arms around me and said his goodbyes; said he enjoyed working with me and hopefully we would work together again. Noel, well, as I said earlier, Noel is Noel, he said goodbye. Jimi and I embraced each other. I was a little teary-eyed like the last day of camp. We talked for a while about his next trip out to the west coast. He placed his right hand on my shoulder and told me that he was pleased with everything we had recorded and said, "Good work; we will do this again." I said I enjoyed myself. I thanked him for his patience and for choosing me as his engineer.

I said, "Jimi, whatever you need, I'm a phone call away. I will never forget these sessions and all that went down."

We walked slowly down the hall to the front entrance; it felt like the longest walk. He said to stay well, and I said, "You too, my friend." Again, we embraced. That would be the last time I would speak with Jimi or see him alive.

I started to check all the tapes, and legends were placed on each reel with the appropriate track breakdowns, ready for shipment. But as soon as I finished, word came from the front office. Warner Brothers had just phoned and requested that I transfer all the 2-inch masters to 1-inch 8-track tapes to accommodate a 1-inch 12-track machine, which was what Electric Lady had in New York City. We had well over 30 reels of 2-inch tape that took up most of the wall in the rear of the control room. Time to set up our eight-track machine.

I complained because I was concerned about the loss of quality. I wanted to retain as much quality as possible. Sometimes things are done that don't make any sense, and you have no control. There was no way of stopping or getting around it; they had a 12-track machine that they worked with, so the result was the 2-inch 16-tracks would become the safeties. A few days went by and finally, as I sat in the control room doing these transfers, many memories kept coming back to me of the many other artists that had stopped by. What a blast; it was not a job, just a music extravaganza of professional artists that filled this room. Many nights I wish we hadn't finished recording the album; boy how I missed the band and all the great times we spent in that room. The consistency had me hooked; they were great times.

I had gotten used to the long recording sessions, every day going till 2:00 or 3:00 a.m. On my way home all I could think about was the following day, and what new tunes we would record. I had often hoped that Jimi and I would work together again. In a very short period, we had become really good friends, but unfortunately, fate made it all impossible. Jimi died two years later; a very sad day in my life was Friday, September 18, 1970. At the age of 27, one year my senior When I heard the news, I was completely frozen in my footsteps. All I thought was what a loss to his family, his fans and the music industry. But the show must go on is a saying I've always hated; but it must and it did. It would take me a while to come out of it.

I was assigned to a variety of recording sessions, and at this point, for me, time was just dragging, but I kept going. Music was all that was on my mind. I would not have time to mourn. Things were looking up; TTG was slowly stepping into film work with another client that supported the studio an arranger and composer by the name of Stu Phillips; who had done a lot of TV work with such shows as Quincy, Knight Rider and the Monkees, just to mention a few. Stu loved the studio and would, whenever possible, record here with his wife Dory as a contractor. All the sessions were always large orchestra, and Stu was always moving fast through each cue. Stu said to us one day, while at the console, "You know guys, I was in England and there the consoles have a producer's desk where I can play around with all the tracks, add echo, etc., and it doesn't alter your tracks at all." He was always great about sharing information, unfortunately for us we had an older console and there was no way that it would ever be replaced. Stu was very patient with everyone and dealt well with it.

We were now doing the story of Evil Knievel starring George Hamilton; it was now 1971. I was familiar with George Hamilton; he had also done The Hank Williams Story, which I loved. I enjoyed these sessions. During our breaks, George always hung out with us in the control room, and I was able to ask him all sorts of questions. He was always a gentleman; never acting as if we were imposing on him. He would answer whatever I asked him, and boy was I elated. Never had I been able to converse with a star. Thank you, George; it meant a lot.

I loved what we were doing, and again, it was short-lived but very educational for me. I never in my life ever thought for one instant I would be writing about it. I remember that George never had any small bills, or so he claimed he didn't. We would often order from Martoni's, the Italian restaurant on Cahuenga Blvd, which was a favorite of ours. But when the delivery guy would arrive, George would say, "Anyone have change for a hundred?"

We'd laugh and say, "We got it." That was funny, but we ended up picking up the tab on every session, and why not? The man was treating us right. These were great sessions, very comfortable, and great music. And what can you say about Stu Phillips and George Hamilton but thank you, guys.

Time just moved on and so did we. It was now 1971. I had a meeting with Sonny Bono who had switched labels from Atlantic Records to Decca/MCA. Their A&R man at the time was Johnny Musio, a very helpful and likable guy. I was introduced to Dennis Pregnatlaro, who was Sonny's assistant, a young talented and very resourceful man. We hit it off right away; any questions about anything I would just go straight to him, and the results were always great. He was always very accommodating and resourceful. He knew the business really well, and I enjoyed working with him, because whatever the situation, he always had a solution, which became an asset for their project. And who could forget the team of "Sonny & Cher?" they were both great entertainers who were made up of a husband-and-wife team in the 1960s.They had started their career as R&B backing singers for record producer Phil Spector, and had achieved fame with two hit songs in 1965, "Baby Don't Go" and "I Got You Babe." Signing with Atco/ Atlantic Records, they released three studio albums in the late 1960s. They had now signed a recording deal with Decca/MCA and here we were at TTG recording a tune called "Somebody."

Sonny brought in their road band, who were pretty damn good musicians. This is where I first met Dean Parks, a wonderful talented guitar player. In addition, we used some of the great brass players in town. The arranger was none other than Harold Baptist, who had worked with Sonny on their previous records. We were all very excited; this was a new label deal for Sonny and Cher. Our intentions were like anyone else, to record a hit record. I stayed away from the normal setup, so I didn't use any tight miking on the brass. I wanted to use the room; we were looking for a certain sound. I started by placing 2 Neumann AKG C-12s under the portable vocal booth outside in the room, which I aimed at the brass section. I moved the mikes around a few times to get what we wanted until both Sonny and I were satisfied with the sound I was getting. We knew we had locked it in. We rehearsed the tune a few more times and, during this process, I took a step back and thought to myself what a great opportunity to be able to do this. I felt great that Sonny was giving me all this time to experiment; we weren't being rushed. For me this was a great gift. I was always very particular about levels. At all times I would look at the meters to make sure we were recording properly; making sure that what I was reading at the console corresponded with the machine, making sure it was responding well.

I was accustomed to maintaining good eye contact with my second engineer; on these sessions it was Nye Morton. We had certain signals just in case something was not happening, because later when everyone was gone, if anything was wrong due to lack of attention, it's on you and no one else. And you would have hell to pay. Sonny was very excited during the session; he loved the sound we were getting, and during the process he got a piece of paper and covered the meters on the console and said to me, "Fuck the meters. I love what I'm hearing, it's a hit." It was a great evening; a lot of excitement all around. I did a rough mix and made a few copies for Sonny, unfortunately it was never released. I think I'm the only one that still has a copy of that session.

After the session, during a playback, Sonny wanted to know if I was available to record them live at the "West Side

Room" in Century City. I was blown away. I said it would be my pleasure; to me it was a great compliment. The very next day we started to go over the dates. I was very excited again, what an opportunity. The West Side Room at the time was a very prestigious room trying very hard to make it; so, it was presenting all sorts of acts trying to see how much of an audience they could capture on the west side of town. It was a great sounding room, beautifully done, located right next to The Century Plaza Hotel. Sonny asked me to secure whatever I needed and that MCA Records would pay for it.

I called Wally Heider and made arrangements to rent their truck for two nights, two sets each night. I told Wally that I would like to see the truck, check the equipment, and meet with their tech. I received a little flak from Ami, not directly but by word of mouth, that I should've gone through the studio. What if something should go wrong was the word. I was very confident. I felt that if something went wrong then Wally Heider's maintenance engineer would take care of it. He was more than capable; that was his job. They had been doing remotes for the longest time and they were the best game in town; not to mention the fact that they also had their own 2-inch16-tracks that Tom Hidley had built for them. He had built three, and one was for Wally; who was always ahead of the game. I didn't listen to any of the rumors and went ahead with the project. I didn't realize it at the time, but this would be the start of my independent engineering career. We had a meeting at The West Side Room, and we went over the show. There was an awful lot of excitement about this live album; lots of meetings and very careful planning as well as selection of equipment. We scheduled another meeting and went over the entire program with Sonny Bono, Dennis Pregnatlaro and their musical director, Mike Rubini, as well as the house engineer.

We discussed Cher's entrance, which would be stage left, and Sonny's entrance, stage right. I made arrangements for a stool to be placed on the side where Cher could pick up a vocal microphone upon entering. However, I wanted to cover all bases, so I decided to put an additional microphone stage right; just in case she decided to come out that way. The head of sound from the club decided he would just take an audio split from us and leave the mixing to me. This way we would all be listening to the same feed, and it would make it a lot easier for everyone.

Finally, after careful planning, here we were; ShowTime. It was a great turn out; a full house with lots of excitement. The house announcer did his bit, I'd taken a separate feed from the house engineer's microphone, but Dennis Pregnatlaro, who is producing the album, felt at a later time he would use someone else's voice. So we begin, "And now, ladies and gentlemen, the Westside Room is proud to present Sonny & Cher. The band played a fanfare, Sonny came out to applause. He did his monologue and introduced Cher, and she came out, not as planned but stage right. I was glad I added the additional microphone. Applause and the crowd goes wild as they start to sing "I got You Babe." What a show, great performance, they were fantastic. What an act. It was a great night with a great reaction from the audience.

We recorded two great nights without a flaw with enough music to choose from when I started to mix the album at TTG it was all good because this in turn gave the studio a good amount of work, we tried many things and used nothing but the best money was no object everyone was happy with the sound.

During the whole process Dennis says to me, "I think you should do the announcing."

I almost fell out of my seat. "Are you serious?"

He said, "Yes, I am. You have the right voice for it."

I argue for a bit but I lost, and finally I went out in the studio and the rest is history. We mixed for a few days with very little editing; my only concern at the time was time restrictions; the time element per side. I must tell you that when you're recording a song in the studio, which is a controlled environment, it's a lot different than when you're recording a live performance.

We had a lot of dialogue to deal with; not to mention the audience reactions and applause. In a situation such as this, time was eaten up fast. I had to be very precise, and I had to make edits that made sense. Sonny Bono was making a lot of things possible. There was always something new. He told me that they were going to have their own TV show, "The Sonny & Cher Variety Hour," and he wanted me as their sound engineer,

I had to belong to the local union IATSE local 695; it was a union job. He also told me that whatever the cost, he would pay for it. I called and I was denied a card, which was typical of the local. They claimed that they had mixers on the roster who were out of work, which is their common bullshit line. The truth was that I didn't fit their profile of nepotism, which they are well known to practice. I knew very well at the time that the local didn't have too many sound engineers on the roster that could handle multi track recording. It was all new, but dealing with that bureaucracy and politics was not my cup of tea. I was not allowed to join the sound local. I could've gone to Sonny, and he would've raised hell with the union, but then my seat at that show would've been a resentful one. Knowing what I know now, I could've taken them to the mats. I was very well aware that Sonny needed to work on his show. He didn't have time for that, so unfortunately, I was not able to do the show.

I still continued to do some recordings for Sonny, but soon it all ended and we just drifted apart. As is often the case in Hollywood, their album was a big seller. I'm proud to have been part of it. Time passed and one day, as I was walking into the lobby, I ran into none other than Richard Perry. I knew both he and his wife, Linda, from New York City. He was now producing an artist upstairs in Studio A by the name of Tiny Tim. Richard had become a highly successful record producer with an enormous amount of hit records to his credit.

I would be second engineer on this album, which was really great for me. Although I was still doing a lot of other recording sessions downstairs in Studio 2. Whenever I was free, they wanted me in Studio A. I would often try to hide in the tape library. I don't know how Richard would find me, but he would and he'd say time to record Angel! I was Ami's assistant on this album, which I must admit for me was great. There were times while we were waiting for either Max Bennett, one of Richard's favorite bass players, to do a bass overdub or a keyboard player. We would hang around the piano and reminisce about lots of things.

I can still remember seeing Tiny Tim perform in the Village back then. Whenever possible, I would ride down to Greenwich Village. Tiny would put on quite a show, very entertaining, I guess that's why Richard decided to record him; it was an interesting concept.

I had always loved going down to the clubs in the village, just to hang out and listen to all the great acts that appeared at The Bitter End, Café Au Go Go, or Cafe Wha? The Gaslight Café. I loved the folk scene, and, throughout my career, I have attended a few recording sessions where there would be a folk music group doing their recordings. The very first folk group that I saw in the studio was The Serendipity Singers, later followed by The New Christy Minstrels, The Highway Man, and the one and only Peter, Paul, and Mary, all pretty much in that order. I was instantly smitten and blown away by the whole folk scene and I've always felt very fortunate to meet Peter, Paul, and Mary.

I had been a fan of theirs for so long, and to have spent time in the same room working and witnessing this group at their best while they were working on their album completely blew me away. I was in seventh heaven seeing firsthand how meticulous Peter Yarrow was about their sound. At the time, he was working with Roy Cicala and, if you ask me, a great match. They had only a 3-track machine, and they were selecting takes, and editing various pieces together. It was amazing, and I as always was taking it all in.

They were mixing tunes not in any particular order; the sequence of the album, as always, would take place at a later time. I remember seeing tape all over the control room floor; this was always a sign that work was in progress. A few years had gone by but now here I am in the West Coast. I'm working at TTG and, to my surprise, I have been requested by none other than Mary Travers, one of my favorite ladies, whom I'd had a crush on for many years. The group wasn't touring too much, and she was now doing a radio show out of New York City. She had come to town to interview one of her friends, Bob Dylan. I was honored and very pleased to be doing this session, working with her and Bob Dylan; well, what a rush.

I loved the fact that Mary was very vocal about what she wanted, which I always found very helpful. There was no bullshit with her, no second guessing. We both love New York City, so while we were waiting for Bob Dylan to arrive that's all we talked about. The people; the restaurants and the food, the music scene and the attitude, transportation, everything. She loved New York City and made no bones about it, and I must admit I agreed with her, not only because I admired her, but because it was all true. and I'm still a New Yorker at heart.

We talked at length about the group; it was out of this world. This was the most comfortable time I had spent in this room in quite some time. She went on to tell me about Bill Schwartz, their engineer, his microphone placements, and the many recording sessions. Mary was very observant; she knew what she wanted and knew her way around a studio. I remember one of their sessions back at A&R where she took a guitar and showed the musician how she wanted a certain part played.

Mary was very precise; she had requested two mono quarter-inch full-track machines and 131 low noise tape set to run at 15 ips, and room tone to be recorded at the end of the session for editorial purposes. She had done her homework and had gone over everything with her engineer back east; she always wanted to work with the best, and I was glad I was added to that list.

Mary was very pleasant, I must say. It was a great time for me; I loved that she had booked this session, and I was very touched knowing Roy Cicala back in New York City had made it a point to recommend me.

That evening we all started setting up Studio A; we were scheduled to do another of our weekly TV specials. As always, we would be doing pre-records for "The Hollywood Palace," which was produced and contracted by none other than Johnny Fresco, with nothing but the very best of musicians in town.

The morning would start with coffee and donuts and a slew of salutations from the musicians and production staff. We had the routine down to a science. Once music was passed around to all the musicians in the room, and the script along with the show order in which the musical numbers needed to be recorded was handed to us. Johnny Fresco would set the score down next to Ami, who was the first engineer. I was the second engineer, not to toot my horn but by request; I was ready at my station.

The studio, as always, was packed with musicians and all their instruments, and an abundance of percussion instruments and crates filled the back of the room; there was a lot of excitement. As always, we were all glad to be there; these were great sessions, and the different artists stood out. It couldn't have been better; we did an awful lot of preparation for these sessions. Headphones were placed in case an overdub came into play, and all the music stands had their music and their lights ready. We were ready to start recording; nothing would change from here on out unless it came directly from Johnny Fresco. It was essential for us to record all the big numbers first to cut the orchestra down as fast as possible; all playoffs and playoffs would be recorded after each number. This way, we would be able to deal with any vocal overdubs and get ready for mixing and sequencing the entire show with ease.

This show moved at a very fast pace; it was very hectic, but it was enjoyable. There was no time to waste once the session started. We paid close attention to the clock and breaks were given on the hour. Johnny would call out, "OK Guys, Take A Five." That would be enough time for all musicians and staff to run into the coffee room and call their answering services to confirm any session calls by various artist or contractors; this was a daily ritual. We would be given lunch and dinner breaks; other than that, there was no time for anything else time was very limited.

We didn't go out at all; usually, lunch and dinner were delivered to the engineering and production staff. There was so much going on during these sessions that we could not afford to be away from the studio, because changes would come down the pike and you needed to answer and work out any problems that might arise.

Variety shows such as this one were a staple for the studio, and we did a lot of them because we had the formula down. We were sought after by every production company in town, because every show we did was done with great speed and accuracy. We had the room; the studio was not a small one, and we were centrally located. Everyone in town knew where we were located and the convenience of getting there was a plus. We were ready to record; it was time for me to announce my slate loudly. There was always a lot of people in the control room, and my slate needed to be heard on tape; it was very important for the mix down. So loudly, I would announce, "Stand by, here we go." The Romero number, take 1. From here on out, all slates would be in numerical sequence.

I could still hear the tympani roll and the announcer, Dick Tufeld, with his announcement that we would record for the start of the show. "And Now, Ladies and Gentlemen, Live from

The Hollywood Palace." This show was a very popular one; it was broadcast weekly on Saturday nights it ran on ABC from January 4, 1964, to February 7, 1970.

I remember one evening while I was at Capitol Records, which is right across from The Hollywood Palace building. I was recording Raquel Welch, and she started telling me that it was there where she was cast during the first season as the "Billboard Girl." The series used a different host each week, which meant you had to be on your toe's week after week. We were working non-stop with a very high-profile and demanding group of performers the very best in show business. These were long recording sessions with lots of stars, each with their special musical number and demands.

The host and performers on this weekly show were Bing Crosby, who made the first and the most appearances as guest host (31 in all, including his family on several of the annual Christmas shows), Dean Martin, Liberace, Frank Sinatra, Milton Berle, Sammy Davis, Sid Caesar, Peter Lawford, The Rolling Stones, Groucho Marx, Joan Crawford, Bette Davis, Tony Bennett, Judy Garland, Jimmy Durante, The Supremes, Ginger Rogers, The Temptations, Dusty Springfield, Phyllis Diller, Elizabeth Montgomery, and many other famous faces.

Although they were very long hours, it was always made fun of by Johnny Fresco, who had a career that went back to the 50's with none other than The Jack Benny Show. "The Hollywood Palace" was a mid-season replacement for the short-lived Jerry Lewis Show. These specials usually required us to start early, around 6:00 a.m., with a downbeat at 10:00 a.m., and would go till finished, which meant the very next day. We'd done a great deal of shows, but the one I recall in particular was a special we did with a well-known piano player, Peter Nero, who hailed as one of the premier interpreters of Gershwin. Peter Nero started in the Emmy Award-winning NBC Special "S'Wonderful, S'Marvelous, Gershwin." Many of his TV credits included performances on PBS-TV's "Piano

Pizzazz" and with the National Symphony in Washington, D.C.

Well, there we were in Studio A, and during one of the numbers Johnny Fresco asked Peter if he would play his number solo. Sometimes for TV, production wants certain numbers played solo so they can play around and try different techniques during post-production. We never knew what those intentions or maneuvers might be, so we often tried getting the performers to play with the band, and although we tried to maintain as much isolation as possible, we often tried to have them play solo, trying to get it as clean as we could; meaning no leakage (Bleed Through) from the other instruments. Peter refused to do it. He said he would only play it with the band. Johnny said OK! He asked me if the piano was well isolated, to which I replied, "Yes, there's a blanket on top and he's behind the baffles away from the brass, drums, and percussion." I slated the number, and after we finished recording the number, Johnny asked Peter if he wanted to hear it. Johnny asked me to mute all the other tracks, Peter came in the control room, and I hit play. You should've seen the look on Peter's face when he heard it, and he asked what happened to the rest of the band. He was not aware of what could be done with multi-tracks. Johnny asked me put in the band, which I did, and Peter turned around, looked at Jonny Fresco and said, "You prick."

We all laughed and continued with the show. Johnny Fresco was a tall Frenchman, well over 6 feet, but what a character; very, very funny. The man knew how to run a show; he was the funniest man in any control room and knew his craft very well, and working with him, for me, was a great experience. We always had a big cast to record; well-noted artists. In those days you never knew who was going to be in the lineup. It was important to move very fast, because live taping would usually be scheduled the very next day. We either recorded the act live or pre-recorded a track for them to perform live on stage, because of all our hectic schedules we had to be ready at a moment's notice.

The days were long; 16 to 18 hours on your feet; but with all the excitement they always seemed very short. We were kept busy with all the production people making all the changes and requests, and while musicians went on their breaks, I would be playing back whichever tune or cue needed to be reviewed possibly-sneaking in a bathroom break whenever time permitted. We did a lot of different shows. For the most part, all the popular ones that were televised weekly were either regular shows or their replacements, such shows as "Laugh-In," "The Carol Burnett Show," "The Dean Martin Show" "The Golddiggers" "The Andy Williams Show" "The Glen Campbell Goodtime Hour" "The Flip Wilson Show" "Sha Na Na" "The Smothers Brothers Show"

"The Lennon Sisters" "The Redd Foxx Comedy Hour" Bob Hope's 1976 Star-Studded Special" and many others.

We'd record everything as fast as we could, with many sound-alikes. If you had an artist with a big hit out you had to simulate it as best as possible, luckily TV did give us some license. We had very little time to run tunes down, unlike a regular record date. At times, some artists would forget that this was TV. This was also a side of the business that kept the studio alive, and it became a great calling card for us because, once an artist saw the studio, they would inquire what else was available, and the next thing we knew we were working on either their album or single. This happened with such noted artists as Barbra Streisand, Dean Martin, Johnny Cash, Diane Carroll, Andy Williams, and Glen Campbell. We were very proud of this accomplishment. The talent that we handled was out of this world; there is no way that any of us that were involved during this period will ever forget it. I continued doing many record sessions with various artists that frequented the studio; it was nonstop, and I loved every minute of it. Many rock artists came our way. The Association was another group that fascinated me; I loved their harmonies, "The Velvet Underground" with Lou Reed, and my mix down of "The Who – Magic Bus" that I had completely forgotten about. If it hadn't been for Gary Fradkin, who years later after finding documentation in the tape library, said, " I didn't know you did this?" I had forgotten about it. I had also recorded some other single artists as well as some great groups in Studio 2 : Led Zeppelin, and Fleetwood Mac this was before the group changed and added Christine McVie, Lindsey Buckingham, and Stevie Nicks, one of my favorites, "Roy Oberson" "It Takes All Kinds of People" "The Cowsills" "HAIR " and Sammy Davis Jr.

In 1969, the trades made a big announcement: MGM Records was now under the direction of their new president, 25-year-old Mike Curb. He would become the youngest president MGM Records had ever had. They had purchased the Andy Williams label Barnaby Records. The purchase of the label included the signing of "The Osmond Brothers," who had been under contract to Andy Williams for years. They were now being produced by none other than my dear friend, Bill Cowsill. I felt this was a great opportunity for both Bill Cowsill and the Osmond's. Like any other group they needed and wanted a hit record really badly. The Jackson Five during that time were very hot in the charts and the Osmond's wanted that spot badly. I knew Bill would be a great asset for them. He was into pop music and always into new sounds. I felt, as Mike Curb did, that it was great for all. I was really happy that Bill would produce these kids who had been doing barbershop quartet songs for so long and wanted to break out of that venue. The Osmond's were now finally being produced by a guy who could also sing, knew his way around the studio, and was no stranger to vocal arrangements. He was the talented lead singer of a group his family had formed back in Rhode Island "The Cowsills" in the spring of 1965, which included Bill, Bob, and Barry.

Bill and Bob both played guitars, with Barry on drums and when their other brother, John, learned how to play drums,

Barry switched to bass. They would later be joining their other siblings, Paul and their young sister Susan. Richard, Bob's twin brother, became their road manager. They ranged in age from 8 to 19 and, as time went by, they would later on be joined by their mother, Barbara. The Cowsills were the inspiration for the 1970 television hit series "The Partridge Family..." My first encounter with the Cowsills started at TTG in the same studio where in 1969 we recorded the tune "HAIR" from the hit musical, which told the story of a group of politically active, hair hippies of "The Age of Aquarius." Coincidentally, the play was playing not too far from the studio on Sunset Boulevard across from the Palladium at "The Aquarius Theater." They came in, I set them up and we cut the track pretty quickly. They played their instruments and then we set up for vocals. Bill went out in the room and started singing, and when I heard him sing the first few lines...

"She asks me why, I'm just a hairy guy, I'm hairy noon and night, Hair that's a fright, I'm hairy high and low, don't ask me why, don't know, It's not for lack of bread, Like the Grateful Dead, Darling...." Right then and there I just knew we had a hit.

I fired up the B-3 organ, put my Neumann U-47 mike through the Leslie speaker set in my echo chamber, and we recorded all the vocals live with echo. They sounded great; it was a big hit for them under the MGM label. My friend, Roy Cicala, who had recommended me for their session, had previously recorded another hit with them, "Indian Lake." I was excited about it. To this day, their gold record hangs on my wall along with a few others.

The kids were very nice and polite. It was like being in a candy store. Alan Osmond, the leader of the pack, was the oldest, in charge of his brothers who at all times respected him and paid very close attention to anything Alan had to say. They were ready and well organized at all times. They were well mannered, no playing around. They were here to record, and they meant business. No fooling around; it was again all business, and they conducted themselves well in the studio.

We started recording and everything was going well. Then we reached a point where they had a song where they wanted a natural fade-in. I suggested that they should walk very slowly from the very front entrance of the building's lobby towards a couple of AKG C-12 microphones. I had placed the microphones at the end of the hall by the sound lock, which led into the studio. They were singing a cappella for an actual real live fade. It was great and very natural; they loved it. The office personnel just watched in disbelief as they performed this task.

I must say there was a lot of excitement during all these sessions. The group was happy; the label was happy, and most of all, we were pretty much left alone. Things could not have been going any better. I loved experimenting and we were getting great results. We had a lot of fun putting Donny Osmond on a Coke box to get some presence on his vocals. He was so small, but no objections; they were great. I had a great time recording these guys. I felt they would soon become big stars, bigger than they were on The Andy Williams Show.

The Osmond's were having the time of their lives. Other groups out there had their sound, like the Jackson Five, but these kids were on the move. They were ready to top the charts, and MGM and Mike Curb were right there all the way. They would record as a group and as well as a solo for Donnie Osmond ("Poppy Love") and Marie Osmond ("Paper Roses"). The family was always around. Their father, George, and their mother, Olive, were there to make sure that things were done right, and they were very respectful of everything and were open to any advice or suggestions that we provided. They were looking for a hit record focus, so the search started with new songs, new sounds, and arrangements. They were hungry for that hit and were determined to do it right. What I liked most was that if a suggestion was made that was valid, they would pursue it. This made everyone feel like part of the team. Suggesting the walk from the lobby towards the mikes is a perfect example. When I suggested it, they just jumped to it and it worked fantastically.

We spent a lot of time in the studio recording various songs, doing a lot of vocal overdubs, and just mixing and trying all kinds of audio processing techniques. MGM Records was about to finish their studio on Fairfax Avenue in West Hollywood, a new "State-of-the-Art Facility," and they were building a separate room for the Osmond's.

I had started to work with Perry Botkin, who at the time was producing "The Mike Curb Congregation," a vocal choir that Mike Curb had put together. They were doing a lot of covers of very popular tunes. This was a very easy gig. We all knew the lyrics and the sounds or had worked on the original. I was no stranger to Perry Botkin since I had been either the first or second engineer on all his recording dates here at TTG.

Ami and I worked as a team whenever there was a session. For the most part, it would be the two of us, just like we did back at A&R in New York City. Those were the most enjoyable times for me in a recording studio, and we as a team enjoyed every minute. We just made it look very easy and pleasant for everyone in the room. We kidded everyone, and they, in turn, laughed and played a lot of pranks on us, and the jokes were plentiful. It wasn't work, at least not to us; those were great days, and we enjoyed every minute of it. Ever since I arrived in Los Angeles, once again, I was Ami's guy. All the sessions that were scheduled either large or small were handle by us. Composers, musicians, producers, as well as the artists, expected us in the control room at all times. There are a few credits where we are both mentioned, and to me, it was as always, an honor.

I learned so much from this man who was 15 years my senior, and we enjoyed each other's company, I'm so grateful to have been in such great company for so many years. Ami was a colonel in the Israeli army, which was something I was not aware of for years. He didn't talk about it much, at least not to me. My feeling was that it was his business, so I never questioned him about it. His wife, Ellen Weston, would drop by to see the studio, but they were rare occasions she was an actress, so she also maintained a busy schedule.

Ami didn't take time off too often, but when he did, he would always make sure that whatever project was going on at the time would run smoothly, and that his plans did not interfere with our clients. We were doing the very first album for MGM, and it so happened he had business to conduct in Israel. It would be for an extended amount of time, so without any questions or doubt, he had decided that I should finish "The Mike Curb Congregation album." He spoke with Perry Botkin, who was OK with the idea; he didn't see a problem with it at all. Cliff Goldsmith, for the most part, would be my second engineer, which made me pretty happy. I enjoyed working with Cliff, I was very confident that he could handle it. We had done a few recording sessions together and after that we became inseparable.

Cliff had produced a group called "The Olympics" in earlier years with his partner at the time, Fred Smith, and I had now become the group's manager. Dick Clark was doing an oldie show on NBC. He was showing a clip from the group's earlier performances, but to show it he needed to get a release and being the group's manager, I had to secure one of the member's mom's signature, since tragedy had befallen him. Charles Fizer, who was one of the early lead vocalists, was shot and killed during the Watts riots by the police in 1965.

I felt odd; I would be opening up old wounds, but I was sure Charles would've loved for his mother to get something for the short time he did spend with us. I asked Cliff Goldsmith for help since he knew everyone, and I was not familiar with the area. So, Cliff and I took a ride to Watts, and believe me when I tell you that it would've been nearly impossible for me to find this place. I had no clue how to get there. Cliff was my only resource and I felt safe with him by my side. When we finally arrived at Charles Fizer's mom's house she invited us in. His sister was there. I introduced myself and told her mom about the special Dick Clark was doing, and their requirements. We talked for a while and I explained that I was now the group's new manager, and that I needed her signature to get clearance for NBC to show the clip of the group. Also that any future payments would come directly to her, not to me or anyone else. She agreed and signed the document.

We chatted for a while; it was very pleasant, and I knew that I was doing something right for this woman who had lost her son to such a tragic death. After a while we said our goodbyes, we left with paper in hand, and a lump in my throat; it was a sad day. I was able to deal with this and many other situations since "The Mike Curb Congregation" Album was put on hold for a couple of weeks.

We were now at NBC Studios in Burbank for a day of taping of "The Dick Clark Special," but now there's another hurdle to climb. Little Richard, who was headlining the show, has decided he's not going to do the show. Who is the buffer? None other than Bumps Blackwell, who has been on the phone for well over an hour, and would continue for a few more, desperately trying to convince Little Richard to show up or there wouldn't be a show.

I noticed Big Joe Turner walking by us with a big bottle of J&B Scotch, and everyone was asking for some. I was hoping he wouldn't share because then we would have problems. Joe goes down to the green room; I keep my group upstairs. About an hour later we're still on hold; things have not changed at all. Everyone is hungry, tired, and there's nothing anyone can do about it.

Cliff and I were just hanging and waiting to see what could happen at this stage of the game. Cliff said, "Look, this is not the first time this has happened." He started telling me stories about other incidents that happened in the early days. I knew right then and there that I would not last long on this gig. It was a different world, and to top it off, you made no money; you just made sure everyone got paid. I found being a manager to be very stressful and demanding.

Bumps Blackwell is still in the phone booth pleading with Little Richard to show up for the taping, but Richard won't budge an inch. Everyone now wants some of Joe's scotch, and they are constantly asking about it. Big Joe Turner turns around and says, "It's all gone. You should've asked earlier." And now, after a few hours of waiting, Little Richard has decided that he would show.

The green screen is up, the track is playing, and we started taping. Seeing my guys doing their act gave you chills; these guys could put on a show. I was glad we waited. Walter Ward is leading, with Eddie Lewis and Mack Starr at his side, performing the tune "Western Movies." That's why Dick Clark wanted them real showmanship. The Scotch tasted good; I needed that, thanks to Big Joe Turner.

I thanked Cliff for being very resourceful; he knew exactly where to go, and I was more than happy to see that Charles Fizer's mom received that money. Cliff was, as I've said, very resourceful. He was the one who found Big Mama Thornton for a film Jimmy Bowen was scoring, called Vanishing Point. He said you had to be careful; she hung out in the ghetto and was a pistol-packing mama. So, like I said, he was very resourceful and a very humorous guy to be around. He could light up a control room at a moment's notice; I miss my dear friend dearly.

I was busy at the time; I was doing a lot of R&B acts. I was constantly just seeking as much information as I could gather from Cliff Goldsmith, who earlier in his career had produced such hits as "Holly Gully," "Shimmy Like My Sister Kate" and "Western Movies" for The Olympics, which became their signature hit. He would accompany me on many occasions to Magic Mountain, which had just opened, and NBC Studios whenever we had a show. He was with us when we did the last concert at "El Monte Legion Stadium" with Jim Pewter, who is an authority on "Oldies but Goodies" as well as in the pop, rock and blues fields. Whenever I had any questions, Cliff was my go-to guy. I spent many a day with him; we became really good friends.

I remember back in 1967 we had just finished the Animals album; I was assembling the master with Eric Burton and Vic Briggs in Studio 2 when Cliff walks into the studio. Vic turns around and asks me, "Are those mikes out there live?" I said, "Yes," and he said, "Roll tape." Vic got on the talkback and asked Cliff, "What did you do in the war?"

Cliff answered, "I was a fighter pilot," and went on to give us a little of a recitation of his adventures in the service. When we were done, I went into Studio 3 with Eric Burton and started doing some more editing and inserting Cliff's vocals in their new release "SKY PILOT." That's how things usually went; just off the cuff, no rehearsals. We loved what we were doing, we were having a great time the music business was really at its peak in this country, especially in L.A. Everyone seemed to be recording at TTG. They came from all over the world; it was amazing. All these groups and solo artists we had the pleasure of recording.

I would like to attribute it to the sound we were getting. I remember Chris Stone saying he couldn't believe it, and everyone else wanted to know how we were getting such levels on tape at the time. Everything was mainly recorded on 3 or 4 tracks, so I'd like to think we had to be doing something right. Multi-track would follow later on down the line.

Ami has left for Israel on business, and I'm left in charge. I approached all recording sessions with the utmost care, especially the Perry Botkins project, which we had talked about at length, and now I have to finish it. I loved the songs we were recording for the album; they were all covers of popular ones, and I knew them just as well as anyone on the date. I knew the artists who had recorded them, the stories behind them and the lyrics. It was fantastic. I still think it was a great album with a lot of popular songs with professional studio singers who, at the time, were the busiest in town. We had "The Ron Hicklin Singers" which consisted of all the great vocalists in town, including the Bahler brothers, Tom and John. We had kids and non-pro singers who later on down the road would continue to do their projects for MGM Records.

I remember there was an intro to one of the songs that Mike Curb personally sang, and I was later requested by him to delete it from the album, but I was always the one who could not erase or delete anything. It seemed like Ami had been gone forever; I never got a call from him. I was really on my own. We had just started mixing down the album, and one day, to everyone's surprise, Ami showed up in the control room. After all the handshakes and salutations, he asked Perry Botkin how things went. Perry responded, "They went great! It was just like you being here." Ami liked to hear that; he was proud of me, and to hear it from a client, especially Perry, well it meant a lot to him. It was good for business, and it would also free him to do other projects. The business was thriving; everything was going well.

Perry Botkin was really happy by now; he felt very comfortable with me and told me that we would be scoring a feature film titled "Kelly's Heroes" with Clint Eastwood, Donald Sutherland, Telly Savalas, Don Rickles, and Carroll O'Connor. Everyone was excited to have Lalo Schifrin as the composer, who was well known for the hit TV series "Mission Impossible." Time went by quickly, and finally, after much anticipation and planning, here we were at last. It's early morning, scheduled for a 10:00 a.m. downbeat, the room has been set up, and all the best musicians are in the room. We are scheduled to record a major recording star, none other than Hank Williams Jr., who will be singing the main title "All for the Love of Sunshine." It will be released as a single and will also be part of the album that we had just completed, "The

Mike Curb Congregation." They had put a lot of work into this group of singers, this was going to be the first release for

MGM Records under Mike Curb's banner. There was a lot of excitement all around; we couldn't wait to start recording. When you have something like this going on, one of the first things a studio will and must do, is check everything possible to make sure nothing falls through the cracks.

When Lalo Schifrin entered the studio, we talk for a while regarding his requirements. This would be our first meeting; we had never met before, but he was very complimentary about my work. He had listened to some of my recordings and said he liked what he had heard. We spoke at length; I just picked his brain. Lalo told me he had written a few cues where he would feature the percussionist Ken Wild; he wanted to pay close attention to them, and I let him know that he was on a separate track. This was very typical of Lalo, he's a master at it, and it always works. I went with it on this and all future sessions. He also loved the fact I spoke Spanish, so we spoke Spanish during some of the breaks. He asked where I was from, and I said I was Puerto Rican from Brooklyn, New York City. He told me he was from Argentina, and the fact that we both spoke Spanish instilled some confidence in both of us. He told me many stories; one in particular about when he played with Dizzy Gillespie, they had been up for hours the previous evening and the following day they had a parade for the band. When they announced Dizzy, who had passed out in the back of the open limo, and with all the commotion that was going on, he thought it was him they were talking about, so he just stood up. He said that when he did that, the crowd just went nuts with their cheers and applause.

This is now 1970, and multi-track recording is being used an awful lot. I wanted to be sure that whatever was needed for the film's dub was addressed; that's why in my earlier conversations with Lalo I just picked his brain. We again addressed certain elements that needed to be separated; I had no intentions of missing anything at all (i.e., percussion, piano, or guitar licks). Lalo would always write certain percussion parts that later the editors would use to put some emphasis on certain scenes or moves from various characters. I was aware that this film would require nothing but the best as far as sound was concerned, and I went for it. I spread the orchestra out in the room, making sure everyone was comfortable and used all the best microphones. I had aligned my machine very early and checked every channel very carefully. I wanted this to be a great date for all concerned.

Lalo informed me that one of the players that would be featured throughout was Tommy Morgan on harmonica. I knew Tommy well; we weren't strangers. I had worked with Tommy on many projects. I was adjusting all my microphones on the drums, making sure the microphone on the snare drum was not in the way so it would not be hit by the drummer. I wanted him to feel comfortable. I walked over to Lalo; we talked about some of the music cues and my track layout on the multi-track, we were always in agreement about which player to separate, and as he would always say to me without fail "sí con confianza" (yes with all confidence), it was time to start getting sounds. Hank Williams Jr. walked into the room; you should've heard all the musicians. They all knew him as a big man sporting a beard, what a legend. I was thinking at that very moment, man, his dad had also recorded for MGM and was one of America's biggest music legends. So, for me, it was a great honor and privilege to be working with his son. You could hear all the musicians greeting him warmly, and all the jokes just going around. This was a great session to be doing. I knew it was going to be a great day; we had nothing but the best players in this room.

Lalo introduced me to Hank, and we shook hands. I said, "I'm a big fan. Glad to meet you." I knew all the songs associated with Hank Williams Jr and here I was ready to record him. Lalo was surprised because when Hank asked me which vocal booth I wanted him in, I replied, "Are you comfortable here?" which was at the podium in the middle of the room where we were all standing. He said he was, and I immediately responded OK.

I had Cliff set a small boom with a microphone for his guitar, and another with a wind pop filter for his vocal. I went inside the control room. I wanted to get a level on Hank's vocal with the band just for a few bars. When we were done, I signaled Cliff, who started the machine, and I gave them a slate. "All alright everyone, please stand by. This is M1, take 1, 'All for The Love of Sunshine' and we started recording right then and there.

When we finished, Perry asked for a playback; everyone wanted to hear it. Lalo and Hank Williams Jr. came into the control room, and we listened closely. Leakage was minimal; his vocal was very clean with lots of presence. Lalo was very pleased, as well as Hank, he was done singing the main title. We continued with the session, recording various cues till lunchtime, at which point Hank bit his goodbyes to everyone and thanked me for the sound I got on him.

When we returned from our lunch break, we did a few more cues. It had been a great session; everyone was very pleased. We would overdub The Congregation at a later time. The rest was history. The result was that Lalo Schifrin had his first ever major country record, a very big hit, which he would always comment on, taking both him and Mike Curb by surprise. We became very good friends. There was never anything requested by Lalo Schifrin that was too impossible; the man knew what he wanted and how to communicate with an engineer. I was proud because the soundtrack of the film itself has so much energy. I'm very proud of that movie score, and all the people I was privileged to work with. It was great being in the presence of such great talented people as Perry Botkin, Lalo Schifrin, Mike Curb, Don Peak, Jesse Kay, Val Valentine, and Hank Williams Jr. Years later, while at the theater, I heard where Quentin Tarantino had used one of the cues "Tiger Tank" from that session in his movie "Inglorious Bastards." It still holds up.

I kept working with Perry Botkin on more sessions, and it was during this time that we recorded another icon superstar, none other than "Roy Orbison," who was doing a song titled "It Takes All Kinds of People" for a feature called "Zabriskie Point." Again, I used the same technique I used on Hank Williams Jr.; right in the middle of the room. Roy Orbison sounded great. Don Peak, who was the leader, loved it, all in all, it was a great session; no glitches at all and, I might add, very little leakage. Nothing you couldn't work with. I had a great time recording with these great artists, those are recording dates that you never forget. The fact that we were doing everything simultaneously helped; there was never any guessing about other parts, it was all there, and when you listened back to the tape you knew exactly what you had, which helped, and it was very comforting. I will never forget those sessions that went so well; I had a great time working with so much talent. The only drawback for me was that other sound engineers who were not even in the vicinity of the studio were given credit for it. Things had not changed, but we must go on. In my heart I know it was my recordings, and to me that's all that mattered.

I never had a clue who I was going to be assigned to work with back then. One particular evening, I was requested to work with The Righteous Brothers, another one of my favorites. A duo that consisted of none other than Bill Medley and Bobby Hatfield, two Orange County guys that had been around for some time and had a vocal style that was referred to as "blue-eyed soul." We were doing vocals for their last album together on the MGM label. What an experience, and what a night. Our guest engineer that evening was Tom Nixon, with Mickey Stevenson producing. This was their first time at TTG.

I was assigned as his second, a really pleasant guy that knew his craft well. While we were recording, I noticed smoke coming from the 16-track. I stopped the machine as fast I could; we could not afford their 2-inch master to be damaged. I pulled both reels off the machine as fast as I could. After carefully checking the machine, I found that one of the solenoids had burned out. Tom Nixon claimed he had maintenance experience and that we could replace the part from one of the other machines in the room, all he needed was a soldering iron. I couldn't let him do that, I needed approval from Tom Hidley. We were not dealing with live musicians, which helped; there was no pressure. So before we canceled the session, I put Tom Nixon on the phone, and after a few minutes we did the next best thing. Out came the soldering iron; we swapped parts from another machine, and before you knew it, we were on the air.

The evening went as planned, and we continued overdubbing vocals on some great tunes. One tune, in particular, Bobby Hatfield found very hilarious, "Baby You Bent My Mind," and what a catchy groove there were times when we would get to a verse and Bobby would just start laughing, which in turn set us off in the control room. This was a great session and what an experience. When it was all over, everyone thanked me, they were pleased that it had all worked out. What a great night. By now I had become accustomed to running into artists and composers that either Ami or I had worked with back at A&R. The exodus from New York City had grown a lot by now and I was getting used to seeing lots of familiar faces.

Don Costa, one of my oldest and most respected friends, happened to be one of them. We had met earlier in New York City where he had recorded and produced many hits with such great artists as Steve Lawrence and Eydie Gorme, Lloyd Price, and Paul Anka. Don also arranged Tony Bennett's 1965 album "If I Ruled the World: Songs for the Jet Set." It had been quite a while since I had been in the studio with Don, but by now he had also made the move to Los Angeles, had been here for some time and had become a regular client at TTG. He had formed his own company, Don Costa Productions, and had great success with his label, DCP, by reviving the career of a very popular 1950s act, "Little Anthony and the Imperials," and had also discovered Trini Lopez in 1963. While Trini was working at "PJ's," at the time a popular West Hollywood nightclub.

Don liked what Trini was doing, latinizing contemporary hits, he liked what he was hearing. Right away, he signed him to Frank Sinatra's record label Reprise, which released his debut live album "Trini Lopez Live at PJ's." This album included a version of one of Trini's signature songs, "If I Had A Hammer," which quickly reached number one in 36 countries (No. 3 in the United States) and became a radio favorite for many years.

Don was now doing quite a bit of recording at TTG. We were busy recording Kenny Rankin as well as doing numerous tracks with Trini Lopez when he suffered a heart attack and required heart bypass surgery. He spent some time at home recovering, and a short time later he resumed working with Mike Curb at MGM Records, producing and arranging material for the Osmond Brothers, Sammy Davis Jr. "The Candy Man" and Petula Clark's cover of "My Guy." I was very fortunate to have worked with Don on those sessions, which were great days, the very best and the most exciting sessions I have ever worked on. Don's brother, Leo, was a charm, and the players he would contract for Don's sessions were the cream of the crop. They came to play, and they knew playing on a Don Costa session had lots of perks. He always took great care of his crew. He had chefs who would cook meals and deliver them to the studio. I have said, you haven't had Italian food till you're fed at one of Don's sessions; it didn't get any better. They were unforgettable sessions and once you got there you didn't want to leave—the hours would just pass you by. Luckily for me, I was not that far from home, I lived just right across

Mulholland Drive and down Laurel Canyon in Studio City.

Then in the early 1980s, Costa scored again as an artist with another hit with his 10-year-old daughter Nikka, titled "Out Here on My Own." The two had high hopes and were planning a follow-up. Regretfully he died of a heart attack in New York City on January 19, 1983. I was saddened, I had lost a very faithful and dear friend I could always count on and my hero. It was a sad time for all of us in the music industry, but for us who knew the man personally and shared such beautiful times, we had lost one of our greatest mentors. It would never be the same for any of us. On January 20, I was called by Guy Costa and Nick Perito to assemble tapes for Don's memorial, which was being held in Beverly Hills. I arrived at the house early and started making copies of tunes that he had recorded, and whatever else I could find. I quickly arranged each tune in the order Nick Perido wanted them. When I was finished, I started making audio cassettes for Flip Wilson to play at the church. I had made several cassette copies just in case something went wrong I took one copy, and I gave the rest to their guy, so they would have them at the service the following day. I suggested he give Nick a couple and give a couple to Guy Costa and the kid could deliver the rest to Flip Wilson at the church.

The next morning, when I arrived at the church, there was mass confusion. The kid was not there, and he never distributed the tapes as I instructed him. It was raining. Finally, he arrived and locked the keys in the car. The services are about to start when Flip Wilson's boom box won't work. He quickly runs across Wilshire Blvd looking for batteries. I have no idea where he found batteries at that time; everything was closed. He runs back across the street to the church and is now waiting for the cassette tapes. They can't open the car it's still raining Guy Costa arrives, and he puts his fist through the glass and opens the car door and the funeral takes place like nothing had ever happened.

Nick Perito was a very special and close friend of Don Costa and myself. We had met in the early days in New York City when he was Perry Como's arranger/conductor, and through the years we recorded various records and TV specials. I remember Don telling me about Nick's first association with Perry Como. How he became Como's arranger, at the time Nick had his band at Jack Dempsey's Broadway Restaurant in New York City in the early 1950s. Perry Como had recorded a novelty song called "Hoop-De-Doo," and Nick was hired to accompany him on accordion for all his television performances. In 1963 Como's musical conductor, Mitchell Ayres, wanted to hire a new arranger for Como's television show, and Ray Charles of the Ray Charles Singers who were feature on Perry Como's shows, who was a fan, recommended Nick for the job since Mitchell Ayres left to take a job as the conductor of The Hollywood Palace. Nick became Perry Como's personal musical director and conductor and in 1970 he recorded Perry's hit "It's Impossible." Perry Como credited Nick with the idea of making his 1987 album "TODAY." He worked with Como through his last performance: his Irish Christmas special in 1994. Nick was very special; he was a kind man who was also very fast in the studio. He knew his musicians well and loved to be in the studio. In the early days, either at A&R in New York City or TTG in Los Angeles, I was always accustomed to seeing various composers. Sometimes they would do a special arrangement for whatever record or show we were working on, and it was great because they all had a special feel and style of their own.

I remember my dearest friend, Billy Byers, in New York City coming in on a Leslie Gore session with his arrangement; those were special days. Billy hanging out in the control room holding a Heineken beer, and just shooting the shit with me and Phil Ramone; very memorable times. I will never forget the time Nick booked this Japanese female artist for RCA by the name of Kazuko Matsuo at Group IV Recording. I sent for a dozen red roses for her session. I walked into the booth and handed them to her. Well, needless to say she was blown away. They took lots of pictures of us in the booth as well as the sign we had at the entrance to the building. When the album was finally released, the sign is the cover and I'm on the back of the album with the artist holding the roses. One day, Nick shows up at the studio with a copy of the album, throws it on my desk and says, "Here's your fucking album boy." How we laughed that day. He was one of a kind. Sadly Nick would leave us all on August 5, 2005.

Through Don Costa, I was also honored and privileged to meet Ralph Ferraro, and in a very short time we became very close friends. I ended up working with him for a very long time. Ralph worked on "The Virginian" and the cult movie spoof "Flesh Gordon," in addition to working very closely with Don Costa who was his idol; he was one of Don's favorite orchestrators. Ralph was also well known as an orchestrator to many other composers and directors, such as Leonard Rosenman on such films as "A Man Called Horse," "Bound for Glory," and the animated "Lord of the Rings." He was well liked and he was also very fast. He worked very closely with Randy Edelman on such films as "Gettysburg," "Dragon Heart," "XXX," "MacGyver," "The Wiz" with Quincy Jones, and Bill Conti on "Masters of the Universe." There were many scores that Ralph did; he was a sound engineer's dream, tremendous help in the booth. He was also the happiest whenever we got together, and for me, it was a joy spending time with him at his home in Malibu; enjoying his company as well as his Lamb.

Ralph was a pal; every year without fail, he would call me during the holidays to wish me and my family a happy holiday. He became a very special person to me in many ways, and his wife, "Manny," was a wonderful and pleasant lady to be around. Unfortunately for all of us the workload was in short supply after Don Costa's death. Ralph had a saying: "When Don Costa Died, we all Died." I will never forget him; what a wonderful man. Sadly Ralph also left us on April 3rd, 2012.

There were many sessions that I was involved in, many that I recall, and I'm sure many that I have forgotten, not to mention the albums that were never released or are not available and many TV specials. We were kept extremely busy doing a lot of record dates with very popular groups and single acts. In 1968, we were recording Jackie Wilson with the Count Basie Orchestra for Brunswick Records at TTG. a very straight-ahead big band recording, the dates (or sessions) were being produced by none other than Teddy Reig, a colorful character and one of the most important jazz producers of all time who was a very big man who, for me, brought back lots of memories from our sessions back in New York City. He was well known for his bags of pistachios and pumpkin seeds, which I found amusing. Whenever he walked into the control room at A&R the first thing he did would be to ask me to put the bags on top of the electronics of the Ampex machines to keep them warm. He would always be requesting more bass from the engineer; there was a rumor going around New York City for a long time that he could be heard through the glass in a control room yelling at a sound engineer, "More bass mother-fucker." I knew Teddy could get out there, and he was not a small guy by any means; he was a big man about the size of Big Joe Turner. He would often get excited, but he was a pussy cat. The only time I saw Teddy scared was when we were mixing the Basie Beatles album. Frank Zappa walked in; Teddy took one look at him and ran out of the control room saying, "What is that?" Zappa just wanted to hear Basie's band, but he looked so weird that Teddy didn't know what to make of him.

It's Thursday, January 4,1968, this is the gospel truth. On this particular evening, Benny Carter is the arranger, and he's at the podium, Nat Tarnopol is at the console next to Ami, Jackie Wilson is next to Benny running down one of the tunes with the band. Teddy, being the massive man he was needed to speak to Count Basie, therefore he as well as everyone else needed to step down the three steps from the console section which was elevated. We all had to deal with these steps; there was no way around them. He found himself asking a groupie to please get out of the way. Teddy explained to her in a very charming and gentle manner, "Look, I'm a big guy and I need a lot of room." Then he smiled, but this continued several times, and he was constantly being faced with the same situation. Teddy was always a gentleman about it, and very apologetic, but I sensed trouble coming because it had reached its limit. The girl just kept blocking his way, she would move out of the way but as soon as she could, she would just return to that very same spot. I was witnessing this situation from my recordist station, and I knew trouble was just brewing. Well, finally, as Teddy is coming down again, oh, I don't know, I guess it's the 3rd or 4th time now, he's upset. The girl is still blocking him so he yells out at the top of his lungs, "COULD YOU PLEASE GET THE FUCK OUT OF THE WAY?" You could hear a pin drop, even though the band stopped playing; that's how loud it was. The young girl turned beet red and, embarrassed, she just disappeared. We were doing a lot of recording sessions; this room was the busiest in town. It never seemed to stop. We were recording for a lot of labels, including Buddah Records. One artist that comes to mind was Tony Bruno, who was not a great singer, but well connected. That day when Teddy Reig came in to record Jackie Wilson, he said, "That guy's not a singer. He's a Plummer." He couldn't believe he'd hired The Basie Band to perform and debut his new album at some theater in New York City. Teddy was annoyed and was very vocal about it; he knew his stuff; he'd been around various great jazz artists in his lifetime. We also had Bob Krasnow and none other than Captain Beefheart (Don Van Vliet) who was a friend, competitor, and collaborator of Frank Zappa. Captain Beefheart in 1964 had joined the original Magic Band line-up, initiated by Alexis Snouffer. In 1965, the group drew a lot of attention with their cover of Bo Diddley's "Diddy

Wah Diddy," which became a regional hit. It was followed by another acclaimed debut album, "Safe as Milk," which was released in 1967 on Buddah Records.

I was by my station in the recordist area. Both Bob Krasnow and Captain Beefheart are agitated; it had something to do with who was in charge or had control. I don't remember how the argument started; what I do remember was hearing Krasnow say to Captain Beefheart, "I'll show you who has control here. I'll erase that fucking bass track." This went on for some time; they were mad and kept exchanging a few words and staring each other down. Krasnow would say to me, "Back that tape up and erase that track." This confrontation went on awhile, but it never did come to pass. Thank God, because I was the one that Krasnow was giving the command to; he was after all the producer. I sure didn't want this to go down. It would've been a terrible thing to do; erasing the bass track. The night progressed and I remember Don (Captain Beefheart) showing me how he was going to use a flour sifter to sing through for an effect; they were great times, with great innovators and thinker's magnificent artists.

These sessions were always great to be involved in; they were always a great experience. There was no way you could not learn something on these recording sessions. We experimented a lot, and secrets, there were no secrets, we shared everything. I had a lot of R&B clients that I was working with at the time, and if I was not their first engineer, somehow, I'd wind up being the second. To me, it didn't matter, I enjoyed it all because no matter how you cut it, after all was said and done, it was all about music. Back than we were creating music, music which is still heard today, music that we played and recorded together with everyone in the same room. There was no mystery or guessing about what we would add later.

Another night we were recording in Studio A with Bumps Blackwell, an American songwriter, arranger and record producer, who was very well liked and respected among his peers,

He was producing a gospel singer, which was his love. Bumps, as he was called, was also well known for producing and co-writing hits for Little Richard, including: "Long Tall Sally," "Good Golly Miss Molly" "Ready Teddy"; and "Rip It Up." He was very active, he'd bring his dinner with him and eat right at the console, constantly asking anyone if they wanted some fried chicken. I must admit it really looked and smell great, but after all it was the man's dinner. He was also responsible for producing Sam Cooke's hit "Me."

When he left Specialty Records in 1957, he took Sam Cooke with him to Keen Records. He would later become the West Coast A & R director for Mercury Records from 1959 to 1963, producing Little Richard's Gospel recordings for that label. He became Richard's manager and continued to work with him into the 1970s. They had spent a considerable amount of time in the studio and by now knew each other really well. It's about 8:30 p.m. and we're recording when Little Richard walks in with his entourage. The minute Ami sees him, he's outraged; claiming Richard owed him money. He was mad as hell and said that if he didn't leave the studio, he was closing the session down. In fact, he told me to turn off all the machines. Ami had a few words with Bumps, explaining the fact that Richard owed him money from previous sessions. I've never seen Ami so furious. Bumps pleaded with him, and after much heated conversation, Ami told me to turn the equipment back on. While all this was going on everyone's eyes are on me, but I had to follow orders. Bumps was worried and asked Richard to please leave, but Richard would not leave. Now he was pissed at Ami and things were really heating up; and Ami, in a loud voice, tells me again to shut the equipment off. I pulled the lever, and all the machines went dead; things were not looking good at all. I felt this evening was going to turn into a complete disaster; you could hear a pin drop and everyone was keeping their eyes on me. I remained really cautious. I had no idea what was coming my way, and I had to back Ami up, that was more important to me-he is my friend, and boss; no way was I going to let him down. I had never been a witness to anything like this in a recording studio. I had no idea how it was going to turn out, but if a fight broke out, I was definitely more than ready. I'd been here before. I was standing very still with my eyes on everyone; the Brooklynite in me showed. It became very obvious to everyone in the room. Little Richard walked into the control room and asked, "What's the problem?"

Ami turns to Bumps and says, "I want him out of my studio."

Richard responded by saying, "I'll take this sissy wig off and whip your ass."

Bumps said, "No, we're not going to have any of that. Come on guys."

They argued back and forth but eventually Bumps, as always, was able to handle the situation and calm the two of them down. I was caught in the middle, but I worked for Ami and that was who I owed my allegiance to. I waited to see what the final outcome would be. I was told by Ami to turn the machines back on. Everyone apologized to each other, and we resumed recording with Bumps, as always after every take, yelling, "Baseball," which was his signature saying whenever he felt a hit record coming. We continued to do a lot of sessions for Bumps and, as always, they all had some mystique about them, but all in all they were great recording sessions with a lot of laughs and experience for everyone involved. The man was a genius in the studio and knew his craft, no doubt about it.

The last time I would see Bumps was at the 1977 Grammy Awards. I had just arranged for the busboys to add another table for our group. The Biltmore was full, but I refused to stand and eat in line, so I turned around and gave them a twenty-dollar bill, and they just brought in another table and a whole setup, which pissed a lot of people off; specially Ken Duncan who came over and asked how I did that. Eric Miller and I were talking with Count Basie when I heard Bumps calling me amongst the crowd. I excused myself and went over; it was great seeing him after such a long time. We shook hands and he gave me a hug. We talked for a while and he asked about everyone, and asked how Ami was doing. He was very pleasant and was wearing dark glasses; when I asked him why, he said he'd lost his eyesight to diabetes; he was completely blind. I couldn't believe it; in a crowded ballroom at the Biltmore Hotel, Bumps had heard my voice among the crowd; that's how he knew I was there. Life is strange. Unfortunately, I never saw him again; he died in 1985. What a loss to the music industry; the man was a genius—and again very little was mentioned in the tabloids about him. I felt a big disappointment.

The year is 1969. The Association is my first project with this seven-piece band consisting of Jim Yester, Jules Alexander, Brian Cole, Larry Ramos, Ted Bluechel, Russ Giguere, and Terry Kirkman. We're recording music for the soundtrack of "Goodbye Columbus," the film version of Philip Roth's best-selling novel. The title track was written by Jim Yester and John Boylan. John, who was one-third of the Hamilton Streetcar, is producing the track with the group for the movie, and will stay on board for their next album, which started right after we completed the soundtrack. We have been recording the album now for about a month, on and off. Many of the tracks on this album have a country-rock sound.

These guys were really hard workers. They rented a small office across the street for rehearsals. Once we finished a track, they take a tape copy and start vocal rehearsals in order not to waste any studio time. We were working lengthy hours in Studio A and Studio 2, doing vocal overdub sessions as well as mixing. I enjoyed working with this group of guys, and John, in particular, because I must say working with someone who really understands the recording process is really a saving grace for any engineer. There weren't too many questions being asked; everything, for the most part, has been eye contact, which in fact helps while you're mixing. There isn't much being said; the music is the most important thing happening at this point, unless you have a very complicated tune, and you're rehearsing your moves. We had no automation, so if you had a lot of folks in the control room, they became your automation mixing a track. If I was having trouble bringing up the strings, John would say don't worry, I'll bring them in. He knew when something was not working, which made it possible for all sessions to go well. He was a very bright, young and energetic talented producer with a great sense of humor. This, for me, was a great album to have worked on. The whole group, as well as their manager at the time, were so professional, which made it all happen really fast—no time was wasted at all.

I worked with none other than Eddie Brackett when he first came to TTG to record Sammy Davis Jr. It was for his new album "I Gotta Be Me" with Jimmy Bowen producing, arranged and conducted by Richard Wess. The days were long, but the years went faster, and yet it seemed like a long time. Scott Lookholder had decided to leave TTG after a short period; the music business was not for him. However, he did approach it from a different end with a Patch Bay label company he would start a few years later that was sought after by every recording studio in the country. I loved seeing Scott, along with his partner Charlie, every April at NAB in Las Vegas, with a big crowd around their booth—all the different styles of labeling, and the services they were providing. It was fantastic and really well done. I miss him, as well as his parents and grandparents who were so gracious and wonderful to me in my early years in California.

Dave Brand, who previously worked for Liberty Records, came in as a tech. Dave, a very conscientious person who could deal with any problem on any session, was there when he was needed, and afforded you the time and comfort to express your needs. You knew they would be taken care of. I could say, "I'm hearing something strange," and he would take over and solve it, because now it was personal, he would not just brush it aside. You cannot go wrong when you're working in a recording atmosphere that generates so much pressure and you get this kind of attention.

I don't know if it was because he, Mark, and Scott came from the same place or not. I have always loved being in their company. I always felt a sense of ease whenever we worked together. That's the way it should always be; especially in the studio because when a crisis comes up, believe me, the last thing you need is for someone to be completely unsure of themselves. We've had our share of things gone wrong, an amp hissing, the multi-track not working because of the take-up reel not engaging, or dropouts from grease pencil marks and various things, and you can't just go home and deal with it the next day when you have musicians that are on the clock. It has to be dealt with right then and there.

These guys had a friendship that when extended to others came from the heart of good Jewish boys. I feel privileged to have come across them and honored to have worked with them. There were days when we just hung out and joked about the dumbest things, but when it came to work and dealing with a client's project, we were always very professional—to this day we remain friends but sadly Scott left us in May 29,2023. Time and events just kept changing, and now more new clients and acts kept coming to our studio. The notoriety that the studio had was tremendous. Linda Ronstadt joined forces with Bobby Kimmel and Kenny Edwards who were the original creators and members of a group called "The Stone Poneys," and she became their lead singer. This successful folk-rock trio would be known and billed as Linda Ronstadt and The Stone Poneys.

We were very fortunate and thrilled to be part of their album. Capitol Records had booked Studio A; they were now recording their album here at TTG. Who could forget our sessions with Linda Ronstadt and The Stone Poneys, with none other than Eddie Brackett as their engineer. Eddie was a show all by himself. He would be stomping his feet on the floor, with his body arching with the sound, rocking to and from, back and forth, feeling every bit of the music. It was indeed a show all of its own. If you have never witnessed one of Eddie's sessions, you have missed one of the rarest and most spectacular scenes in any studio control room from an engineer. The man as a recording engineer knew his way around any studio in town. For me it was great to be part of some of his sessions with Sammy Davis as well as Dean Martin.

I personally enjoyed my time being his second engineer. I found it amazing that he still edited tape with scissors; he carried them in his briefcase along with a demagnetizer. He would often comment on how important it was to keep your scissors sharp. He was always there ready to use them; it was a trip seeing him cut quarter-inch tape. I had heard of guys using scissors, but he was exceptional; he was really good at it. What a sight, the man knew his craft and was never ever reluctant to show you anything.

We had set up the band per Eddie's instructions to the right of the studio on the east-north corner of the room, with Linda singing right into a Shure 545 with a windscreen that worked really well. The microphone was very directional so leakage was not a problem. The rest of the band was set around her. It was a live stage act performance right there in front of you. There was a lot of excitement in the room and she, as always, sounded great. We just kept recording and enjoying the session. The band sounded great. It became a win-win situation; these were great sessions. To this day I feel very fortunate to have been part of it.

Eddie was always getting a great sound, and there was room for everyone who wanted to learn something from this pro who had no secrets. The studio's control room was always full; we enjoyed every bit of it as well as Eddie's performances at the console. We had a lot of other sessions come our way because of all the friends that Linda invited to visit and see the studio. Word of mouth, which is always the best way. Eddie loved the studio and the staff; this would not be the last time for him at TTG. He was a freelance sound engineer who had a great following; the man was well known throughout the music business and that in itself was a great advertisement for the studio. We stayed very active with another client, "The Letterman" with Jim Pike, his brother Gary Pike, and Tony Butala. They had block booked Studio time with their own engineer, Joe Polito; another independent sound engineer who came from Capitol Records—perfect for the group, since they had just moved from Warner Brothers to Capitol Records.

Joe had been around for some time and they trusted him. He had a great reputation and had worked with Glen Campbell on the "Wichita Lineman," which got him a Grammy. He had a great deal of credits under his belt, and could handle himself really well in the studio. The Letterman did a lot of punch-ins; we would record every song, line by line; the advent of the multi-track was a saving grace for them. I think just about everyone did second engineering work on all their dates. Joe was always very nice and pleasant and would say, "Watch me for the punch-in," and that's what you did. These sessions were long ones, but they were not hard at all; they were fun. Everyone was always very pleasant, which made the day go by quickly.

The Letterman were very particular about their pitch and vocal sound. They had come here to make a good-sounding record, as was expected of both the studio and Joe Polito. We provided nothing but the best at all times and were always elated when they would call to book time. They had become family at TTG and very popular with the whole crew. We loved the guys; they were the nicest people you would ever want to meet, which was always important. After all, you were going to spend many hours in that room; it was best to be working with someone you like or it could lead to very long uncomfortable nights, spending hours and hours—best to be on a friendly basis.

We had another person within TTG, one of my favorite people, Julie Losch, who did sales and used to be a record promotion guy. He was very instrumental and prided himself, and rightfully so, for breaking one of Jimmy Rogers' biggest hits, "Honey Comb," which stayed at the top of the charts for four weeks. He was a great promoter of hits by Jimmy Rogers that reached the Top 10 on the charts; such records as "Kisses Sweeter than Wine," "Oh-Oh, I'm Falling in Love Again," "Secretly," and "Are You Really Mine," and many more artists.

The man was always dressed impeccably and looked great with his silver-gray hair. Whenever Julie walked into the studio, we would all stop working and just be ready for whatever he was into, which was always something different and enjoyable. Julie was always selling; he got us an awful lot of TV Variety Specials. One day while we were working on a John Wayne Vietnam Special, I asked him if he would put his voice on one of the tracks. We proceeded to put sound effects on this track. It was the funniest things you ever heard. We started with a whip, nice and loud striking a couple of times, and were saying things like, "Hey! Where we going? Vietnam? Hell, no we won't go," and then the whip striking a couple of times. Julie's voice just knocked us out when he started in saying, "Now why you want to send these boys over there to die? Please give them a job and keep them here, don't send them away to die. Please, please," and then we segued to "What the World Needs Now." Julie was a prankster, and he loved all the attention.

He was a very interesting man, the nicest person you would want to meet. He had dealt with the gangsters in New York City, being a promotion man, how could he not? He and I often would just spend hours sharing stories about many characters, incidents and people we had both known for a very long time when we lived back in New York City.

He would tell me stories about promoting records. He told

me how one day he was told to visit someone at their house, and when he arrived, he was escorted to their backyard, which, he said, was enormous but needed lots of care—it was just full of weeds. The owner took a small transistor radio, put it on a rock, and said, "That's where I want the diving board." It was very simple; the next day bulldozers arrived. What followed was very simple new landscaping, a swimming pool would be built, and a record would be climbing the charts.

We had some great days at TTG. We were consumed by the music business, working and enjoying it each and every day. Whenever possible, if any of us had the time, we would just hang out and enjoy each other's company. Julie was very instrumental in pushing me to do independent engineering work. He was a promotion man and would often show up with a singer, and I would engineer for him. He was very generous, and it allowed me to make a few extra dollars on the side. What he made I don't know; I never asked. It was none of my business; you wouldn't ask such a question. Both of us being from New York City, we knew the rules and besides, as I mentioned earlier, he was always very fair and generous with me and the studio.

I began doing many recordings with well-known athletes, the likes of Rosie Grier, who at the time played for the L.A. RAMS, and Deacon Jones, who was being produced by my old friend Marshall Leib, and many sports giants like Tony Conigilerie from the Dodgers organization.

We were also doing all the national commercials—Chevron Gasoline Spots for B. B. D & O. They, for the most part, frequented our studio, particularly the ones from New York City who loved coming to California. It was here where they could take the ties off, cruise the strip, and have a great time with all the groupies while they were getting all of their work done—all in one place.

I felt at ease with these guys; we knew each other from New York City. These clients were just great to work with;

everything was always laid out very efficiently. They provided us with scripts without even asking, not to mention all the label copy needed. The work was very easy; it was after all our comfort zone. It wasn't brain surgery; we had been doing this now for years. We were doing Radio and TV commercial spots, and when completed I would edit and assemble a Master reel ready for duplicating and shipping to various radio stations. Sometimes we would get different performers, one after the other, and they were all for various products; so documentation was very important and a challenge.

I would deal with an assortment of different products, all in one day, that would often change at a moment's notice. You had to service producers from various agencies all in one day; you could not forget a thing. These were very High-End Clients who were very demanding; accuracy and speed was the name of the game. I was always booked on these sessions because of my familiarity with each client; it was very important. The same way we were accustomed to working with agencies back east. I had spent a great deal of time on numerous advertising campaigns, and I knew what was expected. There were always different disclaimers, depending on the states—you had to be very careful not to confuse any of the copies at all. We had the experience and, coming from New York City, we knew their routine better than anyone else at the studio. Both Ami and I prided ourselves in that. If there was music, I was probably involved from day one. We both knew a lot of the agency guys from The Darcy Agency, McCann Erickson, Leo Burnett, J. Walter Thompson, Benton & Bowles, Lennon & Newell and B.B.D & O, which was one of our biggest accounts, and they would just let me go ahead and do my own thing.

Commercials paid very well. There was only one drawback; you had to wait for your money, which usually took a good ninety days. Their procedures were always very strange and different to say the least; you have to make it your business, no matter what, at all times to get a purchase order, a physical one (a hard copy) and job number. That's an essential part before you start anything—it is a must. No matter what you're told, you must not ever forget that your relationship with the client is entirely different when it comes to their accounting department; which happens to be another world. I cannot stress how important that is, and the role that it will play down the line. I'm not making any vague statements about ad agencies; this comes from firsthand experience, and believe me, I lived it. We had an agency that did a great deal of work with us, practically all year round, and always paid their bills; but it took a long time. They would initially, per my insistence, give us a hard copy Purchase Order Number and Job Number; that would either be hand delivered or American Express overnight. This was before FedEx came into vogue. When the work was completed, we had to bill the job in quadruplicate copies. The bill would arrive at their offices in New York City, they would review and verify everything, and I mean EVERYTHING. At this point they would send it for a signature to be OK'd.

The bill would then be sent to another office across the street for payment; this is after a good 90 days, and numerous calls. They would then send the check back across the street for a final signature and finally to their mail room. You had to stay on top of them; they are not like film or record companies. The four questions you had to ask yourself were: how fast? When? Do I really want the business? And would you be comfortable with their methods? This was their procedure; it was not a game; we were very lucky because of the relationship we had with a few of the agencies, so fortunately some of time we were able to avoid these hurdles.

We were a hot commodity; kept very busy with Ad Agencies, Record Dates and TV Variety Shows—it seemed like we would never see our homes. Julie Losch knew everyone that was anyone in town; he kept us really busy with the great following that he had in the music business. His clients and friends came from the same place; they had worked themselves up the ladder in the entertainment and music business, and they consisted of some of the best artists, some of which he managed, musicians, producers, music supervisors, music editors and contractors, the biggest in town and once they used the studio they kept coming back to us. The consistency was really great. He kept bringing one show after another, and word just spread from coast to coast that we had a great sounding studio and a staff that was very capable, efficient, and fast.

We had plenty of room to house large orchestras and production staff; which was a big plus for us. You couldn't ask for anything else. Julie brought in "Rowan & Martin's Laugh-In" a television program that had a good run on NBC from January 22, 1968, to May 14, 1973, with 140 episodes. The show was hosted by none other than comedians Dan Rowan and Dick Martin. It first aired as a special in September 1967; it was such a big hit that it became one of our many weekly series. We were on Monday Nights; we were a replacement for "The Man from UNCLE." The title of the show was a play on the "love-ins" of the 1960s hippie movement. It had terms that originated from love-ins as well as "sit-ins," that were common in protests that were associated with civil rights, and all the anti-war demonstrations at the time.

Laugh-In was a very busy show with an enormous cast and an array of different performers every week, such as Ruth Buzzi, Henry Gibson (who coincidently Julie managed), Larry Horvis, Judy Carne, Arte Johnson, Gary Owens, who was the announcer, Goldie Hawn, and many special guest stars. Who could forget Richard Nixon doing "Sock it to Me" or Sammy Davis Jr. who did "Here Comes the Judge," which was hilarious and a very big hit?

We were scheduled for pre-records usually around 10:00 a.m. Sometimes when a cast member had a solo number or skit, as soon as they would arrive, we would either, if we had the time, record them right there in Studio A with the band, or, if we had done their track, go down to Studio 2 and do vocal tracking; but Studio A was kept busy. This was an advantage that we had over various studios in town. We had the room and could move as fast as we did; the clients just loved it.

We had another special treat, at least for me, when we were scheduled to do another TV Special with none other than one of my favorite people from the cast of "Cat on a Hot Tin Roof," Mr. Burl Ives. Let me say, to be in the same room and hearing him singing "A Little Bitty Tear Let Me Down," it's different when you're sitting next to such an icon and he's singing songs you've heard most of your life. What an experience.

These were sessions that have always been treasured by me because it was like being in another world; the performances were outstanding. To say the least, time just flew by. I found Burl, as he had asked me to call him, to be a great person and a great performer. I remember during our lunch break while everyone went out, he just hung around the studio. Tommy Tedesco was in the room, and they just started talking and playing their guitars. Man you couldn't buy tickets for something this precious. I asked Burl what other songs he was going to do, and he started playing out of nowhere doing "Call Me Mister In-Between," and also went right into "Funny Way of Laughing." Tommy and I just displayed satisfied grins and were thankful to be in the same room.

I found this to be a great day; where else could you witness something like this and at no charge and get paid? When we were finished doing his part on the special, I proudly walked Burl Ives to his car. I feel very privileged to have witnessed all these giants of music doing their thing, and to have had a part in participating in one way or another. I had come a long way, and although I had many obstacles in my way, I had come into my own. So whenever things were right and time allowed, I would spend time with many of the artists, and I was able to share many things with them and they in turn with me. It was always on a one-to-one basis. I found many of them to be just like us. The laughs that we sometimes experienced on some of those sessions I will always treasure; because they always made things pleasant, which gave us lots of comfort.

We never felt alone, as far as we were concerned, we were with family. We've often said, "We spend more time together than we do with our own families." And although we were not on the road, that's the way it worked out. I can't find any other way to put it. I have experienced it, been there, and again, I must say it didn't feel like work at all.

Every morning when I would arrive at the studio, I would have my first cup of black coffee. I never knew who or what I would encounter; the clock was not something I kept a close eye on. I was never in a hurry to go home, and I never worried about having time off. I enjoyed the business at hand and the people. In those days a recording session was a recording session; you heard everything right then and there, every instrument Lead and background vocals. The business was really different; overdubbing was really not that common back then. You could invite someone to a session, and they would really enjoy themselves. It's not like today, where someone might be laying down a rhythm track or guitar parts, vocal parts or percussion, doing auto tuning all technically to perfection, then possibly lay vocals on somewhere down the line and mix in another country. The process of some recording sessions today is very fascinating technically, but very boring to the common person, and unless you're personally involved, you're not going to enjoy it at all, because the process wears out quickly.

In the early days, the artists, musicians, and producers were respectful of one another; there were times when things got a little out of hand, but for the most part these were really great times in the music industry. I feel very grateful, honored, and privileged that I was able to enjoy them and contributed to it.

I never knew who I would meet at TTG, it was like the main concourse of Grand Central Station; you never knew who would be there or when; the friendships that I made became lasting friendships for years to come. It was one of the greatest rides of my life, and I will, as long as I live, be thankful to all the people in my life who made it possible. I'm grateful to have been in the company of such greats as Phil Ramone, Roy Cicala, Ami Hadani, Tom Hidley, Tommy Dowd and Val Valentine; without them I would not have been able to be part of such monumental events in the music industry. The times were changing, but I kept on recording, because music was a big part of my life and I enjoyed every innovation that came with it. There were many changes, and we always found ourselves to be either part of that change or the innovators of it. As I've said earlier, the studio had such a vast clientele.

Ami, Tom and I just forged ahead. All of our sessions had such notoriety, and the artists were such that they just made our work pleasant, which in turn made us put a little extra something into it than we normally would have. The airwaves, oh yes! That played a big part because you were either seeing or listening to your product on a consistent basis, and our clientele knew it and complimented us for it. There's nothing more gratifying than being a part of such a movement, as we were at that time in the music industry. Being able to listen to something you've recorded over the air is such a rush that you can't really explain.

The music sessions at TTG played an integral part in the music industry. I feel very fortunate and blessed to have been part of it. I had never been happier in my life, given the way things turned out for me. I loved California—the weather and all the artists and musicians I was dealing with on a consistent basis. I could not ask for anything more. I found all recording sessions, although long, were enjoyable and just part of our daily life. We were dealing with the very best talent in town, numerous musicians that later on would be nicknamed "The

Wrecking Crew," by one of the best drummers in the music industry Hal Blaine, and as I have mentioned earlier, who could forget such greats that would later carve their own successful careers as solo artists, composers, band leaders and song writers: Glen Campbell, Barney Kessel, Tommy Tedesco, Al Casey, Billy Strange, Rene Hall, Don Peake, Howard Roberts, James Burton, Jerry Cole, Bill Aken, Mike Deasy, Doug Bartenfeld, Ray Pohlman, Bill Pittman, Irv Rubins, Louie Shelton, Steve Douglas, Jay Migliori, Jim Horn, Plas Johnson, Nino Tempo, Gene Cipriano, Roy Caton, Tony Terran, Ollie Mitchell, Bud Brisbois, Chuck Findley, Lou Blackburn, Richard "Slyde" Hyde, Lew McCreary, Leon Russell, Mac Rebennack (aka: Dr. John), Mike Melvoin, Don Randi, Larry Knechtel, Al De Lory, Mike (Michel) Rubini, Carol Kaye, Joe Osborn, Max Bennett, Chuck Berghofer, Ray Pohlman, Larry Knechtel, Lyle Ritz, Red Callender, Jimmy Bond, Bill Pitman, Hal Blaine, Earl Palmer, John Rynes, Paul Humphreys, Jim Gordon, Ed Green, Julius Wechter, Gary L. Coleman, Victor Feldman, Frank Capp the brothers Alan and Gene Estes, Tommy Morgan.

I will never be able to forget working with such great, thoughtful, and talented arrangers and composers in the studio, such as Billy Byers, Don Costa, Nick Perido, Ralph Burns, Ralph Ferraro, Van Alexander, Lalo Schifrin, Mike Post & Pete Carpenter, Pat Williams, Bill Conti, Rene Hall, Harold Baptist, Tommy Oliver, Jack Elliott, Allan Ferguson, Jack Nitzsche, and many more. The background studio singers who always, after everyone had left the studio, made us laugh and contributed so much to every piece of music that was placed in front of them, just to name a few who were the very best in town. It was a pleasure for me personally to have worked with such notables as Sally Stevens, Jackie Ward, Sue Allen, Darlene Love, Ron Hicklin, Tom and John Bahler, Bob Tebow, Thurl Ravenscroft, Gene Morford, Myrna Mathews, The Waters. They performed backup vocals as well as sound-alikes on many jingles and songs that were recorded for records, commercials, motion pictures and TV Series. They were the fastest when it came to sight reading, had a great deal of credits under their belts, and could handle themselves well in any situation or studio recording on any given day. It was out of this world; it was an amazing feeling to have participated and to have witnessed such a great era in the music business. I was always in the studio, and to be around all this talent was fantastic.

You can't imagine the feeling you get working with such talent. There would be many articles written about all these artists, performers—call them what you like. It was all talent who became great accomplished artists in their own right. They were just like us, ordinary people, and they treated everyone as a person with respect. No one looked down on anyone; that was one of the things that, for me, made it enjoyable. They were all just very professional, straight ahead—no egos, beautiful people that enjoyed life and loved music to the fullest and never missed a beat. Times were different, and people were more thankful that they had such opportunities to record their songs. From a musical standpoint, it was fantastic because they played, and they produced, and we were their music engineers. We never stepped on each other's toes; it was, for me, a musical era, not a technical era. We were given time to get a sound, and we didn't rely on the fact that we could fix it later. I've seen others spend so much time trying to duplicate sounds we got in the past, and it won't happen. There was a lot of planning that went into our recording techniques and there was very little time that was allocated to getting a sound; yet we were able to achieve it with the musician's candor, patience and participation on every session. This was always part of the music we were recording; a very creative process by everyone involved in whatever given room. We were assigned to work, and they were the most memorable days of our lives.

Those were the days when it was possible to present a song to a record label, and in a few days, you would be making a few phone calls to go into the studio to record your songs, deciding on your A and B sides, mastering your record, and turning it over to your record company—hopefully within budget. Before you knew it, you were on the airwaves. Many times, things didn't go as planned, but we made music, and we enjoyed the time we spent together. There were many people that we dealt with that became a big part of our lives.

There are many songs I hear now, and I can still picture precisely where everyone sat in the room. TTG had these 20-foot baffles that were wrapped in yellow burlap, which cut off about a quarter of the room, but this was a big room. You were still able to fit a very large piece orchestra with no problems, even with all the baffles. We also had, in the middle of the room over the percussion where the drummer usually played, what Ami and Tom called a saddle. This consisted of a sheet of burlap that stretched across the room, and it sagged at various points so that when cymbals were hit, they would bury themselves—believe it or not, it did work for us. We never talked about it because it was never an issue.

The baffles in the back of the room kept sound from just bouncing around the room. We also had very high ceilings with acoustical tiles, our portable booth that we could place anywhere in the room, and one that was completely isolated from everything with a great eye view of the room. We had our coffee room where we brewed coffee, usually at least three pots ready for the breaks. I would often, if at all possible, hang out with the Kats (musicians) in front of the building during our 5-minute breaks, just to get a breath of fresh air or have a smoke, tell a few jokes and listen to a few stories of what was going on in the music business. This, for me, was a really enjoyable time, hearing of different places in town where other studios were located and their conditions. It was another part of the business that I enjoyed hearing about. The genuine, respectful, and graceful friendships were pretty apparent. I had become friends with many of these guys. One of my fond memories was my friendship with Eden Ahboz.

I wasn't aware of his reputation, he was, for me, someone who was always around on our breaks. It just so happened that one day we started a conversation; just like anyone else in the crowd right outside the building, which was a normal thing. That's where everyone went to hang out. I noticed that he drove this old Volkswagen Bus that had a lot of strange-looking things on the side. The ones that fascinated me most were cattails which are plentiful wetland plants with a unique flowering spike. But being from the concrete jungle (Brooklyn, New York) I had never noticed or paid attention to them except when we headed west at some of the marshlands. I had never really held one in my hand. I was very inquisitive, and Eden was very generous with them. From that day on, whenever he came by the studio, he would bring some over to me because he was taken by surprise that I had no idea what they were.

We started hanging out at the studio after a session. We would share a joint and I would do some playbacks of the sessions for that given day. We would just talk for hours. I wasn't aware that he was a songwriter and that he was a "proselytizer of love and peace". This was something I had read somewhere. I don't remember where, or maybe someone told me that, but it's a word I can't even pronounce. When I first met Eden, here was this guy in sandals, long beard and hair. I was not intrusive, never have been if someone wanted to tell me something about themselves, but I have never been one to question anyone. I had no idea Eden had written "Nature Boy." I was blown away when I found out that it was a song that was made famous by Nat King Cole, which he had written in 1947 when I was 3 years old. I knew he was a writer, but the fact that he was born in Brooklyn was really what created our bond.

That first day when he asked me where I was from because of my accent, I said I was from the East Coast. I was born in Puerto Rico and raised in Brooklyn, New York, in the Red Hook

Section. He said he liked that I was descriptive about myself. We continued, as always, with a very busy schedule doing what we did best, recording Records, TV Shows, Commercials, and Variety Shows, as well as some motion pictures. One that comes to mind was when we recorded the main title song for the popular 1967 drama "Valley of the Dolls."

We were scheduled to record a singer by the name of Tony Scotti. He was another actor who had received so much notoriety from his performance in a movie that Liberty Records decided to put out a soundtrack album, just like everyone else in the business was doing. If you had a star that became very popular then the film or record company would exploit it. Many film and TV companies were doing this with their stars, it was very customary.

I had already finished recording an album with Greg Morris of "Mission Impossible" fame in Studio 2. We would do it again, this time it was Tommy Oliver and Dave Pell producing. We recorded "It Must Be Him" for Vikki Carr which reached number three on the U.S. pop chart and spent three weeks at number one on the easy listening charts. The album would do well, it reached No. 12 on the Billboard charts and is the singer's most successful English-language release to date.

Tommy had many credits to his name. He had arranged and produced hit albums by Doris Day, Edie Adams, Donny and Marie Osmond, Charles Boyer, Franky Avalon, Joanie Sommers, Eddie Fisher, and The Jefferson Airplane, to name a few. Unfortunately, for us all, Tommy left us on May 2, 2006. I miss him very much; we had become very close and dear friends—a big loss.

All the sessions we were working on, I might add, were done on 2-inch 16-tracks. It wouldn't take long before every studio would have 24-tracks, and eventually would come the synchronization of a few multi-track machines. The demand for more tracks was unreal; we were using the machine to full capacity. When we would run out of tracks, we would just play the tune down to see which tracks were empty in a particular section, and how much time we had to punch in and out, which created a lot of work on the mix down as far as muting, opening and assigning tracks for the stereo mix. One way would be to assign tracks to a multi position with a few outputs and bringing them up on a few faders on the console to set-levels, equalize it differently, add Echo and Panning position and, after a few rehearsals, it was all hands on deck, usually three or four people. This was all done manually; it would be a few years before automation would come into play.

The way we achieved this was really fun. It was very natural in those days, and you'd be surprised how many albums were done in that fashion. Well, enough said, we continued working and taking our routine breaks, hanging out, getting some fresh air, and on our smoke breaks, you'd be surprised who you would meet here in front of this building.

When I was a kid, one of my mother's favorite shows was "Name That Tune," which was hosted by George Dewitt. I remember one evening seeing this talented kid with red hair appear on that show. His name was Eddie Hodges, and he sang and danced; the kid was fantastic. The audience was so captivated by his performance on the show, and because of his charisma and talent, he was asked if he would fly to Hollywood to star in Frank Capra's "A Hole in the Head," a major motion picture with Frank Sinatra, Eleanor Parker, and Edward G. Robinson in 1959. He was twelve years old. I never forgot when the MC of the show announced that they wanted Eddie for the film; it just stayed with me.

I'm walking down the hall, and here's this kid going in the same direction. We greet each other and go outside to have a smoke. We started talking, and to my surprise, I was blown away when I found out that I was talking with Eddie Hodges, the real Eddie Hodges—that same kid that I saw on TV. Here we were in front of TTG, the two of us sharing war stories. We talked about dropping acid; he said he had done some and liked it. I hadn't tried it yet, but it would be just a matter of time.

Eddie said he had become a songwriter and had done some recordings. He hung around our session for a couple of days. What a nice guy. Unfortunately, I never saw him again, but for me, it was a trip meeting him and sharing some great stories. He was three years younger than me, so we had pretty much the same interest in music. The groups that we were recording were playing what we were into musically. I loved every minute of it. I never thought for one minute I would ever meet Eddie Hodges, this, to me, was a trip.

There was a lot of young talent that headed for Hollywood in the 60s. It had become a big haven for an opportunity in the music industry. You could get a deal overnight; the record companies were taking more risks. Before you knew it, you could be in a studio recording your project. The musicians in Hollywood were the best, they were big contributors and very creative. All of our sessions were fast and always just a bundle of fun. I knew I had hit town at the right time, and I was enjoying every part of it. I was doing what I liked, working in music and making friends for life.

This was a saving grace for me. I had my family well-situated; everyone was doing great, and here I was recording music and meeting people I liked. I still felt very fortunate being here and glad I had decided to make the move to California. Ami and Tom had kept their end of the bargain. I had no complaints at all; we were doing all our regular sessions for Capitol Records, Liberty Records, Uni Records, and MGM Records. They kept us busy as well as BBD&O, who kept us busy with their commercial campaigns.

We were busy; various sessions were happening every day. It was always something new, and interesting. I could invite anyone to a session, and they would enjoy themselves and be thankful for it. There were a lot of changes coming to all the recording studios in the music industry, such as new recording consoles, outboard gear, and newer and faster machines.

It would be a matter of time before we would feel all these changes; not only would our recording equipment and techniques have to change, but because of the times, like any other business, TTG was also facing stiff competition.

I loved the move I made here. I would not change it for the world. So, I would also have to adapt to the times. Monday morning, our receptionist, Stephanie Murray, announced she was leaving TTG; she was indeed our first receptionist—you couldn't count Ami's nephew David, or me. Stephanie was our jewel who had come from Colgems. Cheri Wagner would be taking her place. She was a very different but intelligent girl from the valley, had been hanging out with us awhile and was well liked by all the staff. She was not a stranger to us, and she got along very well with all the clients and musicians. She knew how to run our office. Stephanie taught her well; she knew how to book all our sessions, which was very important, she had a certain way about her of putting us all in our place whenever we got out of line, in a nice way, never out to embarrass you at all, and was aware of our needs during any recording session. She didn't work 9 to 5; she was always around when needed. Stephanie had done us well, so it became a really good change for the studio and staff.

There were times when we would work an all-nighter and have a 10:00 a.m. session booked the very next day, which we had to do. You couldn't just sub it out to another engineer, or it could be a project you had started or were starting, so sometimes you reached for a little help. I remember on my very first all-nighter, which was a variety show, I had finished doing vocal tracks with the Johnny Mann singers. Both Johnny and I approached Cherie, and Johnny said, "You got an upper, a Benny," and it was here that I tried my very first Upper, and I must say it did help me. I was given a Benny and I got through the day without any problems at all. This was my first time, and I felt strength I had never felt before or thought I had, and I feel fortunate that I didn't abuse it, because in those days they were very easy to get. Things were going very well at the studio, but at home, we needed changes. I needed to earn more money; we could not afford to live in the same apartment we were at; we had outgrown it. The children were getting older. We had to move, there was no question about it, not to mention the fact that we all needed more privacy.

When you're in the music business or studio recording business, the days are long, but the years go by really quickly. If you don't take a step back to analyze your situation you can lose sight of what is most important. I must say, in my situation I was extremely fortunate because I had found someone to help me out, since I was in debt up to my ears. I had become friends with someone who literally and willingly was there to help me whenever I needed anything. Stan Broder, who was related to Cherie Wagner, she called him her big brother, but I don't think they were blood relatives. I could always bounce things off Stan and he, I must say, was a great listener. He'd helped me get creditors off my back and was very helpful in helping me get around town as well as advising me about various places in the valley. Stan had come to TTG as our night desk operator. Before long he was doing the books while he was still studying during the day, and I believe he was in the Naval Reserve. Eventually he would take over as our traffic manager. I could never repay him for all he did for me. I will always be indebted to him; the man knew what he was doing, and he was very meticulous about anything he would encounter. Stan and I spent many hours together. He took us trapping for crabs at Venice Beach pier one day. He had asked me if I had ever gone trapping for crabs, to which I replie "No Stan. I don't even know how it's done."

He responded, "Would you like to try it?"

"Yes," I replied.

So here we were; three of us: Stan, Danny (my stepson) and me. It was a warm summer evening with a nice breeze blowing. We rented some traps and bought some bait. You were not allowed to trap crabs off the pier, but we were very determined and did it anyway. We were now waiting for time to pass; both Stan and I just hung around the pier discussing many ideas, and to be more precise, my next move just talking and making plans. I knew it was time for me to make a few decisions: first, find an apartment or house to rent. I wanted to be away from Hollywood, rents were cheaper in the valley, and it was a better place for kids. So, we kept talking about various moves I could make. Time passed and finally we realized we had given the traps enough time.

I reached over and jerked on my rope a few times. It didn't help; it wouldn't move. The first thing that came to mind was, "Oh no! I'm stuck on a rock or something; I'll have to pay for the trap I've rented." As always, lots of things just running through my mind. I kept on pulling and tugging my line with all my strength and finally it came loose. I heard something snap, and I thought, "Oh God, I hope I don't lose it." So here I was in the dark on the Venice pier struggling with my line trying to pull this trap over the railing. I had decided to get my trap back at any cost. Time had passed, and it was now pretty dark; the only lights we had were the lights on the pier and the moon. It was getting a little too cold for my taste.

I kept pulling on my line over the railing, all the time looking down at the water thinking I probably do have a tire stuck to the trap. I turned to my right and kneeled on my right knee, pulling as hard as I could on the line. As I was doing that, I could see the waves on the beach below me. I'm looking up through the railings and I can see the lights from the pier in the breakwater. By now I've reached the very top of the railing, and I can feel a little less weight on my line. As I look up, to my amazement, I see the biggest crab I have ever seen in my life. This was a Spider Crab. It had to be at least ten-fifteen pounds maybe more. I kept struggling and I must admit it scared the living daylights out of me. There was a lot of excitement on the pier; this thing was very big. Some bikers came over; I had let the line fall halfway down the railing. They helped me pull it up and finally it dropped over the railing onto the boardwalk. This thing was huge; it was gray in color, moving slowly, but very scary, it was enormous. I'd never seen anything like it; the claws were as big as a large baby's arm. Some more bikers rushed over; there was a lot of commotion by now and I was hoping the cops would not show. The bikers asked me what I was going to do with it and I said I had no idea, I'd never seen anything like this before. They asked if I would like to trade, and I quickly replied yes. I gave it to them for some pot and they started a fire and proceeded to cook it right then and there; what an evening.

I had never done or experienced anything like this anywhere, not even in New York City. I never took any time off. All my life all I'd done is work. I didn't stop working once I arrived in Hollywood, my interest was solely music and establishing myself. If I was not working for the studio, I'd be working on some project of mine. I was always working weekends. The only problem with it was that I wasn't making enough money to justify the long hours. I never complained, that's not me. I was way too busy working, and I was blind to the fact that I did need to make more money to pay our bills. I had not seen an increase in pay since my arrival from New York City, the studio was doing very well so it could afford to raise my pay. We were working so much that certain situations that needed to be addressed had fallen through the cracks. I needed a raise and a bigger and better place to live. Stan went to Ami Hadani and said, "Look, this guy can't make it on what you're paying him. Look at his track record, he has a good client base."

I felt strange about the whole thing, that it would be Stan to negotiate and get me a considerable raise. We were finally able to move over the hill to Studio City, where we found a small house west of Laurel Canyon with a great backyard. I loved Studio City; at the time it was still fairly small, and you saw actors walking the streets since Radford Studios was but a few blocks away, and the restaurants were all really close. Who could forget Dupar's, the car wash on the corner of Laurel and Ventura Blvd, the school on Carpenter Avenue was very close, so we had made a great change again, everything within walking distance and great neighbors. Everything seemed to be falling into place.

Time passed quickly, we lived there well into the early part of the seventies until our daughter, Denise, was born at Valley Presbyterian Hospital on June 3, 1972. We needed to move again, but now I would put a lot of time and effort into it. I would spend as much time as I could looking around the valley. I didn't want to go too far, but after a few months we found that what we needed to do was purchase a house. The move was timely; now we purchased a 3-bedroom house with a big yard and swimming pool in Canoga Park. I would no longer be that close to Hollywood, but I felt the family was safer and commuting into Hollywood was not a problem, which changed me on the freeway. I had to time myself carefully, on my first session I was booked to record a commercial early Monday morning for The Gas Company. The arranger was none other than the eccentric Claire Fischer. He had written for a big brass band that consisted of some of the best players in town, which were always Claire's choice. The orchestra consisted of Guitar, Piano, Bass, Drums, Percussion, 4 Trumpets, 4 Trombones, and 5 Woodwinds. It was a good session. We had picture up and everything was going as good as it could. I got a balance as always really quick.

We began to record, and after a few takes, I could sense from the agency guy's comments in the control room, that they weren't happy with the session. It had nothing to do with the sound; they felt it was way too big for the visual picture they had shot. What they were expecting was something gentler, so they wanted to change the band. The feeling was it had to fit the picture, which showed pasta being thrown into a boiling pot of water, and there was a great shot of the blue gas flames under the pot on the stove, which they wanted to feature.

The big brass sound didn't do the picture any justice at all, which made the agency guys uncomfortable. Sometimes this happens; it's not rare. Claire Fischer walked into the control room, and after carefully listening to a playback and the client's concerns about the piece said, "Hey! I'll send the band home, no use continuing. We can start fresh early tomorrow morning. Let's check the studio's schedule." I called downstairs; it was a go. Everything was paid for the day it; added an extra recording day, and I was able to get out early.

The next morning, we had strings, harpsichord, woodwinds, and percussion. Now when you saw the pasta being thrown in the steaming pot of hot boiling water, you heard the shimmering of the bell tree, strings along with the woodwinds, and when the flame came into focus it all made sense; all the hits were right on. Everyone was happy; this was typical of agency dates, and Claire Fischer knew how to handle them; he was a master at it. We recorded several spots and mixed everything; the agency got what they wanted, and we were all happy as can be.

We continued doing other sessions, the studio was never idle at all; it was constantly in demand. The only reason we were able to leave early the previous day was because that time was being paid for by the agency. That was just a treat that rarely happens, and thanks to Claire, he was all for it; he went home to write. Agency dates are tough in the sense that everyone wants to impress the client because there's always a lot of money on the line, and the product or products at all times are very important. They are the stars and will be treated as such. You have to be able to deal with critique and all the changes that will come with it. In this case, Claire was right on, and they loved him for it.

Claire was an extremist about language, very quick to correct you or anyone, especially when it came to the Spanish language. We were in the studio one day, and I had said something, and when he heard what I had said, he quickly jumped in with his correction. I said to him, "Look, Claire. I'm the Spanish guy, not you."

He quickly responded, "Yes, but your pronunciation is incorrect."

God love him; that was Claire. I was doing a lot of recording dates with Claire. One day he called me out of the blue and told me he had decided to record and release his album. He booked Studio A, and he decided to buy some black hash that he suggested we smoke during our breaks, it was a trip. Our breaks were now taking longer than most sessions because Claire wanted to go next door to an abandoned house to smoke. The house was adjacent to our building, next to the Chinese laundry, which was owned by my friend, Tom Hung. We would walk in there, Claire would shave the black hash into a glass pipe he bought and just light up. We were aware that we were taking more time than usual on our breaks, but it didn't matter as far as time went; we were doing very well. But after so many trips, we grew tired of the house; we were tired of walking down the long stairs, so we decided to smoke in the back of the studio behind the tall baffles.

A few weeks later, Claire showed up with the LP in hand. Because they had forgotten, or so he said (I think he forgot), to print engineering credits on the album, he took it upon himself and had written on the cover, "The only engineer I have never argued with," and handed it to me. I miss him; I liked Claire, and although he was a challenge, it was good because you learned an awful lot from him.

It was the start of a new week and I was not booked on any sessions. I hung around the front office and decided to go through the traffic book. I was turning pages to see what sessions were booked, and to my surprise, I noticed one session that stood out with one of my favorite producers that I had met back in New York City at A&R Recording; it was none other than Jimmy Bowen. At that time, he was married to a very talented lady that I liked, none other than Keely Smith, who was mostly known as the duet partner of Louis Prima, who put on a great show and was best known for their top 20 hit in the 50s, "That All Black Magic," which I had seen a few times and enjoyed.

When we first met back in New York City, Jimmy was producing Morgana King; most of you would remember her from The Godfather, she played Carmela Corleone, the mother of the Corleones. In the mid-60s, Jimmy worked with Frank Sinatra, Sammy Davis, Jr., and Dean Martin at Reprise; since then, he had high posts at Capitol, MGM, Elektra/Asylum, and MCA, concentrating mostly on country music. So here I was at TTG and I just couldn't wait to see both of them; they were great people. On the first session, I was right there; I greeted them, and we just hugged and said our hellos. Keely said, "So this is where you ended up, always being very cheerful." Jimmy was now producing Kenny Rogers and the First Edition in Studio 2; it was a total lockout. He was also bringing in his engineers, Eddie Brackett and Chuck Britz, who were great engineers with great track records. The upside was that we would be experiencing a great deal of new recording techniques as well as meeting new acts.

Jimmy brought us a lot of business; we were busy working with a few members of Elvis Presley's rhythm section, such as Ronnie Tutt on drums, Glen D. Hardin on piano, and James Burton on guitar. Kenny Rogers and Cliff Goldsmith hit it off, as well as the rest of the group. They were doing a follow-up psychedelic song, "Just Dropped In (To See What My Condition Was In)," very timely for the times, which earned them a little fame, to say the least. The arrangement was done by Mike Post, with Glen Campbell playing the backward guitar intro and Mike Deasy, who was providing various psychedelic sounds. The tune became a hit early in 1968, climbing to No. 5.

I remember that while we were recording "RUBY," a song

written by Mel Tellis, we were searching for a particular sound to use on the break. We searched and searched all over the building for something. Finally, we went outside; we kept looking all over the alley next to the Chinese Laundry. We looked all over the place, and finally, we found a big cardboard box in good shape. We brought it inside the studio and put a mike on it; Ron Tutt played the Break, and "Ruby, Don't Take Your Guns to Town," which hit number 6 in the US and number 2 in the UK, was born.

These were long sessions, but the pay was great, the musicians were the best, and Jimmy, as always, was a gentleman. I enjoyed the time I spent with Kenny Rogers and The First Edition; what can you say about the guy? Kenny Rogers was the funniest guy you would ever want to meet, a very respectful and extremely talented man. I miss those sessions; they were an experience I will never forget I feel grateful and honored to have had the opportunity to be part of their sessions. In 1971, a laid-back disc jockey by the name of Tom Clay was playing a tune he had assembled: "What the World Needs Now is Love/Abraham, Martin and John," which he created at the radio station he was working at KGBS in Los Angeles. Motown Records head, Berry Gordy, thought it was great and decided to release it as a single. I remember that morning leaving my house; I'm driving in my 1960 Corvair. The freeway was packed, so I decided to go South on Laurel Canyon. As I reached the corner, I made my left on Ventura Blvd, headed East, and as I crossed Lankersheim Blvd and started up Cahuenga Blvd into Hollywood, I turned on my radio, and I heard this tune—rough, but I'm liking the concept.

I pulled up to the studio, parked, and as soon as I walked through the front door, I'm told to call Dave Pell at Motown; he had already left a couple of messages. I called him back, he said that he had a record he wanted to do and asked if I would engineer it. I said yes, and he said he would book the time as soon as he spoke to his contractor, Ben Barrett, and that it would be a fun session. Within the hour he called and booked the session. Gene Page would be the arranger/composer. A short time later I spoke with Ben Barrett and I knew by the size of the orchestra that this was a serious session.

The following day I was really in for a surprise. I had no idea that I would be recording what I had heard the previous morning for MoWest, which at the time was Motown's West Coast label that was active from 1971 to 1973. They had a small roster of artists on that label, such as Rare Earth, Frankie Valle and The Four Seasons, and Bobby Darin. This would be a first for Tom Clay; everyone was very excited.

MoWest would close after the parent label made its final move to the West Coast, and some of the artists, most notably the Commodores, which at the time included Lionel Richie, would now switch to the main Motown label.

We were very fortunate to have a great arranger such as Gene Paige, who I had worked with numerous times. He made it very exciting; this would bring in another hit for me, as well as the studio. I had a surprise visit during the session; none other than Guy Costa, who was Don Costa's brother and head of production for Motown. We knew each other very well; he had dropped by to check things out and say hello everyone was happy.

I was creating sound effects live, lifting flute parts from the woodwind tracks on the multi-track machine to a mono machine so that when a president was mentioned, I would fly it in to make a statement. A recording that was done of a young kid, and Dave Pell insisted on keeping the genuineness in his voice. He was being asked the following questions:

What is segregation? I don't know what segregation is.

What is bigotry? I don't know what bigotry is.

What does hatred mean? I don't know what that is...

What is prejudice? Hmm, I think it's when someone is sick.

It was such an honest statement coming from a child

answering these questions from an adult. This was a great session; the mood in the control room was a bit somber because of the subject matter. When we finished mixing, we knew we had a record that said an awful lot of things; it had a very chilling effect on anyone that listened to it, and everyone, Dave Pell, Tom Clay and Gene Paige, was very complimentary. The session had gone very well, and we knew we had ourselves a hit record.

I was doing very well at this point in my career. In addition to engineering, I was also producing a lot of sessions of Leon Haywood for Capitol Records. Leon was a funk and soul singer and best known for his 1975 hit single "I Want'a Do Something Freaky to You." He was one of the nicest guys you would ever want to meet and working with him for me was really the best of times in the studio.

We had hit it off on one of Cliff Goldsmith's sessions while he was producing him for VJAY Records, a very exciting session where we recorded "Ever Since You Were Sweet Sixteen." I would go on to produce with Leon such tunes as "Blues Get Off My Shoulder," "You Know What," "You and Your Moody Ways," as well as a few others; all written by Leon Haywood and arranged by Ray Jackson.

We were spending anywhere from two to three days in the studio and having a great time. There were times when I would keep him in the studio so long that by the time he arrived at the club where he was performing, he'd have a sore throat from singing for so many hours. I enjoyed working with Leon; to me he was exceptional, and I loved the songs he was writing. I put my heart and soul into those sessions. It was a different time for me; I ate, breathed and lived nothing but music. It was all I thought about; you couldn't take me away from that console. I was spending numerous hours in that room session after session.

We had recorded a song called "There Ain't Enough Hate Around." After the session I went ahead and did a rough mix.

The following day I called Ron Kramer, an old friend and producer who was heading a small label, and I went over and played it for him. He loved the song. I left him a copy. The following day when I arrived at the studio, I had a stack of messages from guys like Bill Trout from Chicago, saying, "Don't forget your friends." There was total excitement; everyone loved the song. Ron Kramer was very enthusiastic about what he heard, so I arranged a meeting with him and Leon the following day. We arrived early and chatted a bit; there was a good feeling about this record. Everyone felt we had a hit on our hands.

Ron asked what was needed to finish the record. I said that we needed some brass overdubs and a final mix. We were done with vocals; probably a good 6-hour session at best. We left Ron's office very enthusiastic with high hopes and the possibility of getting a good record deal. Something else came into play; Cliff Goldsmith convinced Leon to put a prayer on the record, which Cliff said he would overdub. The minute I heard the idea I was totally against it. My feelings were that it would bring the record down, and it would definitely take away from it. Well, needless to say it killed the record. When Ron heard the mix, his words were, "That's not what I heard before in the rough mix. This is entirely different; the rough mix was better. The deal, if there was going to be one, was dead..

We continued recording, but eventually we just drifted apart. Leon Haywood, sadly to say, died at the age of 74 on Tuesday April 5, 2016. I still play his tapes. As far as I'm concern those were really great sessions for an artist that didn't get the exposure he deserved. I still miss him, as well as those great sessions in Studio 2. We both knew that room really well, and I had spent many hours recording the cream of the crop there; the likes of Phil Everly and his pals, Monk Higgins, Jimmy McCrackling, a lot of different artists. The room was small but it had a very unique sound. If you setup the room correctly you could fit up to fifteen men. I never heard any complaints.

There was a great deal of recording done in this room, and I was fortunate to be in control of it. I was always working this room and requested by everyone that came to record here. I did music for such TV shows and films like "Barney Miller," Bruce Lee's "Enter the Dragon," "Police Woman," "The Streets of San Francisco," "Hawaii Five-O," "Adam Five," and so many other TV shows.

This continued for a while. Then things all of a sudden turned for the worst. TTG was no longer able to meet its payroll. We went for a period of time where we were not paid, and sessions were now far and few in between. I needed to make a change; the money wasn't there. Other studios were springing up all over town, and competition was fierce. I had a family to care for. Although I continued doing a lot of recording sessions; I knew deep inside, I had to make a change. There were newer studios that had state-of-the-art consoles and equipment. It was imperative that I learn how it all functioned; my livelihood depended on it.

MGM Records finished building their studios on Fairfax Avenue in West Hollywood, and I was approached by none other than Val Valentine. He wanted me to move to MGM Records. I had brought my family to California. I could not fail them. I was very concerned about my next move because I was faced with a very difficult decision; one that I didn't want to make. It had been some time since Tom Hidley had left, and I didn't want to just jump ship when the chips were down. I felt I owed both the studio as well as Ami something. When I spoke with Val, he told me that I didn't owe TTG and Ami anything; he wanted me to join his staff, and he made no bones about it. He said I would most likely end up doing the majority, if not all, of Don Costa's sessions. MGM Records needed an engineer who could work with the roster of artists that Mike Curb was signing to the label, that Mike Curb liked me and he wanted me there.

I was being pressed by Val; he was very persistent and

asked me numerous times to join their staff. I found it a difficult decision for me to make, and by the same token, I also felt the welcoming mat would soon end and that offer would not be on the table too long. I had come a long way, and I still didn't want to leave TTG. I was very naïve in thinking that Ami had taken care of me. I felt I owed him something, while everyone else said, no you don't and kept pushing me to leave and go to MGM Records. I had never been a person to move around from job to job, although things didn't look too promising for me at TTG. I was hoping for a savior; I was heartbroken seeing how things were going, it was not a pleasant sight. I had often been offered many opportunities and yet I found it very hard to accept them. I couldn't and wouldn't switch jobs; I was very loyal, but reality was slowly sinking in, and again I began to worry about how long this offer would remain on the table.

I had already turned down Wally Heider and Gary Kellgren at The Record Plant; how many more offers would come along before I would make a decision that was solely mine to make? I had to make a decision; I couldn't just keep people waiting. I knew deep inside it was time, because of the way things were going at TTG. I didn't see it working out; we had no health insurance, what if something happened? I knew MGM would provide us health insurance. It was a no-brainer; I had a wife and children to consider—It wasn't all about me. Finally I accepted Val's offer. I felt funny; it was a heartbreaker for me, but I was fighting a losing battle. I had no choice; there was nothing I could do to justify staying at TTG.

All I kept thinking about were those early days, so historical and all the great sessions we'd done with notable artist, producers, bands, all the TV shows—so much history. I knew that I would miss my surroundings in this part of Hollywood; I had been here a few years, and I would also miss all the convenience and ease of getting here. I loved these rooms. Although they were not that modern, they had a unique sound of their own, but there were other things I had to consider, and that first and foremost was the family. I wouldn't sacrifice that for anything in the world. There was a lot on my plate; it was one of the biggest decisions in my life, but I had to do what was best. Everyone was very supportive. I knew that I was making the right decision, but at the time there was this reluctance in me that always brought me back to those early days at TTG—but it was time to move on. I will never forget this place and the projects, with all the notoriety that I was involved in as a sound engineer.

Album	Artist	Year
Freak out	The Mothers of Invention	June 27, 1966
Animalism	The Animals	November, 1966
Winds of Change	Eric Burton and The Animals	March, 1967
Big Boss Bones	Trombones Unlimited	June, 1967
Free	The Mothers of Invention	April, 1967
The Velvet Underground	The Velvet Underground & Nico	July, 1967
Basie Straight Ahead	Count Basie	January, 1968
The Sound of The Seventies	Tommy Vig Orchestra	July, 1968
Jam Session at TTG	Jimi Hendrix & Jack Bruce	October, 1968
The Jimi Hendrix Experience	Jimi Hendrix	October, 1968
A. B. Skhy	A. B. Skhy	December, 1968

Album	Artist	Year
Crow by Crow	Crow	February, 1970
Longbranch Pennywhistle	Longbranch Pennywhistle	April, 1970
Copperfield	The Dillards	May, 1970
Sunday's Child	Sunday's Child	October, 1970
Slow Down	Crow	January, 1971
The Last Time I Saw Her	Glen Campbell	July, 1971
I'm Gon' Git Myself Together	Jimmy Smith	October, 1971
Doing What Comes Naturally	Charles Wright	January, 1973
Inside America	Juggy Murray Jones	April, 1976
Concert in Blues	Willie Hutch	October, 1976
Bahiana	Dizzy Gillespie	February, 1977

I often think about that first day when I arrived in Hollywood on that holiday weekend, running into the building by accident late at night. I didn't know California at all and registering at the motel on La Brea and Sunset Blvd, calling Ami and hearing all the excitement in his voice because I had finally arrived. What I had accomplished here in such a short time, with all the help from him and Tom and so many other people. I was going crazy just thinking about it. Many memories kept running through my mind; I couldn't sleep, and I just couldn't let go.

The memories of my first day, walking in the front entrance and the greeting I received from Ami's nephew, David. Tom Hidley coming down the hall to greet me and my family, Fred Borkgren showing me around the building; all this was running through my head constantly. It would not be that easy for me to forget this place. Perhaps in time I probably would, but deep inside I knew that I would always be a part of TTG, and that the men that offered me this job would forever remain a big part of my life. For me those were memorable and remarkable times. We had come a long way, and it was not that easy for me to just brush aside.

I will always remember walking through that front door and how I felt; and how these two men that I had met and had become my friends back in New York City, had taken me in, taught me the art of recording, along with many other things. They had introduced me to Hollywood and helped me further my career, which was something that at the time would not have been possible back east. I kept fighting with all these thoughts, but reality just kept staring me in the face. It was time to close the books on TTG. I had no idea what lay ahead for me, but I would take it one day at a time. There were a lot of believers on my side, but I was not totally convinced. I kept fighting it and the more I did the more I kept coming up with the same answer; my family needed all my support, that was very clear. I could not sacrifice their wellbeing as well as my own. I hoped and prayed that hopefully things would work out; it was time for me once and for all to start thinking more positively about what lay ahead on my new venture.

MGM was very promising. All I had to do was think of better days ahead. My new job and position at MGM Records would definitely be a change of pace, and the pay was a plus. We were expecting a child, so health insurance, which was provided, really helped. I had never worked for a corporate entity before, but I felt that with Val Valentine's support, I could succeed. Who knew it would just be a matter of time. There are no guarantees in this business. Although I had been at TTG for a very long time; the oldest employee always hoping for the best and look what happened. I knew it wasn't deliberate; times had changed, and it was all economics—we needed equipment. We didn't have a good selection of microphones, and when it came to outboard equipment, we didn't really have any; by now our machines were outdated. It had become a 24-track standard in all the studios and Dolby noise reduction had also entered the picture—these were essential tools that were needed. Yes, you could rent them, but who would have to cover the cost? Clients wouldn't pay for it; but at MGM it was all inhouse.

I had always hoped for the best. It wasn't there, and I know everyone was well aware of what I was feeling. We had lost our edge, and I often wondered, like everyone else, where did all the money go? Certainly not on equipment or salaries; no one was really making that much money. The place was hanging by a thin thread. I knew that if I didn't make my move, I would really be left behind and really in bad shape. Yes it was time to move; I didn't even say my goodbyes. I was too choked up; it was a sad day. I just walked out the front door and looked at the house and auto repair shop across the street. I looked up at the building, made a right turn, and got in my car that was parked under the big Loquat tree next to my dear friend's laundry. I was hurt, and I thought maybe someday I would return; who knew? Anything is possible.

That evening when I arrived at the house, I had a headache that wouldn't quit. I was all stressed out and I needed to rest. Monday would be my first day at MGM, and I had to be at my best. The worst was now behind me. I had made my decision; it was time to move forward. I spent the weekend at the mall and purchased new clothes. Val and I had lunch at Martone's, and we talked for quite a while about the studio. He was very excited and said that nothing but good times was all he saw down the road. I had never worked for a label before; this was all new to me, but the fact that they did have the resources had made it really tempting for me. Taking care of my family was a must for me, and it was something I did not want to fail at, so this made it a lot easier, I said I'd be there bright and early and ready for whatever comes. We shook hands and I headed out the door, got in my car and drove up Cahuenga Blvd towards the 101 freeway.

MY MOVE TO MGM RECORDS

My first day at MGM Records, I showed up dressed in coat and tie; something Val Valentine wanted me to do to see if the rest of the crew would follow in my footsteps—but that would end very quickly. I was greeted by my new boss, Val Valentine, along with the front office gals, Rita Hagen and Rosemary Frenchimonie, mastering engineers, Edwin Atwater and George Miller, and Ed Greene, who was second in command—he hailed from Washington D.C. The Osmond Brothers were present, and Jay Osmond said, right in front of everyone, "Ed, this guy is a real good engineer." That really boosted my ego. Hearing that coming from their own artist really made me feel right at home.

I was also very surprised to find out that Jack Hunt would also be working at MGM. He had decided to leave TTG and followed Tom Hidley when he went to work at Record Plant Studios; but somehow it didn't work out. I never really found out the real reason why they had transferred him to their facility in New York, but I know Jack had become so disappointed with the arrangement that after a short time in the city he quit, which was what they wanted, and he ended up here at MGM Records. I must admit that I was glad to see Jack; we had some good times together and had numerous sessions under our belts, and although there was the Jimi Hendrix issue, it never stopped me from liking the guy.

I, by now, had come a long way with great credits to my name, which, I might add, were very impressive. I would no longer be looked on as a second engineer. So here we are a few years later and we're working together again. I started slowly at MGM Records, learning their rules, the new console and just asking Ed Greene our supervisor lots of questions regarding their patch bay, which is the first thing you want to know in a studio. It's very important to know the signal flow.

Ed Greene was from the Washington, D.C., area and knew a lot of artists I had worked with. In addition, he was a bright, honest and a wonderful man. He was very helpful to everyone he came in contact with. I must say that Ed Greene was a great asset; I felt really at home with him, and I was feeling really comfortable. The studio was very well equipped, and if you needed something, in no time at all, if it was valid, they would buy it—buy it, not rent it. I liked that—very professional.

We had two Neumann record lathes at MGM, and Ed personally trained all the staff engineers to work them properly. A record lathe is a complicated piece of equipment that records audio information on blank record acetates. The lathe operates in a similar fashion to a record player, but with some substantial differences: They have a microscope that is attached to the lathe that allows the mastering engineer to examine and make fine adjustments to the depth and width of the groove. Instead of a standard cartridge for listening to records, the lathe is fitted with a strong and durable cutting head. The cutting head is driven by one or more amplifiers that move the head in the X and/or Y axis, depending on whether the record is stereo or mono. As the blank record spins, the cutting head is lowered into the vinyl to begin the first several rotations of groove. The master recording is played back through the amplifiers and manipulates the head into cutting a representative groove.

Although not used as frequently as in the past, record

lathes are a necessary piece of equipment in the supply chain that feeds the record collector. So here we were at MGM cutting our own reference dubs and masters; we had a lathe on the first and second floor. Ed Greene's students were Edwin Atwater, George Miller, Lewis Peters and Humberto Gatica. This whole process saved MGM thousands of dollars daily because we didn't have to wait for someone else to do our masters or reference dubs, which takes a considerable amount of time. We were more than capable of making our own masters that would be picked up by messengers at the end of the day by the pressing plants MGM was using at the time, H. V. Waddell and Monarch in Burbank. This was a process that we, on a daily basis, would perform for all artists on the label; and for our international clients.

I never had the time to learn the system. I, as well as Jack Hunt, were too busy on a daily basis recording in M-1 or M-2; their main studios, which was OK by me. I didn't have eyes on becoming a mastering engineer. The other guys were doing a great job and enjoying it to the fullest. I had no interest in mastering and Ed never assigned those duties to me; I was strictly hired as a mixer.

Our international catalogue consisted of an enormous country catalogue that went back many years. Whenever any of us engineers had any idle time, we would go to the board by Rosie's desk and pull a work order. We would locate whatever masters were needed for the project and head upstairs to the TD Room (tape duplicating room), where you would proceed to transfer whatever LPs were requested, be it by either domestic or international clients. We were the luckiest guys in town because we were given a chance to listen to such great music from their country catalogue, such as Bob Wills and The Texas Cowboys and Hank Williams Sr. MGM Records had an enormous and impressive library. We were also able to listen to our present collection of artists, such as Sammy Davis Jr, Eddie Arnold, The Osmond Brothers, Donny Osmond, Marie

Osmond, The Mike Curb Congregation, and many more. We had a great selection, and it wasn't boring at all. In fact, we would often race just to make copies in the TD Room. The room was equipped with a small Studer Board that sounded really great. The process was very easy, and you weren't disturbed at all.

I would often ask our office girls, either Rita Hagan or Rosie Frenchomonie, if there were any international copies to be made. We would always use this to fill our time whenever we were not assigned to a session. This room was also great for editing your quarter-inch masters, and when finished you just took it down the hall to be mastered. Everyone stayed very busy; there was always something for you to do, and you had the very best of equipment to complete your work.

I was booked to edit a single with two producers who had a rush release. We needed to cut the length of their tune down because the radio stations wouldn't play it if the tune was too long. I aligned my machines and made two copies, and now we were ready. I played it down and we took notes. Well, in the process one of the guys says to the other, "Don't cut that chorus down, that'll make it too short," to which the response was, "No it won't." To this, the other responds, "Yes it will," and before you knew it, they start arguing with each other. "Man, you don't know how to edit." They are screaming their heads off going back and forth. Things like, "Man, you haven't been in the business long, have you? I been in the business for years, I've edited lots of songs," etc., etc. In the interim, there I am standing with a blade in my hands waiting to make a cut, but I can't.

The phone rings; its Val Valentine. They were screaming so loud you could hear it down the hall into the other mastering room and M-2, our second studio, so the front office had called him. Val was a man who didn't take it lightly with anyone screaming at his staff. His first question was, "Mister, is there a problem in there?"

I responded no, and he says, "I don't allow anyone to scream at my staff, is that clear?"

I responded, "Yes, but it's between them, not me."

Val always stood up for his guys; he was a great boss, and I must say he was very supportive of his team. I found that to be a great asset for us having someone on your side, not bad at all.

He wanted a strong staff and there was nothing he wouldn't do for you as long as you followed the rules. He would not tolerate any abuse towards any of us. The session continued, and I took what was a 5-minute R&B tune and edited it to about 3:10. This was very typical for us to do and not rare at all. Our main room, M-1, was well equipped, and whenever we had a session to set up everyone just chipped in. The staff, as I said earlier, was fantastic. All egos were left at the front door. Ed and Val kept us all pretty busy but with their office door always open should there be any problems.

Every once in a while, we would have to take tunes and speed them up, per Mike Curbs' request, so documentation played a big part as to which machine was used and how many wraps we put around the machine's capston, what kind of tape we used, just in case we had to escalate it or reduce it. All this information was extremely important. We would always put this information on the tape box legend so there would not be any guessing.

All this was done by ear; we had nothing else to go by. Some of the rental companies in town would eventually have some great processors readily available to rent, but for now we did the best we could with what we had at hand, and besides, sometimes it was just on the spot; you mixed a tune, and it was ready for mastering, you had no time to find another piece of gear. You mixed your tune, and a dub would be cut. It was sent to Mike Curb at the main office and later word would come we had to put a wrap on it. Sometimes you went through the whole process a few times. After they listened to it, word would come from the main office to either add another wrap or take it off. If need be, sometimes, we would go back in and do a re-mix. This had always been the case on some of Donny Osmond's releases like "Puppy Love" since his voice at the time was changing and Mike Curb and Don Costa were concerned and always wanted to make sure that the single release sounded great.

We did great with the tools we had in order to facilitate the countless records we were recording and mixing; always meeting our deadlines. We never knew on any given day what artist or tunes we would be recording; and if it was a rush release or just a standard release. But the Osmonds were priority at the time; they were the hottest act on the label, along with Sammy Davis (Candyman) which was a hit record, in and out once we overdubbed the Mike Curb Congregation. Very fast, a rush release approved by the main office. Everything always had to go through them, but when it came to these two artists, exceptions were always made, and the results were always really good.

Our main office was located at 7165 Sunset Blvd in Hollywood. This was where all contracts were signed and, after everything was confirmed, then it would come down the pike to us on Fairfax where the girls would issue our work orders.

There were times when you worked with an artist or producer and they would ask if we had time available the following day; at which point, we would dial the front office. This would always happen to me whenever I would be working with Don Costa, Solomon Burke, John DeMarco, Marshall Leib or other producers, but like I said, it wouldn't be a problem; normally we would have an answer within minutes. The workload was awe-inspiring but the satisfaction we felt hearing our work constantly on the air was by far the greatest feeling imaginable. I felt at ease, and I finally felt that here was my chance to expand my talents since our president, Mike Curb, was very open to new ideas, and thanks to Val Valentine, I had finally found a home at MGM Records.

I loved it; the place was run really well, and we had all the best equipment possible. I was excited being an MGM Records employee. Things were different; I had a steady paycheck as well as health insurance for the whole family, which we desperately needed. The staff was top-notch, some had come from New York City and Washington D.C. All the other engineers were local.

Val Valentine was very persistent in bringing me here. I'm glad I took his advice, because everyone I'd met seemed glad that I joined the staff. Every artist is top-notch and willing to experiment, not to mention we have the best equipment money can buy, and if not, like I said earlier, they would rent it or just buy it. This was really a big change from where I came from, and I welcomed all of it. I could not wait till I got to work; there was so much excitement in the building that the minute you walked in, it would just lift your spirits up. Sometimes we look for things beyond our reach. I felt fortunate because I reached out, and when I did an awful lot of people saw my hand and helped me. I will never to this day forget any of them; sometimes I would be driving down the road or just sitting down and their names and faces just popped into my head. I've been extremely fortunate to have been in the company of so many brilliant and supportive people; to this day I applaud and treasure them all.

I was excited and proud being at MGM Records; it was a great place. I started doing a lot of recording sessions with the Osmond Brothers: Alan, Wayne, Merrill, Jay, and Donnie. I felt like I had never left these guys or family; we had spent numerous hours together before coming to MGM, so I was not a stranger to them nor their restrictions, which I found to be reasonable. I had no complaints. We were recording and being heard on the radio, so it was a rush for me as well as the label. Everyone was excited, it was good times working with Donnie. We recorded Paul Anka's hit "Puppy Love," Steve Lawrence's "Go Away Little Girl," and also Little Jimmy doing

"Rockin Robin." All very enjoyable; it was really a treat since they were arranged and produced by none other than my dear friend Don Costa.

I again felt very much at ease. I was working with a few friends, but for the most part with Don Costa. It was a no brainer and very enjoyable sessions. All of his sessions always had visitors from all over the country; a full house of artists, producers, A&R heads and managers, who came to listen and hear Don's arrangements. They were in awe and in great spirits; and Don welcomed and acknowledged them. Our control room was always full. After a session we would spend time making copies or doing playbacks, which would usually take us into the early morning hours. I didn't mind it at all, I was on overtime—yes overtime—a new experience and I was enjoying myself; and since I didn't live that far from the studio, that made it very easy for me. The hours were great, and life was good. There was never a problem as there was always someone around to help on setups, to move microphone booms, baffles and music stands, or make room for your vocalist once your session was setup. They would check to make sure you were good, and they would either go home or just hung out. During evening hours, we always had a security guard, and when the session was over you struck the room; this was normal procedure.

I stayed in touch with everyone at TTG; after all, they were my first family since I arrived in California. But, like everyone else in the business, once you get busy, you lose touch. It's a vicious cycle, but we always hope and try our best. I was engineering, but I was also looking forward to doing some producing, if at all possible, Mike Curb was signing lots of acts, I figured maybe I could take advantage of it, providing I came up with the right act. I kept my eyes and ears open just in case the right situation presented itself.

I was always doing side jobs for Don Costa, and with all his night sessions at MGM, he kept me pretty busy. We were really taken care of by Don, he would provide us a cook, who would cook us some of the most wonderful dinners. These were great sessions with no pressure whatsoever, and for the first time I was getting overtime. Who could ask for anything more? You filled out a time sheet and there were never any questions asked. The place was run with class. Val Valentine and Ed Greene were always there and very supportive of us, and all they asked was that you did your work in a professional way. We were not under a microscope; your word was your bond. This added a plus, as I mentioned earlier; if you needed something and it was valid, it would be provided.

MGM Records was under the banner of Mike Curb, who let go of 18 groups from its roster in 1970 who had publicized the use of drugs in their songs. Some say that it was really an excuse to get rid of some unsuccessful bands. Eric Burton and the Animals and Bobby Bloom did the same, but they were a hot item so they were kept by the label. President Nixon, at the time, would praise Mike Curb for his attitude against drug abuse.

The label moved forward and now we had family entertainers like Sammy Davis Jr, Steve Lawrence and Eydie Gorme, Eddie Arnold, Petula Clarke who I loved working with, Lou Rawls, and the Osmond Brothers. These acts, along with many others, kept the label financially sound in the domestic and overseas markets. We were able to keep the international market busy with our current and distinguished catalogues and we were the busiest studio in town.

Our Transfer/Dub Room had never been busier since the studio opened; it worked at least twelve hours a day. We were shipping tapes left and right to Japan, being one of our biggest markets. They kept consistently requesting various albums and we obliged every request. Everyone kept their eyes on the board and if the TD room was busy, we went into either one of the mastering rooms or studios, wherever possible, to make these copies. We were having a ball and meeting all sorts of deadlines. I had never, and I think most of us never worked at a place like this. We loved it, our tape library was full to the max. This building was rocking with all kinds of music. I was not aware MGM had such an enormous catalogue; and a great one at that. It was enjoyable, where else could you sit down and, in the process, get paid to enjoy great music.

We would remaster old catalogues of some of the most popular artists that were still with us, or who had passed. This enlightened some of the younger staff who were not aware we had such a great catalogue. Some were in different languages, which made it more attractive. We were proud of our vault, and we decided to start making safety copies of any albums or singles whenever they would be brought to the TD Room. It was a wise decision, and we were praised for the move by our front office. We knew we were headed in the right direction; this made it possible for all of us to keep our library up to date.

We had started something to keep all master tapes in great shape, not to mention the fact that now we were able to find anything really quickly. MGM's tape library had moved so many times through the years, and it had become impossible to keep track of anything. The reality was that no one really knew what we had in our archives, what version did we have? Was it a single record version? Or the LP cuts which were the longer versions? We had multi-track tapes that were stored in Culver City at the main lot, and when the lot caught fire in the 70s many folks scrambled to get their master tapes out for fear that they would be destroyed. I couldn't blame them; I'd do the same thing. Why not? If water was to reach any of those tapes it was over.

I heard Michael Lloyd ran to get his Lou Rawls master tapes as soon as he heard about the fire, and I applaud him for it—a great move, not only because Lou was a friend, but why not? The majority of times it was a real drag locating master tapes. Yes, they would eventually be found, but you worked your tail off just locating them. The label had signed new acts, and it became really important for all of us to be aware of where tapes would end up—and that went for either quarter-inch masters or multi-track tapes. If you had a session booked for Vocals or Orchestra overdubs and you couldn't find the master tapes, you would have enormous problems; because talent had to be paid, not to mention we had a release date to meet. The tape library played a big part of the overall picture; you couldn't send out the wrong tapes, that would be total chaos. We had master tapes that were arriving from all parts of the world that needed to be catalogued in proper order. Everything that arrived at MGM had to be accounted for.

We were able to fully take control of all this really quickly. MGM rented a loft on the corner of Hollywood Blvd and Ivar at the old Security Pacific Bank building, and we started to catalogue the whole tape library, which made a lot of sense. Finally, we would have full control of our tape library once and for all, a lot of work, but in the end it would pay off because now it would be feasible to send one person to the vault and have your tape or tapes within hours.

We had some great engineers on board. Aside from Jack Hunt, whom I've describe earlier, we also had Lewis Peters, a great mixer who had worked with Delaney and Bonnie, who was a very good mixer, and fell into the mastering technique really quickly, George Miller who came from Washington, D.C. I gather he and Ed Greene had worked together—a very bright guy and good at maintenance and mastering, and Edwin Atwater, another mastering engineer. A great staff and we all helped and complemented each other.

I remember whenever the whole Osmond family came to record it was really hard finding your parking spot, or even getting into the building. If the groupies found out, they were at the studio; they would just show up in packs. At times it looked like a big parade on 5th avenue. The Osmond's were hard workers and since there was no play time available there were times when there was a bit of horsing around in the studio, but all in good nature, they were just kids, respectful kids. Their parents, George and Olive Osmond, were always at the studio; they would bring their lunches or whatever was needed with them. Alan Osmond, being the oldest, was the leader and kept everything going smoothly. The brothers, as well as the staff, always looked to Alan regarding any and all requests and he in turn was very helpful. I can remember on many sessions turning to Alan and asking, "What do you think? More or less bass? Should we use less limiting or echo on the vocals?" I loved his input he was honest about what he felt and was always very open about any suggestions that we might've had. He knew the studio. I still say that for his age you could not find anyone that was more helpful, and he made our job easier and pleasant.

We did however, at times, find ourselves looking over our shoulders, very surprised, particularly when you had a setting, say on your 1176 limiter, for a vocal or instrument and they would change settings on you. So although they were respectful, they had a habit of sometimes playing engineer, and at times it became very annoying; but looking back it was tolerable—after all, like I said, they were kids. We were really busy with the Osmond's, and now it was Marie Osmond's turn. She had recorded "Paper Roses" in Nashville, and I became very involved doing her vocal overdubs and remixes. I have always liked country and I knew this tune inside out, which gave me an edge over the rest of the staff, who didn't like country. I was very familiar with a lot of the country tunes and that, in itself, made it easier for both Don Costa and I to have the most enjoyable memorable sessions at MGM.

There were sessions where, after so many hours, we were so tired we couldn't remember the entrance or down beats to vocal parts. Don would say "Don't punch in, I'll give you the punch." I would start the machine rolling and wait for his cue, but under the circumstances, more often than not, it wouldn't come. I would look over and there was Don; he had fallen asleep on the couch. He would wake up and say, "Did you get it?" Those were the most laughable and memorable moments, which would break the tension in the room.

Sometimes we would just pass on an edit or punch in; Don would just hire a musician to cover the part. Musically, it would work, but at the cut, the vocal would just sound strange. One night we were recording Tony Bennett, a tune called "Tell Her It's Snowing." I did an edit, but when it came to the down beat it sounded really weird. It was difficult; although counting the bars made sense, it just wasn't working. So Don asked Leo to get Gayle Levant, one of the best players in town. She came in and did a harp sweep, and the rest was history.

However, there were times when we would do all-nighters; no one went home, but they were great sessions that once you started, you couldn't stop, or you would lose the feel—you just couldn't come back a few days later. Don as usual on sessions like these would provide dinner; the very best. You never wanted for anything on any of his sessions. He had a house on Kings Road, right off the strip, with a full kitchen and studio. He would have a cook just put things together and the next thing you knew we were all having a wonderful dinner, with no interruptions to the recording session. We would just keep going—this would happen on many of his sessions.

Don kept us all very busy, while he himself kept arranging, producing and writing for all the acts on the label. We had no idea how he was able to do so much work and yet stay focused; the man was a genius. He was the best of the best. He would listen to something and in no time at all he'd have a sketch of the tune. Musicians were always amazed at Don's speed during all his sessions. He would pay respect to everyone and listen to their jokes or whatever they had to say; but his mind was at all times completely on the session. He would never question me; he knew full well that I had his best interest at heart, and I felt very honored, proud and privileged to be working with him, and by now we had been working together for so long that I knew what he expected and I never deviated from it.

I remember there would be times everyone would be waiting and worried, but they would be in for a great surprise. There would never be any overtime for the orchestra, not with Don Costa. He would be late, but he would walk in and say, "Just hang in there." He would sit down, turn on his little cassette machine, listen a few times, do his sketch, and would hand it to his brother Leo and say, "Here, make me a few copies." He'd go over it with whomever was on the date as his orchestrator, be it Ralph Ferro, Nick Perito or Larry Kellam. He would go in the studio while I stayed in the control room, I had already worked on getting a sound and now a balance. I would ask to hear the rhythm section and, once I had a level, would ask to hear the brass, then the strings, the violas, the cellos, and finally everyone together. We were now ready to start recording and I would wait on my cue from Don.

Sometimes the artist would be on his or her way, so we would take an earlier 10-minute break. Once our vocals were set, we would at times just deal with them maybe by changing a line or try a little tempo adjustment, and possibly adjust an instrument here or there to give whatever tune a little more of an edge. If we felt the track was good enough, we would save it and overdub our vocals at a later time, and if he determined we needed background vocals, we would save it for later. There was no need to waste time on something that could be done later, and background vocals could take a backseat; it was common practice.

Whenever we recorded a good track, and if Don felt that maybe an edit would help, then we would cut the multi-track right then and there and listen to the cut, because we needed to know that it would work. No second guessing, even though we might think the edit will work, we don't really know unless we try it and listen to it.

There were times when other things played a big part in

a song, so it was better to see what our options would be, and we had the tools and talent right there at our disposal, so why not see just how far we could go? At his direction, whatever changes he made always worked; the man was a musical genius. There were times when an edit was made, and you heard a glitch, but by muting a track, the edit worked. You had to explore all your possibilities; that's exactly what I always loved about Don's sessions. Nothing was carved in stone. We had experienced this on many other sessions with Tony Bennett, Petula Clarke and Sammy Davis, where we either muted or added another instrument, and no one was the wiser. I was never afraid to cut 2-inch, not with Don in the room. Sometimes he would say lay a click track down. We would lay the click track to tape, play the tune and start counting, and he'd say cut it on the third or twelfth click. As soon as I made the cut, I would splice the pieces together, play it and all the skeptics in the control room would be amazed that it worked.

This scenario played out more times than you could imagine; but that's life in the studio. We would be booked to record four tunes in a three-hour session; this was not impossible, unless you had problems with one of the tunes, then that would trickle down to the other tunes, but with Don that was never the case. We might've started with a break, but the orchestra would always be out in time. I had to move very quickly, and documentation was of the essence, because I could be doing tracks for Sammy Davis Jr. and Petula Clark all on the same date, which by union rules was not legal, at least back then. The following day the question would arise, "Where's that track for Candy Man?" It could be on an entirely different reel from a different session, only because there was no time to put it on a different reel, or we weren't aware it was for a different artist. I was just the engineer; it really didn't affect me. I just kept track of where things were, the sessions kept us busy, they were good times. Those days for me were also really some of the most exciting times at MGM.

I remember that Don's dream was to have his own little studio in his house with no time limits; that's all he ever wanted. He would often say, "Angel, listen to me. To be able to walk into my own room in my own house when I have an idea. That would be the best of both worlds. I would have so much flexibility being able to put my ideas to tape as fast as possible without ever having to go through all the channels or having to deal with the front office in order to record a song."

I arrived early one Monday morning. I had no jacket, and the tie was gone. Val came out of his office and said, "What happened?"

I said, "It's not working for me," and from that day on I never wore a tie to work.

Everyone liked the fact that I had gotten rid of it; even Don Costa commented. He said, "I didn't want to say anything, but you were starting to look like Val and Ed Green. I like the new look. The coat and tie do not suit you, not in the studio."

I told Val when I first started, I would try. It was his suggestion, but I told him earlier on that if I felt it didn't work, I wouldn't wear it.

It was time to get to work. Don Costa was a very busy man now, producing for almost all the acts on the MGM label. Whenever he would come into the control room, he would say, "Are we ready?" My reply was always, "I'm ready to go," because I had done my homework and asked all the important questions prior to the session. I remember Don saying to me once that he liked that I was always there for him, as well as all his sessions; that if he had to start explaining everything to an engineer it would just slow the whole process down—and I agree, there is a lot of truth to that statement.

I had now started doing a lot of independent recording sessions for Don with a group he was producing for MGM Records. They were called "Orange Colored Sky," and were managed by a wonderful, graceful gentleman, by the name of Don Ceroillie; again, another fantastic cook. Don now had a small studio located on the second floor at 6001 Sunset Blvd, with a side entrance on the Gordon Street side. He had a custom 8 bus recording console which had been built back in New York City by his brother Guy Costa. He was a genius when it came to recording consoles or machines.

I had arrived early at DCP Productions, which was the name of his studio. I walked up the flight of stairs; the group was still setting up their equipment. We introduced ourselves. It was a packed house with lots of visitors and chicks all over the place, just hanging out. The control room and studio were one and the same. The console was to the far right of the room and it was crowded. There were a few adjustments I needed to make to the room before we could get started. Nothing major, but I needed time to familiarize myself with the console. I was accustomed to being alone; it was not anything new to me. I prefer to work that way, so I went ahead and started clearing the console, putting patch cords in place, aligning the tape machine and checking things out.

It was a small room, which was very crowded, and once the group set up there wasn't too much space to move around. Stan Costa, who was Don's nephew, wanted to hear a Carl Worthington tape he had done, so I played it for him. Stan was the youngest of the Costas; he was Leo's son, Don's older brother, and a real rebel; but the nicest guy you would ever want to meet. He was searching and wanted to get into producing so he had recorded Carl Worthington; a successful car dealer in Los Angeles, singing country music. Carl Worthington was best known for his unique advertisements of his car dealerships. Carl's TV commercials were a spoof on Ralph Williams, another big car dealer in Southern California, whose dog, Spot, was a German Shepherd. Carl Worthington was usually joined by "his dog Spot," except that his dog, "Spot," was never a dog. Spot at times would either be a tiger, a seal, an elephant, a chimpanzee, or a bear. In one of his commercials, "Spot" was a big hippopotamus that Worthington rode into the lot for the commercial.

They were now just wasting time, so finally, Don Ceroillie starts screaming, "Come on, let's record. What the fuck! Come on you guys we're wasting time." I had aligned the 8-track machine with a fresh reel of tape and placed a few reels of virgin tape to my left. I pulled a bunch of cables that were lying around, and I hung patch cords where they belonged, and started to get levels when I looked over at the patch bay. I noticed there were no labels—I should've notice that earlier. I asked but no one knew what I was talking about, so they gave me Dave Fisher's number and I called him for information regarding their patch points. Dave was very courteous and resourceful. I went over the bay with him on the phone and it worked out. He said, "Look over to your left. I have a few white grease pencil marks that you can use as a guide. The first one with one dot is for the input to the echo chamber, and the one with two dots is for the output, and to the right the top knobs are for the headphones. That's how all the sessions went. Every time I needed to know something I just called Dave who was, at that time, their house engineer, and a great guy. You could ask him anything, at any time, and believe me when I say it was not a problem. We had a friendship that started back in New York City, a friendship that lasted for many years. Unfortunately, we lost him on Friday May 7, 2010, but he is another that will always be in my heart as long as I live.

The console, although it was old, worked; you just had to be patient and do your thing. It didn't have all the birds and whistles but it did have a good sound. I would take care to carefully record everything with good levels on 1-inch 8-track, knowing full well that after all the sessions I would transfer the master takes to 2-inch 24-track at MGM Records.

Don Costa kept me pretty busy. I still remember his calls

in the middle of the night, which to this day I still find very amusing, funny, and what else can I say? He'd call me and I would always respond, how could you not? He was great to be around, always productive. They were not boring times.

He'd call and ask very politely, "What are you doing?"

I would answer, "I'm just laying back. Why? What's up?"

"Nah, forget about it. I don't want to bother you. Its late."

"Ah, come on Don. What is it?"

He'd say the old man, meaning Frank Sinatra, has an idea. We want to put something on tape. I don't want to bother Dave, meaning Dave Fisher.

"Ok. I'll be right down," would be my answer. "Give me maybe 20 minutes to get over the hill." meaning Laurel Canyon. At the time I was still living in Studio City.

"OK. See you then. Thanks."

There wasn't anything I would not do for Don Costa. He was one of the reasons I took the job at MGM. Money with Don Costa was never an issue; he took good care of everyone. I loved the guy, he was always there for me, no questions asked. You couldn't ask for anyone better. There were always a lot of laughs; not to mention the people you would meet, who were really very interesting. It was said, and there's a lot of truth to it, that you would not want for anything at all on any of Don's sessions at the studio; or at the house—and I can verify that statement. Don would always make you feel very comfortable, and when it was all over, you as well as everyone else wished that it would have lasted a lot longer.

I felt very fortunate because for me, there always seem to be more sessions, and all very memorable ones. Don had a way about him that would draw you in. He was a very honest, likeable man, and a friend; never imposing on you or your family. He never asked for anything that was out of the ordinary and would never take you away from anything that you were doing. He wouldn't hurt a fly. It has been said that one time back in the early days in New York City someone was messing with him, and a few guys were sent over to that person's office. They held him out the window and informed him to please don't bother Mr. Costa ever again. The story is true. It was told to me by a very confidential source and confirmed by the late Nick Perito, who swore by it. I would never ever dare ask Don about it, but I do believe it to be true. It was, after all, a different era back then. His brother, Leo, was the contractor, his nephew also named Guy Costa, who we called baby Guy, was his copyist, Ralph Ferro and Nick Perito his favorite orchestrators. The sessions, although they seemed hectic, were always on time and productive; and I must say time just seemed to pass really quick.

I miss those recording sessions, as well as the artists and musicians and all the many memories that came with them. They are imbedded in my heart forever, and I will never ever as long as I live forget my dear friend Don Costa.

Eric Miller, who was working at the tape library, and who in later years would become Norman Granz's right-hand man and producer of some of the most notable artists on the new label Pablo Records, entered into MGM Records. We had known each other prior to that. We had lots of mutual friends; two in particular were Cliff Goldsmith and Fred Smith producers for the group the Olympics. Eric was now in charge of the tape library. He hired a few of his friends from his neighborhood and he brought in his next-door neighbor's kid, Dennis Sands, to work for us. They had their hands full as far as cataloguing tapes, pressings, moving furniture, and many other things that were being shipped to us from New York City. The studio was in need of someone to do mastering. Dennis was suggested and, after very careful consideration, he was hired and trained by Edwin Atwater. He at the time sported long hair and was always dressed in an Army jacket and dark sunglasses, always asking all sorts of questions. We started spending some time together, the kid, as Eric Miller called him, always wanting to tag along. He had no real job experience and wanted to be a sound engineer. always wanting to be in the mix with Eric Miller and myself. At the time I was very busy recording numerous acts for the label. Socializing was not on the cards, but there were times when it became possible, and we all had a great time; with Eric as always picking up the tab wherever we went. I remember Eric saying to me, "The kid has fishhooks in his pockets."

MGM was really busy, no one liked to record country music. So, whenever there was a country session or anything related to country, they would shy away from it. I would do it; I loved the music. For me it was natural and very easy, and a treat. I was very busy, and it was what I wanted. In addition, I was recording Lou Rawls (Natural Man), Sammy Davis Jr. (Candy Man), Tony Bennett, Petula Clark, Solomon Burke, Richard Roundtree (Shaft), Steve and Eydie Gorme, Duke Ellington, Bobby Bloom, Tommy Roe's "Working Class Hero," and many other artists that passed through the doors; along with The Mike Curb Congregation.

I recorded a couple of albums with Solomon Burke "Cool Breeze-Soundtrack" and "We're Almost Home." I was also able to record and produce my own group, The Olympics. I managed to get them signed through a production deal my friends Marshall Leib and John DeMarco had with MGM Records. The Olympics were a doo-wop group that was formed in 1957 by Walter Ward, their lead singer. The members included Eddie Lewis who sang Tenor; Walter's Cousin, Charles Fizer who also sang tenor, Walter Hammond baritone and Melvin King bass. Walter and I had met years earlier, and I figured that maybe there was room for them on the label. I had played their records for John Demarco and Marshall Leib, and they felt maybe there was a possibility.

Through their production company GTM, which had a deal with MGM and Mike Curb's blessing, we were able to record them. We started listening to a lot of songs, hoping to find something that would lead to a hit. They were a novelty group, so we were limited as far as song selections went. I was very persistent and had already explained a little bit of history on the Olympics to Mike Curb, who was aware of them, and he was excited about signing them to the label. Needless to say I was also excited that I would be able to do something for the group, and if successful I would finally start producing more acts for MGM.

Val Valentine and Ed green were happy for me. I was not in strange territory. I loved the support coming from both of them. The Olympics had a bit of history as a group, and Walter himself had been around for some time. They were not strangers to the music business. They had hit records in the past, but because of bad management, and their labels never sticking by them, they had lost their notoriety; but those were earlier years. I had now come into the picture, and I was looking to change that if at all possible.

The Olympics recorded "Western Movies" on Demon Records in the summer of 1958, which was written by Fred Smith and Cliff Goldsmith. The record climbed the charts to #8 on the Hot 100 on the Billboard charts. The song was a hit because it came at a time when everyone was in love with all the Western TV shows that were much liked by kids as well as adults; and it clicked, they could relate to many shows on TV. Such as "The Virginian" with James Drury, Doug McClure and Lee J. Cobb, "Maverick" with James Gardner, "Gunsmoke" with James Arness, "Sugar Foot" with Will Hutchins, "Tales of Wells Fargo" with Dale Robertson, "Wanted Dead or Alive" with Steve McQueen, "Bronco" with Ty Hardin and "Cheyenne" with none other than Clint Walker. During that time, when those shows came on everyone was glued to their TV sets. You couldn't turn on your set without running into a western movie.

When this group of guys hit the road, their acceptance was out of this world. There weren't many groups doing this kind of act. When these guys went on stage it was a whole different world, they were great. Everyone would just start dancing and enjoying all their performances. I kept pushing for the group, and with the help of John DeMarco and Marshall Leib, we finally were able to get a deal and we signed them to MGM Records.

We started listening to a lot of songs from writers and publishers who were now coming out of the woodwork. I went to see Fred Smith, who was still living at his old apartment in Hollywood. We talked for a while, and I asked him if he had a song that I could record with the group. He sat down at his piano and started to play a song called "The Apartment." As soon as I heard it, I knew it was the song we needed. I got on the phone and called both John and Marshall. I set up a meeting at John's house up in the Hollywood Hills. They loved the song, especially John. The song was right down their alley, and the fact that it was written by one of their original writers and producers I felt it was a plus.

We needed an arranger, so it was time to start looking around. We needed someone who could work with all of us and deal with the various personalities; someone that could feel the group and give us the sound we needed in order to get this group on the charts. Marshall suggested John D'Andrea and both John and I looked at each other and said, "Wow! That is a good choice. Why didn't we think of that?" We never argued; we were really into the music as well as the group. I had earlier on suggested one of my favorites, James Carmichael, but he was really busy. He wouldn't have the time to spend with the guys.

A budget was submitted, and we selected recording dates. As far as musicians went, for the most part that became John's task; my only request was that Ronnie Tutt, who worked for Elvis Presley, be the drummer since I had worked with him on a lot of sessions, and I loved his sound and technique. Everyone was in agreement; John would put out the call.

We had one problem that we had to deal with; the new

member and youngest of the group, Kenny Sinclair, was very eager but vocally he didn't have the studio chops. He would require a lot of work. I knew Marshall, and I trusted him with anything, especially when it came to vocals. If he said he could make it work, he would.

We knew that before any recording was to start, we had to have our act together. The days were getting closer; I spent time getting contracts signed and verifying that there were no outstanding commitments by the group. We had to check things out, because if anything came down and the legal department found out that wasn't true, you were toast. Everything was clean and accurate. Marshal Leib, John DeMarco and I were happy with everything. We were finally on course; we were as ready as anyone could be,

I had to finish an album I was recording with Don Costa, who was producing none other than Tony Bennett, and right after that we scheduled time with the main office. I was in a very good position as engineer, producer, and I had the run of the studio. Really, what more could you ask for? We scheduled a meeting on a Saturday at John De Andrea's house to go over the charts without the group. We would have plenty of time for them; we had to figure out rehearsals, where they had to be. It would be nice to hold them at the studio, we thought maybe the Osmond's room in the back, but that would make it really awkward. Besides I knew Val Valentine wouldn't allow it. The rooms were always busy and we could be bumped at a moment's notice. It really had to be a local place where we could have privacy and be cost-effective. We had a small budget to deal with; there were no ifs or butts.

We were all aware that we needed a room with a piano that was in tune, per John's and Marshall's request, because, in all honesty, the group did have a pitch problem, and that, in the long run could really slow us down in the studio. Marshall, being a professional singer himself, would teach them certain tricks to hit various notes, mainly in Kenny's case. There were no objections and the guys behaved like pros. John D'Andrea was a great young arranger/composer, very hip and energetic. He became a great addition. We started rehearsals immediately in a small studio on Hollywood Blvd.

We were all excited. Kenny, the youngest of the group, couldn't believe we had gotten a deal. Eddie Lewis was happy and ready, Mack Starr as always was very excited and very vocal about it, and Walter? Well Walter was the observant one; he had seen it all and his attitude was, "We have to move; we need a hit."

Marshall kept going over the vocal parts with the group, with John D'Andrea at the piano. We kept this up for a couple of weeks, going over parts, what the horns could do, and as always speculating on the amount of time needed in the studio. We would cut three songs in a three-hour session; all live, rhythm section and horns with a rough vocal track as guide for the band. The master vocals we would overdub at a later date; for now, the rough vocals would serve as a pattern.

I remember how excited everyone was when the horn ensemble came in, and Walter Ward started singing the intro with his scratchy voice, which was the signature sound of the Olympics. "The Sign on The Front Yard Reads Apartment for Rent, Come Live in Luxury, There's Air-Conditioning and A Patio for Your BBQ." I had chills run down my arm hearing this intro. When Ronnie Todd, the drummer, hit his snare on the downbeat, and the horns came back in and started playing with the rhythm section, we just went ape shit. We were so loud in that control room that John had to shut us up; we felt we had a hit, or at least that's the feeling we had. That same excitement everyone feels when you're excited and your emotions just take over.

When we started doing vocal overdubs, it became very apparent these guys hadn't been in the studio for some time, and it was now less forgiving. You have to remember that these guys were working clubs when they could, and there's a certain license that an audience gives you in a club that you won't get in the studio in front of a microphone. You have to be in perfect pitch and tempo at all times. There's no time for forgiveness; you have to sound your very best because you're doing a recording. The audience that you're trying to reach is listening very closely. They can't see you so your performance has to reach them; it has to be very convincing, because you're coming through a very small speaker and again, you're not seen.

When you're on stage, there's a lot going on—girls are screaming, drinks are being passed around and everyone is having a great time. There is this tremendous sound barrier going on, so a lot of things go by you and the audience. The waiters and waitresses, they are taking your orders and your friends, they are all shouting, whistling, talking; so, you have a great license. In the studio you're under a microscope. It becomes a different story. Not even the air conditioning unit can be on, it affects your voice, and it makes noise. I as an engineer will be listening to every bit of sound possible, and since we are over-dubbing your vocals, I must make sure nothing but your vocals are heard. I placed baffles around the sides and a small carpet on the floor. I covered the music stands to avoid any and all reflections and I started playing the track several times to make sure they had a good balance, setting the mood to see what would be helpful to keep them in perfect pitch.

I had set up a table with all the comforts of home: a pitcher of hot water, honey and tea just in case. The vocal sessions were long, and we fudged the work orders so we wouldn't run out of studio time. It took way too long, but we finally managed to get through it. What we had was a singles deal, which meant we had to get a hit right out of the gate in order to be able to record again. The possibilities of an album, well that was a stretch. We mixed for a few days but I didn't like the results, so I asked Ed Green if he would remix it for me—I was way too close to this project.

When we finally finished mixing the tune, we played it for Mike Curb, who said he wanted it cut from 4:35 to at least 3 minutes and wanted a lot of the lyrics omitted; they made too many statements regarding drugs. The label had already dropped a few acts because of their association with drugs. We complied with his wishes, after all, we wanted our record released. We scheduled time in the editing room, and we started editing. We were being really careful not to alter the lyrics too much in order not to lose the story line or the feel of the record. We made so many edits, that to this day I don't know how I did them; especially with a razor blade in hand. We finished editing and had the song master and OK'd by Mike Curb and Eddie Ray, the head of promotion. There was a lot of excitement and everyone gave us their good wishes.

When the release day finally came, February 19, 1972, we could not compete with Donny Osmond's "Puppy Love," a record I had personally mixed with Don Costa and Mike Curb, which was released the same day—and that was the writing on the wall. The promotion department at MGM put all their time and effort into that record, and we knew that was the end. The group was done. I continued to book the group at some venues, and they had one last appearance on a Dick Clark Special; sad to say that was not enough to sustain them. Eventually we all went our separate ways. I was now scheduled to do an album with Eddie Arnold, which would definitely keep me busy for some time. I had no time off, and after spending a lot of time mixing, I spent time with Val in the mastering room, because he was convinced that by the scope standards, Eddie's voice was distorted. Eventually, we just listened and Ed concurred that it was all good and the album was set for release.

Walter Ward would perform with the group again in November 2006 in Long Island, New York, at another Doo-Wop Spectacular. He died that same year in December at the age of 66. I still reminisce about our times together; Walter was a very talented and warm person. The funniest guy you would ever want to meet, I feel privileged to have spent time with him. The jokes that he and Joe Turner would tell me whenever we were together in those green rooms were, for me, priceless and enjoyable. I loved the times we shared together. I have worked with many singers in my career in the music business, but Walter had something that unfortunately we were never able to really showcase.

I kept on working with John and Marshall. We felt bad the group never made it, but we as well as everyone else had to keep on going. Sadly, the show must go on. I continued doing my regular work recording many other acts for MGM Records; the workload had become very demanding. The Osmond Brothers, with their increasing popularity, kept both studios, including their own room, very busy and at times it became very hard to get in any of the rooms to record. The payoff, however, was the sessions we would record with Lou Rawls or Sammy Davis, Jr, and later adding The Mike Curb Congregations vocals to their tracks. I was now doing a lot of recording sessions for John and Marshalls Production Company on a steady basis. On one occasion we had this all-nighter, a session very hard to forget. They had signed a Latin Group from San Francisco; they were called "La Clave," who were very popular musicians from the bay area and had a good following. My relationship with both John and Marshall had really grown. They were handing every act that they would sign over to me, they were really happy with the way I handled the acts and my engineering, and I was always able to complete projects without ever going over budget.

I was able to record each and every act they signed, one of whom was R.B. Greaves, who had a smash hit with the song "Take a Letter, Maria." We were recording La Clave and on their first session we received visitors from all over town; they were coming in droves. I feel very fortunate that it wasn't my own place, and that I was not responsible for all the drugs that were used that evening. MGM had their own security staff at the studio on a daily basis, I didn't have to worry about anything, just what was going on in the studio.

We recorded all night, and various singers and musicians showed up and just sat in. We went around the clock, which was very rare. We were on a roll, and I might add, this was something that was never done at MGM Records since Mike Curb had already let go of many artists on the label that were associated with drugs. But this session, no doubt, was a party, no question about it. There was so much marijuana being smoked in the studio you could not see through the glass in the control room.

I remember returning from the men's room. I walked down the small ramp towards the studio. As I opened the door you could not see anything because of all the smoke. I turned and looked towards the control room; it was also full of smoke and crowded with lots of people. It made it impossible to hear anything. I had to keep the monitors cranked up and at the same time being really careful not to blow them. The security guard, Jimmy, didn't say a word. As far as he was concerned it was OK. The next morning, about 8:00 a.m., everyone has gone home. I was cleaning the control room, fixing legends on the tape boxes, when in walked Val Valentine; as always well-dressed in coat and tie, asked me, "You guys starting early?" Val was always the first one in; a habit that we both had going back to our days in New York City.

I hesitated for a minute, but then I answered him, knowing full well what his reaction and the outcome would be. "No," I said, "we've been here all night." Well that really got him pissed off, and he turned beet red and started slamming his fist on the console. He went off on a tantrum. When he heard about all the grass smoking in the studio, as well as in the control room, he threatened to cancel all the sessions. I called Marshal and asked him to tell John what was going on. I told him that when Val heard about what happened during the session, he just blew up; he was really pissed off and wanted to cancel all the sessions.

We needed to do something. I said, "Look, Marshall, I know it's hard to control these guys, but what happened last night cannot happen again." I continued working, doing various sessions. It was at this stage of the game that a young and upcoming young engineer, Humberto Gatica, would come into his own and finally get his start. He had been here working at MGM for some time, always in the TD Room making tape copies. Val Valentine knew his uncle, Lucho Gatica, who was a big star in Chile, and he was very fond of Humberto.

He and I often spent time together. He became a mastering engineer, again trained by none other than Ed Greene. He wanted to move up in the ranks. He was very inquisitive and had such a hunger to become a recording engineer that he would've done anything to achieve that goal. That's all he talked about. We would often go across the street to the local delicatessen or a Chilean restaurant on Sunset Blvd that he would often frequent. He would just pick my brain. He was very anxious but not annoying in any way shape or form.

Humberto didn't speak English very well, so that made him very shy; but he was a charmer and very well dressed. The one thing he had going for him was that he understood music, so that was a plus. He was also well liked by everyone on the staff. He would spend a lot of time with Ralph Valentine, another great engineer and Val's brother, who had come to work for MGM when Columbia Records decided to close their studios.

Ralph would always show Humberto how to work the 1176 limiters and lots of recording tricks. It became a great school for him, and he paid very close attention to everything. On this given day, boredom would set in—or let's just say take over. I had just met my wife, Cookie. This is May 1, 1973. By now, Val Valentine has left MGM to start his studio in Mexico City, and Ed Greene was now in charge. The studio was not busy at all, work had come to a complete halt and there wasn't much recording going on in any of the rooms. It was decided that if we didn't have a session, we should find something else for the staff to do. Why keep all these sound engineers around? It really wouldn't look good to be seen by anyone from the main office.

We were sent to work at the tape library. All of us drove down in separate cars: Lewis Peters, Dennis Sands, Jack Hunt, and Eric Miller, and once we arrived, we realized that there was nothing for us to do, all the tapes were filed correctly; we were just killing time. Humberto's session went well, and he continued working with Steve Lawrence and Eydie Gorme; they liked what he was doing. Steve was delighted with him, and they continued to use him in a lot of their upcoming sessions—the rest, for him, is history.

Eric Miller, by now, was working for Norman Granz, the impresario of jazz well known for his JATP (Jazz at the Philharmonic). He was now working exclusively as his right-hand man and producer. He was unbeatable; he knew his craft well, and Norman trusted him. The man knew every band, its players, producers, tunes, writers; he was a musical encyclopedia.

Norman had now started a new label called Pablo Records; there was a lot of excitement. He was a pal of Pablo Picasso, who had designed his logo, and now, after being away from the music business for a while, had decided to re-issue recordings of a few artists such as Art Tatum, Billie Holiday, and Sarah Vaughn, and new recordings by such jazz greats as Count Basie, Joe Pass, Harry Sweets Edison, Dizzy Gillespie, Monty Alexander, The Modern Jazz Quartet, Oscar Peterson, and many other artists. This kept the studio very busy. I was in the studio more than I had anticipated; this is where I was able to meet Duke Ellington. We were doing a videotape session for Norman Granz. What a night, and as always very laid back. The pay again was really good; all recordings were done under my production company A L B Productions. We were really busy doing remotes for Pablo Records. The work never stopped; all this with the blessings of Eric Miller and Norman Granz.

We were hired to do a remote recording of "the Joe Pass Trio live at "Donte's." In the 60s, 70s and early 80s, there was no better place than Donte's, which had opened back in June 1966 on Lankershim Boulevard in North Hollywood. This album would earn Joe Pass a Grammy. The trio was really a good marriage; it consisted of Joe Pass on Electric Guitar, Jim Hughart on bass, and one of my favorites and most respected drummers, Frank Severino. The club was a small venue, and on this particular night, December 8, 1974, as always, it was jam-packed. It looked like everyone in town had come out to see and listen to these guys play.

We had a couple of problems, one was their cash register, every time they would ring up a sale it would just come through our console loud and clear. I talked to the bartender, and he was able to help us work around it and we were able to continue recording for two more nights. We kept doing a lot of projects for Pablo Records under Eric Miller's direction. I kept asking him when the label was going to give us credit on all the records; we were recording. He said he would speak with Norman Granz about it.

Eric had a lengthy conversation with Norman Granz, at which point he agreed to give us credit on all his albums. This was great news; credits were always an issue that had never really been addressed, and here with one meeting with Norman Granz and he agreed to it; the man was really great. News started to spread quickly around town, as well as in the trades, that MGM Records was being sold to Deustch Gramophone, a European company.

Mike Curb resigned as MGM president and he was replaced, on a temporary basis, by John Fruin. The main office kept denying rumors of the studio's closure, claimed that it was not true. I knew I was going to miss this place that had given me so much, and all the pranks that we played on everyone.

like the time I was recording George Wallace Jr. in M-2 and Lou Rawls stopped by to pick up a dub.

I said, Lou, guess who I'm recording upstairs?

He asked, -who?"

I told him and invited him upstairs. The room was dark; George was very shy. I turned the lights on and Lou, in his deep voice said, "Hi George."

The kid didn't know what to say, and just shook Lou's hand. We went back downstairs, just laughing it all away.

The main office had scheduled a big staff meeting that consisted of the entire department heads of the studio on Fairfax; it did not look very promising. We were told at that meeting that MGM Records was going to become a black label; one of the biggest in the music industry, and if you believe that then I have ocean property in Arizona, I would like to sell you. Who were our acts? We didn't have that kind of artist roster on our label; all we had at the time was a large catalogue of Country music, Soundtrack Albums, Bubble Gum acts and Rock, and the likes of Sammy Davis Jr, Tony Bennett, Lou Rawls, Petula Clarke, Solomon Burke and The Osmond's, so how was that even possible. I could see the writing on the wall. They were just buying time in order to avoid a big exodus.

There were no quick answers, but I knew I had to do something. So., I started looking around and keeping my eyes and ears open. Again, as luck would have it, my old friend Stan Broder called me and said he had left TTG. He was now working at Motown Records and became their traffic manager at their new studios, MoWest on Romaine Street in West Hollywood, formerly known as Poppi Studios. Don Costa's brother Guy was head of studio operations. Stan called me and asked if I'd be interested working for Motown since they needed an engineer that could do big sessions, I said OK, but deep inside I was still hoping MGM would not close.

Stan set up an interview for me. So now I have this appointment at Motown Records. I really didn't want to work at Motown, I had gotten used to working at MGM Records with Don Costa and hanging out with Eric and doing the majority of jazz sessions for Pablo Records. Unfortunately, there was no consistency, and like everyone else, I needed a pay check and a steady gig. But I figured if I stalled maybe something else would pop up. I took my soon to be wife, Cookie, with me to the interview. I figured they would say, "Who does this guy think he is, bringing his girl to a job interview?" My appointment was with Guy's second in command, Russ Tarana. I arrived for my 10:00 a.m. interview. We went into the control room of Sunset, a small tracking room on the first floor, Motown had names for all their studios in the building: the other was Sunrise, which was also located on the first floor, and Dawn which was on the second floor. I introduced my girl, and we talked semantics for a bit, Russ seemed nervous, I guess because of my relationship with the Costa family and my girl's presence, but he never said anything so I didn't either.

As soon as we walked into the studio, I liked the feel of the room immediately, along with all the equipment I was seeing. I knew they were interested in doing film work and they needed someone with my experience recording large orchestras for film with everything simultaneously. Russ was a great engineer, but he had only done what I, to this day, call stacking sessions: that's how Motown worked on all their sessions, they would record the rhythm section first and then overdubs of percussion, guitars, keyboards, vocals, strings and brass, and even replacing drums then mix-down, which was the norm—and believe me, they were really good at it. The hits spoke for themselves. It didn't make them any less sound engineers, they were great, I mean guys like Russ Tarana, Carl Harris, Joe Atkinson and many more who had worked on some of those historical records at Motown in Detroit, great sounding master pieces in my view. Motown made fantastic sounding records that still stand out to this day as far as I'm concerned—

great work. They only had one room large enough for large sessions, maybe 30 men. I was accustomed and trained to do large recording dates all at once, so that was a plus, aside from the fact that I knew Guy Costa.

They were well aware that I had a good reputation with him since I had recorded an album that was a very big hit for them on their white label, "What the World Needs Now," with a local DJ by the name of Tom Clay. The interview began. We talked at length, throwing various artists names around that I had recorded, and an hour later Russ turned and asked me the magic question. "How much would it take for you to make the move to Motown?" I told him my figure and he said Motown could not pay what I was asking; they didn't have the budget. I knew that would be his answer; it didn't surprise me at all, but I'd been around and I knew what salaries were around town for a recording engineer. I was also aware of what they needed from my conversation with Stan Broder. I was happy, and I said, "That's OK, man. Don't worry." But Russ didn't waste a minute, he said, "Wait, let me go talk with Guy Costa." He left the room, and I looked at Cookie with relief. She had no idea what was going on but stuck with me. We chatted for a while. All studios were new to her. The only other one she had seen up to now was MGM Records, which was where we first met.

I was doing vocal overdubs and I let someone else take over and went to the front office, where we talked for the longest, and I invited her and her son for a weekend BBQ; that's how our first meeting went. I knew that I would be involved with Motown's new movie, no question about it. That's why I was here; there was no doubt in my mind, and the call from Stan Broder had said it all.

"Mahogany" would be an entirely different movie for Diana Ross than her previous one, which had a very historical factor since she had portrayed the late Billie Holiday. I had done some remixes for that movie, and they were happy with them, but this new one was different; it was being directed by Berry Gordy and produced by Motown Productions. Berry Gordy had taken over the film direction after British filmmaker Tony Richardson was dismissed from the film because of creative differences. I knew that they were not going to spare any expense on this new one. They had hired some great producers as well as some great writers and had lots of great tunes. They had a lot of hard work ahead, but I would welcome every minute of it.

Time went by and finally, Russ returned and said, "Guy has agreed to meet your figure, with an increase once 'Mahogany' is finished." I guess they all felt that this one would also earn Diana Ross another Oscar award. I was ready for anything that came my way. It was going to be an adventure of a lifetime for me, and I would be working with people I knew, such as Stan Broder, Mark Kauffman and Dave Brand; all very talented—and I can't forget my dear friend Guy Costa, who OK'd my hiring.

I shook hands with Russ who said, "Welcome on board." I had now officially become a new employee for Motown Records. It was 1974. Russ asked how long before I could start work

I said in two weeks, which is customary. I had to be fair to my current employer, MGM Records. We agreed and said our goodbyes. It was obvious they were a busy studio. I knew I would have to start in two weeks.

I went to work on Monday and asked Ed Green if I could speak with him. I told him I had enjoyed working for MGM Records and, first and foremost, I had decided to leave. I was giving him notice. We talked for a while. He was also aware things didn't look well for the studio. He asked me where I was going and I told him Motown Records. Ed just turned around, gave me a hug and his blessing and said it was great news; he was happy for me. Ed was a great guy no bull there weren't too many guys like him.

Val was in Mexico enjoying his studio. He had tried to entice me to move there, but I had small children. I couldn't just sell my home and move there; it would've been a big mistake as well as a big culture shock for the whole family. And I'm sure my wife Cookie wouldn't stand for it. None of them, except for me, spoke the language, and I was limited. Although Val claimed we would have all the amenities that we needed; it didn't make sense at all. He had also tried to get Humberto Gatica to go there, and when we got together, I said, "Look, if you go there, in time, you would be forgotten here; and right now, you've got a good thing going. But it's your decision and yours alone."

I think it was a great decision on our part, because a few years later Val returned to California. Apparently, he had a bad business deal with his partners and things did not work out well for him. This was a bullet that both Humberto and I had dodged. We never talked about it, but boy were we lucky. Humberto went on to become a great engineer and a Grammy winner on the Michael Jackson Bad album, Celine Deon album a few TV shows and on the famous "We Are The world" recording. So it was, after all, a great decision we both made to stay here in California.

Val would return to California a few years later. He worked for Norman Granz for a short period of time while Eric Miller took a sort sabbatical. The same old Val wanted to take control, but things had changed considerably. Mexico had been one of the worst decisions he had ever made. He would later go to work for Ed Green on Star Search, but it was not the same. I remember Ed telling me that it was really embarrassing, but Val needed the work because he had lost everything, and within a short period both he and his wife finally moved to Lake Tahoe near his daughter.

Val had enjoyed a great deal of notoriety through the years, and although many of us didn't agree with him or his tactics, we went out of our way to please him. I remember back at A&R Val sporting a little cigar, at the time he was a smoker, and Phil Ramone saying to be nice to him, he'll just hang around for a while and then he'll go home. He was always very nice and respectful. He would ask me, "Mister, can you do a Connie Francis date for me?" Which I could not decline.

Towards the end, while living in North Hollywood, he had my wife and me over for dinner. At the time I knew he needed a job, but I could not help him; my hands were tied. I had partners to deal with and things were slowly going downhill for us at Group IV Recording.

The time we had all spent under his supervision at MGM Records were great times; he was great, and I must say he always stood up for his crew. When it came to defending his crew, there was no one better. Unfortunately, he lost a lot when he made the move to Mexico; it was the biggest mistake he had made and I believe that in the end, he was well aware of it.

Ed Green also helped as much as he could, but there was no changing the man. Never the less the man was an institution, and did some of the greatest recording sessions, and he dealt with some of the best artists in the recording industry. He was indeed, when it came to MGM RECORDS, a legend like no other. I think of him often and I must say he was instrumental in helping a lot of us succeed in the music business, I'm proud to have known him, and I hope some of you feel the same way whether you care to admit it or not.

Although sometimes it was really frustrating for me, as I'm sure it was for many other sound recording engineers, especially when you worked on an acid session with a group, spending numerous days and nights, putting your best effort into those sessions. Then when the LP was released, and you looked at the credits, yes, you were angry. There was nothing you could do; you could call Val on it, which I often did, but it was customary; it wouldn't change anything. Some labels didn't list anyone at all. But in time it did change.

If you come across some early recordings from the early

days, you will recognize the heading in the back of the majority of those records, which read Val Valentin Director of Engineering. They had their graphics in house as well as the pressing plants in Manhattan. It was all in house; that's before they made their move to the west coast and, in his defense, that was how MGM had operated for years and he was a company man.

I must give the man some credit. Although some might disagree, he did do some great recordings with Sinatra and Ella Fitzgerald. He was a charmer; his famous line, which I will never forget: "Don't worry mister. When we sell 500 thousand units we will reprint and put your name on it." There was nothing you could really say; it was over. We all knew it would never be corrected; that wouldn't happen in a million years. But again, those were different times, we have learned a lot since then.

Unfortunately, Val was another icon that we lost on March 24, 1999, and regretfully there was very little coverage in the trades. I often think about him and how he personally helped me, as well as many others, may he rest in heavenly peace.

MY MOVE TO MOWTOWN

Well, after many false promises and statements, the doors to MGM Records were finally closed, and in a very short time, it would become Cherokee Recording Studios. I had now been at Motown for over a year. I didn't have a great car to get around in those days; what I had was a 1970 Pontiac station wagon, which was what was left from my previous marriage. I remember everyone would always say how it didn't really fit me. I had a cinder block in the back to keep the front seat from going back too far, because if it did, I could not reach the gas pedal or brakes. This would always happen on my way to and from work, whenever I would go over Laurel Canyon. I dealt with this for a few years, always doing the best that I could.

I was now living in Canoga Park, an hour's drive. I knew things would eventually change. I was very happy because, for me, things had changed. I had re-married, we were all in great health and no debt—all for the better. In a very short time, I had found myself working in an environment that was very demanding but really good. I was working with one of the most popular and active groups at Motown Records, "The Jackson Five," with Michael Jackson always dancing in the studio. We had Social Services representatives who were always present whenever they were recording, making sure that we maintained the control room monitors at what they thought was an appropriate level. If we exceeded that level, they would have us turn it down; they were always present and would sit on the control room couch, which was positioned right in front of the console. It was customary for all child actors in the business to have a welfare representative present, making sure that we observed any and all rules as far as breaks and the hours. The Jacksons were allowed to work, but they were minors, so by law it was mandatory and we had to comply with the rules. That meant all the rules, there were no exceptions at all. This went for everybody. It was great for me, since all our work had to be done during the day, I would have all my evenings free; these were great sessions.

I worked on their last major smash for Motown, the 1974 number two hit "Dancing Machine," a nod to the emerging sound of disco, which also topped the R&B charts. I spent a lot of time with Hal Davis, who was one of their producers. All these sessions were really a party of great music, and great performances by the Jacksons. You really couldn't ask for more. I loved all the microphones and toys they had; it was a new experience for me. I used all the equipment that was available, so whenever possible I would request as much as I could.

The maintenance department was headed by Mark Kauffman, and someone was always a phone call away, not to mention his assistant at the time, none other than Dave Brand, another bright and talented maintenance engineer. I was working with Hal Davis, who always loved to take various vocal parts from different tracks in and out, as well as percussion instruments, which were really good for Dancing Machine, especially when Michael would do vocal overdubs while we were on a roll and had the time. Hal always aimed at getting as many vocal tracks as we could, that's when Hal would say to Michael, "Look, when that part comes, give me some oohs, baby's and ahhs, as many ad libs as possible. Improvise anything, just play with it." And so he did, and so did we on the mix down sessions. That's where Guy Costa's box came in handy, it gave us a lot of choices, be it vocals or percussion tracks, to work with; it became a great tool that we used on all mixes. We only had 24-tracks, but if any track or instrument had a rest and that track was open, I would record and pull out in time to get what we wanted.

All these sessions were a lot of fun but extremely fast and very exciting you had to be on your toes at all times and at a really fast pace, because your time was limited. You had very little time in which to record this group. When the welfare lady said it was time, you were finished, done. We knew that it was important, so we made use of every minute possible. Sometimes we'd forget time, and the welfare lady would stand up and remind us that we had to call it a day. Oh boy, "The Jackson Five"—Michael Jackson at the time had not gone solo yet.

I remember one day we had started really early, or at least I had since I had to leader the 24-track masters, because at the pace we were going it made it a lot easier to find your tunes. We had been at it for some time now with Michael Jackson, it had really been a long day, and both Hal Davis and the welfare lady were in agreement; it was time—we needed to take a break. I went out into the hall, Eddie Kendricks was standing there all alone, so I stopped, and we started talking about his upcoming sessions. He told me that Leonard Caston had requested me. I was more than happy to be recording Eddie, for me it was always a lot of fun.

I told him that I had already listened to some of the songs we were going to record, and at that very moment, Michael comes out of the studio and starts hopping down the hall, and I'll never forget Eddie's remark. "There's something wrong with that boy, but there's an awful lot of talent in the kid." Little did we know how Michael Jackson would change in years to come, becoming the king of pop with so many hits it was indeed a privilege for me to have worked with him. I was surprised to learn that I had even made Jet Magazine with Jermaine Jackson. I wasn't even aware of it till my brother in-law Roy Richardson called to tell me.

Whenever we had a session with Hal, near the end, he would say, "As soon as they leave," meaning the welfare lady and The Jacksons, "lock the door." Then we would turn the monitors up and start doing rough mixes. What a party with all the great tunes we had just recorded; it was undeniably one of the best times in any studio. Not to mention all the rough mixes because they were untouched; those were really great sessions—nothing but the best and Hal Davis, what a guy and such a great producer. I could not have been treated any better. Unlike all my other jobs, I was getting home early, which was odd for me, but I knew it would only be a matter of time before that would all change. I was also working with one of my favorite groups ever, The Temptations who were still recording for Motown Records. They had been with the label for years, still trying for that hit record. David Ruffin and Eddie Kendricks were no longer members of the group; they had gone solo. But the same magic and respect was still there. I had been scheduled to record a solo album with David Ruffin that was being produced by none other than Norman Whitfield, who had a very extensive track record with The Temptations, and it helped an awful lot since he knew David really well. Norman, as well as everyone else on the label, was looking for that ultimate hit record; so, he allowed me to expand some of the recording process.

He wanted to try a different approach, so we were adding effects on the fly to simulate a live sound. Yvonne Elliman came to one of the sessions and I must say what a pretty and nice lady, she had come by to hear what Norman was doing on David Ruffin's session. Norman asked her what she thought, and she said she didn't like it; to which Norman asked why. "It sounds like he's screaming," she replied. He looked at me and I started laughing. To which he said, "Now that's not what I wanted to hear, and now you got him started."

We finally finished mixing David's album, which I found exciting. No sooner had I finished than I was now scheduled on another album with Eddie Kendricks, produced by Leonard Caston and Frank Wilson. I had previously worked with the pair when we recorded a hit for Eddie called "Boogie Down," and here we were again. My only complaint was that you didn't get engineering credits on any of the albums you worked on. The label kept me really busy, and the albums were great, however for me it was a setback. I wanted to get credited for my work, but I did not like the fact that I would spend hours on an album, mixing for hours, and when the album was released, it would read produced by Leonard Caston and Frank Wilson; mixed by Frank Wilson—now that pissed me off. What a crock of shit. Frank wouldn't admit he was not the mixer. I found this to be an insult; how could this be? There had to be a way of addressing this issue; it could not continue. This did not sit well with me. I would spend numerous hours getting a sound that worked for the artist, as well as the producers, and yes at times they would help. We didn't have automation and when we had some complicated moves it was all hands-on deck. But Frank Wilson was not the engineer, he was the producer.

There were many producers that helped during the mix down process, but that didn't make them by any stretch of the imagination sound engineers. There were times when my suggestions, as well as many of my peers, helped on a record but we were the engineers, not the producers. It didn't earn us the credit of the producer, which many times it should have, but we never crossed that line. That was the thing that really bother me. When you worked for Motown Records you always worked your butt off, and some producers became the ones that received the credit for engineering. I became more and more annoyed, because you sat in the same control room for countless hours with someone who had no knowledge of the whole recording process, and he would get engineering credit.

I thought we'd gotten passed that, but we hadn't and guys like Frank Wilson thought it was funny. I didn't find one bit of humor in it at all. I made it a point to speak my mind because I thought it sucked, and I found it insulting.

When I started working, I was told it would only be till 6:00 p.m., there would not be any night sessions, but it all seemed to change really fast, and here we were again working very long hours. I didn't mind it at all, I was used to it by now. As far as I was concerned it came with the dinner, especially now with the new movie, "Mahogany." Fortunately, I was accustomed to working all-nighters, so for me it wasn't a problem. I had managed to form a good friendship with Norman Whitfield, whom I called the rebel. Norman, who loved to intimated engineers. But I never bought into it. He knew that I had worked with the best and the roughest of them all, so in a very short time we became friends. We had exchanged a great deal of ideas during David Ruffin's solo album. He would often come to visit us while we were recording Eddie. Everyone was accustomed to having visitors on their sessions, which made for some really good times. I was working with the best of all the producers at the label.

Another one of my favorites was Leonard Caston. Earlier on, when I started; every time I was heading towards the front office, I would see this black guy in a black leather jacket and a tennis hat just hanging around the front office. I didn't think much about it since everybody there seemed to have more or less the same attire. I saw this guy several times, but I didn't inquire, I just kept on working and always kept to myself; but I must admit I was curious. Finally, one day I was assigned to work with Caston and Majors, a husband-and-wife team, with Leonard Caston. They were producing their own album; the mystery was finally solved. I found Leonard to be a great person, and his wife Carolyn a joy to be around. I liked their album concept and felt their project had a lot of potential. I even imagined it being a big seller, so I put all my time and energy behind it. I thought it was great material with great potential and recorded very well; but yet it sounded like the orchestra wasn't allowed to breathe and demonstrate the blending of their tones. The arrangements were fantastic. I knew this could be fixed; it was all down on tape, recorded very well. I loved this album, which was called "Let There Be Love." to this day I still believe it was some of our best work.

I remember on our first session Carolyn was out in the studio. I went out into the room as I listened, I knew right away that the microphone that was placed in front of her was not suited for her sound. They had placed a R E 20 on her and she didn't sound natural. There was nothing wrong with the microphone, it had become a habit from other sessions, but after two takes I said, "That mike is not for her. It has no presence. It's not what she's putting out." I walked over to the closet, and I pulled out a Neumann U-67 and changed the mike. Leonard was taken aback to my reaction. He had never experienced anyone doing that, and ever since that session we developed a mutual friendship and respect for each other, and since then I was requested for all of their sessions. This is how I always worked in the studio. Very important, I'm accustomed to listening in the studio, out in the room, and then in the control room before I start recording. I always found it important to listen, let your ears work for you, see if what you hear out in the studio is the same as what you're getting in the control room.

We had ourselves some great times during all of their sessions. Although I had worked with both Leonard Caston and Frank Wilson as a team, I always felt more comfortable with Leonard. He didn't put himself down as the recording engineer on any of the projects, and I must say he was more technically knowledgeable than Frank. The front office commented on the project and my work, they said that it really had a great sound. I was also assigned to work with a lot of the other artists on the label, such as Stevie Wonder, Smokey

Robinson and The Commodores, who were an American funk/soul band, who at the time were at their peak. They had met as freshmen at Tuskegee Institute in 1968 and had signed with Motown in November 1972. It was an easy transition for me, we hit it off right away, since my wife was from Alabama, and they being from Tuskegee, Alabama, well they loved it, they asked what part of Alabama she was from? I said a small town called Leroy, and they all said they knew it really well.

They were always real gentlemen in the studio; very easy to work with. We spent a considerable amount of time in the studio; they were great guys. Their arranger/producer, who I had known for years, was none other than James Anthony Carmichael, he and I had worked on many recording dates with a mutual friend of ours, Fred Smith. At that time, I was recording a female group called "The Merritt's." I was always busy and in the short time I was at Motown, I must've worked on just about everyone's projects. I worked with Tavares, Yvonne Elliman, The Four Tops, Rick James, The Undisputed Truth, G.C. Cameron, you name it; so, the introductions for the most part were not needed—this went on for some time.

I was kept very busy and then Motown started slowing down. The Jacksons had left the label. "Lady Sings the Blues" had been finished; Diana Ross had gotten her Academy Award, and "Mahogany," her second film, although it was received well at the box office, didn't do what Motown had expected. The workload was getting really slow, there were evenings when we would just spend our time making international copies of various albums and playing ping pong or just doing safeties of master tapes.

We had just gotten this amazing pot that was so strong we claimed it gave you polio. You just couldn't move; you just seemed to lose your legs. Ralph Lotten, our telecine engineer, and I had gotten into a conversation about the grass with the security guard at the front desk. We told him how strong the stuff was, and we were really convinced that there definitely was no comparison to anything else we'd gotten in the past.

As soon as we said that the guard just chimed in by saying, "Man, you guys don't have anything that strong. I don't believe it,"

Ralph replied, "I know you can't handle it."

The guard said, "Shittt, try me."

Ralph rolled a joint and when he was done, he handed it to him and said, "Be careful with that."

The guard, acting tough, replied, "Man, I can handle it."

We went about our business. We resumed our game of ping pong and completed a few other duties. A short time later, Ralph and I went to the front office, and we asked the guard, "Hey man. What you do with the joint?"

He replied, "I smoked it!"

We were startled and asked him, "The whole thing?"

He said, "Yea man, I can handle it."

We went away but we were concerned, so after about an hour we returned to the front and asked him how he was feeling. He didn't look that good. He said, "I think I'm going to have a heart attack. I just called an ambulance."

We were in shock and our response in unison was, "You what?"

So, before we knew it the ambulance arrives; but there was a slight problem. Apparently, there was a county ordnance where they could not come across the street to pick the guard up; news to me, but that's what we were told. We had to think quickly. We got everybody to pick the guard up and we carried him across the street and put him in the ambulance, and they drove off. We now had to be very careful here and think fast. We had to call security because we were in need of another security guard. When we call for another guard, their reply was, "Why? What's wrong with the one you have now?"

We replied, "He got sick, and an ambulance took him away." I know nothing.

Time passed and now we were spending time doing solo

albums. I was booked in Sunset, the small studio, mixing Eddie Kendricks' new album with Leonard Caston. Frank Wilson is recording our background vocals in the other room (Sunrise). When they would finish with the multi-track tape, it would be walked over to us in Sunset and Leonard, and I would mix it. We were working really fast on the single from Eddie's new album, a song called "Shoeshine Boy." We'd been at it for some time and I thought we would never finish mixing this single; just getting the rhythm down and locked was really tough.

The front office was in a hurry to release this album. Everything—the single and album—we were being rushed. We were spending a lot of time on the single because we wanted it to sound just right, which was always a very important issue for us. I was personally feeling the pressure from everyone else. We didn't have much time, and aside from all that was happening the promotion department, as well as the front office, kept constantly pressuring us to finish mixing in order to meet their scheduled release date. We decided to go late and wrap this album up. The mix for the single had already been completed and shipped. We were now doing the LP version, and while we're busy working, the security guard went into Guy Costa's office, kicked the drywall from the inside out and took all of his stereo equipment and put it in the trunk of his car, which he had parked around the corner at the Boys Supermarket on Santa Monica Blvd.

We worked all night. Frank Wilson had finished all the background vocals across the hall and had gone home. Leonard Caston and I decided to continue mixing the rest of the album, it was past 3:00 a.m. we were burned out. When we came out of the studio, we noticed all this commotion going on. The guard had placed a call to security and reported that there had been a burglary. Guy Costa's office was at that end of the hall behind the guard's station, and no one had heard or noticed anything. We'd been here all night and certainly had used the restrooms which were at the very end. When the head of security came to the studio the first thing, he asked the security guard was if he had heard any noise at all. He said no, claiming the music coming from the studio was too loud throughout the building and that it was impossible to hear anything at all. I was taken by surprise as I always insisted the doors to the sound lock, which led into the hall, always be kept closed at all times.

We were working on a special project that was very important. We were mixing a single for Eddie's new album. When you're mixing you don't want any distractions from the outside; therefore, you always keep the doors closed. You don't need any noise coming from anywhere in the building at all. The few people that were around that night stayed in the control room quietly just listening to the song, no one was wandering around, and yes we did play the music loud, that was the norm, but the control room doors were always kept closed.

They asked him where he had parked his car. He said down the street, so they took a walk with him to his car, and there it was—all that equipment in the trunk of his car. He was handcuffed and taken away.

Although a lot of childish incidents did happen at Motown, the staff always kept working; no one ever slacked at all. It was a great staff, all very professional. If you needed something it was always provided for you. I kept on working many sessions doing vocal overdubs with Diana Ross for her soundtrack album from her new film "Mahogany." I had spent a lot of time working with Berry Gordy, all his sessions were very long ones and very involved, but you were afforded time to set your room and get a head start, since they always arrived an hour later. Great for us engineers, and I think they knew that.

Berry was producing, and as always, there were a lot of yes men around, including bodyguards. I loved all the work and the challenges that came with it. Busy days and nights and all the excitement made it worthwhile. I had been promised a raise when I was hired and was told it would be coming as soon as we finished Mahogany. We had worked our tails off on this feature with long hours and lots of changes; which often happens on any feature. I was setting up the studio for background vocals on a Smokey Robinson project when Mark Kauffman, who at this point his position had changed, so I knew he would have the answer to my question. He wouldn't lie to me. There was no reason for him to do that, and besides the time seemed right.

I asked Mark about the raise, and he said that there was no more money available; it had all been spent on the film. I asked what that had to do with me? He said the money was not there, so I responded, "I have to resign, that's not what we agreed on." A week later I gave Motown my two weeks' notice, effective immediately. I started making calls and just looking around town. I was not nervous; I knew I'd find work. It wouldn't be that difficult and I knew I would prevail. I was leaving.

TTG had hired a girl by the name of Kathy, who was a law student and had now become the new traffic manager. Kathy had called me on various occasions to either first or second on some of the sessions whenever she was short of staff, which constantly happens. I gladly had accepted the calls and clients kept asking if I was coming back.

I decided to keep taking calls, and I returned to TTG on a freelance basis. The only familiar face on staff at this point was Nye Morton, who by now, after spending a few years at TTG, had worked his way up to mixer status and was doing very well. Kathy was now chief, cook and bottle washer. She would call me as much as possible. I was not a stranger at all; their clientele knew me.

I kept taking many calls for sessions, such as the popular "Carol Burnett Show" with Peter Matz, who I had known a very long time. I was able to work on a new film; the Robert Redford film "The Sting," and as time went by it became convenient for all my clients as well as myself. I started making calls all over town and the response was great. I was busier than I had ever been, so I decided to take advantage of the situation. Studio 2 was completely empty. I was freelancing now; Ami had a new console install in Studio 2 in order to attract more business. I started soliciting as many clients as I could handle.

My return had started more curiosity than ever, and now Studio 2 became busier than it had ever been. Now it was very rare for me to work upstairs in Studio A, which was OK with me. My client base was growing at a fast pace. I couldn't believe it; I was working on weekends and lots of night sessions.

I had Leon Haywood, who I was producing for Capitol Records, and more clients, the likes of Phil Everly and Willie BoBo, who is best remembered as one of the key players who fused influences from Jazz, Latin, Soul, and Rock in the late 1960s and 1970s, helping shape the evolving boogaloo style. Willie was a dear friend from New York City who would say we're YorkeRicans. Sadly he would leave us in 1983 due to cancer. I had Juggy Murray, an old acquaintance from Sue Records, Monk Higgins, and not to mention my old friends who followed me from MGM Records, John DeMarco, Marshall Leib and a few Agency guys from BBD&O whom I had worked with earlier on.

I now had a nice client base that kept growing with a lot of artists I had worked with at Motown, and although Motown artists were not allowed to record outside of their own studio, Guy Costa was very supportive of all my sessions, and although I was no longer an employee, we still remained good friends.

TTG at this point was making some progress. They became a little busier and were able to pay their bills. I was keeping Studio 2 so busy that now they had to have two maintenance engineers. They had one who was very sure of himself, very opinionated with no results or drive, and a bright young guy just out of high school, Gary Fradkin. He was full of life, and he knew quite a bit about studio electronics. If there was anything I needed, I would just ask him and I was always amazed with the end results.

I had started bringing in many acts from Motown, one of them being none other than Diana Ross. One day while I'm recording her, I noticed that my microphone was losing gain. I could not let anyone become aware of what was happening, so I danced a bit till I could solve it. When my session was over, I called Gary Fradkin in the shop. He came in to check my microphone. and he told me my battery was low; to which I replied, "What battery?"

He said, "There's a battery in that mike (Neumann U87), didn't you know?"

It was a big surprise to which I replied, "Why? I can't believe that in this day and age we're still dealing with batteries. This is a new console."

Gary replied, "The phantom power supply needs to be installed, that's all we need to do."

I asked Gary why Jimmy hadn't done it, and he said that he (Jimmy) just had not done it. I said, "OK, so the problem is really Jimmy, because there's been ample time." I asked Gary if it was a difficult thing to do and he replied no, it's just two wires: that's all. So now I'm going crazy, and I ask him if he could hook it up now? His answer was, "I have to see what's involved, but it shouldn't take long. Let me see, maybe tomorrow. I'll have to check the book." (Meaning the schedule.) Well I already knew, since I was aware of all the sessions that I had booked, I could allow him enough time, this was important.

Gary at first was very reluctant to install the power supply. He said, "I don't want to get in trouble with Ami." I replied that I'd take the blame for it and asked when he could install it? And how long would it take? He said less than an hour and I said OK do it. Gary installed the phantom power supply the very next day, which ended the use of batteries once and for all. Ami later tried to tell me that he could have blown up the whole console, but in the final analysis the truth was it worked, the kid knew what he was doing. There was nothing wrong with the install; it took maybe a half hour.

I told Ami that he was sticking up for a guy that was just plain incompetent and lazy. I was aware that Ami had a lot on his plate financially. I was trying to help as much as I could; that was solely my mission, and I was trying to make him aware of what was happening. I said, "Ami, look I don't believe that would've happened at all; the problem here is that we have two maintenance guys and there's only one getting the job done. We need things to run more smoothly with no glitches. It's my name and the studios out there and as you know really well in this business you get just one chance; that's all. I need everyone to understand this. I have gone to various lengths to get clients in from Motown, and I will protect that at all cost."

We have had problems on more the one occasion when one or two earphone boxes did not work, which created a short in the system and not to mention the time factor; it delayed the session, and no one owned up to it. I can remember numerous times trying to figure out which headphone boxes were bad or for that matter which headphones. If I turn in a headphone box, Jimmy would not bother to check it, he would just put it back out hoping it would get lost in the shuffle, which now created a bigger problem.

The sessions were all very important to me. I couldn't afford a bad rap to get around, and speed was of the essence. I was recording a lot of music for the likes of such noted TV shows as "Streets of San Francisco," "Hawaii Five-O," and "Police Woman," just to mention a few. The word on the street was very complimentary, so I could not take the chance of losing that clientele.

I was really happy because I was working with composers Jack Elliott and Allyn Ferguerson on a very popular T V series called "Barney Miller," a situation comedy series that was set in a New York City police station, Precinct 12 in Greenwich village. The series was broadcast from January 23, 1975 to May 20, 1982 on ABC TV as well as some features like "Enter the Dragon," the Bruce Lee feature.

I found myself having technical problems during live sessions. Our headphones would not work because of the maintenance department's lack of understanding of the importance of keeping our equipment working. I don't know if it's because Jimmy's pay checks are not being covered or what, but it had become very annoying and a hassle, particularly during live sessions. I couldn't handle it anymore; it was driving me out of my mind. I would throw a tantrum every now and then and, to show that I was serious about it, I would just throw the headphone boxes against the wall, and I'll admit there have been times when I would just jump up and down on them at least 3- or 4-times hand them back and say, "Jimmy, the box doesn't fucking work. Fix the mother fucker." I knew Studio 2 very well, this is where I had recorded many hits, but now I also had to think of my family with things again not being very promising at TTG.

GOING INDEPENDENT

I had decided that since I was doing so much freelance work, it was time for me to form a legal company of my own. I went down to the local paper in Burbank and applied for a DBA. I had decided to call the company A L B Productions. I started booking Studio 2, and now I would personally start paying for all the costs of studio time and labor, but it would be my clientele and my staff. I would not be on the studio's payroll any longer. I quickly started to do work for clients on an independent basis, which at first wasn't easy. I had to make the deal, book the studio, provide the crew, bill it, collect it, and pay everyone on time. This really kept me extremely busy, but it was survival.

I started to establish a good reputation as the guy to go to. People were calling for my services. I was very careful and never turned anyone down. If I couldn't do it, I would send them in the right direction. I would personally make the call for them. This usually brought them back—it was as if I had my own studio. We never, or at least it seemed like we never, leave the studio. My time was really occupied, and I was also very fortunate, because weekend work was very rare, which gave me a chance to work on the books, which was all manual work, no computers. This also allowed me to do work around the house and spend as much needed time as possible with my family.

I was doing the billing of all sessions done during the week and followed up with phone calls for the coming week. I was still doing a lot of recordings for Norman Granz's new label Pablo Records, which took a lot of time. He was recording a lot of artists and fortunately I had become his first call, which was really helpful, but it did take me away from a few things. However, I had to take care of him; this was our bread and butter. Norman was always very accommodating, he didn't care where I wanted to record, he personally told me himself; he said just give the address to my secretary Pam and I would be wherever you want to record—but I didn't want to abuse the situation, I wanted to make sure that it was convenient for him and his artist at all times. That, to me, was really important. Whenever I needed something, Norman wouldn't bat an eye, he had also personally said to me at various times: "If you need money just call my office." He was really one of my best clients. I loved the man; he was always straight and good to me.

One of our most memorable sessions for Pablo Records happened at TTG during the recording of Louie Bellson's album that, to this day when we talk about it, brings so much laughter and joy—it seems like it was only yesterday. We had set up the band, removed all the baffles, as per Norman's request he always wanted the bass in front of the piano, and the guitar to the right; that's what he preferred, oh and the lid off the piano. We started recording Norman as always doing the slating and providing master numbers for each tune. Everything was going well; everyone, including Norman, in great spirits. You couldn't ask for anything more. Louie started us off, and when it was his turn, he took his solo. During the solo, he was so into it, unbelievably just playing away—what musicianship. I was fortunate to be doing this. He kept going, hitting the cymbals, hitting all the toms that surrounded him, his double bass, drums, a very long solo. I remember Norman saying,

"He can't get out of it." He continued to play and during the process, as he's riding the cymbals, his wig starts falling off slowly. He's trying to keep his head up, so it won't fall, but all of the sudden, it falls onto his snare drum and Louie hits it with his drumstick. Norman starts laughing, the band and everyone else in the control room just bursts out laughing. It was hilarious, what a night. One of our best sessions in quite some time. You very seldom saw Norman laughing that much; it was so amusing and funny and when it was all over the whole studio was still laughing like there was no tomorrow—what a great session to have been part of.

I was really busy recording other artists for Pablo Records; Big Joe Turner, Jimmy Witherspoon, Clean Head Vincent, The Trumpet Kings, Ella Fitzgerald, Count Basie, Oscar Peterson, Joe Pass, Dizzy Gillespie, Monty Alexander, Harry "Sweets" Edison, MJQ (Modern Jazz Quartet) and many others; it was time well spent and with Norman, money matters were never an issue; all he cared about was that he'd get nothing but the best. That was all he ever cared about; that and no-nonsense. I was in the best situation I had ever been in my life, and the man was always very supportive.

Things were really starting to change, but a bigger change was coming. One day, during one of our recording sessions in Studio 2 at TTG, I received a call from Michael Lloyd, a confidante of Mike Curb and a very successful music producer with whom I worked many times during my days at MGM Records. Michael was calling to see if I would be interested in servicing a client he had because he really didn't have the time to service them. He said it would be a big help to him. The client was Sid & Marty Krofft, a very busy and demanding client, but they paid their bills, and he again expressed it would be a favor to him personally. I could not refuse this offer; it was a gift; I needed the business. I wanted this; I could not turn him down. Michael said he had spoken to their head guy about me, and asked if I would be willing to call him. I said I would be more than happy, I'd call him right away. He said his name was Rich Heller and that he would be my contact, I thanked him, and I said I would call him right now, and thanks again. I knew I had to make this call fast. I headed towards Studio 3, which was always empty, but had a phone and lots of privacy. I didn't need a crowd around me, and I didn't want anyone aware of what I was doing—this was serious business. Little did I know at the time that this call from Michael Lloyd would take us all a very long way.

I called and their secretary, Trudy, answered. I introduced myself and I politely asked to speak with Rich Heller. We had a pleasant but brief conversation. I arranged a meeting for us the following day at their offices, which at the time were located in the San Fernando Valley, 7200 Sherman Way on the corner of Vineland Avenue. The following morning, I took Dennis Sands with me, as soon as we arrived at around 9:45 a.m. we walked upstairs and down a long hall to their offices, where we were greeted by Rich Heller—a tall slender guy sporting a curly brown hairdo and beard, he was very well-dressed, friendly and pleasant. He introduced us to Jimmy Haskell, their composer, whom I already knew from various recording sessions I had done with him through the years, their whole staff of engineers, program guys, and finally to the brothers Sid & Marty Krofft who would become our new client.

I was taken by surprise. These guys were well known and had a lot of TV shows under their belts. How fortunate we were to be given this opportunity. The brothers were very cheerful and pleasant and I took a liking to Sid Krofft instantly; he was very friendly, pleasant and very sincere. We spent some time talking about their needs and what they expected; we were now properly introduced to their personal Secretary, Trudy, a wonderful lady, and Sid's brother Harry, who was their bookkeeper. Finally, we sat down and then one of their designers pointed to a mechanical hand on top of a credenza behind us. He pushed a button, and the hand stretched slowly backwards and threw a baseball across the room, that's when I realized, at that very moment, that we were now in a different league. Everything from here on out required our full attention with a lot of care. We had to be very careful; there definitely was no room for error. Sid & Marty Krofft were supplying original music programs to the Six Flags Amusement Parks in the South.

We had to be on top of everything; there was no room for error. We had to be very careful how we handled this client and their product; this was a very important step we would be taking. We could not be lighting joints in the studio anymore; this was serious business. We would all be working under the supervision of Rich Heller, who was always very calm and would have an answer to any and all questions.

The next day when I returned to TTG, I went to the front office, negotiated a good rate with Kathy, and booked Studio 2 on an open-ended basis. I had no idea how much time we needed, but I knew we were going to be busier than ever, which was definitely a good sign.

One of our first tasks was buying plywood that we needed for a finale number we were going to record with tap dancers. We immediately started by editing and transferring pre-recorded music and building various sound effects for one of our very first projects that would take place at the Six Flags Amusement Park located in Williamsburg, Virginia.

We were now in charge of all music recorded for any and all of Sid & Marty Krofft's TV shows, Puppet Shows, and their Six Flags Amusement Park Shows. This was a great challenge as well as a great opportunity; lots of work. I had a staff to train; it would not be easy. I started slowly recruiting a few guys that had some experience, not much but enough that they could be trained very quickly.

We now had a good amount of editing to be done, and an awful lot of music and effects to put together in a very short time. My production company, in a very short period, had become very busy, with a few guys working for me on a free-lance basis; I was paying them really well. We were recording music and making sure it fit whatever projects Sid & Marty gave us. Believe me when I say there were lots of them, and we had to meet their deadlines without any problems.

I found it to be a great challenge and at the same time very educational, learning new things all the time; a great experience for everybody. I had never imagined it would turn out this way. Michael Lloyd had really turned me on to something really great. I will never ever forget that day when he called and asked me if I would be able to take care of Sid & Marty Krofft.

They had a lock on the amusement park venues that kept us consistently busy. I made sure this was done; meanwhile I'm training Dennis, who would eventually become a partner. We had not shaken hands on any deal yet, but I kept on going along with all the other work. The only requests were good quality, and all deliveries had to be on time.

The first show was for Six Flags, an amusement park in Atlanta, Georgia. On this show Kermit the Frog is at the piano he is lip-syncing "Georgia on my Mind," the state's national song by Ray Charles. This is a very funny and entertaining sketch. Kermit is playing the piano, and while this is going on you hear a saw in the background sawing away in tempo, the legs of the piano are being sawed off. I was using sound effects that I personally created with the help of my wife Cookie. I had timed it just right, as we were approaching the end of the song the piano falls off the legs on to the stage with a loud BANG! The curtain opens, MUSIC starts and we're into the downbeat of the show.

Now we needed some tap dancers for the finale. While we were recording them, we realized that the tempo was faster and Rich Heller wanted the dancers to go faster for this particular number. He looked from the control room and started wrapping his hands around really fast, signaling them to go faster to increase the tempo. The dancers were not really pros, they didn't know what Rich really wanted, and they were confused; they start running thinking that's what he wanted. We all just looked at each other and burst out laughing; we needed that every once in a while. You need a good laugh in the studio. What can you say? It was hilarious and much needed. We finally corrected the tempo, and the tap dancers doubled the tracks. They sounded great and it was a good day.

Sid & Marty Krofft were commissioned to develop an amusement park for the new Omni International Complex on Peach Street in downtown Atlanta, Georgia. This project was new to everyone involved, and it would be a theme park that would be called "The World of Sid and Marty Krofft." The world's first indoor Amusement Park due to open on May 26, 1976. In keeping with the highly creative nature of the name, the park featured elaborate attractions such as a large carousel adorned with mythological creatures of crystal, and a giant pinball machine-themed dark ride in which the riders would sit inside large ball-shaped pods and be ricochet through the "machine."

Visitors would enter the park at its uppermost level via a multi-story escalator, which was listed in the Guinness Book of World Records as the longest freestanding escalator in the world, supported only at its ends. Moving down from the reception level was the first carnival level, presided over by a stilt-walking master of ceremonies, and featuring three circus trailers, each with a different performer. These shows were presented in circus "trailers"; performers in costume usually did a 2-3-minute show to a different narrator/performer's voice. The middle trailer featured Betty Broadbent, and a purple belly-dancing rhino that was voiced by Ruth Buzzi.

The next floor was a transition level and included a caricature artist and an overlook for the stage show below. The following floor featured a live performance stage and a number of different shops and artisans. The Shows included a tightrope walker, a trio of break dancers and a song-and-dance show that starred Patty Maloney. All the events throughout the amusement park featured other "little people," including Debbie Dixon (who was in Star Wars), and they also had twin brothers John and Greg Rice, who were listed in the Guinness Book of World Records as the "World's Shortest Living Twins," until John's death in 2005.

The Park was full of surprises. Wherever you went there was something for you: gift shops, food emporiums, the glass blower/shop completed this level. The lower level featured the Krofft forest-theme "The Living Island Adventure" which also incorporated a theater with a live-action Krofft characters. The show also had a craft stall with a leather crafts person.

I remember Sid Krofft saying to me that he really wanted John Lennon to be the first to ride the pinballs; but unfortunately, that never came to pass. The floors of the park were gorgeous, largely open to the main atrium of the Omni, especially the ground level which also featured a great skating rink. Sid & Marty had come up with another idea; they wanted to use robots which they had named the "WalkArounds. Inside a space suit who would walk around wearing gloves that had magnetic contacts on each of their fingertips, so that by pressing the thumb to any of their fingers the robot would trigger an 8-track machine which was attached on their costume; very futuristic.

When kids in the park would ask any question like, "Can I go in there?" The Walk-Arounds would press an index finger with their thumb and the answer would be fast. It went something like, "The answer to your question is no," or "Why is the sky blue?" and again by the pressing of the index finger they would have another answer quickly.

We were now faced with recording various answers to quarter-inch tape and putting them in sequence, but with the music recording and everything else at hand, I needed someone that could do tape editing very accurately and fast. We had a lot of work to do, and at this point I'm introduced to

Mike Julian, a family man and musician who had come out to California from Syracuse, New York with his wife and kids and an urge to work.

I asked him, "Can you edit tape?" and he said he could. Finally, I had found someone with experience that I could leave completely unsupervised. This project needed nothing but the best and needed to be finished on time, there was no room for errors. We were using a quarter-inch 8-track format, you needed to attach a silver tape that was part of the triggering for switching tracks at the correct time.

Mike just happened to be available, and the fact that he was knowledgeable and not a stranger to studio work made me hire him on the spot. It was our busiest time in the studio, and while we were recording music in the studio, I had set him up in the vocal booth editing, where he would assemble the quarter-inch master's. There were times when we would be doing two sessions at once and all with different subject matters. I kept my whole crew really busy working on all of the Krofft shows.

Whenever Sid & Marty had anything that had to be recorded, we were always called in to attend their production meetings, given a script, and off we went totally unsupervised. We were all working very long hours on such shows as H.R. Pufnstuf, Land of the Lost, Electra Woman and Dyna Girl, WonderBug, Sigmund and the Sea Monsters, Witchy Poo, Stupid Bat, The Lost Saucer, Krofft Super Show, Kaptan Kool and the Kongs, The Bay City Rollers and The Brady Bunch Hour. I was really busy booking studio time and engineering personnel, collecting receivables, paying vendors, employees, mixing and keeping track of all tapes that needed to be shipped.

We stayed really busy, which was the name of the game. In addition were spending time with Jimmy Haskell, the composer that Sid & Marty were using for the amusement park in Atlanta. I was called in one day by Rich Heller because there seemed to be a couple of problems in Atlanta that we had to address. The Living Island ride had problems; every time one of the cars reached a certain section their hits were off, where "Stupid Bat" was to face you whenever your car made its turn it would be facing in a different direction. Additionally, the musical show with Kermit had its own set of problems. The crews were constantly asking that we add more treble or high end to the tapes.

I felt this was an odd request. Why was this coming from them? Why were they making such a request for brighter tape masters? I became very curious about this issue because, from day one I had personally made sure that the final master or masters were done on the same type of tape and machines that were being used at the park like for like, with the same configuration. We could not have anything different on either end, this was extremely important. If a client was using Dolby noise reduction that would be what we would provide but, in this case, it was DBX and that was exactly what we were using. I felt very strongly that somehow the wrong application was being applied. I was very confident that it was not on our end; it was not possible.

This became a sore subject with me with so many changes and the consistent request for new tapes. I sensed there was something very wrong going on, but I couldn't put a finger on it. I said to Rich Heller, "Look, there's a problem here. These tapes sound so brittle, there's no way that we should be adding so much high-end end; it doesn't make any sense." Now we started getting requests to make adjustments for another venue, "The Living Island Ride," which had its own set of mechanical and technical problems. I expressed my concerns to Rich Heller and told him he needed to send us to Atlanta to see what the problems were firsthand. I expressed my concern we were using the same machines here in Los Angeles that they were using in Atlanta for the ride; in the park as well as the stage shows. Our routine was as follows: after we made our master tapes all copies were done on the same make and model machine, I did this in order to avoid any and all mistakes such as the ones that we were now facing.

I felt that was the best form of quality control, but with everything that was going on, I knew something was definitely wrong; there had to be. We had to get to the bottom of these problems and really fast, so I asked for a meeting. I again explained my concerns to everyone and finally Rich Heller convinced Sid & Marty that it was imperative for us to go out to Atlanta. I felt that it was really important in order for us to solve any and all problems. The most important thing now was the ride "Living Island." I had tried everything possible that I could here in LA after so many requests regarding the problems they were experiencing with the ride. I was very persistent and finally on a hot and muggy day, both Dennis and I were at The Omni International on Peach Street in Atlanta, Georgia.

We checked into the hotel and without fail quickly headed down to where the shows were being performed. We introduced ourselves to their engineering staff and went over the problems they were having. I had a complete set of new master tapes that we wanted to play. We loaded the machine, and they were right; they sounded very muddy with a little high end, so I played a second set I had with extreme high-end with same results. We talked for some time with their engineers and went over their maintenance procedures with regard to their equipment, and as it turns out their head engineer there had told the operator that the heads on the machine did not have to be clean, he claimed the magnetic particles released from the audio tape would take care of it. He was claiming the accumulation of the particles acted as a cleaning agent.

I could not believe what I was hearing, so I reached into my kit and pulled out a cotton swab and some head cleaner. I put the swab coated with head cleaner on the heads of the machine and it came out completely black. They were not cleaning the heads on their machines at all, as per their instructions; no wonder they kept requesting for more and more high end (treble) on all the tapes that we were shipping from Los Angeles. Their machines with dirty heads were not reproducing a true sound, and in the process, they were accumulating more dirt since they were not being maintained properly like they should have been doing in the first place.

We checked everything on all their machines, de-magnetized, cleaned the heads on all their machines, and did a complete overhaul. All the time and effort was well worth it. We instructed their staff, and I emphasized how important this process was. It had to become part of their daily routine, and I made it a point that it was important for them as well as the company, that it was a process they needed to put in place in order to maintain the quality of sound. It was a good thing we had come out; now their problems for their playback machines on stage were finally solved.

When we finished cleaning the heads on all their machines, we put the new tapes on and hit play. The sound was so piercing; it just hurt your ears. It was a good thing that we had arrived with two sets of new masters. I destroyed all the other tapes they had. We had finally corrected all their problems once and for all, and we educated their engineering staff in keeping their machines in shape. In the end everyone was happy.

We finally got to our rooms, and needless to say, we were very tired. I called room service and Dennis reminded me that our deal was we pay for our own food and beverages. I completely ignored him I ordered food, wine and beer, and when it arrived, I just signed for it. I filled the tub in his room with ice and filled it with all the beverages we had. We smoked a joint, no we didn't pay for it.

Atlanta was different; the people there were the nicest we had encountered in a very long time, and the hospitality extended to us was really great. Neither of us had ever been to

Atlanta before; it was all new to us. I remember Dennis drove me crazy because he wanted to buy travelers checks. I said, "It's not like we're going to Europe, man, we're in the USA." But he was very persistent. I said, "Not me, I'm taking cash; that speaks in any language or accent." I knew our work was cut out for us. The reason why we were here, and an important one, was none other than "The Living Island Ride." From day one we rode and timed this ride several times very carefully in order to determine what was wrong with it. The problem that we were facing with the ride was that at certain points when the cars were supposed to turn and face any given character per the script storyline, they were out of sync, which was a issue. (Synchronization is timekeeping, which requires the coordination of events to operate a system in unison from top to bottom.)

We rode this ride at least 30 or 40 times with their electrical engineer to see if there was a voltage loss of some kind in regards to weight. He was very accommodating, taking timings and notes as to how many passengers were on the ride, but we knew it wasn't a weight factor. This was going to be a really difficult task and time would prove just that. We needed a Recording Studio that was close by, so we went to the nearest room, Master Sound Studios located on Peach Street. The studio was owned and operated by Bob Richardson and his wife (BABS), and they were both very accommodating. A great team and wonderful people who knew how to take care of clients. We were in good hands, and they went out of their way to help us. Time was of the essence; we needed this ride to be working. Bob Richardson took it upon himself and bought his own machine so that he could load cassettes for us. We spent a great deal of time testing the ride constantly, just going back as often as possible; but in order for us to confirm our test we had to wait till closing time. A big disadvantage because it would've been really useful to have other passengers on board at the time since their engineer at the time claimed it was also a weight factor involved. We were told that we couldn't disturb any of the patrons, which was really apparent to us; after all they were paying customers, but again the ride's accuracy was based on how many people were riding at any given time. We had been in town just a few days and during that time for the most part all we did was work on the "Living Island" ride, working in the studio doing all sorts of adjustments day and night.

One morning we arrived really early at the studio. We spent a few hours going over our notes, editing, and making adjustments to our master track while the cassettes were being loaded by Bob Richardson. We decided it was time to take a much-needed break from the studio. I told Bob we would pick up the cassettes in an hour and we went for a walk outside to get some fresh air. I noticed while we were inside that it had rained, so as we stepped outside and the sun was just blazing, the rain was starting to dry, and you could see steam just rising from the sidewalks. It had become very humid, oh yes, we were in the south. We noticed a bank across the street from the studio; it was a "City National Bank." Dennis wanted to cash one of his traveler's checks because he wanted to have some cash in his pocket. We walked across the street, and he went up to the teller who said, "I can't cash this, you have no local ID." They would not cash his traveler's check; needless to say, I was hysterical. I said, "No worries, I have plenty of cash on me. I have your back. Look, you're a Jew from Los Angeles in Atlanta, this is after all the South. What do want?" We just laughed all the way back to the studio. After everything that we were going through we needed a laugh. We were very concerned about this ride. I spoke to Rich Heller back in LA and I explained the problems we were having it. It was never-ending.

We were trying to fix something that was impossible to fix. The ride was just a bad engineering design and there was no way to sync these cars to the program. Nevertheless we kept trying our best, working non-stop day and night, taking all sorts of timings with my Minerva stopwatch in hopes that we could find the answer, fix it, and settle all the discrepancies. It seemed like it was taking us forever. After going on this ride numerous times, we would return to the studio for more mixing, editing, and creating new masters, but it was a fruitless attempt; we could not come up with a solution. It was impossible, there were too many variables. The hits were off and it was always different; unfortunately, this was before Time Code Synchronization.

We could not fix this. Each and every car was running independently, and out of sync. There was no way to lock these cars since each one was performing off its own cassette. Finally, we had decided it was time to head home; we said our goodbyes to Bob Richardson and his lovely wife Babs, who really wanted us to stay for their July 4 celebration. I wish we could've stayed, I'm sure it would've been a great one; but we'd been away from home way too long and it was time. These folks had been nothing but the best and their hospitality was impeccable.

The next morning, we parted a bit teary eyed and flew back home to Los Angeles. It was July 4 and the plane was completely full. I was a smoker, so I asked the attendant for some cigarettes, back then airlines still provided cigarettes for their passengers. The stewardess returned and said they were completely out. I had run out of cigarettes, and I needed another smoke. Nothing was available. The stewardess was really nice, and she asked some passengers for some and was able to come up with a few cigarettes. I knew I was going to run out, this was a long flight. I tried, but it didn't work finally I whipped out a joint and lit it, and that solved the problem.

There were a lot of folks heading west on this flight. I remember the choreographer, Joe Cassini coming over and saying, "You didn't?" At which point we just nodded our heads. When we finally landed at LAX, we headed to Cloverfield Avenue in Santa Monica, where Dennis lived, and I called my wife Cookie to come and pick me up.

This was a very memorable trip and a hard working one. It was time to rest and put it all behind us. It was the last time we visited Atlanta or dealt with "The Living Island Ride." We certainly owed a great deal of thanks to our hosts Bob Richardson and his wife Babs. What great people; they knew their business and how to treat their clients—it was indeed an honor to have dealt with them, they could not have treated us better. In conclusion, from an audio standpoint, we were right on, but from a mechanical standpoint, well, let's just say that it was not on us.

Upon our return from Atlanta, I again sat down with Rich Heller, and we went over our findings. He agreed with us that we had done what was expected. He said that it was time to move on and he informed me that Sid & Marty had a new TV Show, "The Brady Bunch Variety Hour" with musical director George Wyle, a great guy to work with who had written "The Ballad of Gilligan's Island," the theme song for Gilligan's Island with Sherwood Schwartz. He had also written the Christmas song "It's the Most Wonderful Time of the Year," which was first recorded by Andy Williams in 1963. I had met George way back when he served as the musical director for "The Flip Wilson Show" during the early 1970s. He also served as the musical director and arranger for John Denver and the Muppets' A Christmas Together.

We would have many orchestrators, but one in particular was my friend whom I had worked with on many occasions, Sid Feller. I loved Ray Charles and Sid was responsible for a great deal of Ray's hits. He did his first album, which was "Genius Hits the Road" and featured "Georgia on my Mind." He had also recorded another song for Ray, "I Can't Stop Loving You," which would become Ray Charles' biggest hit. The man was a genius and knew what he was doing and was a hard worker. This was not our first time working together, and this meant a lot to me. What an honor and privilege to have Sid in the control room.

I think, out of my whole crew, I was the only one that knew these guys, and I respected their company to the fullest. I would now be in total control; all the pre-records would be done at Sunwest Recording Studios on Sunset Blvd. I had to find a studio where the mix-down would be done; it was entirely up to me as long as all deadlines were met.

I started looking for a room where we could do our final mix-downs for each episode. I was very excited; I knew this would require a lot of work. I needed to get my crew together; we were going to be doing "The Brady Bunch Variety Hour." We were scheduled to record our first show on Wednesday, November 24, 1976, that eventually would lead to eight additional episodes that would air from January to May 1977.

I was very excited, we were now working with Sid & Marty Krofft on a weekly basis, which really kept us quite busy. We needed to be available every Wednesday very early in the morning to record the band and vocals. We were also required to spend part of Thursday as standbys when the shooting would take place at KTLA. We had to be available to attend whatever meetings would come up, especially production meetings.

We were always recording a tune that was popular on the radio charts for that given week, which was sort of a theme for the show. For example, if Glen Campbell was hot on the charts with a tune like "Southern Nights," we did record that for the whole cast to sing.

These meetings were very important, and they gave me information that was needed as far as tracks were concerned since we only had 16 tracks to work with, so it was very important. I needed to make sure tracks were available for the entire cast when they would record their musical numbers.

I made my arrangements known to everyone in my crew. I had set it up so that I would arrive at 6:00 a.m. every Wednesday at Sunwest Recording Studios. Once I arrived, I would put my show binder in the control room and start setting up the band with Roy. If there were any changes for the studio, I would go over them with the studio's head tech, Phil Serrate, and Gary Fradkin, our tech. I would check all microphone lines and wait for the musicians to take their places ready to record. The downbeat was at 10:00 a.m., and this whole process was exciting. I was working with the cream of the crop, the best musicians in town.

There were no strangers in the room; I had worked with all these guys throughout the years at various recording studios. We had done many sessions together. I was very proud to be working with all of them and I respected any and all requests that they might have. I also found it an honor and pleasure to be in the same room with such notable composers and arrangers like Sid Feller, and Tommy Oliver, and our musical director George Wyle.

During the recording, it was always a good practice to have someone who could read the charts or score as we were recording. I was very fortunate to have none other than the maestro himself, Sid Feller, sit alongside me and read the chart as I was recording the band. He would call out the entrance of various instruments, be it percussion, brass, or woodwinds, anything that would make a statement for that particular music cue or number. This was always extremely helpful, and he was a master at it. If Sid said we needed a pickup, we could cut it; that's what we did. He was always right; there was no second-guessing. Editing at that time was all done with a razor blade.

We had a very special vocal coach present at these sessions, none other than Ray Charles, who was a fixture on The Perry Como Television Show and had written special material for some of the world's greatest entertainers—the man we all called "The White Ray Charles." He knew every performer's singing potential and whether they could hit a certain note or not, because the only professional singer we had in The

Brady Bunch was Florence Henderson. Ray would handle all the vocal charts for The Brady's, and once we recorded a number that needed vocals and George was happy with it, I would make any and all notes for the vocals. I would send that multi-track to the other room down the hall in Studio B.

I had previously made arrangements for Dennis to come in around noon and I would have him record all the vocals. The vocal recording sessions would go on usually till 6:00 or 7:00 p.m. until all the vocals were done, but usually no later than 7:00 p.m. When all the vocals were done recording, all master tapes would be gathered and then we would be ready to mix the entire show. I had already made arrangements during the course of the day with Roy Richardson to have food and drinks for our entire crew. Enough so that it would last us till morning.

Roy's duties were very timely and important, although they often changed, he did perform them really well. They consisted of gathering all the multi-track tapes and any working materials and delivering them, no questions asked, really quickly to Paramount Studios on Vine Street and Santa Monica Blvd. We would often try to have dinner at "Moulin's Chinese Restaurant" on Sunset, "Martoni's Italian" or "Musso & Franks" on Hollywood Blvd, depending on how much time we had. If we didn't have enough time, which was often the case, we would head straight to our mixing location.

We were working at Paramount Recording Studios, which was built back in the late 1960s by the Brolin family. Rumor has it that Brian Brolin was encouraged by his brother, the well-known actor James Brolin, to open the studio after he gained some renowned popularity of his own from his recording work with his former classmate Ritchie Valens. There was also another rumor going around that at the time James Brolin was under contract to Paramount Pictures, and he named the studio after his employer as a way of poking fun at such a large corporation.

Paramount's studio manager, Don, and I had struck a great deal that was really hard for any of the studios in town to beat. Not to mention there was a great convenience factor built in that no other studio in town could offer. Neither Johnny Mercer's studio on Western Avenue or Sun West Recording, which would've been great since that was where we were recording the shows, or TTG, they couldn't beat the deal I made. We could bring all the food we needed, personnel, tape, and equipment. As long as it was done in an orderly fashion there would be no ins and outs. Don would lock us in, and we would start mixing, usually around 8:00 p.m. until the early morning hours, usually no later than 8:00 a.m. the following morning.

Don would arrive about 7:00 a.m. in the morning, we would go over details or complaints, if any, about equipment. I would pay him for the time used, pack all our gear, and leave till the following week. This arrangement worked great for both of us; a guaranteed booking, we couldn't be bumped, and I would pay them right then and there on a weekly basis. I always insisted that we take care of everything, never abuse any facility; they were very important to us.

We had tried TTG, but that was very distracting. I had also tried Johnny Mercer's studio on Western Avenue; that was a disaster. We had to provide our own pens, pencils and razor blades, and like I said earlier, SunWest was way too busy. We had a good reputation, and we wanted to maintain it, so in order to survive and for the sake of our show, we stayed at Paramount.

Some of my crew consisted of some really good and bright talented guys with little if any experience in the music business. They knew very little about it but they were really hungry: they were sponges with an urge to succeed. I had to teach them all the various applications and methods of recording. I had Dennis Sands, who was just starting out; we had met back at MGM Records. He had been with me the longest and, by default, became my second engineer. Another fast learner, a hard worker who would later become a partner in my production company.

I would, on many of our sessions, have Dennis relieve me from doing vocal overdubs and rough mixes. He could edit tape and that was a good asset because back then, all the work was done analog; there was no such thing as automation, This was the mid-70s. Whenever there was a complicated production number, it was all hands on the board. He was very helpful, and I must say, good at it.

We also had our own tech, Gary Fradkin, who was right out of high school and enjoyed his work. He had a great deal of knowledge when it came to electronics. He would research whatever we needed and would always come up with great results for us, although his time was limited. Gary was still employed by TTG. but he would spend a great deal of time with us on all our sessions. He was a loyal individual and remains a close friend to this day. I could always rely on him whenever we had a session; he was always right there and he would contribute a great deal of support to every session.

We had another second engineer, Paul Aronoff, who was very methodical and a great person very dependable, punctual, reliable, and very trustworthy. He was a childhood friend of Dennis. When he recommended Paul, although he had no music experience, I was thrilled because the man had great work ethics and was looking to grow. I felt Paul would go a long way. He was married but had no children, which would work for all of us since we worked all kinds of weird hours; and long ones.

We were very busy; it was the era of variety shows. Since we were all working on an independent basis, there was no telling when you would be home, and having children, well let's just say it wouldn't be fair to your kids, and your wife would have something to say because you do lose your social life. I was very fortunate; my wife was dedicated and extremely helpful. She understood that side of the business.

I had also decided to hire Roy Richardson, who was my brother-in-law, he took no bull. We had nicknamed him Reverend Skippy because he was often quoting a bible verse, but when it came to Pot, which we all smoked he was right there. I knew he was out of a job and was looking for work, and I needed someone that could be reached really fast; and it so happened he lived right smack in the middle of Hollywood, which was a plus and worked for us. I gave Roy a lot of responsibilities, which I never regretted. He was a joy to have around. I put him in charge of procuring all of our supplies. He would shop for us and would also serve as our setup guy, front desk receptionist and driver; a man with many duties it was great to have on board. He was very friendly and helpful; the man—knew how to handle people and never missed a day.

Our schedule was very timely, there was no room for errors. Every Thursday morning, once we finished mixing the show, master reels were assembled in show order. Once we made safeties, we had Roy deliver them to KTLA-TV, which was located not far from us on Sunset Blvd and Van Ness Avenue. The location was just a few minutes away from us. I had set things up so that we could be close to everything, as well as everyone else on the show; another reason why I had chosen Paramount Studios on Vine Street and Santa Monica. The studio was very convenient for Rich Heller, who was our main contact as well as the production staff, producers, composers, runners and, most of all, Sid & Marty Krofft. They never came around, not during the mix sessions, these were late hours, and no one really wanted to be in Hollywood; not during those un-godly evenings. It wasn't safe, but we were accustomed to it.

Once we were finished, I would dismiss everyone. At this point Dennis and I would hang out in Hollywood on call, usually back at Studio 2 at TTG. This was a safety measure, just in case some changes needed to be made, which never came to pass, but we were ready willing and able. We were recording various clients and continued with the same routine till May 1977 when the show finally came to an end. I continued working with my other clients; one in particular was Norman Granz's new label Pablo Records. I continued recording a lot of great jazz artists such as Ella Fitzgerald, Oscar Peterson, Joe Pass & Niels Pederson "The Trio," which had earned them a Grammy for best performance by a group, and Count Basie "Prime Time," which also earned him a Grammy in 1977 for best performance by a big band.

Norman Granz kept me pretty busy; he was a very strict producer. But if you paid attention, you could learn so much. The man who was a legend and contributed so much to jazz. As a matter of fact, he was jazz; all of his sessions were always filled with some of the greatest artists of jazz. Norman always insisted on nothing but the best from everyone. There were times when the musicians would start with their complaining because they could not hear one another, and Norman would say, "Get rid of those baffles," or "Take the lid off the piano, get rid of the headsets," which I must say I loved. He never gave me a hard time at all, and he was not too demanding. I must say working with Norman on all his sessions taught me an awful lot. I always felt they were very historical.

Norman also played a big part in my life as well as everyone else's; and he was very generous, whatever you needed, if it was essential to the session, it was never a problem. I made sure that all the musicians on my sessions were comfortable; especially on any of Norman's dates, which he in turn appreciated. With all the effort that we put into it he kept calling me back. I was able to establish a good relationship with Norman which lasted till his death in 2001.

I loved hearing my old friend Harry Sweets Edison, who always called me Angel Eyes, and would always say, "Man, you get a good sound." A very sweet man and always very cheerful. All the bands that I recorded for Pablo records were in their own right the best the world had ever heard or seen.

I liked Sunwest Recording Studios. I used the studio for some of Norman's sessions. It was there that I recorded "Primetime" with Count Basie. Norman would always say to me, "Wherever you want to record is OK with me. Just tell me where and I'll be there." A great compliment coming from him personally.

We did other sessions at Sunwest. One of the most memorable ones was for Louie Bellson—really exciting. We had such notable musicians as Alex Acuna from Peru, Cuban bassist Isreal "Cachaio" Lopez, Manolo Baderrena a great Brazilian, Cuban Francisco Aquabella on Bata drums, Wilfredo Reyes Sr. and Jr. on percussion, Louie Bellson drums, and Emil Richards on Marimba. The album was called "Ecue Ritmos Cubano." It was a great session all done in one day. Norman was so happy that he was dancing in the control room to the Latin beats, and wanted to take everyone out to dinner at Packita's, a Puerto Rican restaurant not far from the studio on Sunset Blvd. I had never seen Norman like this. It was very rare, and it was a great sight to witness. The musicians, all of them, loved it and you could hear it in their music, a great recording session. The mood that evening was out of this world. All the performances were magical—another treasure which was released on the Pablo label.

MGM's closure was what pushed most of us in different directions. We had no other choice but to seek other employment. My short stay at Motown Records, and again my short return to TTG, didn't do much for me; that's when I had decided to start freelancing and I became very successful at it.

Ed Greene was another who, on many occasions, would call me to record "The Donny and Marie Show," which for me was an honor. Tommy Oliver was the arranger, composer, and conductor for the show, which saved everyone an awful lot of time and money. I can't express what a pleasure it was for me to be working with Tommy again. I had worked with him on various projects, and he was as always, a very happy, pleasant and outgoing guy. One of the best. Our relationship went way back; we shared a lot of memories in the studio.

The Osmonds had built a studio in their condo, which was not that close to Sunwest Studios; it was located in Westwood off Santa Monica Blvd, behind the Mormon Temple, so it was a bit of a drive, especially in my old Pontiac station wagon.

The control room was not that great, but we were there to mix and perform a task, not to re-design or bad mouth anyone for it. We were hired as sound engineers, and we did our very best; and it worked. They had installed a Soundcraft Recording Console. The speakers were not matching, but we knew what we had, so you had to be careful on your mix downs. Their studio was in a residential area, so you could not play your monitors too loud, especially in the middle of the night, and smoking was not allowed anywhere in the facility. Both Tommy and I were smokers; if we wanted to have a smoke, we had to go outside, no matter what hour of the night.

Then we had the issues of recording formats. The Osmonds had a 24-track machine at their studio; the format at Sunwest was 16 tracks. When we would finish recording the orchestra, they would take all the 2-inch 16-track tapes home to do vocal overdubs. They would place the 2-inch 16-tracks on the 24-track machine, and at this point they would record on the outside tracks where track 1 (one) would now become track 2 (two) of your 24-track machine. They could record on track one of the 24-track and would skip every 2 tracks and so forth. You had to be careful and always check your layout, but in the long run they were able to gain 8 tracks on our 16-track tape. This made perfect sense; it did work, although there were times when Donnie would erase the bass drum for a few bars, which we would fix later during the mix down.

They did their own vocal recording unsupervised, which they managed to get done before we would arrive for the mix down sessions. We would usually start around midnight and work till 8:00 a.m. in the morning. Their messenger would pick up the master tapes for taping at KTLA. At this point I would gather my briefcase and all my notes and head down to the 405 North home to Canoga Park.

I received a call to do some brass overdubs at the Osmond's studio. I had Dennis sub for me because it was near his home in Santa Monica, since I was already booked with Norman Granz. The following morning, I received a call from Merle Osmond personally. He was okay about the switch of engineers; he wasn't upset, I apologized and told him I would talk with Dennis about our conversation and would let him know they were happy with his work and the switch. I also took the time to explain to Dennis that we could not handle any of the Osmond sessions like all the other sessions that we were doing. We were at their home, and they were calling the shots. The Osmonds were hard workers, very strict, and did not like any playing around, and we had to respect that because, directly or indirectly, they were providing us with a lot of work.

If Ed Greene was not available, I became second call. We had to act really carefully how we conducted ourselves. This fast-paced activity continued. ALB was very busy; in addition to the Osmonds we were now doing a great deal of live sessions and remotes that took us as far as Palm Springs. I had an agency client from New York City who had a lot of trust in me, and asked if I would go to Palm Springs to record some radio spots for him. He didn't have the time and was anxious to get back home. It would be a simple job taping Sandra Palmer, who would be playing at "The Dinah Shore Golf Classic." This was a yearly event that his agency covered. It was important for us to tape her, and assemble some radio spots that would be played on various radio stations. The next day I met with him. I was given the script for Sandra Palmer and the timings for each radio spot, as well as her location. Bright and early the very next morning we packed our equipment in my 1970 Pontiac station wagon and headed out to Palms Springs.

We had arrived early, had some food, and just hung around

town. Finally, we headed for her bungalow. When we arrived, I asked where we could set up our equipment and we were directed to a small area in the living room. We didn't have much—just a microphone stand, tape machine and a small Ampex console. We went over the script with Ms. Palmer and started recording her. She was very fast, and it didn't take too long. Fortunately there were no gardeners working nearby; it was very quiet.

When we were finished, we thought we would just hang out to see if we could get lucky. We started packing our equipment slowly, but we were just ushered out the front door. So much for our expectations. We cruised around Palm Springs for a while and headed back to LA. I had booked studio time, so as soon as I could, I started editing and building a master reel. I made safeties and shipped the masters out to our client at BBD&O back in New York City. We were constantly talking about building our own studio. We had for some time now faced a problem that was not going to go away; the problem being that the majority of studios in town really were record oriented and either too big or too small.

The format for TV was very different, so when you requested a mono full-track machine it became impossible. At the time most studios were not interested in TV work. For them it was a different world. All record sessions were done much differently than your typical motion picture, TV Commercials or Variety Shows, and the pace was definitely different and not very demanding. The majority of record sessions by far were at a slower pace and now, since the advent of the multi-track machines, you had the flexibility to record the rhythm section first with usually a scratch vocal, and do all of your instrumental overdubs at a later date; be it strings and or brass overdubs. Lead vocals and background vocals usually followed, which took a considerable amount of time, and finally your mix down to stereo 2-track or whatever format was needed; and that could take some time. Those were the multi-track days. I knew this because I also functioned in that manner when I was doing record dates.

The TV programs we were doing at the time requested that you deliver your masters in a quarter-inch mono full-track format yesterday, and ready for taping. Most studios in town didn't own a mono machine; they would try to convince you to use their 2-track machine, which was all they had. We were doing a considerable amount of tape editing with razor blades, which in most cases we had to supply. Most studios in town at the time didn't understand or weren't interested in TV work, and because of it, a lot of work was being referred to us. I must say we were very good at it, and we manage to stay very active in the TV Variety circle because we made it our business, and we understood what was needed.

I knew that whenever you were doing a TV show you had to be ready for any and all changes. You had to be aware of what the final format and delivery of the masters had to be and quick. We had tried a few different places, and as I mentioned earlier, we had tried Johnny Mercer's place on Western Avenue, but that didn't work. Johnny's son was managing the place, but his heart was not in it. We had sessions where we had to supply our own equipment, which was another inconvenience that we didn't need. I had so many other things to deal with, and that was the last thing I needed. But when there is no other choice, you deal with it.

TTG and Paramount Studios were more affordable than any other place for our needs, as well as our clientele. TV production companies could not afford higher rates. At times when Dennis, my partner at this point, would want to go to a different studio, I would have to remind him that it was not feasible. I had negotiated the deal, and I had to stand by it. I could not let anyone just change that because of their ego or no knowledge of the business at hand. I would always stand by my word and deliver exactly what was agreed to in any meeting. As I would often tell him, you can't just change a deal in the middle of everything. A deal is a deal; you have to stick to what you agreed. Your word is your bond, and you cannot get on the phone and say, "I've changed my mind."

This also gave our clientele a sense of confidence, which gave us a lot of creditability. That to me has always meant an awful lot—stick to the deal. I was, without a question, overworked trying to keep all this together, but I was enjoying myself, knowing full well that I was doing what I liked the most, music. I respected every customer that came our way, and they in turn gave us more work, which is what we wanted. I knew things would change, but for the moment I was doing my very best and staying on top of it all. The only drawback that I faced was that my crew didn't have the experience or notoriety. I had to be around at all times, it was a one man show, but I must admit it was fun. In the long run everybody worked and earned their money, no question about it.

I had always done R&B sessions (rhythm and blues). I was doing a lot of R&B sessions which from day one kept me very busy. I had a friend who had started his own small label in Hollywood called HDM Records. He was an ex-disc jockey from Phoenix, Arizona, Hadley Murrell, who I had met at a recording session I was engineering for Fred Smith. When we first met at TTG, he was introduced to me by Fred as his business manager, which really surprised me that Fred had one. We were recording a female group called The Merritts, which was arranged and conducted by non-other than James Carmichael. Time went by, and a few days later I received a call from Hadley, who said he and Fred Smith had decided to part ways and he had decided to return to Phoenix.

I liked the guy. I said, "Look, stay in LA; the business is here. I'll do all your sessions for a good rate." He agreed, and in turn, kept me pretty busy. He signed a few acts to his label, and we started recording a lot of different bands and groups that kept us really busy. We recorded Freddie and Henchi, Richard

Cason, Smoked Sugar and many, many others. Hadley's decision to stay in town would eventually help me in keeping Studio 2 at TTG busy. I was also able to teach other up and coming engineers how to do record sessions with R&B groups; this included Dennis Sands. This continued for some time, and eventually when I was asked to record a group called Black Ice, I asked Hadley if I could use another engineer that I had been working with. He agreed, but he wasn't aware that Dennis was just starting out and had not matured enough to take care of things in the studio seriously. When I completed all the live recording, I showed Dennis how to record the vocal group using an AKG C-12 and a U-47 microphone overhead, which I often used and ran through a Leslie speaker. I did a few tunes just to show him how simple the process was and then, when the vocals were done, it was time to mix. I booked the studio that evening for mixing and turned the mixdown duties over to Dennis. During the course of the mixdown he lit a joint and offered it to Hadley and he, not being that aware or a smoker of pot, completely lost his point of reference. The very next morning I get a call.

He was frantic, apologizing to me and said, "I would never do that again, man."

I asked, "Do what?" and then he proceeded to explain to me what had happened during the mixdown session and what happened later.

He drove home thinking he would never make it and went straight to bed. When he woke up in the morning, he played his mixes, and he knew immediately he had to re-mix everything. I had to have a talk with Dennis. I said, "You can't do that with him. We could've lost the client and who knows what else. He's giving you a chance." I said, "Man, we have to be serious about our work." We were busy-bee's and had a good run going; it seemed like it would never end. One day while we were recording, I was asked by Hadley Murrell what it would take to put a studio together to do exactly what we were doing. He said he would be interested and could probably put some monies and people together and that we should pursue it; which have always been his famous last words. I wasn't that comfortable with the thought of owning my own studio and having more partners. Although we were busy, I felt it would be something out of our league. Who would run it? Certainly not Dennis. I was already overworked with no weekends free; it just didn't make sense. I thought about it for some time. I really didn't want any more partners, but after careful thought and being pushed by a lot of people, I got on the phone and had a lengthy conversation with Brian Cornfield, an ex-TTG employee who had formed a very successful company called "Everything Audio." I talked at length with Brian, and I explained the needs and the situation and I asked him to put a quote together for me. The project would be called "In the Pocket Recording." It was a name I really didn't care for, but never the less it was a start. Hadley said he would look for the money, which he never did and I was not surprised at all..

Time went by and we started really getting serious about having our own studio. I said that if it was really important that we should look into this very carefully since I was the one that would have to be pounding the streets in order to sell it. We started by arranging meetings about building a studio. Since we were always busy recording during the week, it made it impossible for us to have any conversations or meetings, or even come up with any plans towards our goal. So I set meetings on weekends, usually early Saturdays. I felt it was important that we all be on the same page discussing manufacturers and their equipment, personnel, the size of the room, and clientele. These meetings were held whenever possible at my house. Just the three of us, Dennis, Gary and myself. My wife Cookie was very supportive, she would always cook us great dinners, and we'd just sit around and throw ideas around. I felt it was important if we were going to do this, we needed to know what our options would be. I must admit that it wasn't easy getting together on weekends, but it was the only time we had available. There were times when Dennis did not want to show; he felt it wasn't necessary and that it was all bullshit. This was what Gary and I had to put up with, but I was really persistent, and after much coaching he would come around, especially if A L B Productions had money.

I felt that there were many other things we had to address if we were really serious about putting together a studio; one being collateral. I was the only one that owned a home and had credit. Dennis didn't have any at the time; he didn't even have a credit card, and he had no credits as far as recording went. I was the only one with the credits and a homeowner, so I knew that I would eventually be on the hook.

Another issue I felt was important was that most orchestras were now being cut to a smaller size. The powers at hand didn't think big orchestras warranted the high cost; even Johnny Carson's Tonight Show had cut down their band size, which was the highlight of his show. The norm was now about seventeen men. It was a big factor that played a big role in what we wanted to build. We decided the room would have to hold at least 35 musicians, always thinking of TV variety shows. I knew exactly what type of equipment would be needed down to the brand of music stands; to me it was a no brainer. I felt the place had to be plush, with all the bells and whistles. The best gear in town with a large control room in order to accommodate dancers.

Brian Cornfield from Everything Audio finally came up with his proposal for us. While in the process of putting our proposals together, other folks were inquiring and wanted to go along for the ride. I was a good earner, and from their perspective, that's all they saw, but there was no action from their side, as always, a lot of talk but no action.

I was very popular in town, there wasn't anyone in town that was associated with the music business that I didn't know. I had a considerable number of artists I had worked with, and my client base had grown and kept on growing. Whenever or wherever there was a party, I attended because it was important to stay visible, and in the long run, it brought in more business.

I needed to get some commitments, either verbal or in writing (preferably in writing); that's what bankers always want to see. I started to make appointments with as many clients as possible.

The ones I felt had the most notoriety and pull in town who were doing popular films, records or shows. I decided to go after agents, arrangers, artists, composers, managers, music contractors, music recording labels, production companies and publishers. I solicited letters of intention from all of them, stating that if I built a studio, they would use our facility. That in fact our studio would become their home for all their recording sessions as well as all their clientele. I felt these letters would look great to a banker or any lending institution, so on my own I started to pursue them.

I decided to call on an old friend just to get things rolling. I knew I could count on him, no question about it. Plus, he was very well known, influential and respected in the industry; so I placed a call to see if Don Costa was busy in order to set up an appointment with him. I called his home and asked what time would be good to see him, and he replied, "Jesus Christ, leave me alone. You know better. Anytime, just come by." Boy did I get a big scolding. I loved his reaction, his very words to me were, and I quote, "Friends don't make appointments. Why don't you just drop in. I would love to see you. Is there anything wrong?" He asks me what have I done? Aren't we passed all that bullshit? Just come down here you don't need a fucking appointment.

I remember walking in the front door of his office and there sat Leo Costa, Don's brother, with a big smirk on his face. Leo was a riot. I don't remember exactly what was on Don's desk, but I touched it, and I asked him, "What is this?"

Leo reached in his pocket and pulled out a big stack of bills and said, "Don't touch that, you want this? You can have it but don't touch that." He was always playing with me.

Don walked in and said, "What the fuck are you guys doing?"

I responded, "Leo is trying to bribe me."

There wasn't a time when Leo would not want to mess with me. He was a great kidder. I loved this man who would always ask me, "You got any porns? We had known each other a long time. I personally enjoyed all his pranks; it was always like this.

Don and Leo were two of the kindest people I have ever known. Boy how I miss those guys. We've known each other from early New York City days. They were always there whenever I needed something, and it was never mentioned to anyone. I explained to Don what I was doing and why I wanted a letter. His response was, "I don't know what to say. Tell me what you want me to say." I spent a few hours there dictating what I wanted him to say for the bankers' benefit. His response was, "You know you have my full support. We go back a very long time and you've earned my respect, and I mean it." I was teary eyed. He hugged me and said, "You know I wish you nothing but the best, now get out of here."

Don, as always, was very sincere; he was a man of his word. I walked out of his office, and when I did, who do I run into? None other than my dear friend Dave Fisher. I will never forget the surprised look on his face. It just so happened that he had come to the house on that particular day to go over some vocal charts with Don. He was his main guy because he was really good with vocal arrangements. Now, when it came to vocal parts, he was always the first call. I remember Dave saying to me later on that when I came out of the office with a letter in hand, he wished he had been a fly on the wall because no one ever approached Don the way I did.

When I left Don's office, he had a great big smile on his face, and I knew not to say what most people say that we've always found really insulting. "This is between us." He would not let anyone know what our business was about; what we spoke about would always stay with us. He was proud of me and had seen me come a long way, but little did he know that he himself had played a great part in my wellbeing.

I knew Don Costa would eventually bring a lot of business without being asked, and if there wasn't time available that day, he would reschedule. I will never ever forget that he did that just for me, not for the studio, which he liked very much. He was a man of his word and very supportive.

Eric Miller was also very persistent. He said several times that we should run the idea by Dennis's uncle, who claimed he had a lot of money—Dr. Ben Eisenstein, who was a skilled radiologist at UCLA. We all took it for granted that he did have lots of money, but I was reluctant at first since it was too close to home. Eventually, we put that aside and scheduled a meeting with the doctor on a warm summer night at his home in Santa Monica.

When we arrived, we were greeted at the door by the doctor, a very tall man well over six feet, sporting a gray beard and bald head. He was very cordial, and his wife Jean, who stood about five feet tall, greeted me with a nervous smile. The Eisenstein's had a beautiful home, very well decorated and very expensive. They both seemed a little nervous at first, especially his wife. I couldn't blame them; this was our first meeting. But after a few drinks and as the evening progressed, everyone became more comfortable and spoke more freely.

Dennis, who was his nephew, had spoken to both of them about me before our meeting. They were very inquisitive and rightfully so, this was an expensive venture that they, as well as their nephew, knew very little about. But I had the answers to all of their questions. I was well prepared; this was not my first meeting regarding the possibility about building a recording studio in Hollywood. I was very confident about it and had all the numbers and projections to prove it. I welcomed all questions; it was better to get it all out in the open now.

We all talked for a while. I had never met the doctor before, but he seemed very interested. Word had it, he was very wealthy and that he was looking for a good investment to put his money in, and that he was looking for a long-term venture, and that was precisely what we were after. I had made it a point to bring along some documentation with me, and after talking about the industry, its needs and what my idea was, I showed the doctor a copy of my ledger. He was startled. I did the books manually, no quick books back then, and I must say very clean. I accounted for everything. I explained to the doctor that if we had a studio, we could double, even triple the figures, because there wasn't a studio at the time that really understood the requirements for TV Shows, which was precisely what we were doing. TV Variety shows; this was the brunt of our work. I had the clientele to prove it, and not only that, I was very confident we could succeed, and I was very aware of what was needed to service them.

I did all the talking at this point, since I was the one that knew the business. He was impressed and said he would like to think about it. I wasn't sure we would hear from the doctor again and obviously he needed to run it by his wife, who really asked most of the questions at the meeting.

We continued working on our variety shows and kept meeting at my house on weekends, all the time keeping the conversation of a studio a secret between us. I was not going to spend any time thinking about our meeting with the doctor. We were very busy and on schedule doing our recording sessions for Sid & Marty, which kept us really busy.

A couple of weeks went by, and we received a call from the doctor, who said he was interested and that we should meet and talk some more. We met again at his house, but this time they were more relaxed. He prepared some steaks, and we had some drinks. We threw a few things around, Ben wanted to know what should we called the studio? Which was a great question and would help when we would file papers, corporate papers with the secretary of state. He asked should we call it A L B, which was what had really originated this whole thing, but Dennis immediately took issue with it. We kicked a few names around and finally I said, "Look, there's four us involved; you, Esther, Dennis's mom, Dennis and myself. Why don't we call it Group Four, but the four should be a roman numeral, IV. After careful thought everyone agreed the studio would be called Group IV Recording.

We discussed other issues. The doctor was very concerned about the economy, and I remarked, "Ben, people listen to music no matter what state the economy might be in. TV Networks won't shut down and entertainment will always be needed." He was also concerned about his nephew being so green in the music business, and asked if he could handle it? I said, "That's also my worry, but I'm not concerned. I've been training him. I had the same conversation with his brother, Barry Sands, and I told him that in a matter of time I will personally make sure he would have enough credits, and that through my efforts he would become a well-known recording engineer." I had to sell it, he was family and I wasn't, and they had their concerns and rightfully so. They didn't know me from Adam. It was a touchy situation, but I had a handle on it, and I meant every word of it. I wasn't out to deceive anyone.

As the meeting progressed, Dennis said he wanted to bring in David Michaels, he asked if I knew him. He started to describe him, and we talked for a while about him. After a while I realized yes, I knew him. We had met years ago at a recording session I had at TTG when I was recording "Rolling on the River" with Ike and Tina Turner. At the time this David Michaels went by the name of Bernie Ross. I said, "For now I'm OK with it, but what bothers me the most is that he is now going by the name of David Michaels. I hope there aren't any left hooks." The fact that he would bid on our studio package and have a lot of confidential information really bothered me, and knowing Dennis I knew he probably spilled all the beans about wanting to build a studio.

I said I didn't trust him. Why the different name? Dennis claimed that he could put a turnkey package together for us and that he had talked to him about it. Well, there you go. As I said, spilled the beans. This was something that later on would come to hurt the business, this attitude of Dennis always talking out of school. I knew that somehow; he would do it again. He really didn't know much about the guy. Dennis had met him in passing at Ike & Tina's studio, Bollick Sound, just a few times while he was doing freelance work. This was after Fred Borkgren, who was Ike and Tina's personal recording engineer, had decided to leave. Dennis had a bad habit that he would meet someone at a party, or any get together, and he would always let the cat out of the bag. If he liked somebody, he would swear by them; in his eyes they could do no wrong. But gut feeling told me something was not right, he didn't have the credentials, yet Dennis assumed Bernie could do this project. Reluctantly, I agreed. My feeling was that Bernie was a cynical person; at our very first meeting I immediately recognized him with the greasy hair look and he flat out lied. He claimed he would provide us with an architect (Harry Newman) to put blue line prints together. He also claimed that within a few weeks we would have a design of the studio, or some concept that would be presentable to a bank; and that as far as permits were concerned it would not be a problem, they would just walk them through. That should've been a big red flag right then and there, because it was another fucking lie.

How can you really do that? Not in this city. They didn't have that kind of muscle; and time would prove it. I still had my doubts; I didn't trust the man, and I knew I had to keep an eye on him. We still needed to find a location; it could not be in the Valley, and I also stressed that it could not be west of Highland Avenue or east of Western Avenue. The search was on for a location that would suit my clientele. We, personally, could not go around town looking for a building because this would tip our hand to other studios; and we could be cut off from the ones we were doing business with, which put me in a very peculiar position, since I was doing all the bookings. I could not express my concern enough to everyone on staff to keep their mouths shut. We were in a very strange position and we needed to keep it a secret—they all wanted to know why? I had kids to content with and they just wanted to brag about a studio; but in the end I prevailed. We had several meetings with the doctor and his wife, Jean, who was like white on rice, always with a very nervous demeanor and smile.

She never missed a meeting. I showed them the equipment list, and Ben said he was ready, that he would put up the money. There was a lot of footwork to be done, but what we didn't know then, and would find out later, after the fact, was that Ben just wanted to play the big man with all the money; but he didn't have that kind of money. He was leasing the equipment; what he had was a good credit line, and good contacts with bankers. This would later come to haunt us in a big way. I now had a lot on my plate. The sessions we were doing kept me extremely busy, a possible studio now to book and selling my crew to new clients, who did not know them; not to mention additional key personnel we would need. I was taking on a great task and no one ever said, "How can I help?"; but I was more than capable.

Time passed and one day I received a call from David Michaels, aka: Mr. Bernie Ross, as I always in my mind addressed him, saying that he had found a building for us and that it would make a great studio. It had parking in front, two loading docks and lots of room for expansion. He claimed we would love the location; it was really good, and the owner was willing to lease it with an option to buy. It was a prime location. I asked when we could see the building and he said he would have to set it up with the realtor. After a few calls back and forth to everyone, we all decided to gather in Hollywood. We wanted to look at the building that would become our studio, located at 1541 North Wilcox Avenue, right next to the Citizen News building and across from The Hollywood Mercedes Benz dealer, which later on would become SIR.

This, I must admit was a great location, right smack in the heart of Hollywood. You couldn't ask for anything better. Bernie had done well, but I still didn't trust him. The building would certainly meet our needs; Martoni's, a well-known Italian restaurant. was right around the corner—it was frequented by everyone in the music industry. Sal Salvatore, whom I knew personally, had opened this place in the 60's; the food was great, and the service was outstanding with a great atmosphere. You would always run into top musicians and singers; it was always a packed house. This would be a great asset to our business, where we could take our clients safely for either lunch or dinner. I spoke with Sal about our venture; he gave me his blessings and said anything I wanted all I had to do was ask. We now needed to look at the plans. Bernie said he would meet with the architect, Harry Newman, and after some careful and accurate measurements they would provide us blue line drawings.

A few weeks passed and we met with Bernie at Ben's house, and went over plans which showed the studio and control room, the offices, bathrooms, air-conditioner units, elevation of ceilings in the halls, studio, the control room, main front office area, lunch room, rest area for musicians, and our private office. We discussed each area very carefully. We OK'd and initialed every page; from here on out there could be no changes at all. We had chosen Jim Lumsden, who was Ben and Jean's decorator, to choose the furniture and colors for the front and private office only. We all agreed that any changes, within reason, were OK; but that any major ones would be over and above and would be charged accordingly.

We all agreed and felt that we had negotiated a great deal for Group IV Recording's building with the owner, who was really a proud old Hollywood man, Mr. Harlan Palmer.

It would be a five-year lease with a buyout at the end of five years for $172,000. Harlan Palmer was a great businessman, an honest one, who was very helpful and informative and very eager to help with anything we needed. The fact that he knew Hollywood and had done business here for years was a plus for us. I could call him at a moment's notice, and he would have an answer for me; no hesitations at all. It helped that he knew everyone in town—it was a plus for us.

We had a meeting in an existing office on the north side of the building, way in the back, and it was apparent that we needed security. We needed to keep things very private; no one was to know I was involved in this project. We also noticed that we needed to secure all the windows in the front of the building; as the area of the loading docks was wide open and could be subject to burglars.

Roy Richardson had suggested a couple of masons he knew in Carson who worked for Caltrans. They were great at masonry work and knew what was needed. When we met with them, I told them I wanted to cover the windows in the front of the building. I suggested something in the form of little boxes with weeping mortar to match the existing bricks so that we could still get some light from outside. They were really great about it and understood what I meant ,so I hired them on the spot. I had them remove two industrial fans and block their openings from what would eventually become our private office.

I was informed that materials for the builders would be delivered on a daily basis, so we gave Roy a full-time job as our security guard. I requested that he keep a log detailing all activity in the building. I was very specific; I wanted to know who came by the length of their stay, and the purpose of their business. No one at all was to be excluded.

When we were confronted by anyone about a studio, my answer to them would be, "I don't know." It was not the time to admit anything. We really had nothing to show; we hadn't begun any construction. If I admitted to anyone that I was building a studio, as I've mentioned earlier, it would jeopardize all of our scheduling because now, we would be viewed as competitors, and the last thing we needed was to have any of our sessions canceled by any studio. We had a few shows to record and deliver in a timely manner, and all of them had a deadline. We could not afford to miss those schedules, so I had to make sure that no word would not leak out.

I would check Roy's log on a daily basis to make sure that I was aware of anything that was going on in the building. He was doing his job thoroughly; he never missed a beat. I was very happy that he became the man for the job. Roy was really good; he really took it seriously.

3M, our local audio tape dealer, when they got wind of a new studio being built in the Hollywood area, immediately sent their rep to check it out. It was becoming very hard keeping it quiet, but nevertheless I tried as hard as I could to keep my name out of the mix and at the same time drumming up business and getting new clients ready for our opening, which was a must. This became one of my biggest hurdles, but I knew deep in my heart that in the long run it would all work out.

Time passed, and finally, I decided that it was time to let the word get out, and I proceeded to finally admit to a few people that the rumors were true. I could not believe how well most people took it. They were very excited and thrilled for me and stated that they could not wait for the opening to use our studio and, I welcomed all the praise.

We were at Sunwest Studios recording an episode of "The Brady Bunch Hour." Melanie, who was doing a guest appearance on the show, was down the hall with her manager, Artie Ripp, who I had known for some time. I went over and spoke with both of them. I was very cordial and invited her to the studio opening party. I told her that I would love to add her name to the invitation list; Melanie agreed and said yes. I thought it would not hurt; it would be impressive to have her there; it would be good to have as many recording artists as possible. Melanie was very popular; she had her biggest American hit: "Brand New Key," on the neighborhood label, which most people would often refer to as "The Roller Skate Song." My feeling was that it would be a nice touch to have her attend. Both she and Artie knew I was a good friend of Don Costa, which for me was a great calling card. I had many encounters just like this, so whenever possible I would invite various guess and, being very careful how I would approach them, I didn't want to come off too pushy. It had to be done in a friendly and courteous manner.

The very first sign of any construction came on Monday morning, December 13, 1976, when all of a sudden, a laborer, a tall black man in coveralls, showed up without any notice at all and just started taking down the acoustical ceiling material and piling it in the center of the room. I called Bernie, and he told me that it was one of Rudy's guys; not to worry, and that permits would be issued soon. Bernie was playing a game; there was no doubt in my mind he was doing very little and was trying to mask it as if there was a lot going on. Perhaps in his mind, he thought he would be getting away with it; the man always had a story; he was a salesman. He was never on site with Rudy Brewer, maybe once, but all his dealings as far as I could tell were on the phone.

I noticed that rolls of insulation and lumber were now being delivered, and finally, to our surprise, workers showed up to cut the floors for cable runs. The following day, Tuesday December 14, 1976, more workers showed up again and this time they started framing. The teamwork of these carpenters was amazing. We had been waiting for the permits to be pulled for some time; it had become very frustrating. We could never get a straight answer from Bernie, so I didn't know if all this was just for show. But all of this started a bit of excitement. The following Monday morning, December 20, 1976, when I came into the building, there was no activity at all; it was very quiet. I didn't see Rudy Brewer or any of his crew—they were nowhere to be found.

I went to my office and called Bernie, and he responded with one of his favorite lines, which he became known for, "I'll look into it." This bothered me to no end, but I was being nice; I didn't want problems. I had no idea what was happening, and nor did anyone else. I knew that Bernie himself had no clue at all. I made a note of this situation on my calendar, and as the day when on I also witnessed one of Rudy's helpers drive up in a small pickup truck, he loaded some of the insulation stored in our building onto his pickup truck and drove off. I was tempted to stop him, but I promised myself I would be cool; after all this was Bernie's job, not mine.

We were to find out later, to our surprise, that Rudy Brewer was on another job. In addition to building our room, he was also working elsewhere since he was not being paid in a timely manner. He was using whatever time and resources he could get his hands on, and unfortunately, our materials had become part of it. Bernie was hardly around; I was constantly calling him and again his favorite answer was, "I'll look into it." I didn't want to rock the boat, but I must admit it was getting to me. I was really annoyed with Bernie, but I needed to stay calm in order to have this project finished. I couldn't fault Rudy Brewer; he had a living to make and building studios was his business. I understood it fully; why should Rudy Brewer refuse any work? I wouldn't if I wasn't being paid.

Things were now surfacing way out in the open; everything was beginning to make sense. It became obvious to everyone, not just me, that Bernie Ross, aka: Dave Michaels, was not meeting the payment schedules. Brewer told him he would not do any work till he was brought up to date. I confronted Bernie. I asked him if there was any truth to this, which he obviously denied, and now we were spending hours going over figures. Bernie had been shuffling monies around; the delays came from his failure to be straight with everyone. It was obvious that Studio Maintenance didn't have sufficient funds and Bernie Ross, instead of coming clean, tried to say that additions to the project had caused all the delays. These were not changes, we were sticking to the letter; they were things which we had all agreed to and had been initialed by all parties on the contract way before any work had begun.

He claimed that the air conditioning units had to be increased from what the plans called for, and that the ceiling heights specified in the plans had been changed, which again we had all agreed to, initialed and signed prior to any construction as per his request. How could they add additional materials to the project? I had personally spoken with the air conditioning contractor, and he told me that they had installed what was on the plans; they had not changed from day one. I was very angry. How could this guy say all this and make all these claims? I wanted to hurt this guy. I said to Phil Diamond I should drop a dime on him; his response was just, "Hang on. Your career and family are worth more than him."

We had a meeting with our attorney Ben Breitman, and Bernie's attorney Moses Luna, who came on very strong at this meeting, claiming that we were not meeting our obligations as per the contract, which we had all signed, and that his client had every right to shut the project down. Ben Breitman became unglued. He advised Moses Luna that we were within our rights; that his client had received a considerable amount of money and that if it was a lawsuit they wanted, we were willing and able. Given the chain of events we would prevail in any court. At this point his attorney backed off and the meeting continued. Bernie agreed to our demands. The work schedule would continue without fail, and the meeting ended.

When the meeting was over, Dennis and I sat in my car across the street from Ben Breitman's office and we talked for the longest time. I could not believe what I was hearing from him. He was convinced that we needed to keep everyone away from Bernie. I disagreed with him. I said, if anything, this is when we all needed to keep an eye on him. I told him that I was not comfortable with the chain of events and what really scared me was the fact that Studio Maintenance Service was storing our equipment in Bernie's garage. That all the equipment should be delivered to our building, and all the wiring and harnesses be done on our premises; this would allow us to keep an eye on Studio Maintenance's crew, as well as all the equipment that we had paid for. I really wanted to hurt this man, but Phil kept me calm as much as he could. It was really hard for me, but I remained calm. Bernie's crew didn't really do much; they showed up whenever it pleased them and would never answer any questions. We were always directed to speak to Bernie, who was never around or had an honest answer.

We tried to solve the situation, but it was obvious that we were dealing with a lunatic who was now holding our Trident Recording A Console for ransom. We eventually decided to give Bernie more money because he was holding back payments to Rudy Brewer; we needed Rudy to keep working, as well as Bernie's crew. We had another meeting, and I pointed out to everyone, "We need to keep Bernie Ross happy; this, no doubt, is going to turn into a big lawsuit." I felt very confident about our position; we had all the needed documentation from day one: who had come inside this building, at what time, for what purpose, length of time, name of their company, and what work they performed. I had photos taken at every stage of construction, etc.

I had asked Bernie at this point if the console had been shipped and he said no. I called the manufacturer in London, and they confirmed that it had. I was really curious, so I asked my sister in-law's husband, Lytton Duffus, who worked for customs, if it was at all possible for him to check it out for us. I gave him the shipper's number, and he confirmed that there was in fact a bill of lading. I found out the console was being held at LAX by customs, and that it would only be a matter of time before it would be released to Studio Maintenance.

Bernie, in order to extort more money, kept saying the console had not been shipped. It was very apparent that Bernie was going to hold the console for ransom again; he wanted more money; it was the last card he held. He had two key men working for him, but they were just condescending slaves; you could never get a straight answer from them. I felt very confident with all the documentation; it would strongly support us for any given lawsuit Bernie might dream of because he, on many occasions, claimed he would sue us. I said, "Let him. Let's wait till the console is in the building. I will personally throw them out of the building; let's just remain calm, people. Be kind. Don't let him intimidate you."

I have been very cool, and don't think for one minute that it hasn't been hard for me. We sat down with Gary Fradkin, who was very well aware of what was going on. I explained what I was planning. I said, "Gary, it's your show. I'm counting on you to do the install. It's your baby now." I always felt very confident with Gary. He knew just as much as Bernie Ross's guys, if not more, and unfortunately, he had to take a back seat to these idiots. And I, to this day, blame Dennis Sands for that decision. I didn't want these idiots involved in our project. I had sensed trouble from day one. We were all afraid of a lawsuit, but it was impossible; we were dealing with an egomaniac. The only ones that had anything to lose were the doctor, his mother and me. Dennis didn't have a dime to his name. We, on the other hand; we had our families and homes to protect. We needed the console, so eventually we caved in and gave Bernie more money; enough to keep him happy. I reiterated, "Stay calm people. It will all be over soon. We're going to get this mother fucker, one way or the other."

The console was finally delivered to the building on Friday, March 4, 1977. Everyone was very excited, and it was all hands-on deck. There was Gary at one end, Dennis, Roy, Paul Aronoff, and me, along with some of the workers. The glass in the control room had yet to be installed and workers were framing, so before any other work was done, we uncrated the console and we got a forklift in order to put this very fragile piece in the control room, through the frame where the glass would eventually be installed. We had to be extremely careful because of the danger of possibly damaging the console; and yet it was a very exciting moment for us. I have pictures, which I had taken during this whole charade, of everyone in awe; the whole crew just drooling over the console. These were later entered into evidence at our civil trial, on August 10, 1983.

I had earlier on, before any major construction started, invited Larry Pike, a well-known photographer I had met years ago at TTG while I was recording The Dean Martin Show, and asked him if he would come by and take pictures of every phase of all the studio construction, and date them. I knew, deep in my heart, that they would later play a big part; little did I know at the time that it would be in court.

There were various things I needed Bernie's crew to finish since we had already paid for them: the harness on the console for the microphone inputs and outputs; as well as the Dolby triggering for the 24-tracks. At this point there was no need to show our cards; we had our console in place. On Monday April 25, 1977, as always, I arrived early; all the carpeting and parquet flooring in the studio had been completed, and the modules in the ceiling had now been installed. All we needed to do now was check all the equipment and tune the room; we were pretty close; this was the day of reckoning.

I walked into the control room as usual, there was not too much activity going on. Bernie's crew, as always, were working at a snail's pace, I'm sure per Bernie's orders. There were some frail wires on the floor from the harness that had to be made, but again, as usual, this was another one of their projects and they intentionally made sure that it wasn't completed too quickly, which was an ongoing problem with Bernie and his crew. I asked Brian, who was one of Bernie's men, "Where's your boss? Is he coming down?" He said he was home, and he had no idea if he was coming to Hollywood. I was really looking for a fight, but fortunately for them it didn't come to pass. I made my final announcement right there, looking everyone straight in their eyes. I was ready for anything; I told his men, "Look guys. The show is over. Pack your tools and leave the premises immediately." They asked me what the problem was, and I answered, "I'm looking at it. Get out of my sight, and if you know what's good for you, don't bother to return."

When I was done, I walked over to Rudy Brewer, who was by the rear loading dock waiting for a check, and I told him the game was over; there would be no more money for anyone and that if it pleased him, we would also see him in court, we have had it. I was hot and I guess it showed, because no one wanted to take me on. But they knew they were wrong, even my partners stayed out of my way, the only ones that I knew had my back were Gary Fradkin and Roy Richardson. They hung in there watching every move, and within minutes I received a call from Bernie asking me what was going on. I responded by telling him, "The party's over my friend. I will see you in court." And I hung up on him.

I remembered what my old friend the late Chris Stone said to me, "Angel, you got to hit them hard." He had also used Rudy Brewer on a project and had his own set of problems. There was nothing else for Bernie to say; the wrong thing said and I would've gone to his house and who knows what might have happened. Gary was Johnny on the spot. As soon as we got rid of all the rats, he was right on top of everything, and it took him very little time to install everything without failure. Everything was working just fine now; all that we needed was to test the console as well as the studio.

NO END IN SIGHT

I called my friend Ray Jackson, an arranger and trombone player whom I had worked with for years. I asked him a favor: I wanted to know if he wanted to do a session in our studio. There would not be any charge at all. Without any hesitation he said yes. I blocked the whole evening out and scheduled the session. I will always be indebted to Ray; he was there for me as soon as we finished talking. He booked musicians from all over town. He brought musicians who had played with the Watts 103rd Street Band, Earth Wind and Fire, singers, songwriters, all familiar faces. They all came out to help me out, and it did help; this was our first session in the studio, and it was fantastic, the room sounded great. We had to test all the gear before we went public. This was very important, and with the help of these guys, we were able to proceed at our own pace. It was a great evening and I felt blessed, grateful and privileged having all these friends and great players come out for me. God bless them all.

It was time to move on now. I had to secure a studio manager that could work hand in hand with me. I knew I needed the help since I was going to be extremely busy most of the day securing more work for the studio. I needed someone I could trust, who could also do sales and was knowledgeable of the studio business. I started looking around town and asking everyone I knew for suggestions. This was an important position that needed to be filled. Eric Miller recommended the traffic manager that worked down the street at The Sound Factory, which was a very busy place. After a few meetings with her I decided to hire her. Kim Paladino became our studio manager. She had studio experience, was well liked and well respected in the music business. I just felt she could become a great asset to our studio, and as it turned out she ended up spending more time with us than was expected, a great worker. I didn't have to hold her hand. Immediately she started to work on our press releases and putting together our open house invitations.

We had scheduled our opening party for Thursday May12, 1977; and what really surprised me was that Kim was bringing people in to see the studio, people that I hadn't even thought would be approachable. She was really good, there was nothing this woman couldn't do. What a gem! The constant bickering and pressure of dealing with Bernie was over and our studio was ready for business. Both Kim and I were working and spending numerous hours trying to come up with an idea for our open house party, so after numerous meetings and late hours, Kim came up with some verbiage for our invitation that we all felt was very presentable and unique for our opening party. She came up with something that stuck and made perfect sense. I, to this day, personally give her credit for what she came up with. She wrote what, to this day, I thought was a brilliant quote; and I know it took a lot of time. With so little time to spare she came up with the following:

"Great expectations. There are some things that are expected of a first-rate recording studio in Los Angeles: Technically Precise State-of-the-Art equipment that is Fastidiously maintained. A staff of talented professionals who understand that a studio provides a vital service with the attitude that nothing is impossible. This is expected. And then there's the unexpected. Group IV Recording."

This became part of our invitation, which we carefully inserted into paper tubes and mailed out to all prospective clients whom we wanted to attend our opening party. We were finally ready for business; we threw an amazing party with a great caterer. We had a nice pen, which had our logo imprinted on, as a giveaway to everyone in attendance. Our opening reception brought people from all over town. Anyone who was anyone in town showed up to our party. Artists from various labels: Capitol Records, Columbia Film and TV, Lorimar Pictures, MCA Records, Motown Records, Warner Brothers Records, Universal, Disney Film and TV. Composers, arrangers, producers, heads of music departments, engineers, even Chaka Khan showed along with my all-time friend and producer Bob Monaco. It was a night that I will always remember as well as a sigh of relief because we were rid of Bernie Ross.

I had hired LAPD off duty officers as security that evening; just in case anything went wrong. And believe it or not, during the early part of the evening a couple of Bernie Ross's guys had the nerve to show up uninvited. It gave me great pleasure to have them escorted off the premises. I knew it would get back to Bernie, but I was not playing; everything else that evening did go smoothly, the food, the guests and entertainment, it was a great party and it was unforgettable.

Time passes and we started enjoying a lot of sessions from new clients, and everyone's talents were tested. A new studio has a lot to prove. We were definitely under that microscope, but we loved every minute of it. The only thing that was now becoming very annoying was Ben Eisenstein constantly putting us down, claiming he was working his ass off having to secure cash. I felt that was his job. After all, he had claimed he had more experience in business than we did. That might've been correct in his mind, but when it came to the music business, I did not face any competition from any of my partners. I didn't see why he was so upset, but it was a constant battle.

His wife, Jeanne, who we had to take under duress as our bookkeeper, whenever a receipt was turned in by anyone for a legitimate expense, she'd claimed that we were nickel-and-diming the studio. She even had issues with Kim for such minor things as a Tampax dispenser in the ladies' room. I had always hoped that we, as a group, would stay on course and see the studio succeed, but again greed was slowly entering the picture.

Ben Eisenstein, who did not have a clue about the music business, was very eager to take money out of the studio. All he talked about was that he wanted to invest in an avocado farm, and claimed there was money to be made in California Avocados. I agreed with him, but my focus was the studio business. Ben on the other hand kept bringing this subject up quite often. I never thought much about it because all my energy and time was geared towards the success of the studio. That's where my interest laid, not to mention I had a staff to sell in order for the studio to succeed. I had no other interest, but little did I imagine that Ben would put so much pressure on us I guess he wanted us to join forces with him, but again my interest and loyalty lay solely with our studio. As I recall one day, it's very early in the morning, I believe it was midweek, we received a call from him. He wanted both Dennis and I on a conference call. When we finally came online, Ben, with his nervous cough, started by saying he wanted to withdraw $30,000 dollars; he was very direct and demanded it. I don't know what commitments he had made, but he seemed desperate. He really expected to take money whenever it suited him. I became the bad guy, because I was not about to let anyone do that, He thought he could do whatever he wanted, this became very apparent by his demand, and If I was to allow this to happen the studio would definitely suffer. We were busy and making some money, but he was getting ahead of himself. We had only been open a short time, and we were barely surviving since we were undercapitalized, which didn't help. After much conversation, Dennis and I both just sat there looking at each other back and forth. This was very odd for Dennis; this was his uncle, and he never had to stand up to him. I guess they all looked up to him, but this was business and I felt it should be conducted as a business. I responded by saying that as president of the corporation I could not let this happen; the answer is no! There was dead silence; you could hear a pin drop; He suddenly became very agitated and angry. He said, "Well, I guess I'm going to have to sue you both." I responded by saying, "You do what you have to do Ben, but the answer again is no; the company cannot afford it." What followed was a chain of events that certainly had no merit or truth to them; his son went crying to Dennis's mom, saying they were going to lose everything. Jeanne came in the following day with a record from Johnny Paycheck, "Take this job and shove it," played it, and announced she was quitting. This made everyone very happy; it was not a great loss. Ben claimed I had locked him out, which was not true; everyone had a story not valid nor an inch of truth to it. He was now soliciting anyone who would listen to him; he was all over the place, trying to sell his part ownership to anyone who would listen to him. I knew he was desperate. Cherokee Studios came into play I have no idea how he came in contact with some of these people; he even solicited a producer I knew, Jerry Goldstein, who arranged to meet with us at the studio. I remember Jerry asking me, "What do you want to do, run the studio?" What did I have in mind? I really couldn't answer him; I was being pushed and I didn't like it. I had a lot to lose; my home was on the line. Dennis didn't really contribute much at any of these meetings. He didn't know any of them and they didn't have a clue who he was. All questions were directed at me. I really didn't trust any of these potential buyers; my home, my job and savings were at stake.

Ben had also solicited Bob Liften from New York City, and how he made that contact, to this day, was beyond me. Bob Liften had his own studio in New York City. When we met, his only interest was how to cut down the crew on film recording sessions. This showed me where his interest was and it was definitely not in Group IV Recording; and I doubt that he had any money. We did not show much interest to anyone; or at least I didn't. If they bought his stock in the company, we would still be the majority stockholders. In the end the sale never came to pass. So much for his so-called knowledge of business. Time did fly by. He never filed the lawsuit; it was just a charade. We continued working, and after many meetings and negotiation attempts, thanks again to Phil, we found out that Ben had lied. He did not put up his own personal money as he always claimed. What he really did was lease the equipment then turn around and lease it to the corporation under a leasing company he had formed. He was getting all the tax breaks—very self-serving. He finally agreed on a deal that Phil Diamond put together. Ben at this point was no longer talking to any of us; which was OK by me, it wasn't a great loss. I stayed on course soliciting more business for the studio, doing some sessions, selling Dennis to new clients and dealing with the daily chores of the studio.

Time just flew by, and after a few long and stressful years, Bernie Ross finally surfaced, and we were served court papers. We were to appear in Superior Court in Van Nuys. Oh well, we knew this day was coming sooner or later and I was prepared for this conniving crook. On February 16 and 17, 1983, we had our first arbitration in hopes of resolving all differences, which in my heart I knew would not happen. But it was a sign of good faith, which was recommended by the court before we went to trial. Bernie showed up, as always very confident of himself, with his lawyer, who proceeded to read us our rights. I felt that it was just a replay of days past and again Ben Breitman was annoyed with the accusations. I knew it was a waste of everyone's time; it was a replay of prior meetings. The meeting ended very quickly, and everyone went their own way. There was no way we would come to any decision; this was going to court. I knew this before we had arrived, we were dealing with a man who had such arrogance and an ego that was so big you could not reason with or do anything—he wanted it his way. Bernie wouldn't stay long with his attorney, Moses Luna, he fired him. I gathered he didn't agree with his beliefs and, before we knew it, we were in Beverly Hills for our first deposition at the offices of his new attorney, a Mr. Grush.

These were long, grueling, and exhausting hours. The depositions just went on; and trying to schedule everything around our business did become very exhausting. I was constantly drilled by my partners after a long day of dealing with all the session bookings and attending the depositions for the trial. I had to recount everything that was asked or said, word per word. It was very tiresome, but important. First, I was questioned at the attorneys, and now here we were at the office doing the same thing; it was a real pain in the ass, but I understood it. I would've done the same to them. Ben Breitman, to our surprise had decided to resign; he didn't feel he was that strong for the case. He claimed he was not a litigating attorney and would not be that useful or effective to our case; even though he felt we did in fact have a strong case.

Bernie Ross, to no one's surprise, switched attorneys again, and now the process would have to start all over. He kept on switching attorneys at the drop of a hat if they didn't agree with him; or maybe they felt he didn't have a strong case. Where he was getting all the money from, who knew? But I'm sure it was very expensive. This time it was a new attorney who was located in the valley, a Mr. Lipschutz at the offices of Tabor & Lipschutz in Van Nuys. The switching, at times, worked in our favor, because in the time it took the new attorney to be up to speed, we were able to take care of the studio and all of our business. We could always say within reason that we needed more time because of their changes, and they had no other choice but to buy into it. Phil Diamond had recommended earlier that since Ben Breitman wanted to resign, we should retain the services of another attorney, Sherman Lentz. I loved it since I was the one spending a lot of the time with all the attorneys at their offices. They were close to my house on Canoga Avenue in Woodland Hills. We had a few meetings and depositions at Sherman Lentz's office, who also felt we had a strong case, and as always, I would be the one to spend a lot of time with Sherman, the lead attorney. We would go out to dinner with our wives. It was, so I thought, a good relationship, but then things took a turn that was really a letdown, and it confirmed my belief that you can't trust all attorneys. My 1970 Pontiac station wagon had finally died on me, and Phil Diamond said, "Why don't you get a new Mercedes Benz?"

I replied, "I can't afford that."

He said, "Your banker will finance it. Since the company won't lease you a car, give it a shot; it'll work." Phil was really referring to the fact that I was going all over the place representing the studio in an old, dilapidated auto, a 1970 Pontiac station wagon, and the fact that it didn't look good for business. I really didn't care; it was the furthest thing on my mind. I'd had this wagon for years. I'd been just about every place with my wagon. I understood Phil but I was OK with it.

Whenever we had any meetings, and this subject came up, everyone didn't really care; the focus was always on keeping the studio booked.

I finally took his advice; we went across the street to the dealer. After looking around, I drove out in a new 300D turbo Diesel Mercedes. I knew I would struggle with some of the payments, but I felt good about it since it was my own doing, and the company was not footing the bill. Monday morning, both Sherman and I, as usual, had an early breakfast meeting at Jerry's Deli. I was so excited, after our meeting I asked Sherman to come outside and see my new car.

When the weekend came, I was taken by complete surprise. There was a knock on my door and a woman stood there carrying a bunch of papers. I was served, Sherman Lentz was suing me for his bill. He sued me personally because he thought we were trying to avoid his bill, and how could I afford a new car. He didn't even have the decency to talk to me about it. I was really surprised by his actions. I went to the office Monday, wrote him a check and interviewed a new attorney. Shame on that maggot, Sherman, how presumptuous of him. I had personally taken out the loan in my name and would personally be making all payments; the studio could not afford it. The studio would not be making any of the payments and never did. It just go to show you.

We decided to retain the services of Robert Young, another attorney, a young fella from Brown University. A very likeable guy and who seemed to understand our frustration with this lunatic that we had been dealing with all this time. Phil Diamond had dropped by. We were in my office going over various documents for the trial. He asked me who was the insurance company at the time all this happened, and I said Allstate Insurance. He asked to see the policy. I went to my file cabinet, pulled out the policy and handed it to him. He started to examine it. After carefully going over it he turned around and said, "I think they're on the hook for the lawsuit."

Phil proceeded to explain to me that business interruption insurance, although it was very expensive, was in our favor. It was really the best thing that Ben had done for us. This could be a saving grace. We called our insurance agent, and sure enough they were on the hook. They immediately came to see us. They looked at all the documents we had, at which point they decided to appoint their own litigating attorney to the case, a Mr. King, who knew our business inside out; he had handled more litigations than you could imagine.

We met with Mr. King, and on our first meeting he got the ball rolling. He said, "There won't be any more depositions; we're going straight to trial." I felt very confident this was what we needed. Mr. King was very positive and seemed very capable and confident about our case. He was a man that was all business and understood what Bernie was trying, or had tried to do all along.

The weekend prior to our court day, as per everyone's suggestion, I went to Montgomery Ward's and bought myself a new set of very conservative clothes. I also shaved my beard at the suggestion of Phil Diamond and Bob Young so that I would not look that threatening to the jury. So, after much preparation, here we were in August 1983 at Van Nuys Superior Court – Department C, Room 530, with Judge Den Kauffman presiding along with Allstate's attorneys Mr. Jeffrey King and our corporate attorney Bob Young. We were ready and as soon as I got off the elevator, I was approached by Allstate's legal counsel; they wanted my permission to make Bernie Ross an offer. "I said OK, but I doubt he will accept it." They went to the other side of the corridor and made him their offer of $75,000.00. Bernie, always thinking the world owed him something, and finding that now, since we were covered by insurance he could get more money, became greedy and said he wanted $150,000.00. When they came back to me with the response, I said, "I'm not surprised. Tell him I'll see him inside the courtroom."

Bob Young and Mr. King decided on who should take lead handling the case during the proceedings. Mr. King decided he would take the lead and Bob Young was more than comfortable with the idea; he felt that since Mr. King had more experience with litigation it was a good decision. We spent one day selecting a jury panel and then the prosecution took their turn. The trial started, there were various witnesses that Bernie brought to court, but after my first day on the witness stand Allstate felt very confident that we had him. They liked my testimony on the stand and said I should just be myself; that I was doing just fine. They seemed very confident with everything at this stage of the game. It was their money.

Those were very long days for me, since I was also constantly in touch with Kim and our clients, and also leaving Van Nuys after a day in court, returning to Hollywood to check things at the studio. Bernie Ross was overly confident that he would win, although he was now on his fourth attorney. He was having a ball. He felt he had us. He'd walk by us in the hallway with his arm around his wife just laughing, with the biggest smirk you ever saw. You could see right through the man; he was greasy and sleazy looking, and although he was wearing a suit and tie, you could tell he didn't belong in it. Something just didn't look right.

There were a lot of funny things happening during this trial, but somehow, I knew in my heart and gut that we would prevail. But again, you never really know what could happen. I had nothing to hide, although Bernie was trying to portrait me as a gangster from New York City. I had to be very careful; that's another reason why I shaved and got into some very low-key attire. I didn't want the jury or anyone to start drawing the wrong conclusions.

I wanted my two youngest kids to experience this, so I asked my wife Cookie, who had to put up with all this drama, if she would bring them to court. It was early morning, and the judge was in a really bad mood and was snapping at both attorneys. I was on the stand, and then we witnessed one of the most memorable and funniest things to ever happen during the trial. My daughter Denise, who was in the audience, suddenly dropped something which made a loud noise in the courtroom.

The shock brought everyone to attention in the room; especially the Judge, who again was not a happy camper. When he heard the noise he raised his head, looked around the room and said very loud and firm, "What the hell was that?"

My little girl answered, "I dropped my Tic-Tacs."

The judge responded in a kind way he said. "You can pick them up, go ahead dear..." This brought lots of chuckles and relieved some of the tension in the courtroom.

The trial continued and Bernie produced several witnesses who were not there of their own accord. I understood it and I didn't hold it against them. One of them was the builder,

Rudy Brewer, whom our first attorney Ben Breitman had said we should cut loose because he felt he had no merit to the case; but during the trial Mr. King said we should've never let him go. He had another witness, the most surprising one of all, Ami Hadani. I was shocked to see him, but he was there as a character witness; he knew nothing about the studio. I could sense Ami's discomfort, but I knew some deal was made here; maybe Bernie offered him equipment, who knew. Mr. King very carefully asked him a few questions. They were simple ones. He asked him why Bernie would do what he did, and his answer was, when you hire a pro you hire a pro, that was it. Mr. King said, "Your honor, this witness has no bearing on this case. I would like to dismiss him." At which point the judge said, "The witness is dismissed."

Bernie had shown up in court with charts, big charts with all kinds of figures and dates that made no sense and contradicted all his notes. They only made sense to him, and him alone. The question we were all waiting for, especially me, was now being asked by Mr. King; where he asked Mr. Michaels, "Have you ever gone by another name?" I could see Bernie turn ash white and, after moving around in his chair very uncomfortably.

The judge said, "Please answer the question."

He replied, "Yes."

Mr. King then asked, "And what was your previous name or alias?"

He answered, "Bernie Ross."

Mr. King asked, "Why did you change your name?"

He claimed he'd filed for bankruptcy and wanted to start a new life, so he changed his name to David Michaels and moved to California. This turned many heads in the courtroom and did not sit well with the jury; especially all the women.

Mr. King was a brilliant attorney; I would hate to go against him. He had now shown the jury what we had to deal with, and Bernie for what he really was, a fraud. His attorney,

Mr. Lipschutz, asked the judge for a recess. He said he felt very dizzy with some queasiness. Perhaps it was what he had for lunch. The judge called a one-hour recess. We resumed after an hour, but the questions just kept coming. Mr. King was on a roll, he was relentless, and Bernie just kept confusing everyone; it was really hilarious.

The studio was functioning very well and fortunately for us any sessions that we were booked on happened during the evening, so that part was working for us. I held my breath, hoping it would remain this way, at least until the trial was over; but who knew. I figured should any sessions be booked that required Dennis or I during the daytime; one of us would remain in the courtroom. At least one of us had to be here, and that person would be me. This was important, we were being sued by this maniac to the tune of $6,000,000. He wanted our blood. In his mind he figured he'd get the entire studio, as well as everything else; the man was out there with complete tunnel vision.

The final day of the trial and now closing arguments from both sides. It was the end of the day and everyone was exhausted. The judge gave his instructions to the jury; they would begin deliberation the following morning. We left the courtroom and I headed for Hollywood to check things at the studio, and then went home. I was up all night. Who could sleep? So many things ran through my mind, way too many scenarios.

The following morning, we went inside the courtroom. The judge asked the jury if they were ready to begin deliberation; they said yes, and he sent them away to their room. We headed to the cafeteria for coffee; we sat there wondering how long the jury would take. It was a crapshoot; it could take a couple of days, who knew? Everyone was nervous, you could hear it in our voices. All the attorneys had their own opinions as to how long it would take. I had figured this was going to take forever. I bought some coffee and sat down; I was really nervous. I couldn't eat, my stomach was tied in knots, and as I sat there, I kept thinking we'd come a long way, and now the possibility of losing my home, as well as the studio, was really on my mind.

We were not in the cafeteria that long when we were called to the courtroom. I became very nervous; why so quick? We took the elevator up and quickly entered the courtroom and sat down, awaiting the judge. Bob Young figured maybe the jury had a question, but before you knew it, the judge entered the court-room, and the jury was called into the courtroom. I watched as they walked in single file, one by one and took a seat. Then the judge addressed the jury with the words that I have heard so many times, mostly on the screen. When your part of it, and it's your turn, it sure has a different sound.

"Members of the jury, have you reached a verdict?"

Before I knew it, the foremen stood up and said, "We have your honor."

I was scared. There was no going back for anyone. It was all up to what these twelve jurors have decided. What if they believed Bernie? What next? My mind was racing a mile a minute, and then the moment of truth, the verdict was read, and each juror was called one by one. I don't remember anything else, all I remember was our attorney Bob Young saying loudly, "We won, we won."

So, on August 12, 1983, the final analysis. Bernie Ross, Aka: David Michaels, lost 12-0 on a jury trial. I was ecstatic. I didn't think it would turn out this way; we had prevailed in a court of law. I thank God we had been vindicated; we had finally gotten rid of this idiot. I shook hands with Mr. King. He had done a fantastic job for us, and as far as I was concerned, he was by far the best attorney we had ever had Very relaxed, the man was a real professional that from day one understood what we were up against.

Phil Diamond was not present; he and Dennis had a tiff going on after Phil negotiated the buyout deal with Ben. He wanted to reduce Phil's fees, which was very typical of him; again, changing the deal. He also had other matters to take care of; he had his accounting firm to run. I called him, gave him the good news and thanked him for all his help.

I had decided to take all the jurors out for drinks at a bar on Van Nuys Blvd, called Otto's Pig. during the celebration some jurors said they wished we had asked for more money; one even went as far as saying she was hoping I had looked her way so she could give me a sign. I'm glad I didn't, that could have really opened up a can of worms. Everyone on our side walked out with a sigh of relief. It was over.

Ben Eisenstein's grievances were settled, so on the same day, I handed him a check for $180,000. He would no longer be a part of Group IV Recording. That was the last time I would ever see him; he was paid off right there in the hall of the courtroom.

We won a judgment that was not really big, but that's not what we were after. We just wanted what was rightfully ours, and the attorney fees to be paid by their side.

A few days later we received a call from Bernie's attorney. I wondered, "What's next?" He said Mr. Ross wanted to know if we would accept a note for payments on the amount due. I said I'd like to think about it. I wanted to make him sweat it out. The following week I responded. I told him I would, but to add insult to injury, I said, "Yes, as long as his wife also signs on the dotted line." So now it was business as usual for Group IV Recording. We were finally back on track. From here on out we wouldn't have to deal with Bernie Ross or any of his cronies.

I had a lot of friends that I had known for years who were very helpful. They loved the studio, so it was not a problem booking time for their companies. These were great contractors, arrangers, engineers, and artists who started to use our studio. I, to this day, am very grateful and thankful to so many of them. Don Costa, Jack Elliott, Allyn Fergurson,

Billy Byers, Bill Hughes, Dave Fisher, Marty Berman, Marian (Dopey) Klein, Ben Barrett, Michael Feinstein, Jack Hunsaker from Paramount Music, Raul Perez from Columbia Pictures TV, Dick Berris from Lorimar, Ed Nasour from 20th Century, Billy Goldstein, Nat Kaproff, Johnny Fresco, Johnny Mandel, Pat Williams, Harry Loweskie—who later on brought Alan Silverstri to do the series "Chips," Herbie Hancock, Ralph Burns, Bill Conte, Earl Hagan, Steve & Eydie Gorme, Gary Smith, Dwight Hemion, Rita Scott, Peter Matz, Lee Decarlo, Hank Cicala, Don Hahn, Val Valentine, Bud Fenton, Ed Green; the list just kept on growing.

I had started to seek big paying clients. When we first started out, we were doing small sessions for record labels, then a few larger Variety shows; but now the list just kept on growing and we were on a roll. Kim was able to get Stanley Clarke to record his album at Group IV, but he wanted to bring his engineer. Very commonly it bothered my partner Dennis, a small ego problem but there was nothing either he or I could do about it. And since it was their call, we had to honor it, everyone else in town did; it was take it or leave it. We had no choice. We had to accommodate all outside engineers, or we would lose a considerable amount of business. There was no two ways about it, although outside engineers became a bone of contention. Dennis was not a happy camper with it. He wanted to be the man behind the console, but he had yet to pay his dues in the music industry, as we all had, but he was the new kid on the block. We didn't invent this; again, this was a common practice in town.

What about when we used other studios? We never ever received any flak from their staff. We we're always welcomed with open arms. One evening after a very long and exhausting day I decided to go home and have dinner with the family, which was rare for me. I usually stuck around until the last session was either on the way or over. I was sitting down having dinner with the family when the phone rang, which was not rare, it was either that or my beeper, I was on call and this was the life of a studio owner. I would always be getting calls at home. I knew I had a 24/7 job.

Whenever I assigned anyone to do a date (a recording session), I had to be around to please the client, because if they were not happy, and something went wrong, I would take the blame and I would have to take over; that was my guarantee. On this particular day, we had a guest engineer. The call was from Dennis, and he sounded frantic, saying, "You're not going to believe what's going on?"

My response was, "What is it?"

"Stanley's engineer, Ed Thacker, wants to shoot a 45 magnum in the studio."

At this point Dennis is all freaked out. I asked him, "Do you know why? Have you talked to Gary?"

"It's an effect they want for one of the tracks and we don't have an effects library."

To be really blunt I said, "Who gives a fuck? Ed is smart enough. He's not going to shoot that into the glass or anything major. Give the man some credit."

I could sense his resentment, since he really was not comfortable with outside engineers, which again made no sense at all. I said, "OK, hang on. I'll be right down." I don't know why or how my wife put up with all this; it was not the first time.

I drove to Hollywood really quickly and when I arrived, as I walked in, I was greeted by Roy. I went directly to Studio A. I spoke to Gary Fradkin and Ed Thacker briefly; it wasn't a big deal. They were using sandbags and cut the lead of the bullets in half and did the shooting in the rear of the building. After a few shots this seemed to work for them and, in the long run, everyone was pleased. It was illegal, and my concern was that the police would be called, but it never happened. Most importantly, Stanley Clarke was happy.

Whenever anything would go wrong, I was the first call. Fortunately, I was always able to solve the situation at hand. And believe me, there were many situations that came my way. But like I said, it came with the dinner. I was often called for the most ridiculous things. I regarded it my job, and as I would always say, "You took the gig." There were often situations which my partner could have resolved, but no one really knew him. It wasn't his fault, but he just wasn't that approachable. Things like running out of tape in the middle of the night. We had so many studios in the neighborhood that were happy to loan us a case of tape with no problem, but the call always came to me. I would make arrangements to have the tape replaced the very next morning by 3M or I would deliver it personally.

Group IV Recording was getting a good reputation, and we started to welcome a lot of new outside engineers, and with each came many demands, some awkward and some reasonable. When you own a recording studio, your aim is to please the client; and in the studio business you start with their engineers. Fortunately for me, being a well-known engineer, everyone on either coast knew me, which was a great calling card. I was now pushing Dennis, who had no credits, and a lot of folks didn't care for him. A few claimed he was not easy to work with, but I kept pushing.

What I realize was that I really needed to put him and our staff to work on high end projects. I asked for help from various friends, one being Mike Melvoin, whom I, as an engineer, had worked with at various studios. Michael understood the situation and said he'd be glad to do what he could. He managed to bring in Bud Fenton, who had a commercial agency called Grandscale, and they just happened to be doing TV commercials for "Flying Tiger Airlines." They agreed to use my engineer and staff, and I gave them a reduced rate, which worked for everyone. It was good business; Bud Fenton and I would form a friendship that would last to this day. I will always be more than grateful to Michael Melvoin for all his help, and for his continued help and patronage to Group IV Recording; as well as his support to me and my staff.

We began doing numerous music sessions, and word started spreading around town that our studio was a state-of-the-art facility, and that it was capable of handling any or all types of recording sessions, whether music for Film/TV, as well as music for records or variety shows. I made calls to all artist and record labels that I had worked with, and I managed to get lots of support. I kept hearing, "I wish you guys had 35mm projection, then I would book your studio all the time." I figured that maybe it would be possible; that we could do Film and TV music scoring during the daytime hours, and record sessions in the evenings. I was sure it would work. We had no other choice but to try it. I would give clients a good rate to record here, and as Norman Granz would always say, "Nothing but the very best."

I realized that we could not accommodate various clients; we only had the one room. We needed to expand and offer more capabilities that were in demand at the time. Our existing clients would not be able to handle the new rates we would have to charge in order to stay in business, and I knew we would lose some, but we had no other option; we could not continue this way. We needed to add new equipment; and with that came the reality that we needed to recoup the expense. The studio could no longer do sessions at the reduced rates we were charging; it was impossible. I started working on new approaches and soliciting new clientele that could support our expansion.

We had always talked about building another room, but the way we were going about things it wouldn't happen. I remember Val Valentine walking down the hall and saying to me, "With one room you stay busy, but you don't make any money. You need a second room and you need to offer more services." I decided to seek other means of generating income. The studio had to adapt to newer clients and their needs in order to succeed. I started doing research, reading the trades, talking to people that we knew in town who would be straight with us, and going to various trade shows. It was important for us to be seen at as many venues as possible. We joined numerous organizations; we needed the notoriety really badly in order for it to work; I was on a roll. I would not take no for an answer and would not take the advice of any of our clients lightly. We needed to stay focused, so we followed the advice of one of our clients, Brian Hickox from Filmways to the fullest; which meant learning to speak the language and be able to converse with all motion picture and TV composers, their music editors and producers it was important that we all spoke the same language.

I decided to look into Columbia College for film on LaBrea Avenue. The facility is not there anymore, but at the time, it was very close and convenient to the studio. This seemed like a great idea. I called and made various inquiries and finally I made an appointment for both Dennis and I. We went and enrolled; I explained to the dean that we were not really interested in the grades; we just wanted to learn the language. His response to us was instant. He said that he would have to grade us just like any other student; those were the rules. We would have to attend class and take their test, that was what was expected of all their registered students. I knew at this point that we had no choice, it was reasonable, and we would gladly deal with their rules. And besides, in the long run it was good for both of us, and although I had more experience, you never stop learning. I also felt that this would put us right up there with all the other film scoring studios in town; especially TTG. Their clients were the ones asking me personally to get in the film business and that they would support it.

I knew this was a good move for Group IV Recording. We would be able to speak to anyone about their projects at length. We attended all the classes; to me it was important for our new venture to succeed; this way we would be in tune with the motion picture and TV Industry. I had some experience in motion picture and TV shows, which went back to my earlier days at National Recording in New York City. But this was different, and definitely a newer approach for the studio. We spent hours talking to music editors of film about the pops on the film, start marks, scrubbing film, 35mm mag, frames, sprockets, all kinds of film processes and terms. I started spending a great deal of time with my old friend Marshall Leib; he and I had done a lot of sessions together at TTG in the early days when he worked for Liberty Records. Marshall was always holding a Pepsi can in the studio, he loved his Pepsi. He was a great guy who would often tell me some great stories, and they were not just war stories; he was very honest with me. He would often tell me about when he, Phil and Don Everly were in the Marines how they would just hang out.

Marshall would often say that when they were in the service, they did nothing, absolutely nothing. He was a bright guy who in no time at all had become a very knowledgeable motion picture and TV film producer. He had just finished working on the movie "Ode to Billy Joe" with a good friend of his Max Baer Jr. I found Marshall to be very helpful, he didn't care how much time he'd spend with me. We loved to hang, which is something no one does anymore. I loved the guy; he and I would spend hours discussing how to approach a film, Company. Marshall would tell me who it was worth spending time with, and who was responsible for various phases of the film production. We were good friends, and he took it upon himself to teach me a great deal of things. Marshall was great at it. He was also a great supporter and very dear to my heart, I will never forget him.

One day I was sitting in my office reading the trades when out of the blue I decided to call the offices of Irwin Allen Productions at the Warner Brothers lot and requested an appointment. They agreed to meet with us; I was blown away. So, I gathered some brochures with pictures of the studio for our meeting. The following morning, I was ready to go. When we arrived at their offices at the Warner lot, we were greeted very well. Their secretary asked us to take a seat, it would just be a minute. Here I was in Burbank, about to meet Irwin Allen, who was also a New Yorker from a different time, but never the less a very busy man, and we wanted some of his business. I wanted his business; that's how I approached him. The fact that I was from Brooklyn did help with our introduction. He was very cordial. I told him I wanted to do some of his films, and I knew we could do a great job; I was very confident. I knew all about him. I had studied his films and knew some of the music people who worked on his films. I had called his office cold to make this appointment. I was well aware that he was very busy, he was, after all, the most successful science fiction producer of the decade's fad for disaster films, and I felt and voiced that we could participate in whatever film he had coming up; and I wasn't shy about it. I was aware of his credits, which included one of my favorites: none other than the famous: "Voyage to the bottom of the Sea," "lost in Space," "The Time Tunnel," "Land Of The Giants," "The Swiss Family Robinson," "Code Red" and "The Towering Inferno."

The fact that we brought along a few of our impressive brochures helped. As soon as I showed him pictures of our studio, he immediately took out his calendar, and called his head guy, who was also impressed with what he was seeing. We spoke for a while about the size of the room and all of our equipment. He kept looking very carefully at the brochure, and he had a puzzled look. He asked, "Do you fellas have 35mm projection capabilities?" And that's when the whole meeting took a different turn. This was an essential part of the program for this client, as well as many others in town. I had fucked up. We needed to go back to the drawing board. I was embarrassed but well aware that one of the most important things we needed in order to forge ahead was 35mm film capabilities. We were missing the one tool that was very essential for a film scoring stage: a projection room; it was a must if we wanted to be successful in the Film Scoring Business.

Film scoring is not a business you can play with, we were

anxious yes, but not prepared. I should've known better. I knew from my days at TTG, as well as National Studios in New York City, and all the conversations I had with Marshall Leib, that music scoring is challenging and very demanding, a fast pace grueling business. You had to be prepared, if you weren't you could be out just as fast as you got in. I knew that if you didn't have the goods, and that meant equipment and well-trained personnel, you were out, no excuses. I could not wait to return to the studio.

When we returned, I immediately decided to make a call. I got on the phone and contacted Jeff Ward, who was a projectionist I knew and who, at the time, was still working for TTG my old stomping ground. Jeff had been involved in the installation of their 35mm film Projection System a few years earlier, and they were doing very well. They were the only independent studio in town doing scoring, and they stayed extremely busy with a great deal of TV shows, as well as Major Motion Pictures. This is what I was looking for, and that was the league I wanted and hoped to get Group IV Recording into. It was a worthwhile direction.

I met with Jeff Ward; we spoke at length, and I followed up with numerous meetings. I had to figure out how we were going to pay him since he was a member of IATSE local 165, the projectionist union. Jeff didn't want to work non-union; we were not signatories. We had to figure out a way to pay all his benefits into the MPH&W Fund. This was very important to him, and we could not argue or blame him for that. He was thinking of his future, it was all very straight forward. He also had hopes of possibly working for us once the installation was completed. There had to be a way to do this; I felt it wasn't that difficult. I started making calls around town, asking everyone I knew how I could do this. I knew there had to be a way; we could not just let this issue stand in the way. Finally, the answer came to me, we would hire Jeff through a payroll company as their employee to work for us. You do not have to be a signatory to a union contract if you need work done, just hire the person or individuals, put them to work through a payroll company, pay them and they will pay all the benefits due the employees. That could not be that difficult. I called around, no harm in that, we just needed a company that was a signatory. He would submit a payroll time sheet to the payroll company and they in turn would bill us his hourly rate, plus a handling fee for services rendered, as a standby projectionist. This would work; I knew it would. It was all above board, since the payroll company would pay him and do all the reporting and payments to the motion picture fund. The payroll company, being a signatory to the motion picture industry, was able to keep Jeff happy. This way Group IV Recording could pay him, and he would be employed and fully covered, which was agreeable to everyone concerned. So we went ahead with our plans and put this issue to bed.

We quickly found out that you don't just put in a 35mm projector in a room; there has to be careful planning beforehand, and you can't expect not to have some hurdles. After all the researching in our room, we found that one of our drawbacks was the way the room was designed when the studio was built. We were not thinking of film work at that time; our work mainly consisted of Variety Shows and Record Sessions. I met with Tom Hidley and showed him the room, and for a time, all everyone talked about was the speaker placement in the control room, and how the point by the main speakers dropped some high end. This came from Ken Dunken, as well as all the experts that wanted to make money re-designing our control room. That would've been a big mistake, but my dear friend Tom Hidley called me personally. He said, "Angel, there's nothing wrong with your control room. Don't change a thing." I was very grateful to Tom for saying that, and we kept going as usual.

One of the changes that we wanted to make was valid, but we found out after much research that we could not project from above our control room. We didn't have enough room; it was way too small; we didn't have the ceiling height that was required. The weight of the equipment alone made it impossible. The fire department would have a field day with us; it was impossible. It was back to the drawing board. Our only other option was to project film from the side, to the right of the control room, above the vocal booth. Our plan now was to enter near our amp room and place our projector above our vocal booth. This would help with all the cable runs, and insulation. It would spare us all the noise and traffic we would have above the control room, another issue to deal with, and it would definitely be very dangerous and not very cost effective.

After much research and numerous meetings, we decided to build and elevate a room high above the vocal booth, suspend and support the floor because weight was a factor. We had to build a ramp alongside of our amp room, and finally, we would have a projection room elevated north of our control room. This room had to be the very best in town; it would be well equipped for film editors and their assistants; no expense spared. It had to look and work well. There were also other things to consider, and one of the first that came to my attention was visual looks of the picture on screen. Jeff said that since we were shooting at that angle it would give us an awful lot of picture distortion; I was concerned, and Dennis, as always, was really concerned and worried.

I asked how we could solve this problem; there had to be a way. I racked my brain and went around asking and looking for answers from various composers that I personally had known for years. I wasn't afraid to ask; it would just make life a lot easier for them as well as the studio, and as far as I was concerned, they had the answers. So I went directly to my friends and asked them. I was not surprised at some of the answers; particularly coming from such heavyweights in the business as the likes of Billy Byers, Don Costa, Jack Elliott, Allyn Ferguson, Pat Williams, and many others. It didn't seem to be an issue to anyone, all they wanted to see were the pops and the streamer going across the screen. That was it; they had no other issues at all. They felt very comfortable being able to score a film in our room. When I met with Billy Byers, he said to me, and I quote, "Look, Angel. Listen to me. Musicians have no business watching the screen, they should be watching me. I'm the composer/conductor, they should be playing and just grooving to the music. We are not here to watch movies we are making music."

I finally realized after meeting and talking with all these great composers that we needed to keep in mind that this was not a screening room. After numerous lengthy meetings, I had to say something about all the illusions. I finally said, "Look guys, color prints are not an issue; they would be far and few if any. We're going to be dealing with black and white work prints. In addition, the composers, conductors, and music editors, they are the ones who will be looking at the picture. We were spending too much time speculating on images, and it's time we faced reality."

I reiterated, "After all, these are work prints that we will be getting—just work prints, black and white prints. Nothing else. We're scoring music; we are wasting time, meeting after meeting, and we're still coming up with the same answers. Let's get going here time; is of the essence. We are building a projection room to shoot work prints for scoring sessions; again, this is not a screening room. They are not interested in blues or greens," I said. "Jeff, correct me if I'm wrong, but there are times when the projectionist isn't fast enough or the cue would be too long for the projector to rewind as fast as a tape machine. At that point, the composer would say, 'Let's run it without the film, and we'll look at it later during our break,' which will often be the case."

Jeff's response was, "I know. I've been there many times." I had to keep reminding everyone that what we were building was a film scoring stage, that we were wasting time having meetings regarding issues that were not valid and a total waste of everyone's time. We needed to get on the same page. So, after much discussions it was determined that what we needed to do was file the projectors' aperture down by hand. I knew that, for the most part, the untrained eye could not tell the difference. Again, I reminded everyone that nobody had the time, not during a scoring session. What we were building was a scoring stage, not a screening room.

In Optics, an aperture is a hole or an opening through which light travels. To be more specific, the aperture of an Optical System is the opening that determines the cone angle of a bundle of Rays that come to a Focus in the Image Plane. The aperture determines how Collimated (collimated light is light whose rays are parallel, and therefore will spread slowly as it propagates – transmits) the admitted rays are, those which are of great importance for the appearance at the image plane.

So now, while Jeff was kept busy on the apertures, I proceeded to assemble personnel for this new venture, contacting clients, selecting a few and spreading the word to various composers, editors and heads of music production that Group IV Recording very soon would have music scoring capabilities. We now had to penetrate the sound envelope in the room in order to put in the projection room. We installed double glass and both our projector and mag machine were put on floating platforms in order to not interfere with the vocal booth below. You did not want to be doing a main title with a vocalist and have any noise created from above, so we were able to take care of that right away.

We called Magna-Tech in New York City and ordered a 35mm 3-track mag machine with the capability to play back up to 4-tracks simultaneously. Definitely overkill; we never did use it; we had a lot of dreamers. My partner was still approaching it as if we were building a screening room. I still kept reminding everyone that it was a music scoring stage for music, don't lose your perspective and stay focus because, after all is said and done, I'm the one that has to go out and sell it.

We purchased a film editor's table complete with rewinds, 35mm/1000ft take up reels, empty 35mm hubs for the music editor and his assistant/loader. Our projection room was well equipped and prepared for any and all film scoring sessions that would come our way. Gary Fradkin installed a Plantronics unit; both control room and projection room would be in constant communication during any film scoring session.

Our next task was to acquire a 35mm projector; we couldn't afford a new one, but with Jeff's careful research and contacts in town, we were able to find a great deal locally. Jeff Ward, being the most capable and knowledgeable projectionist, was a busy beaver; he was constantly on the go and reporting to me for approval of any purchases. He went all over town, found and purchased a Century Head, and then a Simplex Base. We had Valley Enamel in Burbank match the head color, and when it was completed, it stood as one unit; you could not tell the difference, it looked brand new.

Next, we made a few purchases: a regular 35mm lens, a TV lens, and a Cinemascope lens. We were equipping our projection room; composers and editors all over town were more than happy to help us, and now the tests began.

Time went by; I made it very clear to Jeff Ward that time was of the essence. He was very excited because I had already committed the room in 30 days; none other than Ralph Burns would be here at Group IV scoring music for "Movie, Movie." I was also very excited; finally, we would have our first film date.

I stayed in close contact with Bill Hughes, who was a close friend and a well-known and respected contractor in the music business. His word was a great seal of approval; he was very instrumental in getting us work. He and I had a relationship that went back many years. I could always ask Bill a question because what you got was always a straight answer, and it never came with any strings attached.

I kept him informed of our progress. Bill had said, "Look,

when you're ready, let me know and I will get you your first film." The pressure was on, but I felt great. I knew we could do this; I would not let anyone down; I was very confident of the crew we had put together; I knew time was of the essence.

We were now ready. Dan Carlin of "La Da Music" was the music editor, along with Michael Tronick. They called me and visited the studio. Dan looked around the place, and he asked a few questions. He was very gracious; we talked for a while, and he felt that what we had would certainly work for this film, and said he loved the idea that we would be working together; he was pleased with what he saw and said that he was meeting with Ralph Burns in the afternoon. He would let him know he'd been here.

The next call that came was the one I'd been waiting for some time; from Bill Hughes to book time at Group IV Recording. I was very excited; here we were, 1978, it was our first film music scoring session for a Major Motion Picture. We did it; we are booked. We've come a long way; it's our first film score with the legendary composer: none other than Ralph Burns; we would be scoring a major feature, "Movie, Movie."

Stanley Donen, the director, would be present throughout the entire recording and mix down process. I loved Ralph Burns. One of the unique things I always found about Ralph was that whenever I called, he would always answer my call, and it didn't matter where he was. We had become good friends. Whenever I would call Bill Hughes' office, if he was there, he'd get on the phone, and we would just gossip about what was happening in town. He knew what new composers were doing, and he always gave me advice as well as the low down on them. We would talk for the longest time, and this continued until his last days. There aren't many like him around anymore. I'm very proud and privileged to have known and worked with Ralph Burns. I enjoyed his candor; the relationship we shared was very special.

In the early days, there wasn't any way to synchronize

(lock) a 24-track machine to the projector, so we came up with a small trick. Nothing outstanding. What we did was, during playback of any given music cue, we would carefully, with a White Grease Pencil on tape, Mark the Record Head (Not the Playback Head) of the multi-track. We'd watch the screen and, as the streamer went across the screen, which was our warning sign, and then First pop, second pop and Third POP, when it hit the screen, we would hit play on the fly. That was the downbeat of music and it stayed pretty much on speed, especially on short cues. The music editors usually could tell if it would fit. It was not major surgery; it was something I learned at TTG Studios when I worked with Ami Hadani. Group IV Recording would become one of the few recording studios in Hollywood with 35mm Film Scoring capabilities. I knew we were heading in the right direction, and I was very motivated and excited about the direction we were taking the studio. We were very lucky because we were still doing record dates. Variety shows were very few, if any, but our main staple would now be film scoring. From here on out it was very obvious that we had found a good niche.

Before our first scoring session, we spent a great deal of time rehearsing and checking all mike lines, ins-outs, all our outboard equipment, and mag machine, and we ran our projector several times, making sure there were no glitches at all. I took it upon myself and made sure that we had enough coffee to go around, and I had asked Roy the day before to get bagels with cream cheese and donuts for the session and lots of coffee when we were ready. I came in early. The session was scheduled for 10:00 a.m. downbeat. I was a little nervous. I had sold Dennis to all these folks and all my friends. Although he has never done a film scoring session before I have put a lot of confidence in him. I knew this was a different animal, and it was by far a very demanding session. We never really talked about it, but it was what we wanted, and I knew that my job at this point was to hang out for moral support, knowing full well that if anything went wrong, I'd have to take the fall.

Everyone is very cheerful and glad to be here. It's a fairly large orchestra, musicians are all over the place with chairs, music stands, lights, microphone booms, and mikes being adjusted. The number of salutations is out of this world. I know deep inside that it all hinges on this session. I know that after the first take, it will be all over town, and as for me, it's a long recording day.

Dennis starts getting a balance on the orchestra. Ralph Burns is at the podium, really relaxed, running down a few sections. We are ready to roll. The announcement comes. Our second engineer, Greg Orloff, asks, "Picture ready? Standby. We are rolling, quiet on the set please. This is M-1 take 1. Roll Film..." Streamers go across the screen, then the POP downbeat. Ralph Burns is conducting, turning pages, everything is working perfectly. Music sounds great. I'm a little nervous but things are going better than I had expected. Everyone, including Bill Hughes, looks happy. Dan Carlin, sitting to the right of Dennis, is giving me the high sign. Everything sounds great, picture is on the screen and, without a hitch, end of cue. Ralph announces playback a big smile on his face. Greg rewinds the tape and waits until everyone has walked into the control room. He's waiting for the cue to hit play, and finally the moment we've all been waiting for. Ralph Burns puts his hand on my shoulder. "Don't worry, he tells me things sound great." I give Greg a signal to hit play. Everyone is quiet and just listening. They're all very complimentary, and there's applause from everyone. Bill Hughes gives a thumbs up. I'm appreciative of all he's done for us. Everything is going smoothly, and now it's time for a break. He is very pleased; he had a lot on the line personally.

There is so much excitement in this building. I can hardly speak. I have a big lump in my throat and my eyes are red. I compliment my crew. and now it's time for me to go to my office and start drumming up more film business. Everything has gone as I had projected; everyone, including all the musicians, are very excited. They were, after all, big fans. You just couldn't imagine the support—it couldn't have gone any better.

I thanked Jeff for a job well done, especially after all the pressure I had put on him. He had come through with flying colors. Dennis really nailed it, a great job under all the pressure. This is our first music scoring session and word is going out to the trades. The word on the street is very favorable. The following day, same situation. You couldn't ask for anything better. We took lunch orders and called it in at Greenblatt's. Everyone is happy life is good.

On the third day they have a few cues to score, the plan is to mix the main title along with some other cues that both Ralph and the director wanted to tweak. They start to mix, and as they go to play the main title the film is ripped out of the sprockets and right out of the gate. This keeps happening constantly. Now I'm called into the control room and my reaction is, "Oh my god. What could possibly go wrong now."

When you're doing a film scoring session, for the most part, you're working with work prints in black and white; as per our previous conversations. These films are run many times through projectors, movieolas and flatbeds numerous times for composers, directors, effect's editors, music editors and producers; it's how we are able to bid on projects; you have to see the film several times. There would always be several screenings of the film, so because the film is run many times there is the possibility that sprockets will get damaged, which is what has happened to our print. This had absolutely nothing to do with our equipment. We were all aware of what was going on, unfortunately the concern showed on my face; it was no secret. That's when Dan Carlin said, very loud and clear. These are work prints, guys. They have been run many times; it's not you. The fact that it was our very first scoring session put us under a microscope; but thank God for Dan

Carlin and Michael Tronick, who understood what was going on. We had the best crew and equipment, and I stood by them. I was, as always, very supportive at all times, no room for failure.

The story of that session remained in my head for a few years. I remember it happened several times, and I can still hear the director screaming in a shrill voice, "What is that? What's going on?" I took the heat, but we did however manage to survive; and the rest was history.

I spent a great deal of time just selling. I didn't stop for one minute; I was all over town. If I heard about a new film or show, which in many cases a lot came from contractors, musicians, and close friends, or the trades. As time went by Group IV Recording earned a great a reputation for being the place to go for motion picture and TV Music scoring. Lionel Newman and many others in town congratulated me; and finally, they, as well as everyone in town, were feeling very confident and at ease with our studio and staff.

We started recording a great deal of TV series that kept the studio really busy on a weekly basis. I received a call from none other than my longtime friend Dave Fisher, who was now doing sound-alikes for a series of Glen Larson's productions for 20th Century Fox.

Dave was really a master at it. He would be doing scores and sound-alikes for such popular shows as Battlestar Galactica the series, Buck Rogers in the 25th Century, The Fall Guy, Knight Rider, McCloud, BJ and the Bear, and many other series; and he proceeded to give me contacts for purchase orders. He wanted to do all his sessions here at Group IV and they were great sessions.

I had the pleasure of meeting one of our heroes when we recorded Frankie Lane on one of "BJ and The Bear" episodes. Dave idolized him; you could see the gleam in his eyes as they were going over the music sheet. This day was like no other because it was sessions like these that gave us time to spend with our friends, When you're in the music business, the studio is the only place you are afforded time to socialize and see each other.

I was busy, and so was the studio, and I was constantly either dropping in on potential clients or on the phone. It was a task I enjoyed to no end. Dave bought a certain vibe to Group IV Recording. He taught my crew an awful lot of tricks. He was just amazing; his vocal charts were always right on the money, a real pro; and his sessions were always timely with no messing around. Dave and I went back a few years, so it was just like home for both of us. Everyone in the crew loved him.

I next called on another team of composers, none other than Mike Post and Pete Carpenter, who were busy doing a lot of Steve Cannell shows. I knew them from my days at TTG Studios, especially Mike Post, who had been introduced to me by Jimmy Bowen during one of Kenny Rogers and The First Edition sessions.

When I first approached Mike, he said he would be more than happy to use our studio and asked me, "Who's your mixer, or are you doing it all?"

I said, "Mike, try my place. You're going to love it. I have Dennis Sands, but you're welcome to bring your own mixer; that won't be a problem."

I didn't want any drawbacks; freelance engineers were now in vogue and we needed his business; and I made no qualms about it. I had to face the fact that I couldn't sell time with my hands tied to any recording engineer.

In time, Mike and Pete started using the studio on a regular basis with our in-house engineer. Pete Carpenter always felt the ceilings were not high enough, this started with a little dislike from Dennis, who is a debater and would not let it just rest and practice the old saying, "The client is always Right." No need to challenge them. In no time at all he was replaced by a well charismatic and funny, talented, seasoned engineer that was very personal and liked by the entire crew, my dear friend Gary Lutz. He became very close with the entire staff;

they loved him. It was as if he had started out with us from day one.

I knew this move would bring us more business, and it afforded me the freedom to be away drumming up business without any worries. The payoff was, that in return Gary brought in more composers to use the studio. He respected everyone on the staff and loved the studio. The team of Mike Post and Pete Carpenter started doing a lot of TV series that really became a great promotion for the studio. The word out on the street was, "If you wanted to know where Mike Post and Pete Carpenter, they were at Group IV Recording." What a great calling card! We were very active, scoring many of their hit shows for them, such as "Hill Street Blues," "L.A. Law," "Hunter," "Law & Order," "The Greatest American Hero," "The A-Team," "Baa Baa Black Sheep," "Blossom," "The Commish," "Doogie Howser," "Hardcastle & McCormick," "Hooperman," "Magnum P.I.," "News Radio," "Profit," "Quantum Leap," "Renegade," "Riptide," and "Silk Stalkings."

We were doing a lot of work for all the majors on a daily basis. The Paramount TV Music Department also became one of our regulars. Since their lot was not that far from us it was a great attraction because of our location, right in the middle of Hollywood. We were given a show called "Cheers" with composer Greg Safan, by the head of music at Paramount TV, none other than Jack Hunsaker, who was in charge of their Music Department. He personally gave Group IV Recording the green light, and under Jack's banner, we scored that show for 11 seasons.

This was great for us—a great selling tool. Although I had my bouts with the music department's secretary who wanted to keep the cost down. She suggested that we use a lesser audio cassette for all mixes that went to all the composers and production staff. I disagreed; it made no sense at all. I did not want to sacrifice sound for the cost of an audio cassette. As far as I was concerned, she was counting pennies and wanted to sacrifice the sound of the show, I stood my ground I would not do it.

I was really glad and honored when Jack Hunsaker paid me a visit, along with his secretary. Jack had not been here since the opening; he loved the place and was very complimentary. As we stood in my office, right there to my surprise, Jack said, looking at me and his secretary. "Angel, I want you to know that neither Carol nor anyone else in my office speaks for me." That said it all right there from then on things went well, and the issue of cassettes was off the radar it was never in question again.

Thanks to Jack Hunsaker I was also able to get more TV scoring sessions on his recommendation, not to mention a few features. Jack had been very good to me; he was an honest man and always stuck to his word. David Grossman followed as the new head of Paramount TV Music Department after Jack's retirement. He also became a very big supporter of Group IV. Things didn't change at all and it was a pleasure dealing with him. He was a music fan and loved the studio always very complimentary of our work.

I was dealing with the very best in town: Lionel Newman at 20th Century Fox, Dominic Frontiere at Paramount Feature Dept, Harry Loweskie at MGM's Music Dept, Bodi Chandler at Lorimar, and also Raul Perez at Columbia/Tri-Star features. They were the guys to go to. Giants that knew the business inside out. They could never be replaced they knew their jobs extremely well and knew how to handle people wonderful men, great to deal with—not a funny stitch on them at all. When you dealt with them it was all straight ahead no left hooks.

I'd been very fortunate I had started something that worked for the studio, and it kept us all busy. We were making good money and our reputation was spreading all over the country even as far as England. I was getting a lot of repeat business and new clients all the time. I was really a happy camper because everyone that came to the studio became very loyal, and they would often become return customers for the majority of their own personal projects.

We were dealing with producers and artist that were very popular and particular about their music. They felt comfortable that I would spend a considerable amount of time on their sessions. I went after Hanna Barbera, and I finally convinced Paul DeCort and Hoyt Curtain to use our studio. After a few sessions they became another of our regulars every Wednesday like clockwork.

The first engineer that I put with Paul DeCort and Hoyt Curtain was Paul Aronoff, who did a great job. When he decided to leave that's when Andy Daddario a young guy who had certainly paid his dues came into the picture very fast and quick with a great personality who really got a great sound. They loved him.

I knew all these producers going way back before we built this studio. In some respects it felt like we grew up together in the music business. I was a recording engineer who had spent many hours with them in the studio for many years that's how I managed to get them here.

They were familiar with my work and they trusted me. It was my creditability, and they knew my word was my bond.

We were a very busy facility to say the least I conducted an awful lot of business, and everything was always on a handshake. I was always very helpful to any and all that needed my assistance. If anyone needed help or had a question, they could rest assured I would be there for them, with complete confidence I was very proud of our studio, and very fortunate to have the clientele we had they were the cream of the crop.

I was asked if I would like to join the board of governors for NARAS the LA chapter for the Grammy Awards. Michael Melvoin presided as president, and I was elected second vice president in a very short time. Technology kept advancing, and we followed right along like everyone else.

Things kept changing really fast a lot of other studios joined the ranks so the competition was on the rise I love it to me it meant that with more good studios, we would have a better chance to grow even more. The more music done here meant more work would be coming to town. There was room for everybody. so the more the merrier. I've always felt competition is a very healthy situation, it shows the town has a great pool of talent to pull from, and this becomes very supportive for everyone especially all of us in the music business.

I never forgot the people I had worked with I made it a point and stayed in touch with everybody; especially Guy Costa, who was a friend and had hired me at Motown. We would often meet for lunch to exchange ideas. I was more than grateful for the way Guy always treated me at Motown Records. I was also thankful for everything he personally threw my way. He was responsible for green lighting session projects of Motown Records while I was at TTG, and now here at Group IV Recording I enjoy and always have respected his company.

Guy and I had known each other now for many years. He had taken a long sabbatical from Motown Records while searching for something else to do in the music industry and was now freelancing as a sound mixer. Don Costa, his brother, was busy as always. He was now scoring "The Great Brain" with Donny Osmond. On this particular session they had both spent hours in the studio on a music cue, which had a rough start getting to the downbeat. They had tried various methods, but they didn't seem to work so they were very frustrated about it.

I remember them coming into the office I would put out a bottle of brandy and three glasses and they would sit there drinking and discussing what method to use screaming at each other. But it was all love they were family, and they in turn treated me as one of their own. Whenever the Costa's were in our building I would go out of my way and treat them with all the love and care in the world. I loved these guys who had been extremely supportive of me throughout the years we all went back a very long way.

Don wanted a pop on the film and Guy kept saying it won't work, Don would say you don't know you haven't tried it this went on for some time and neither of them would budge. I knew I had to say something, so after the first bottle I diplomatically sat down with Guy. I opened another bottle, and I said Guy why not give him the pop, it might work. I knew it would but I was careful not to bruise anyone, both of these guys were my friends. So after my careful coaching we tried it and it did work, and now after the session they sat down again in my office arguing over whose idea it was they loved each other. What can be said about Don and Guy Costa a pair like that? That hasn't been said before. I miss them both very much whenever their names come into the picture, I can't help but reminisce about my dear old friends they don't make them like that anymore.

Time passed and after a while more and more large sessions are being scored. It seemed larger orchestras were now in vogue and the RCA building was being leased out to independent studios or engineers for these sessions. I'm feeling the pressure from my partner who has no concept of what is going on except his needs for notoriety which he has an appetite for in the worst way. The majors are taking notice of this, and they are revamping their own facilities with more modern equipment. They do have the best stages in town, and not to mention the funds to weather any mishaps along the way.

Chris Stone had now taken a lease of Studio M on the Paramount lot and was operating under the banner of Record Plant Scoring. He hired one of my favorite ladies from my days at TTG, Stephanie Murray, as his traffic manager. The Gilmore Drive-In, which was opened in 1948 located near the Farmers Market in the Fairfax area, had been vacant for years.

I remember going over to look at it with Dennis who was very persistent. He thinks that we could build a large studio there and capture all the large music scoring business in town boy how naïve.

This was what I had to deal with—Champagne Taste and a Sizzler Budget. There was no way we could support a venture like that we didn't have the capital to support it we would never qualify for such a large loan consisting of an enormous major construction project, not to mention equipment, and personnel we were definitely out of our league. I knew right away we could not do this in the same manner we had done Group IV Recording; it was an impossible task. I went on a search to see who owned the property no Google back then all land line.

I found out it was owned by the city and thank God because who knows internally what grief that would have cost; not to mention loss of time and money, which frankly, we did not have. We had already tried on numerous occasions to see if we could lease the RCA Studios on Ivar and Sunset Blvd, which I knew was also another losing proposition in itself our overhead would've been enormous. Why would we want to do this? To me it made no sense at all. The whole town was going through a phase, and I knew in my heart that this madness about large orchestras wouldn't last for long. Yes, we were busy, but not enough to ignore our present business, yet alone staffing and equipping a new facility but again, ego and just plain madness was in play.

I also felt that we had no business expanding to another location we needed to stay focused to the business at hand. If we needed to expand, why not in our own building? We had the room besides the expense that came with such a move would be enormous. We could not handle such a task what we needed was more capital. We needed money our own business was undercapitalized. There was no question that these plans were not for us; money talks and bullshit walks, and all we had was bullshit. Things quieted down, and after pure exhaustion of time, everyone at last relaxed and we resumed business as usual.

Time just passed, and I received a call from Ken Duncan of KENDAN Recorders. He asked if I would join him and a few other studio owners in Fort Lauderdale, Florida for a symposium. I accepted getting out of town for a while suited me just fine. The symposium was being hosted by MCI. On June 15, 1979, we were flown to Miami, where we were escorted to our hotel. We attended a luncheon that was hosted by Jeep Harned the founder of the company which began equipment manufacturing in 1959. This was great after lunch a few of us decided to go for a ride into Miami; we wanted to see Criteria Studios, where the Bee Gee's had done their famous recordings of their hit album "Saturday Night Fever."

It was a great experience seeing how small the rooms were and all the MCI equipment used. Carl Richardson, their engineer, had done a phenomenal job with the sound he had gotten; especially with what he had to work with. I applaud him he certainly deserved a lot of credit for what he had done; it was very impressive. It was all good, the studio looked great, and Mack Emmerman should be proud. We had to ride across the bridge where the Bee Gee's came up with their drum beat, just smoking away the herb and having a great time. We returned to the hotel to get some rest and shower. Our schedule for that evening consisted of dinner and a cruise around the harbor. I took a beer and laid back on the bed. I was really tired, and I never woke up; the cruise took off without me. The next morning my 3M rep Aaron Berg said how he had been knocking at my door, but since there was no answer, they went ahead without me. I said after the plane and all the running around town. I just fell out. I never heard the phone or knocking at my door. I was later informed I didn't miss anything at all, so I was not disappointed, plus since I'm prone to sea sickness I believe mentally I was not prepared for it.

That same morning, after a great complimentary breakfast with everyone in attendance, we started in with a long discussion on how we wanted to be treated by manufacturers and suppliers who had taken us for granted for so many years. We also discuss how much power we had as studio owners, and that we could make good use of it if we all stuck together and shared more information among ourselves. The next subject at hand for discussion was the possibility of the building of small consoles that could support all the needs of a recording session. Why couldn't we have one that was more cost effective, with at least 60 inputs and outputs with equalization and pan pots on all faders? A small console where you didn't need to build an enormous control room? There wasn't a single person in the room that didn't participate; everyone was very vocal and it was a great, and very informative meeting; the first ever.

Ken Duncan held the gavel. I remember he stood up and wrote a few names on the chalk board. We had to come up with a name, and after many suggestions by everyone in the room the name of SPARS came into play (The Society of Professional Audio Recording Studios) formed June 16, 1979. Ken was very excited and said, let's elect some caretakers and I'll inform the press ASAP, which he did. The caretaker officers were elected that afternoon to serve temporarily until industry-wide elections could take place. The Chairman of the board representing the studio industry at large elected was Joe Tarsia from Sigma Sound of Philadelphia. The regional members elected to the board were Bob Liftin New York City; Chris Stone Record Plant Los Angeles; Mac Emmerman Criteria Sound Miami; Glenn Snoddy Woodland Sound Nashville, Tennessee. The studios that were represented at that very first meeting would pay the initial dues of $2,000 each they were as follows: A&R Studios New York City, Atlantic Studios New York City, Criteria Recording Miami, Filmways-Heider Recording Hollywood, Group IV Recording Hollywood, House of Music New Jersey, Howard M. Schwartz Recording New York City, Canteen recording Burbank, Larrabee Sound Hollywood, Media

Sound New York City, Record Plant Los Angeles, Regent Sound Studios New York City, Sigma Sound Studios Philadelphia, Sound Mixers New York City, and Studio 55 Chicago.

This meeting, as well as others were often a way of staying informed with other studios, personnel and equipment manufacturers. You never knew where you might be asked to record any given project; perhaps you might need to go to Europe, New York City, Chicago, Nashville, Atlanta to do a session, and it would be good and efficient to have a relationship in some other city. I attended as often as I could. My partners didn't see it the same way and were often very critical of them, saying we would be viewed as price fixing; but I forged ahead—I felt that it helped to stay in touch with your competitors. There are no secrets, especially in the studio business. It's all up for grabs, and who can do the best and most expedient job.

On August 21 to 25, 1979, I was again invited to another symposium; this time it was hosted by the 3M Company, at their magnetic audio tape and video division headquarters in Minnesota. Hosted by their national sales manager, a great guy who resembled the actor Walter Matthau, stood well over six feet tall: Mr. Joe L. Leon. We had our local rep, Gordon Menard, who for years had taken care of all the studios in town. Gordon was the man you went to if you had any problems, and he was always there. He had known all of us for many years and knew our studios really well, and Aaron Berg, his protégé, a tall redhead from Arizona, he was new in our area, but had a world of knowledge.

3M outdid themselves; we were taken by private jets to the Decathlon Athletic Club in Saint Paul, Minnesota, for one of the greatest outings any of us ever experience in quite some time.

Again, was put together by none other than Ken Duncan—who had a knack for putting us all together in one room. If anyone could do it, Ken Duncan was the man. That evening I attended a meeting with Chris Stone, Joe Tarsia and David

Teig. We looked at various samples of logos for SPARS After sorting through a few selections of plaques we jointly agreed on the final logo that would eventually be used and released to the press. That was something that very seldom happens; my thanks again must go to Ken Duncan, 3M Minnesota Tape and MCI Electronics. who made it all possible.

In no time there would be other outings very much like this one, but this one was really exceptional, and it became known all over the industry. Because of what we had done, everyone wanted to participate in any way shape or form possible. SPARS would. from here on out would take form; what made it so special was the fact that all manufacturers, including our host, The Minnesota Mining Company, often referred to as 3M, MCI Electronics, as well as everyone in the recording industry, was more than willing to hear what we had to say, which became very important to every studio in the country. We had started a trend and finally all manufacturers became very committed to hearing what we had to say and were listening to our demands. Great companies that stood by all the Recording Studios in the country, as well as many abroad. We had other audio tape manufacturers, but I feel that 3M went the distance for all of us.

I must complement our rep Gordon Menard who, for us at Group IV, did an outstanding job. We were a hard crowd to please and very demanding, it was not an easy job to say the least, but they would always listen and were willing and able to deliver. Audio tape came in various formats, and now here we were at Prince Paisley Park Studios, a complex he built in the suburbs of Chanhassen near Minneapolis. We were able to view his large soundstage where his band rehearsed for their tours—very impressive rooms; the place was immaculate; a lot of planning had gone into this facility, and it showed.

We were testing a new audio tape that was far more advanced than their current 2-inch 250 tape, which we had already become accustomed to using for a few years. Now, with the advent of new recording gear, 3M were introducing a new formula. They had come out with a new tape 9 9 6, as it would be labeled. This new tape gave us many possibilities; we were now able to put more level on, as opposed to their earlier tapes. We could record at +3db, as opposed to the normal 0db level, by adjusting our playback to minus 3db and record at plus 3db. It was a great addition, but since it was new, the availability became a big factor—not everyone in town would have it at hand.

If you were doing a project and ran out of stock in the middle of the night, and no one was available in town to loan you some reels of tape, then what? This was an issue that needed to be solved. 3M guaranteed that sufficient stock would be available very soon. Meanwhile, at Paisley Studios, we recorded and played back various mixes to hear what it sounded like and, needless to say, we were very impressed by the results. We hung out, everyone talking about their facilities and what they provided, clientele, equipment, recording tricks, artists memorable moments and their habits. No secrets, everyone was comfortable and very open; it was really an enjoyable and productive day.

On Tuesday evening we attended a cocktail party at The Decathlon Club and enjoyed numerous presentations by our host. One other thing they had was the new packaging for their new 2-inch 9 9 6 tape. I sat down with one of their local reps, he put this black 2-inch box in front of me and said, "What do you think of that box?" I looked it over and passed it around. The first question that came to mind was how do I put my legends in this box? It was an odd shaped box with no room to really put our customary legends on. 3M proposed a stick-on label but putting our legends on paper was not well received. You had to alter your legends the way the box was made it had a handle with a cutoff on the side, which left little or no room, and if you had a considerable number of legends, which you would if you were doing film scoring sessions (which was the case for us at Group IV Recording), it was very common.

The box could not hold too much documentation if you put your legends in the inside; you got a big circle from the hub and it made it difficult to close, so now you had to attach a manila envelope to the reel, which really worried me, because the chances of that information getting lost was something of great concern, which I was very vocal about, and unfortunately, it was something that never did get resolved. We stayed at the Decathlon Club until Wednesday; on Thursday morning we departed from Holman Field to their resort in Wonewok, 3M'S very private 600-acre estate.

While at Wonewok, we were treated like you would not believe. Our hosts were flawless; the food was out of this world, and as far as accommodations, we were extended the very best. Some of us were housed in the main lodge and the poker table broke out, what an evening. I had never seen this many pros at one table ever in my recording career. Chris Stone from Los Angeles, Bob Lifton from New York City, David Teig Atlantic Records New York City, Murray Allen from Chicago, Howard Schwartz from New York City, Mac Emmerman from Miami, Glenn Snoody from Nashville, and so many others. It was a fantastic evening.

Howard Schwartz entertained us all evening with his assortment of the funniest jokes you've ever heard. The bar was open to all of us for as long as we stayed up; and let me tell you, we stayed up. I found this very evening to be one of the most exciting times for any of us; plus, we were able, for once, to meet each other face to face. We had heard so much about each other but to put a face to the name was the best of both worlds. You heard things like, "Man, we've spoken for years, and I often wondered what you looked like." The friendships that were formed were very genuine and priceless.

I became a big fan of these events, and I looked forward to many more. This was rare, so I made the best of it. The grounds of this estate were very well maintained and manicured really well. The place was beautiful and enormous, and their lakes were out of sight. We all had a great time, Murray Allen, Harry Hirsch, Paul Slowman, Bob Liften and I, and that for me made it all worthwhile. It gave us a chance to communicate with each other. This was something that none of us had ever done. We were given a chance to attend various activities on the premises, but instead we decided to take a walk around the lake and just talk; it was the right place for it. We felt just great. What an opportunity to be able to spend time like this among your peers. We walked around for some time; this was beautiful; and all of a sudden, we came to a spot in the road where we ran into a fawn, and being city guys, we were just amazed and mesmerized—it couldn't get any better.

I remember Murray Allen had a new camera but didn't know how it worked yet, so we settled for my Polaroid. The time we spent together walking around that lake was great; nothing but laughter and pure enjoyment. We walked Murray to his cabin, and he decided we would now take pictures of all of us, which would've been great but he still had not learned the camera well. What happened next was just a spectacle of lights going on and off like a disco ball. We never did get to take pictures with that camera, and then on Friday evening, dinner and presentations.

Saturday, August 25, we left at 10:45 a.m. for Park Rapids, where we departed via private jets again, compliments of 3M, for our return home. One of the most memorable adventures and worthwhile trips, never to be forgotten. Everyone was excited about the new tape and what we had accomplished on our trip, It was something new to talk about and word spread really quickly. The new tape availability was difficult at first. We'd call our reps who didn't live that close to our facilities, but they had their ways, and were always able to get tape to us—sometimes even during the middle of the night. How they did it was beyond me, but they managed to meet our needs.

Everything was going great at Group IV Recording. We had achieved great notoriety; the music industry had certainly accepted the studio, and everyone in town gave us all the work possible. We were by no stretch of the imagination, a big hit Unfortunately, ignorance once more entered into the picture. My partners suggested going into the dubbing business, to which I said that none of us knew that side of the business, and that we would be competing with the majors—the hands that feed us.

We could not forget that we were a music studio. I knew that this venture was not for us, we'd be doomed to fail. I certainly did not know that much about dubbing; none of us did, besides we were being blinded by ego. Group IV Recording was an independent studio, and as much as it had prospered, it really needed to grow a lot more. I knew this was not for us financially. We were not in a great position to try such a foolish venture. Payroll alone would kill us, and our bank wouldn't support this. To me it made no sense at all. "Why should we take such a gamble." I said. "I don't see anyone bringing that kind of work to the table, and besides who is the mixer that's going to attract such a venture? We would have to hire several mixers, and that would cost money. We don't have the cash."

Paramount Pictures, 20th Century Fox, MGM, Universal Studios, Disney, Sony Pictures, Columbia Pictures, and Warner Brothers; not to mention a few others who did this for a living, had great financial backing and guarantee's, which we had none of. We were a small company. I felt very strongly we would be treading a dangerous path; it was not worth it. I really felt very uncomfortable with it and now they wanted me to take what the majors had a hold on and just solicit and book it. This wouldn't happen, especially since they had given us all the music scoring business; a business that we were very good at. For me, this was not a great position to be in, and it was not a prudent move.

Dubbing stages are not cheap to build, and In addition, they required a vast amount of capital, which we didn't have access to—and couldn't get by doing this. We would be ignoring Group IV Recording; the studio was my main concern. I saw no way for us to accomplish this task, again not to mention the fact that I would be the one out there trying desperately to book a new dubbing stage. Group IV Recording did not have the personnel or client base to support it. The building we were in was way too small; it would require massive construction. We would need to build on top of our existing building; it would require a lot of construction; and in Hollywood this would be a major task—but as in all business the majority rules, so I was overruled.

Finally, it was decided that we should contact an architect designer and get some bids, and after much sought out information and boring meetings, wasted time, and an expenditure of over $35,000 for architectural plans, we had to stop this project, hallelujah! They finally saw the light and realized we were out of our league. In my view it was a blessing; a relief came over me because now we could concentrate on what we were good at and not waste time and money in areas that would not help the company.

I continued calling on our clients and staying in-touch with all the heads of music departments at various studios. This, to me, was very important. I had to give them a shout every now and then; these were busy people on the go all the time and it was my responsibility to stay in touch with the major studios. I had to see what new shows were scheduled for the new season, which ones were picked up or cancelled, their demands and possible new formats.

The trades provided a great deal of information, but for me, nothing worked better than talking face to face directly to the heads of production, as well as composers who were an essential part of our business. I was always following the trades, and we continued with business-as-usual, doing what we did best. But to everyone's surprise, a storm was now brewing in the TV and the motion picture side of the business. It was the 1980s and The American Federation of Musicians in Hollywood local 47 wanted to strike against The Association of Motion Pictures and Television Producers. The actors were already on strike and had claimed they would support the musicians, but once they settle their strike, they just went their separate ways.

WE'RE ALMOST HOME

There was a lot of skepticism about the validity of this strike; the producers were not going to just cave in. My old friend Lionel Newman at 20th Century Fox Music released a statement to the trades in which he said the strike by the musicians local 47 would certainly delay the start of the fall TV, and not only that, it would also shorten the number of shows we would be doing. But no one took notice, they dismiss it, not knowing what the consequences would be.

On Thursday July 31, 1980, we were scoring the last episode of "Dallas" for Lorimar Pictures when the press stormed our front door and asked if I would let them in. They wanted to ask Bodie Chandler, the head of music, some questions about the strike. I called in to Studio A and asked Bodie if it was ok with him. He said, "Let us finish this last cue, were running a bit behind." When they finished their last music cue, my second engineer, George Belle, buzzed my office. Finally, the press was allowed in the control room it; was a complete circus, with lots of cameras and a huge crowd of people. Many musicians stayed behind in order to be heard, but no one was listening.

Once it was all over, some of the musicians came into my office, saying, "We got them by the balls now." They felt they had the producers by the short hairs, and they were dead serious about it. Picket lines were all over the fronts of major studios. Mike Melvoin, a well-known and very vocal musician, appeared on TV with a big crowd cheering him on, claiming they were going to take a letter to then-President Jimmy Carter, which never happened. Those musicians that were visible would in the end be hard pressed to find work.

It was a terrible strike. In the long run there were no winners. Artie Butler of Evergreen Studios in Burbank went to his fellow musicians with tears in his eyes, begging to end the strike. They were not hearing it at all. It was the worse strike in the music industry that musicians as well as independent studios had ever encountered. There would definitely be a lot of scars, and it would take some time to recover if at all. This was 1980; the strike lasted 167 days.

This incident marked the year when musicians metaphorically shot themselves in the foot.

However, in the interim, there were some small studios that were owned by musicians with their own synthesizers that were doing complete music scoring package deals for very little money, eliminating the need for a complete crew, orchestra and facilities like ours. I had been approached many times by some musicians, who will remain nameless, saying, "If you build me a room, I'll bring all my business here."

My response was always, "At what cost? In other words, I take all the risk, put our own money up, equip it and staff it, and you bring a show when you get it. Built you a room? Where is the unity in that brother? Now how are you going to pay me? You're getting your benefits and rate, and on top of that you're charging a low rate, and you have a package deal. How do I pay my crew? There's no profit in that. Why would we shoot ourselves in the foot?" This was the mentality that had been going around town for some time.

After the strike we continued to work. Unfortunately, I had to let some staff go in order to keep our doors open, and our workload, as well as in other studios, decreased considerably. Many people lost their homes as well as their savings. It had been the worst strike ever, with a lot of fingers pointing, but the musicians had done it to themselves; no one else was to blame. We, as independent studios, definitely paid the price. In order to recover, it was imperative that we find some other sources of income or close our doors.

We had to put on our thinking caps. Had we pursued the business of dubbing we would have been in the worst shape ever. I didn't bring it up; there was no need to rub it in anyone's face. We all knew it; and if they didn't it, certainly didn't show. We tightened our belts, and again, eyes and ears open; there were other things we could do. We did have a third of the building that was empty; perhaps we could find another area that complimented what we were doing to bring in additional income. I started to talk among my peers; maybe somewhere there was an answer. I searched and searched all over town. We needed something that would not require a great deal of expenditure. We had very little capital and our bank relationship had been exhausted. We were on our own, banks like to loan you money when you don't need it; and if you're a good earner they will pursue you. They always want a guarantee on their money; the slightest deviation in your account and they are all over you like white on rice—because you're only as good as your last deposit; and hopefully it's a big one.

Time passed, and I figured, let me look around. How are the small facilities doing music scoring sessions without 35mm projection? The majority of these sessions were being done at non-union facilities, which was not allowed by IATSE locals 165 and 695, but yet they, for the most part, would not police or enforce those rules at all. Most of the studios were busy, especially MRI Recorders, Gary Ullmers place in Hollywood. They were very busy and nobody held a union card; except for maybe the owner. I found out that they were doing music scoring sessions with TV monitors and three-quarter video playback—everyone was using this format.

When it comes to economics, people will make a left turn instantly, no ifs or butts about it. I was all over town, talking to anyone that had video capabilities. I knew somehow there was money to be made in this area, and I intended to pursue every avenue in order for us at Group IV Recording to make its share. We definitely had the space, and some of the equipment, as well as the personnel. I knew we could do this; it was just a matter of time, and with some good planning behind it and some advertisement, it was a no brainer. I needed to find a niche for us in order for the company to stay afloat, there was business out there to be had, but it had to be approached very carefully. No one was going to just hand over their business, and if they were comfortable where they were doing business, you had to be even better and faster with great rates.

I spent a lot of time just talking and visiting other facilities whenever possible and making very careful mental notes. Somehow, we needed to prevail. There was a lot of competition out there, but that just makes you focus more; you can't fear it, you just have to be better at it. I knew that we could get into that side of the business with a very small investment. I saw no reason why not, as I said earlier, we had all the room in the world plus we did have a captive audience. The majority of music editors in town were working at our place; we were the toast of the town.

There was something else that was happening: most composers were buying their own video machines to spot their films at home. Meetings could now be held without having to hire a projectionist. Big, bulky, and heavy reels did not have to be carried all over town; there was a convenience factor here that could not be ignored, and it certainly contributed to us pursuing this side of the business.

We continued dealing with our daily music scoring sessions with our 35mm Century projector. We had film delivered prior to our sessions, usually ten 1000-foot reels at a time straight up the ramp to the projection room. How long 35mm film music scoring would last no one knew. But for us independent studios, it would be just a matter of time before there would not be too many of these sessions.

I kept hearing from my projectionists, at least the ones I would call on a regular basis, how they were starving. They were not getting the calls they were used to getting, although the local claimed they would re-train them. How could you in all honesty hire a man to perform the duties of a remote control? The truth of the matter was they were being displaced by technology, which you can't fight or ignore in any business.

I had witnessed video projection back at National Recording in New York City at 730 Fifth Avenue, where real estate is very expensive. I remember when we were doing commercials with Joseph Cotton; we had monitors. We would setup the monitor in front of your announcer or actor. We had four monitors that we could set in different rooms, and from the small projection room in the back, we ran the film projector. That was back in the 60s, three quarter U-Matic video cassettes were not around then. We were now in the 80s and I was glad I had experienced this earlier on because it would now serve my purpose.

I was well aware that placing a monitor in the room would present a problem. It would take the room of three musicians, so, it cuts your room down. We started calling dealers all over to find the best video machines on the market and their availabilities, capabilities and cost. These machines at that time were bulky and very heavy, but changes were coming. We didn't need recorders; all we needed were players. Monitors were another issue, as I said, they take up a lot of room, and these puppies were really heavy. You had to build cabinets for them; AV carts were too big. So now you were into constructing something with wheels from the ground on up that had to move safely with ease and very fast. Most carpenters and machinists that we knew had no idea what we were talking about. We had to educate them. It becomes very difficult to explain to someone who is not in the business what you want, and for what purpose. You also need to explain what supplies they need to make any item for you.

When we first opened, having baffles and just a simple Podium for the conductor in the main room was a really big deal, which was something we really needed really fast. We started attending various trade shows, especially the NAB Show (The National Association of Broadcasters) in Las Vegas because when the time came, and it was coming, we would have to move really fast. Fortunately, we found a great deal of vendors at the show that could supply us with any equipment we needed for this new venture at a moment's notice, and it was becoming very educational for all of us.

Time passed really quickly, and now I started seeing music editors about transferring their films to video. I knew there was a niche in the film to video transfer world, which was confirmed by none other than Bob Badami, a well-known music editor who told me all the films he was working on were transferred to three-quarter-inch video cassettes; the composers he'd worked with loved the convenience and speed. 35mm projection was not being used much. We were also doing a lot of scores to video while our perforated screen occupied the back wall of the studio and our 35mm projector just sat there.

Video was now allowing other studios to synchronize (lock) their multi-track machines. The process was a lot faster, and you didn't need a projectionist, which the union local 165 was against. But there was very little they could do about it. The times, boy they were indeed changing.

I did some research and some projections, which I was very good at, and I found that if we had a Telecine Transfer Room, we could do transfers from film to tape. Whether the session was being done at Group IV Recording or not, didn't matter. We would still make a profit and we would be servicing composers and music editors. We also needed to find out the different formats that our clients had in order to keep everyone happy; you didn't want to make a transfer and when it arrived at anyone's home, they couldn't play it or the tracks were reversed. It was another thing you definitely had to pay attention to; there was no room for errors.

We decided that we would tear down our old acoustic echo chamber and transform it into a Telecine Machine Room; we would run cable from our amp room through the attic of the building from one end to the other. Our new Telecine Room would now allow us various capabilities transferring 35mm motion picture film to video in any format, and additionally, we would be able to do video streaming for any and all cues on any film that would need music scoring. This process would work great, and we, for the time being were the only ones in town capable of doing it, and we were very fast.

The Telecine process enables a motion picture, captured originally on film, to be viewed with standard video equipment, such as TV Monitors and video cassette decks (VCRs). This would also allow producers the advantage to use video production equipment to complete their film projects much faster.

I kept notes on everything and made sure that if anything was being scored in town, I would know who the composers, music editors and producers were, and I would offer our services 24/7; we were going to do this come hell or high water. We started to work on an advertising campaign targeting anyone I could reach; we had to spread the word all over town. Our techs were really on top of everything; nothing was overlooked; hours didn't matter; they were very persistent. It was important to all of us; the excitement of adding a new phase to the studio was really important and, as always, everyone wanted nothing but the best for the studio; and it showed. We were working as fast as time would allow us while doing sessions during the course of the day; no one took any time off; we worked on this project whenever possible.

Time and time again I would just take a step back; I was the only one doing sales, and now on very rare occasions, I was mixing unless I was requested; it was really hard being behind the console with so many other things on my mind. I was a good earner for the studio and my time was better served with my head solely into the daily operations of the studio. As always, any and all sessions that were booked were approved by me. I knew the personnel on the sessions, the production staff, how many musicians, and what instruments were being played; there could not be any second guessing, everyone depended on this information.

Once we decided that film to video transfers would be our next move, I just went full blast with it. I would not take no for an answer; this was what we were going to do, and why not? I had heard that telecine was performed in a color suite; well, I didn't care; it would be done in our new machine room with room to spare; we would be transferring 35mm film to three-quarter-inch video, and as long as we took care of all transfers with the utmost care, I knew we would succeed; there was no doubt in my mind.

We had gone through various phases in this building; we had tried numerous things. Eric Miller, my pal, and I don't use that term loosely, especially when it comes to him, was very supportive during this time as well as through all of our crises, and we had many. Eric by now had become Norman Granz's right-hand man at Pablo Records. Because of Eric we were able to establish the Pablo Room in the back side of our building, and the work that Eric threw our way helped us in many ways, we could never ever repay him for all his help and advice, he never asked for anything from us, and we had a regular client where we were able to generate a substantial amount of monthly billing.

During his working relationship with Norman Granz in the Beverly Hills office, he kept Group IV Recording busy on a daily basis, and would continue even after the label was sold to Fantasy Records. Eric Miller had been a really big supporter of Group IV Recording from the very start, always helping us to make a living. He was also very instrumental in getting

Dennis in the music business, for which he was never really acknowledged. Not that he looked for it or even wanted it, but I found it odd that his old buddy never recognized what he did for us.

Eric and I would travel to New York City on various occasions and do remote recordings; always keeping Group IV Recording in mind. We recorded Jimmy Smith at Fat Tuesdays on the east side; and when the remote was over, we shipped all tapes to Los Angeles to be mixed. This was always the case with so many other artists on Pablo Records, such as MJQ, also known as The Modern Jazz Quartet, Ella Fitzgerald, Joe Pass, John Coltrane, and many other artists on the label. And because of Eric, jazz recording and mixing became well known and a main staple for us at Group IV Recording.

He would continue to support the studio as much as he could till the very end. Group IV Recording would be up to speed soon; it was as if we were just starting all over. I loved every minute of it, working with our techs was always a great feeling; they just made our life much easier.

The word telecine is a Portmanteau of Television and Cinema. Within the film industry, it is also referred to as a TK, as TC is already used to designate time code. This would be a plus for Group IV Recording, and again as always, it would put us at the cutting edge. It wasn't impossible for us; we already had a lot of connections and the support of various clients. It was a win-win situation.

All we needed now was a 35mm projector. We could not use our existing projector as it was too big. What we needed was a smaller projector that would not take up so much room. I began asking around till finally, I found a guy in New York City that had one in storage and was willing to sell it. I called him and asked him how much? his answer was pound for pound. I said, "Where are you? I would like to look at it." He gave me his address in mid-town Manhattan on the east side.

After much research and going over things with my partner and our tech Gary Fradkin. I started inquiring about converting the 35mm projector to do film to video transfers. Jeff Ward said he had a guy that worked at Paramount who could do the mirrors on the projector. I knew it was now time to take the red eye to New York City and see the projector; time was of the essence. I didn't want to lose this deal. Dennis decided that there was no need for three of us to go. I said, "Well, you can stay. I don't know about you but I'm going. I have way too much time and effort invested, I've been working on this project too long and negotiated the deal. I can't take the risk of anyone blowing this deal, and this is a very aggressive New Yorker I'm dealing with. I'm ready to go."

The very next morning, on a cold and windy day, there we were at JFK at 8:00 a.m. Because of our early arrival, we had to wait at the airport cafeteria till about 10:00 a.m. Our contact was expected in his office around 10:3 0a.m. so we made the best of it. We arrived by cab promptly; we looked at the projector and it was in great shape; Gary gave it his blessing. We discussed crating it and all the possible shipping procedures. I took out a blank check and paid for the projector; and we finally confirmed all the necessary arrangements to have it shipped to Los Angeles.

We were not able to spend much time in Manhattan due to prior commitments and sessions that were booked. So, after closing our deal we went straight to the airport. We had a layover in Denver. Dennis, Gary and myself kept nodding off. I tried to keep everyone alert as much as possible, so when four Rabbis were approaching where we were sitting, I asked Gary, "What are they speaking?"

His response was, "I don't speak Hebrew."

As they got closer, I heard them talking and to my surprise they were speaking Spanish, which we found really humorous.

We flew back tired like you would not believe; but our mission had finally been accomplished. We had hired a consultant by the name of Neil Harrison, who had experience finding money for private parties, and after numerous meetings he directed us to a leasing company, TOPA Leasing, and, before we knew it, we were signing on the dotted line. Everything was happening really fast; finally, we would be getting the money we needed for the rest of the equipment.

We built our large transfer room and in no time at all we were able to start doing 35mm film transfers to three quarter and half-inch video. It was exciting, I had always wanted to do this. I knew it would become very lucrative for Group IV Recording, because not only could we do video transfers for our own projects, but for other music editors as well as other studios. Shortly after, things started to change a lot in the business. We now needed another studio because, once we finished recording, if additional time was needed for a rough mix or say a vocal overdub, we had to either delay the incoming session if at all possible, or just pass on it, which at times was not always a good idea for us. Now little did clients know that I always gave them at least an half hour buffer; the office as well as the crew knew that. I remember many times when composers like my dear friend Earl Hagan, as well as many others, would call me and say, "Angel, when and where are we supposed to mix?" Dennis used to say, Earl can't make up his mind, that was not the case, you had the buffer, use it, composers like him are preoccupied with their score. When you have that kind of pressure, the last thing you think about is mixing or re-mixing a cue; and sometimes, although you're doing a half-inch 4-track recording simultaneously, you need options where you might want to tweak a certain cue, because we missed an entrance of say brass; or you wanted more of the percussion. That's why you're recording with a 2-inch multi-track simultaneously in case a change is needed, or let's just say the producer in the room came up with a different thought and felt that remixing a certain cue would give him what he was looking for in the mix.

The first engineer should be on top of it and inform the front office of a possible re-mix. That additional time might be needed; don't just turn around and say we don't have any more time, that's bad business. We were a service business, we shouldn't forget that. Earl Hagan's response would always be, "Can you get me Angel on the phone?" And the next thing I'm being called, and I was always able to find time for him, it was never a problem. Earle Harry Hagen was a very well-known composer who had created music for various movies and television. He was well known for such TV themes as "The Andy Griffith Show," "The Fishin Hole," which he personally whistles and, Earl told me, it took him just ten minutes to write, "Make Room for Daddy," "The Dick Van Dyke Show," "I Spy," "That Girl," and "The Mod Squad."

I had by now known Earl for many years. He, to me, was a straight shooter and was one of the composers who gave me a letter of recommendation for the bank. Whenever he needed additional time, I would speak with the incoming producer, these guys all knew each other, so if I said I need some time for Earl, they would more often than not oblige us. It was just a matter of asking and the next thing you knew they were greeting each other; I truly miss the guy.

We had another great composer and friend, Gil Melle, very eccentric, who always wanted to re-mix. There was no question about it, so whenever he booked a session, I would always add additional time to his sessions. I would not charge him, if he didn't use it then it was just another buffer.

Gil was a well-known composer and jazz musician who did "Night Gallery." Gil was good friends with Rudy Van Gelder, another well-known studio owner and recording engineer whom Gil introduced to "Blue Note," the well-known jazz label. We met when he and Charles Patty, who was friends with the owner of Marino's, another one of the great Italian restaurants in Hollywood, the brother of Sal Salvatore, who also owned an Italian restaurant on Cahuenga Blvd Martonie's, which was a popular music industry hang out.

We never did spend any time socially; unfortunately, we were too busy. Besides, we spent way too much time here at the studio, which was very common. When that is in play, the last thing we do is get together on weekends, which is very typical in this industry.

One day, we started talking about Blue Note Records. He started to tell me how he was the first white musician signed to the company in 1952, that lasted thru 1956. He was a young guy at the time he signed with Blue Note, and if memory serves me right, I believe when he was maybe 20 years of age, he became a composer for film and TV.

He was the very first composer to compose a Main Title for a TV series, Rod Serling's "Night Gallery." The man had done over a hundred films and had worked with the likes of some of the best jazz musicians: Zoot Sims, George Wallington, Max Roach, Tal Farrow, Oscar Pettiford, Ed Thigpen and Kenny Dorham.

The subject of Gil possibly doing an album came up, and I was more than happy to entertain the thought. Why not? He was here a lot. I said let's do it and we can split everything 50/50.

We started the album, and Gil brought in his keyboards and some iron posts, and lots of other items he wanted to use in the recordings for effects. We were happy campers, so after all recordings were done for the day, we would start, and fortunately, we had time to spare. We would turn down the lights in the room. It was great hearing him play baritone sax. He definitely had his own style.

During some of the music, Gil would just grab a bunch of the iron post he had brought in and just slam them on the ground; man, what an effect! Man, what talent; he really had it down. We recorded a few tunes; we had maybe a couple of multi-track tapes done, not a big investment. I, as well as everyone else, was pretty excited about the project; but then, all of the sudden, we all started to get really busy.

We had various clients to concern ourselves with who were our bread-and-butter, such as "Cagney and Lacey" with composer Mark Snow, Phil Ramone my old boss from my A&R recording days who, after my chasing him and calling while he was at A&M Studio's, eventually came in with "Flashdance," and Dick Berris who had also been very supportive of me for years, and was now doing an NBC special. Pat Williams called me, he was doing shows called "Me Too" and "Mr. Smith" with engineer Don Hahn.

When I said we were busy, we were; there was no stopping. We had a tremendous following, and it seemed like it wouldn't end. Even Gil came in with another great friend from years past, none other than Johnny Fresco, who was doing a show called "Voyager." We continued working and servicing such clients as Norman Granz, Mike Post and Pete Carpenter for Steven Cannell's shows, Hunter being one of them, Pat Finnegan doing "Movie of the Week" with composer Angela Morley, Dave Fisher and his sound-alikes, and Brad Fidel.

We also had Steve Lawerence with his Stage Two production company, with composer Alan Ferguerson, and another dear friend, Tommy Oliver. This place was hopping; we were working day and night. We had no time to finish Gil's project, although we had spent a considerable number of hours on it, no one, including Gil, was upset about it. So it was decided that Gil would take the multi-track tapes home; which was ok with me. We never did finish the project, which was a shame.

I always felt that it had such potential but then again who knew, it was a record project and the labels at this point were not putting out too much product. I look back at those days, as well as everyone's involvement in the project. They put as much time and energy as they could, but we needed to earn a living and, unfortunately, records don't always do it. It's always a gamble for everyone involved, so we had no choice but to move on.

We had an enormous roster of great clients; we were now in need of another room. How could we go about this? We were spending long hours into the evening, smoking a joint or two, bouncing ideas around about another room. We owned the building, and it finally hit us both; we could sell it and lease it back from the new owner. This would allow us to build and equip the second studio; it would also give us some working capital. We would be able to get the additional machinery needed.

Why would the new owners object? This would make us more of a permanent tenant, the trick was finding a buyer. Our accountant, Dennis Rose, said he had a realtor that might be able to help us. I often, if not more than once, ran ideas through Phil. He knew how to put things together; my partner didn't. He was afraid to take chances. He would run things by his wife, and who knew who else, before he would agree to anything.

The realtor that Dennis Rose spoke about did just that, she found us a buyer who could possibly meet our needs, and here entered Peter Ahn, a young Korean gentleman who was looking for an investment. He had an attorney who was his partner, but we would be dealing directly with him at all times. We met several times, and after many negotiations Peter Ahn decided to purchase the building. He would lease the building back to the corporation as agreed, but there was one catch; the monies of the sale would be put in an escrow account at Security Pacific Bank, and it would require two signatures to access it.

The deal we made was that in order for us to use this money it would have to be for new construction, or any new equipment purchases. Only both he and I would be the signatories on the account. I was more than delighted. I welcomed the restrictions because of my partners; too many things kept changing. This way we were assured to use the monies only for what it was targeted for; and not for anything else. I liked it, so during construction we went around town to various vendors and started looking at the equipment we needed for the new room.

We really had to be very frugal, we were on a tight budget. So we figured maybe we could squeeze some money for operating capital without sacrificing the quality of the equipment. There were an awful lot of choices to be had, but again we needed to be careful. We search and talked to just about everyone we knew in town, visited trade shows where we were welcomed with open arms, everyone knew what we wanted so they were competing among themselves.

The time was right because new equipment had just come out, so all half-inch and three-quarter video machines that were being held by some vendors were very affordable. We could've bought used machines, but it would've been like buying a used car; you don't know what to expect and, in our business, we couldn't afford to be labeled. Word would get around town really fast. We had a reputation to maintain after all. We would be dealing with master tapes. What if something went wrong? What would we do? We knew that it was imperative that we buy nothing but the best; there was no way around it. I knew that when we would showcase any equipment it would be nothing but the best. That's what we were known for in town.

One thing that we kept in mind was to ask for a discount, and that it be given to us as in the form of a rebate. This way we would be able to accrue additional working capital. All the equipment dealers were more than happy to oblige. We started wiring and equipping Studio Two to do music mixing, vocal overdubs, and film mixing, although the thought or idea of it still made me very uncomfortable, but we put it out there anyway. The room had complete access to the new machine room.

I had a lot of work ahead of me. I had to book this room, which was not really that attractive, to most of the clients. The console was different and most clients wanted to mix their music in the room it was recorded in, which now presented me with a different problem. One of the first sessions that

I booked was for vocal overdubs, but the ladies being large ladies could not fit in the vocal booth; it was too small. This became an issue. Quite frankly, we had just fucked up, also in the handling of the console. I should've also been on top of it because, after it was delivered and installed, Dennis said, "We have a problem. The patch bay is on the wrong side." This cost us a lot of downtime and money.

We had to fly out the manufacturer's tech from New York City, put him up in a hotel in order to do the changes, and all on our dime. I would have to deal with clients, trying my best to entice them to use this room; but as much as I tried, it wasn't working. We had to move forward; we had no other choice. I felt that the only way to resolve this was a hit show or star engineer. This room had become impossible to book—no one liked the room or console.

I approached an executive, who I knew from MGM, who was a music editor/producer. I had worked with him on two popular TV shows, "Chips" and "Fame," the American television series which was based on the motion picture by the same name, which was based heavily on the actual High School of Music & Performing Arts in New York City. He was now actively working for a small motion picture company; it was very convenient they were down the street from us, so it would cut a lot of traveling time. I asked him to come and look at our room; I needed the room to get some notoriety by someone in the film industry, and he had the notoriety, not to mention a lot of work. He looked at our room and, as always, he was very critical. But that was his style, so after much talk and putting up with so much criticism, I asked him to try the room out.

The first movie we would eventually end up working on was called "The Wild Pair." It was about an uptight FBI agent, Joe Jennings, played by Beau Bridges, who is forced to team up with a reluctant local black officer, Benny Avalon, played by Bubba Smith. It was a great experience for all of us. We did

ADR right in the room. I needed to keep this room busy. I had the staff but no work, so I was trying anything that I possibly could. Again, we were not known as a dubbing studio, I had to get word out, and the best way was to have a show or several shows under our belt.

He gave us some work, not a lot, but enough to keep the room busy. One day he came in after lunch; I knew he had a few under his belt and quietly he asked if it was possible to get some stereo equipment he wanted for his home. Time passed and we kept working together doing various reels for the picture. I came in early one morning and there was no one around, we waited, "What the heck, we thought. Maybe they were at a meeting?" I was concerned because we needed to know what we were going to work on in order to set the room up correctly. I called the office, because now it was midafternoon, and I was wondering what was happening. When the receptionist came on the line, I was told our contact no longer worked for Trans World; that was her answer.

The next day I received a call from their legal department, and they proceeded to drill me. "Did he ever ask for any favors? Was he ever compensated for anything personal?" They were really asking a lot of questions that I had to plainly say no to. It appeared the executive had asked for kickbacks from numerous vendors and the company got wind of it. I told their legal department, "My hands are clean and I would like to retain your business." And we did. I must say the sessions were a lot mellower, but eventually, like most independent companies, once they had a new head of post-production, they found a new home and moved on; which is typical in Hollywood. It's all about relationships; and sometimes you're not it.

A few weeks later, I was sitting in my office going over the schedule, and wondering what I should do with this room. Elisa, my studio manager, buzzed me and said, "You have a call from Lee Decarlo." What a pleasant surprise! I knew Lee from

New York City; he had now become Bill Conti's personal engineer. I quickly picked up the phone and said hello and he, as always, said, "How you doing?" and said hello from Roy Cicala, to which we both started laughing. Roy was our mentor, and well respected by both of us. He wanted to know how my new room was doing and if I would be interested in booking the room for a series 20th Century Fox was doing with Tracy Allman: which featured "The Simpsons." We talked for a very long time and he told me he was busy with Bill Conti, whom I had been trying to lure back to the studio for some time after recording "Rocky III" with us. I knew Bill from my TTG days, where Ami and I had recorded the first Rocky, and since he had done "ROCKY III" with us I wanted Bill to continue using our studio. Steve Hope, his music editor, also wanted Group IV to become his home, because it would've been very convenient for all. I had asked Dennis on many occasions to take Bill Conti out to dinner to help, since he had engineered Rocky III and perhaps it would entice him to start using the studio again. I knew he was busy; there was no question about it. I really wanted Bill back I would've done it, but I was trying not to step on anyone's toes. He claimed he did and said his famous last words, "You know Jew's and Italians. We're tight." But I doubt it because it never came to pass.

I liked Lee Decarlo; he was a New Yorker and a straight shooter. I knew he would like the studio very much. Dennis on the other hand, well he was very insecure, since now Lee was Bill Conti's personal engineer. I went over all the particulars with Lee, he told me what the show needs were and their drawbacks, and the fact that he would probably do two shows, but then he would be stepping aside, and we would have to take over. He again reiterated that he was too busy with Bill Conti. He asked me if I would be willing to meet with the show's producer, Peter Schindler at Fox, to discuss the show and their needs. I told him that I needed the rest of the week to come up with a proposal.

The following week, Lee and I got together. I showed him the room and capabilities; he was pleased and said it would work for the show. I expressed my concerns to him, the fact that sometimes it's not that easy to throw a different engineer into a show once it has been established. Lee said he was fully aware of it, but he had already laid the groundwork. I strongly felt this show could become a problem, but I would give it a try. What the heck, we needed a show in this room. I had faced other challenges; so, before going to Fox to meet with their producer, Peter Schindler, to get a budget approval, I went over very carefully on the cost factor of the show. I did not want to use Dennis on this show; he was too valuable to waste on dubbing a show. He belonged in the live room doing scoring music sessions. I knew we needed to use a different mixer because he had a tendency to get too creative, we couldn't pass overage costs over to the client. This show had a limited budget, which we had agreed on, so whenever it went over it was going to cost us money. We needed sound effects for The Simpsons cartoon, so I hired Travis Powers, which was a mistake in the making. I went down and met with Peter Schindler and showed him my numbers. It was a very simple deal; two 8-hour days to prep, mix and layback the show—any overages would be billed separately. I would allocate Tape Rental Stock and once the show aired, we would re-use it.

The meeting went very well. Peter signed off, and we were given the green light. The show already had a music editor by the name of Eddie Norton, a well accomplished music editor who had great credits, and an impeccable reputation as a music editor on such shows as "Here's Lucy" with Lucille ball (120 episodes), "Tony Randall TV series," "The Bob Newhart show," and "The Andy Griffith show." We had worked together years back on many shows including, "The Mary Tyler Moore Show." He was now renting a place on Cole Place in Hollywood; he had been there for years, and I felt that an editor with his notoriety could do nothing but help us. I asked him if he wanted to move into our building. I figured since we had space to spare that was not developed, we could use it to our advantage, and he would now be more visible, plus we could certainly recommend his services.

Eddie knew just about everyone in town, and we were more than able to do all his transfers and possibly the music scoring for any show he might bring. What more could we ask for? He also had an enormous sound effects library, and Movieolas that we would have at our disposal. It was a good deal for all. I would make it known all around town; it would be in the trades, and we would all benefit from it.

Dennis, Lee DeCarlo and I knew that it would be a matter of time before we would need another engineer to take over the show, as we had discussed earlier, but who that would be was still up in the air.

Time passed and suddenly Lee DeCarlo had to leave for Rome to score another movie with Bill Conti. Unfortunately, Dennis became the mixer, and now the time being wasted was unreal. This show had become a total disaster. Everything was taking too long. They would sit and discuss things like the sounds of a telephone, and everyone had their own opinions. Even the runners chimed in with no one really taking charge, not even their own supervisor.

Whenever it was time to lay-back the show; instead of waiting for approval to lay-back, they would go ahead do the lay-back, and then they would take a dinner break and wait around for the producer to arrive, who would now screen the show from top to bottom; more time wasted. This was a one-hour show, so after watching the show, the producer would come up with changes. We now had fixes; we would do the fixes and redo the lay-back. We were not making any money on the show. It had turned into more additional work. They were exceeding what we'd agreed to. I had to do something; it was costing the company money. I was able to recoup some overages after a few battles with Ed Nasour at 20th Century fox, who didn't want to hear about overages. Dennis kept saying, "Bill them for everything." Which wasn't that easy; we had a deal, and we had to stick to it.

I had hoped initially that Bill Conti would not be busy in order to keep Lee on a little longer, but that became an impossible task. Dennis was not suited for this show; he didn't have the chops for this. I had to do something. Finally, I was able to put one of our engineers, Scott Weber, on the project. A very capable engineer who had been on the show since day one as an assistant, so he knew the show very well. I gave Scott very specific instructions. He was not to get lost in the shuffle, he was representing Group IV Recording, and I made him aware that speed was of the essence. We were providing a service.

One day, it was early morning, we're getting ready to start dubbing and everyone is looking for Eddie Norton. They had called his house and didn't get an answer. He didn't have a cell phone, most people didn't back then. "Well, don't worry." I said, "He'll be here soon." It was getting late, the waiting had gotten the best of everyone. We became very concerned. I called one of my engineers, Dann Thompson, to my office. I said, "Go up to Eddie's house, here's his address, and bang his door down. He probably got smashed last night. call me from there."

Time went by. My phone rings, I pick up and Elisa says Dann is on the line. I picked up the phone and Dann said, "You're not going to believe this. Eddie took a gun and blew his head off. We found him in the bed. There's blood all over the place and the police are here. We're waiting for the coroner."

I apologized to Dann for putting him in that situation. I immediately informed Larina, the producer, that perhaps everyone should go home in Eddie's honor and we would start fresh first thing in the morning. I had lost my place for a moment; this was Hollywood, and that line, "The Show Must Go On," it's true. Within an hour, they had another editor at the studio ready to go. There were lots of incidents that happened during this time—too many to really get into. What a shame; you think you know a person, but you really don't. Eddie never showed any signs at all; he drove a nice car, but I found out later that he was in a lot of debt; he owed everyone in town.

Time went by, and after a few shows and all the bickering back and forth, we lost the show, which, in a way was a blessing. They finally moved to a facility they had built, and our effects editor went with them, which happens a lot in this town. But it was time to move on. I had to regroup because now I had an empty studio. The good news was that it was not a lockout for two days—long days with no room for any profit at all; just money going out the door on labor.

My partner initially didn't want me to mix any sessions because it would get in the way of his notoriety, which he was looking to rack up as many credits as possible. But now that the room was empty, he wanted me to continue mixing. He was freaked out, he just kept saying. "I'll lose my home." It was slow all over town—very slow. We had very few sessions coming in, but he was behaving like it was only affecting him.

I couldn't do both. It was impossible to sell and be behind the console; although there were times when I was requested, and I had no choice. Whenever Don Costa or Norman Granz, two old friends and clients who had supported the studio for years called, I had to be there for them. To me that was good business. He didn't understand that at all.

I remember Don Costa calling me early one morning. He said, "You got a minute?"

I said, "What's up, Don?"

He said, "Listen, the old man (Frank Sinatra) wants to record, and I'm planning on doing the rhythm section first with him, and I'll bring in the horns and strings at a later date. We can mix at your leisure." I was excited. My first reaction was this would work, and it's a great credit for the studio.

Don said, "There's one catch, and that's why I'm calling. I want you to do it. You're more experienced and have the know how to deal with all of this. I don't want to use Dennis. I hope you understand. I don't have time to teach, and he's not mature enough for this type of a session. The old man knows you and you've been around us a few times. Is that ok with you?"

Gospel truth those were his very words. I said, "That won't be a problem, Don. I understand. I really appreciate the work, we need it." And we left it at that what else could I say? He was right.

I went to the traffic book, and we checked studio availability. This was going to be a great session. After our conversation, I thought about it; the schedule would work. I had nothing else pending; I was really excited. I felt very honored that Don thought that much about me, but we went back a ways and had worked on numerous projects. What occurred later on during the course of the day when Dennis came in really told me where I stood.

When I told him about my conversation with Don, I noticed right away that it didn't sit well with him. I sensed a great deal of envy, jealously and resentment. He couldn't even look me in the eye. All he said was that it wasn't fair for the studio.

I asked myself, had I been wrong all these years? What happened to the days when we would just hang out as friends? I remember it like it was yesterday; we were accustomed to just taking off to see movies. It reminded me of one of the funniest things when we decided to go see Star Wars at Grumman's Chinese. He had suggested we smoke a joint, like I've always said, Dennis always had the best grass. We parked, and we just talked and smoked. We purchased our tickets, and as we entered the theater it was very dark. There's a wall in front of us, which we are not aware of; we can't see. So we decide to wait and adjust our eyes. The picture has started, but we're just looking at the wall, and still think it's way too dark. Well, needless to say we missed the opening of the picture before we finally realized we were looking at the wall. Alf Clausen the composer for the Simpsons had said to me that when he heard about it, he couldn't stop laughing.

We used to have fun earlier on, and now things with him were changing really fast. I remembered what Jean Eisenstein had once said, that it was all ego. I was the one who wanted to get out of this business, and he was the one that convinced me to stay. Now this was my payback. What was I supposed to do? Don Costa was a client, and first and foremost a friend who has helped us get started, but it didn't matter. His ego was shattered, and he just walked out of the office and left right after his session, without even saying goodbye.

I went about the business at hand. I knew something was in the air and sooner or later it had to come into play. The next day, Leo Costa called and gave me the setup for the session, and we proceeded as usual. On the day of the session, I said, "Dennis, look. I've been really busy and I could use a little help, just to get off the ground on this session., I have no idea what mood Frank Sinatra will be in. Can you hang a bit till the first take?"

The answer was, "No." He wanted to get home and left. He would not hang, forgetting all the years and days that I hung around till his sessions got underway when no one knew who he was. I supported him and guaranteed that there would be no problems. I just went ahead, and I didn't let it get in the way of business. But now I knew where he was at; but the show must go on, and it did.

The reality of it all was that the Costas did not like him, and that also included Dave Fisher, as he himself would tell me later, when Dennis was out of the picture. Time went by and one day Harry Loweskie, who was head of music at MGM, knocked on my door and asked if we could talk for a while. He asked me if I knew Eric Estrada, I said yes. Harry said, "I'm going to bring his show 'Chips' here."

I said, "Wonderful, Harry. Thanks, we can sure use the business."

He knew we did and since I had worked on a few of his shows, namely "Fame" when I worked at TTG. He asked me if I would do the show. I said I was already booked and told him I would schedule our house engineer. Harry said he had a new composer they wanted to try by the name of Alan Silverstri. He asked if I knew him. I said no, I hadn't heard of him. Harry said, "They are very impressed with him and wanted everything, as always, to go smoothly and I guaranteed they would."

I booked Dennis on the show, and everything did go well. Harry was very happy, there were times when Eric would show up in his CHIPS uniform just to listen to the score. His manager, Helen Acevedo, would come by and have a drink with me in the office; it was all one big happy family right up till the show went off the air. Harry continued to bring us business till his retirement.

Alan continued using the studio, where we did some Chuck Norris movies with him, and smaller stuff such as "Predator." He followed by bringing us the "Back to The Future" trilogy. During the first score, some the orchestra was too big for our studio, so it was decided that they would book Warner Brothers scoring stage, and later we would mix at Group IV. The session, as well as everything else, went according to plan; there would be two more large sessions, which also went very well. Alan eventually bought a Synclavier and kept bringing us more business.

We started working on a few pictures with him (he was now a hot item), one that comes to mind was "Clan of the Cave Bear," mainly because we never got paid. We were stiffed to the tune of $35,000. What made it worse was we never got any support from anyone at all; we were on our own. The final mixes became an issue. I didn't want to release any of the master mixed tapes for fear of bankruptcy rumors, but

Dennis, who worshiped the ground Alan walked on, wanted me to release the tapes. It was, "Oh! Man, its Alan." I had to meet with their head of production, Hal Harrison, who kept assuring me that the company was sound. He claimed that we would be paid, but I still didn't trust them. I felt I was being set up, and I was not convinced. The signs were all there; I knew they weren't going to pay us. But all I kept hearing from my partner, who was very short sighted was, "Alan is cool."

I said, "It's not Alans' bill."

I remember that during his session breaks, he would come in the office and we would continue discussing the movie. It was a never-ending subject. They kept chasing me and my partner would not let it go, he was really into releasing the tapes. I reiterated that it would be a bad move on our part. We needed to make payroll; that was our only calling card. I shouldn't have listened to him.

I tried keeping everyone happy, but we also had a client that I didn't really know. Alan never said anything, he stayed out of it. I thought that maybe we could possibly lose him, so reluctantly I released the tapes to them. In the long run the only one that got paid was Alan Silverstri, and it was a shut case the company filed bankruptcy. They didn't need the multi-tracks, which is what we ended up with. It was one of the dumbest moves I have ever made. I should've trusted my gut feelings, but I just let my guard down and it cost us dearly.

We would never, ever recover from that loss. Everyone went about their daily business like it never ever happened at all. What a costly lesson. No one ever said a word or apologized, at least not to me; but I was the bad guy. We even went to court to no avail. When we walked in, it was nothing but attorneys in their expensive attire. We were small potatoes. Shortly after, everyone in the production office just disappeared, never to show at our studio again. A very costly project for us, Alan Silvestrie; however, he did continue to keep us busy. But the whole incident had put a bad taste in my mouth.

I often wonder what if we had stuck to our guns, but the support was never there. So, I had to make do with the outcome and continued with business at hand. What else could I do? I didn't have the support I needed, I was running a very busy studio making sure all sessions went well, and I was blind to what was really going on behind the scenes. My partner was heading in a different direction. He was looking out for his own interests. Things were about to change, and little did I know that the writing was on the wall. The thing that was becoming more apparent now was that my partner was not interested in doing any TV shows, which was bad for business, and it became a strain on me. Bookings were also affected. As well as the studio, now I had to promote and sell other engineers to clients that were not used to working with him. He had become a completely different person, and the crew was intimated by his actions. It was bad for business.

I had to reassign some of the crew to different sessions. Fortunately more freelance engineers were booking sessions, which I must say was helping. They had their own preferences, which I had to address. I had to deal with them directly, there was no other way to handle these sessions. Fortunately, the crew was more than capable. We had the best in town; they were all very talented guys, very eager to become recording engineers in their own right and were very accommodating to any and all guest engineers. The hours were long, but they were all great recording sessions with an awful lot of notoriety. I was always very instrumental in making sure credit was given to everyone on my staff; because it matters, and they always earned it. As I've always said, "It's the best resume you can have and great for any studio."

In 1987, Alan is set to score "Predator." They wanted a large orchestra, so they had decided to score the picture in Budapest, because they figure it would be cheaper to get a larger orchestra, as well as a larger string section, at a considerably lower rate. Dennis decided all the billing for engineering services should be done through A L B Productions, our production company. Remember I said Dennis. He was the one that came up with the idea and I thought it was a great gesture.

When we first opened, I had made it possible for Group IV Recording to have a 9 Foot Steinway Grand piano. We set it up where the studio would pay me back, since I had personally taken the loan out and paid for it. At that time, we decided the studio would pay it back through the production company, but I only received six payments, so I thought the situation was great; at least now Dennis, for once, would be bringing in some business to A L B Productions. In the past I was the one who brought in all the business. The studio had not paid me any money for the piano in quite some time, and I felt it would be good. I could recoup some money for what I had personally laid out; at the time it seemed like a good move.

I received all the contact information, and I made all the arrangements for other engineers to be on call while Dennis was away. I covered all bases. We checked our bookings and scheduled their mix down sessions based on their return; allowing for jet lag because it was a long trip. We were set. No problem on our end; everything was a go, equipment, anything needed was gone. We had been very meticulous about it; and when it was time to leave, everyone was very happy. There was lots of excitement. As far as everyone was concerned; all bases were covered.

Upon arrival, the first thing that they encountered in Budapest was that customs had no idea what a Synclavier was. Since it was so foreign to them; they wouldn't even let them unpack it. After a few hurdles with customs, as I was later told by my partner, they allowed them to unpack it and they went straight to the studio to start their recording sessions. But they encountered another hurdle with the musicians; they apparently had problems playing Alan's charts. It was too difficult for them, so after a few sessions, he pulled the plug and returned to Burbank to re-score the score at Warner Brothers.

I'm not sure what really happened; there were lots of stories. I'm just going on what I was told by my partner.

The score was finally mixed; time went by fast. We had received a few payments for the engineering services. Little did I know that everything would change. The deal was off. My partner walked in early in the morning, sat down on the couch and started with his nervous cough. He said that he wanted whatever money was left of Alan's project. He told me that I had done real well, whatever that meant, I could've gone crazy but I really had no time for his ungenerous attitude. I knew where all this was going; he had forgotten that when he became a partner in A L B Productions he didn't have to come up with any money. He just took a free ride, but it was on me. I should've known better. I should've gotten together with Hugh Sommers and made him buy in, just like Phil Diamond had suggested.

There was a lot that he had chosen to forget; that when A L B Productions had tax problems, he was not on record. It was my money that was taken and my home that was attached back then. Phil, who was our bookkeeper, had said to leave him out. No need to involve him, so I took the fall. The state of California took the money out of my bank account, and I would spend years trying to recoup it. I never had a chance. it just cost me more in legal fees till I finally decided to drop the whole thing; I couldn't afford it. While we sat in our office, Dennis said with a straight face, "Don't worry, I'm not planning on going independent. I'm just doing these few sessions for Alan." I responded quickly, and said, "I didn't say that you did."

The next day I gave him his check. What a waste of time! I knew that other things would eventually surface, and as time went by, the music business was changing. Alan Silvestrie wasn't doing anything, and now all of the sudden, my partner again starts to freak out, worried about the business. Times were becoming difficult; it started to get even slower.

Things were really changing fast and with the synthesizers being used more and more, and home studios just popping up all over town, we, the larger studios were losing business left and right. Studios all over town were slashing prices and now it became a cutthroat business. There was no doubt about it, composers were using their homes as studios. Chris Stone at the Record Plant was complaining to the city, but it was no use, you couldn't stop them. Home studios, they were here to stay; it was a losing battle.

We entertained selling the place and tried to see if we could find some buyers, which was not easy, especially with the climate in the music business. Everyone was panicked, and rightfully so. I felt that it was time to tighten our belts. We had to cut back on staff and officers' salaries and just pound the sidewalk. The industry was going through another phase. I knew I was talking to myself, which by now was nothing new to me. As Phil Diamond had once said to me, "You're on your own." But I refused to listen to him. I had put too much trust in my partner and that, in the end, was my biggest mistake. It was time to put on our thinking caps and see what we could really do. There was no point in arguing; that would certainly not get us anywhere. Slowly, after careful thought, we let word out through the grapevine that Group IV Recording was up for sale.

There were lots of inquiries from many folks in town, but it was mainly curiosity. All the potential buyers were not interested at all. I for one didn't want to sell the place; I still felt it had lots of potential. We had a great reputation, and I didn't want to give up what I had worked so hard to establish. I felt that we could survive if we tried harder, but I was the only one that was thinking that way. I didn't want to just throw in the towel.

I talked with my friend Chris Stone at the record Plant, and after numerous meetings and providing all the documentation requested by his accountant, they felt it was not for them. We had another meeting with Dennis McCarthy's business agent. It was not something that I relished from our first meeting; I knew that this was just another waste of our time, and it wouldn't amount to anything. He was a good client, but the studio business was not for him. I knew he didn't have the money we were looking for, and why would he want to take such a risk? It was very uncomfortable; he was, after all, our client—it was a no go all around. We could not sell the place. This was not an easy task.

I had arranged a meeting with Mike Post at the Brown Derby. By now he had become a regular at Group IV Recording, so there was very little to explain. He loved the place and had been doing the majority of his recordings with us. Just in passing he told us he had made 60 million dollars that year, and that he was looking for an investment. We had a very nice lunch and went over our proposal and what our expectations for Group IV Recording were, and when we were done Mike said he had to run everything through his brother, who was his financial advisor. At that point there was nothing else to say except wait for an answer; but gut feeling again told me it wasn't happening.

All these meetings with clients were really embarrassing for me; as well as for them. And we were constantly directed to their financial advisers or agents, who didn't want their clients to take such a risk—and you couldn't blame them; that was their job. We just had to get to work. Unfortunately, timing was not on our side. There was so much going on. I speak for myself; at the time I had no idea what the place could really sell for. None of us did, and if we met with our accountants, all we were doing was wasting our time and generating another invoice; and they took no prisoners at all.

We had no choice but to stick it out the. Time was not right for a sale; we couldn't give up without a fight. We had worked too hard and put in way too much of our heart and soul to just throw up our hands. We couldn't panic; we were not in a very good position. Whatever session or sessions came our way we had to take. We were not in a position to refuse anything at all.

We continued meeting with a few other people that we thought might be interested; but no one wanted to buy a recording studio. For the most part, the majority of people we talked to were in disbelief that with so much notoriety, we were looking to sell and felt that it was not in their best interest. There was a buyer who seemed very interested, but in the long run said that he was not suited for it and said that I should stay with it and run it as I had been doing. The terms were not to their liking; everyone had their own stories.

I had a meeting with Norman Granz. As per Eric Miller's suggestion we met in my office. Norman brought in his attorney and the four of us sat in the office and talked for some time. But again, it was not for him; but I gave it a try. Norman was very cordial about the whole thing, but before the meeting gut feeling told me it was not for him.

We struggled for some time and eventually we had to cut back on more staff; a task that I never really cared for, but given the circumstances, what else could we do? Time passed, then on an early Monday morning, Dennis walks in the office sits down, and with his usual nervous cough he proceeds to tell me that he and his wife were at a party over the weekend where they had met a buyer, and he felt that if the deal went as plan his wife Abbe should get a 10% commission. I said, "No way. That's not right.

His answer was, "Well, let's not fight about it. We don't know if it will come to pass." It didn't surprise me, and I found it insulting.

I kept looking at my children's pictures I had by my desk and just kept my composure. I couldn't believe what I was hearing, so I just sat there in the office, thinking why was his wife, Abbe soliciting for a sale without my knowledge. I was definitely upset; I could not deal with this anymore, and the fact that he wanted her to get a 10% commission—what gall.

I knew it wasn't his wife's idea; it was his, as always, wanting to get anything he could.

He was now claiming he didn't want to come to Hollywood anymore; he wanted to take his home off the guarantee we have with the bank. He was completely paranoid. I called Phil Diamond and explained the situation to him. After a lengthy conversation, he said he would help me negotiate a buyout with Dennis, but in return, he would want a fee and an option to buy 40% of the corporation's stock. I said I was ok with it only if he could come up with the cash, and we had ourselves a verbal agreement.

I knew things were going to get ugly; all these years, what a ride. But my partner was not being upfront with me. After all these years he wasn't speaking directly to me. He could've said, "Look, you keep the business, just buy me out." But now there was someone else involved. I had made a big mistake here, and there was no turning back. I had never really voiced my displeasures about anyone. I was really into making the studio succeed, but in the interim, I shot myself in the foot, and it was too late. I had to move forward.

Phil started the negotiations with Dennis, which really became a chore. I held a staff meeting where I informed everyone that, sadly, Dennis Sands was no longer a part of Group IV Recording. He was heading in a different direction, and from here on out, he was not privilege to any information in regards to studio operations. He was not their boss any longer, and should anything whatsoever come up where he was being insulting and condescending, I was to be informed immediately.

The negotiations started, but it was all petty. He demanded $500,000, an AKG C-24, his home guarantee off the bank, and a computer like the one I had in the office. I said absolutely not! Tough shit, but he kept changing the deal. As I've said numerous times; it has always been his modus operandi. He would make a deal, any deal, and then would turn around and want to change it. We had been here many times; it wasn't anything new to me.

I told Phil I wanted to end this as soon as possible. In the interim, he was out soliciting business all over town and calling many engineers like Humberto Gatica, whom he didn't like, but now it suited his purpose. He was also doing tape transfers out of his house for Steve & Eydie Gorme. I wished him the best. We both had families; it was just the way he was handling things; he had forgotten where he had come from. What could I do? I just waited on the side lines.

I could not believe what he was doing. To put it bluntly he was now kissing up to people he had constantly avoided, people who had begged him for work, people who had sought his help. I would find out much later that he did not have as many fans as he and everyone else thought, but it was best just left alone, I knew time would take its course.

I took care of everything at the studio. I found it interesting that now he was doing what he should've been doing all along, soliciting clientele. I should've been a lot harder on him; as I was later told by both our attorney, Hugh Sommers, and my dear friend, Chris Stone. I should've listened, but I was too busy handling the business. Who else was going to do it?

For some time now I had grown tired of all the hassles that came with some of his sessions. I had to keep the peace. Everyone was always looking for me to resolve various disputes, which were always after the fact. Although some had fallen through the cracks; others were questioned vehemently by the clients. It was always regarding charges for additional equipment that clients were not made aware of, so they disputed any and all additional rentals. When confronted he would often put the blame on the client or their contractors, which didn't sit well because they were the ones who brought us the session in the first place.

I remember when my friend, Frankie Capp, brought us "Remo Williams – The Adventure Begins" for music scoring. The composer was none other than Craig Safan, who was one of our regulars at Group IV Recording. He had already done a few seasons of Paramount's series "Cheers" with us, so the match was really good. Everyone was happy and all sessions were going very well. The producer as well as my dear friend Frankie Capp was very pleased.

We had discussed the possibility of some large orchestra recording sessions. Things were going really well, or so it seemed, and as always being that our room could not accommodate that size of orchestra, it was decided that Warner Brothers, as usual, would be our best choice to record at, and we would mix it at Group IV Recording; as we had previously done with other features.

Frankie Capp, at this point made all the needed arrangements. Everything went well, and we mixed that portion of the score at our studio. The fly in the ointment we were faced with towards the very end was one of the dumbest situations I had to face head on. We found out, after the fact, that unauthorized equipment rentals charges were made without the producer's knowledge. She was not aware of it, or how it worked. To put it mildly, she just went crazy. The production company insisted the bills be paid by Group IV Recording.

I sat down and carefully wrote the producer a letter explaining that the session was conducted at Warner Brothers Scoring Stage, and that any and all equipment rented was not authorized by Group IV Recording. Group IV didn't book the session; it should've gone through their contractor and he should've been aware of the rentals at the session. Group IV did not order the equipment and therefore would not pay the bills, which put a bad taste in everyone's mouth. I knew this client would never return.

The following week at one of our Grammy Governors' meetings for the LA Chapter, Frankie Capp approached me and wanted to discuss the subject matter. He had gotten a copy of the letter and said that he hoped there were no hard feelings. I told Frankie there were no hard feelings between us. There shouldn't, be we'd been friends for years; I wasn't going to let such a trivial in-house matter stand in the way of friendship, and neither should he. We shook hands and left it at that.

There were clients who would say, "Look, I like you guys, that's why I come here. But I told him I didn't need that piece of gear." I had one client that said, "Look, Dennis is very hard to work with." And when I would confront him, it was, "They don't appreciate what I'm doing for them." that was always his answer, bills in question would never show up during any sessions. They would always arrive after the fact. I was the one that had to deal with it, and the client or clients were not pleased. I was always the bad guy.

Time has passed, and now Phil Diamond has decided to sell his practice to our accountant, Dennis Rose in order to join me at the studio as my financial adviser and consultant. Phil is very good at business deals, but he is having problems handling my staff; they resent the way he talks to them, and I understand it. He is new to everyone here. I had to reassure my crew that should anything whatsoever happen, it was me who they would answer to, and that Phil was here only as an adviser.

I had another issue that also needed solving immediately. Whenever we went to dinner with clients, the first thing out of Phil's mouth was that he would have to mention the fact that he had negotiated the deal between Dennis and me. It became very embarrassing, and I had to call him on it. We were hanging on by a thin thread, but business was coming in, not as much as we were accustomed to having, but it was working.

Phil wanted me to sign over an assignment of stock: 40% to be exact. I had agreed to this, but I had made it very clear in the very beginning that he had to pay for it first. There was no secret; the company had from day one been undercapitalized; it had no cash at all, and the company needed the money. I said that wouldn't be a prudent move on my part. I would not make that assignment because, God forbid, if something were to happen to him, I would be stuck dealing with his estate, and that would not be a good move for the company or my family.

This assignment of stock that he wanted was not good news. We had lengthy meetings, and after numerous attempts he decided he would leave and sue me for $5,000. We ended up in court; thank God Hugh Sommers, who was now active with the company, handled the case. I often wished it would've worked. We had been through some awful times together, and I must say he was helpful, and I did miss him, but it would've been a bad move. Phil would die a year later of a massive heart attack. I was finally on my own, so I decided that it was time for a complete overhaul.

Neve had been courting me for some time now, assuring me that my business would go up, and that they would cut me a great deal. I decided to put in a new recording console. I knew that if I got rid of the Trident console, which by now was a maintenance nightmare, and put in a Neve V3 Series console with Flying Fader automation, and a new paint job for the place, the news would spread all over town. It certainly couldn't hurt, and it would boost morale within the crew.

I had been working really closely with Steve Livingston, who at the time was Bill Conti's music editor, and very supportive of the studio. He was really good at pre-laying music for Motion Pictures and TV. When we were not working, we would spend hours at night discussing ways to get more business. I liked Steve; we had formed a great friendship. He was very aggressive, good with people and very bright. Under his guidance we were now doing "The Academy Awards," "Nine Seconds to Glory," and lots of transfers for all of Bill Conti's projects.

Things were going really well for the studio. Eric Cowden, one my most trusted engineers, and I were like sponges, nothing got past us. We were busier than ever; clients were impressed with the way the place looked. They kept returning with numerous projects and were always very complimentary about the crew. The studio at this point, was busier than it had ever been. The new console had attracted new business; it made a big difference. The hours were long, but we enjoyed it; we were learning an awful lot.

Lee Decarlo continued doing a lot of his work here with Bill Conti, and I continued to work with Steve. We had the same work ethics when it came to any given project. I was spending at least three days at the studio, working round the clock, trying to make things work. We had an expensive console to pay for, not to mention the rent that we were behind on, so there weren't many choices. I thank God that my health was holding up.

We were now working on a project that Steve had gotten from New Line Cinema called "8 Seconds." We would be doing the temp score for Bill Conti; a temp score is the music that they want to use that comes from various sources. You take that music, edit it and pre-lay it to picture. You are now laying a pattern, and once approved by the company, it goes to the composer. We primarily used the music from Alan Copland, "Beef. It's What's for Dinner," a circa 1993 commercial.

When we first started, I was told by Dawn, the music supervisor, that they only had money for 2 pre-lays. We ended up doing, in total, 11 pre-lays. There were various bull ride scenes that needed to be covered with lots of excitement within the music. We spent hours making sure that each one was more spectacular than the previous one and, with Steve's help and careful guidance, we were very successful at it.

Bill Conti used a big orchestra; I believe it was 90 pieces. The feature was scored at Warner Brothers stage, and Lee DeCarlo brought it back to Group IV Recording, where it was mixed. Eric Cowden, Steve Livingston and I put it in place, it was great having Bill Conti working at Group IV again, and it took Steve Livingston as well as Lee Decarlo to bring him back.

I spent time with Bill; he was the nicest man you would

ever like to work with. He told me that he liked working with engineers that were strong and that stuck to their guns and showed authority in a session. That was why he now had Lee DeCarlo. He said he liked that type of personality, just like Ami Hadani's, whom he had done the first Rocky movie with. He was back, and I was glad we were taking care of him, and he knew it and acknowledge it.

Time went on and Steve Livingston, for some time kept saying he wanted me to meet this Chinese composer he had worked with, Nathan Wang. Finally, he managed to bring him in for some string overdub sessions. He was blown away; he loved the sound, the studio, as well as the crew, and we hit it off right away. Nathan started to book sessions utilizing both studios.

I scored "China Strike Force" starring Asian actors, Aaron Kwok, Lee-Hom Wang, and the Street seasoned rapper Coolio, directed by Stanley Tong. We were kept really busy on this feature. Lots of work, but worth it. We moved on to another Stanley Tong movie starring Jackie Chan, "Rumble in the Bronx." All the live sessions went well and the mix down sessions were all unsupervised. I did all the recording sessions which for me at the time was a great pleasure; especially when both his dad and mom came to the sessions. His dad took care of anything that was needed. Gene never missed a beat. He was always there for anything we needed and enjoyed it.

Nathan had a lot of faith in me as an engineer, and I took great care of all his projects. His sessions were always great, especially the big ones. On many occasions he would order Chinese food; enough to feed everyone in the building. We had formed a great relationship of trust with Nathan. We took care of him whenever he needed anything, day or night. We would mix these movies and send the finished audio tracks via phone lines to their dubbing stages in Australia, as per their producer, Barbie Tung's instructions.

Steve had done us well, and because of his persistence,

now Nathan Wang as well as many others kept bringing us a lot of work, and now all his projects are being done at Group IV Recording. He continued doing many other recording sessions for records as well as commercials.

One day I'm sitting in my office when Steve called me very excited and says, "I just left 'The Formosa,'" which was a watering hole for music editors, where they would hang out and share stories about projects they were working on. If one of them was stuck on a project, they would offer each other reels in order to finish the project as quickly as possible.

Steve says, "You're not going to believe this. I've been hired to do a picture in Puerto Rico with Lalo Schifrin. I have no idea when I'm supposed to leave, but it's soon. He asked if I wanted to go and score the film." He was really excited and said, "Look, it's Lalo Schifrin. You've worked with him before; it would add some comfort to the session. You speak the language and Lalo likes your work, but I declined, there was no way I could leave town." The title for the film was, "Rice, Beans and Ketchup." Steve said, "You're doing all the music mix down, pre-lay and dubbing." He was very excited. He said, "I've talked about you to the guy who is in charge, and he wants to meet with you, as always." He was really excited for the studio. Whenever Steve was able to get any project and bring it to Group IV Recording, it really pleased him; and it showed. He never asked for anything that was not his style.

The very next day, I was scheduled to meet with Juan Codesi, who was chief, cook, and bottle washer, and was very involved in the project. This was his baby. The picture was being financed through The Bank of Puerto Rico. Juan Codesi was well known throughout the film community in Puerto Rico, and he was also a very close friend of Raul Julia, the famous Puerto Rican actor. The pictured required a lot of work. I was able to book Studio B for the dubbing, under the supervision of Mike and Corolla from Tape Effects, a company where Steve had done numerous motion pictures. They were really a great team, really good at their work and fast.

We worked very long hours on this picture, mixing day and night, being very careful making sure all mixes sounded really good, after all the score was composed by my old friend of Mission Impossible notoriety, Lalo Schifrin. I wanted to make sure, as always, that everything fell into place. I hired two dubbing mixers who had worked with Mike and Corolla. I figured it would work out, but unfortunately, on one of the music cues, their music mixer took the congas out of the mix because he felt they sounded like horses running. When we went to the screening at Paramount, Lalo turned around during the screening and looks at me right away; I knew there was a problem.

When the screening was over, Lalo asked me, "What happened to the congas on the main title?"

I said, "I'll take care of it." I later confronted the mixer, and I said to him, "How dare you take the liberty of taking out percussion; obviously you're not familiar with what's going on in the rhythm sections. That's what the composer wrote."

He was very apologetic about it, but I would never hire him again. We spend hours on this film, worked day and night with all the changes. It would take a month before we finally finished. It was quite a run, and working with tape effects was a challenge, but we got through it and put the feature to bed. I had to move on. It is now 1995; our very last picture is booked by Paramount Pictures: "VIRTOUSITY," starring Denzel Washington, with composer Chris Stone.

They had so much work that we booked every room possible in the building. Synthesizers were set in in the Pablo Room, Studio B, The Mag Room, Studio A (both control room and studio), and the hallway. We worked through the July 4 weekend. Dann Thompson and Eric Cowden had set up a Bar-B-Q in the loading dock and that's how we spent the holiday. Our last session booked was with none other than Patrice Rushen, who had always been one of our biggest supporters.

That evening I told her that I would be closing Group IV Recording. It came as a big shock to her; she could not believe what she was hearing. We had been friends for a number of years, and she was always very complimentary of the studio and staff. Frank Clarke, her personal engineer, who was also a great supporter, could not believe it. Patrice and I had served on the Grammy's board of governors and she was a very creative, and a fantastic musician. I knew I would miss her and her support—they didn't come any better.

I remember when we did the Emmy Awards with her; every year, a new composer is chosen. I have no idea how it's handled today, but when I got wind of it; I immediately instructed my crew, which by now was mainly Eric Cowden and Dann Thompson, to go the distance. They, as well as me were and still are great fans. That session went smoothly; the only question on that day came from Frank Clarke, who wanted to know what "Pres" real name was. They had gotten into discussing jazz artists, and I responded, "Lester Young." We had, or rather, I had, recorded numerous jazz artists so we were always questioned about them. Those are some great memories, but with all that was going on in this neighborhood, it was hard to predict anything.

Patrice asked me, "What are you going to do, Angel?"

I said, "At the moment, I have no idea."

I thanked her for all her support through the years; and she wished me the best. Times were tough, studios all had over lost or were losing an awful lot of business. Our profit margin went down real fast. We had held our ground for some time now, but it was a losing situation. I was still spending countless days and hours at the studio, trying my best to accommodate recording sessions that came our way. They were desperate times for me, as I have said numerous times. I had no support whatsoever except for my wife, Cookie, who put up with a lot; but time will tell.

I had hoped the day Alan Silvestri visited me and asked,

"Does the kid know what you have?" Meaning the new console; might have led to more sessions from him; but it didn't and by now that was a closed case. I didn't know what my next move would be, but I had to figure it out quickly. We had been experiencing a big economic change, and for some time now I had been thinking of closing the studio, but it was a very difficult decision for me to make. I had no one I could bounce any ideas off, and by now Steve Livingston was working at Tape Effects on a regular basis; and not by choice—he had to make a living, so we had stopped spending time together.

I knew the writing was on the wall; too many variables and the economics of running a studio were not cost effective. What we were charging earlier for a 2500' quarter-inch reel of audio tape was now replaced by a $7 digital cassette tape, and you were able to record more time on it. Although quarter-inch tape had a pretty good markup; you were limited as far as how much time you could record on one reel. You were now able to record over an hour on a Digital Dat Cassette, more than on your analog 2500' quarter-inch tape, because you were limited to 20 minutes of music. Even with Dolby noise reduction at 15 ips. It was the same for 2-inch tape and this went on and on.

I called our landlord, Peter Ahn, and I setup a meeting. I explained all this to him, and he was very sympathetic, but the bottom line was he needed rent, and we had been in arrears for some time. I knew it was impossible to catch up. I had to drum up more business, which was not there. We needed a miracle; we had lost a great deal of business to Burbank. Hollywood, with all the crack heads and homeless, had, for some time been driving business away. I had even offered limo service to some clients, but it was a never-ending battle. I had already cut my staff down considerably and I was doing a lot of the work myself.

It was a late evening; I hadn't been home for two days. Everyone by now had gone home, and as I sat there in my office, I heard someone screaming. As I looked up at the security monitor, I saw a man stark naked walking up the street, and police cars just going by; they had become accustomed to this mess in Hollywood. I knew right away what I needed to do; there was no question in my mind. I knew what I was going to do, but I would definitely miss this place that I had put much time and energy into. But time had run its course and there was no remedy in sight. I had tried every possible angle. I was both mentally and physically exhausted and it was time to call it a day; knowing full well that I would miss the interaction with all the people that I had been working hand in hand with all my life. I would certainly miss all the composers, contractors, copyists and musicians; after all, they were the ones that kept me here—no question about it, but it was certainly time.

I called home and said to my wife, Cookie, "That's it my love. It's over. I'm closing the studio for good." It was 1995, sad to say, an end to an era in Hollywood, but no one would really care; to everyone else, it would just be another recording studio gone under. I stood in the hall for a few minutes, and I thought about how many people had frequented this place during the good and the bad times. I stood there just reminiscing for some time, the light from the lamp post outside was shining through the coffee room window. I turned the lights off, walked down the hall towards the back, set the alarm, closed the rear door behind me, and I got in my car. I lit a cigarette, put the car in reverse, drove through the gate, made a right turn and went up to Selma Avenue. I made another right turn, headed towards Cahuenga Blvd and made my customary left; and as I headed towards the 101 freeway, I felt a lot of weight drop off my shoulders. I knew it was time to start a new life. Where it would take me, who knew. But I had my family and friends, and for once in my life I felt very much alive.

I didn't have a clue what the reaction would be from everyone. It was time; where it would take me, I had no idea, but I was very fortunate I had a supportive wife, family, and friends. Group IV Recording was officially closed in 1995, and I opened a small facility in Burbank, which I would eventually close. And with the help of my friend Bud Fanton I switched to the motion picture and TV industry. I joined IATSE local 44 as a set-dresser on Sabrina the Teenage Witch, in order to support my family, as well as qualifying for health insurance. There are no guarantees in the music business, and doing record sessions didn't provide what my family needed. There's no health insurance in Rock 'n Roll. Independent music recording engineers can work themselves to death, get all the accolades, awards and gold records, but health Insurance is something that is rarely addressed or provided, leaving you and your family at risk.

The year was 2000, I was at home when my wife Cookie arrived from her appointment at Kaiser with some startling news, she had been diagnosed with lung cancer. I realized that I had made the right move. Thank God we had full medical coverage to provide for any and all of her medical needs. She was my world and the glue of our family, who had always been extremely supportive throughout my career.

March 10, 2004, while on location at Warner Brothers Ranch on the set of "Without A Trace," I received a call from the Hospice Nurse that my wife Cookie had fallen. I was told to come home; it was time. I still remember the words she would often say to me: "Love. They told me I had two years, but I beat them by two," and as fate would have it, her passing came the morning of March 19, 2004. May she rest in Heavenly Peace. Cookie is truly missed she was the glue of our family. who touched so many of our lives. It has been quite a journey.

ACKNOWLEDGMENTS

I would like to express my deepest appreciation to everyone who has genuinely supported me throughout the years, and shared their words of wisdom and extended me a hand when I needed it most. I have nothing but the most respect and love for all of you. I cannot begin to express my thanks to all who are still here with us as well as those who unfortunately have left us, you're still and always will be in my heart as long as I live and breathe.

Eric Cowden, Dann Thompson, Elissa Kline, Lisa Burrows, Rosemary Franchimone, Linda Bricker, Hugh Sommers, Wendy Sommers, Toshi Sommers, Tommy Oliver, Dave Pell, Willie Bo Bo, Richard Wess, Jimmy Bowen, Keely Smith, Allan Ferguerson, Jack Elliott, Bill Hughes, Van Alexander, Lee Hale, Bill Cole, Artie Kane, Cliff Goldsmith, Andrew Miller, Julie Miller, Washington Rucker, Ray Kelly, Bud Fenton, Vince Edwards, Ron Kramer, Johnny Fresco, Bill Cowsill, Perry Botkin, Don Peak, Lalo Schifrin, Jesse Kay, Dave Sanders, Val Valentin, Don Costa, Léo Costa, Gary Fradkin, Guy Costa, Billy Byers, Nick Perido, Ralph Ferraro, Tommy Tedesco, Burl Ives, Gordon Menard, Aron Berg, Gary Fradkin, Mike Julian, Jim Gandolfini, Ed Greene, Eric Miller, Dave Fisher, Stan Broder, Ami Hadani, Tom Hidley, Tommy Dowd, Don Hahn, Roy Cicala, Sweets Edison, Ray Brown Jr., Jose and Ophelia Hernandez, Phil Diamond, Milo Adamo, Fred Heath, Bob Moore, Scott Lookholder, Dave Brand, Mike Melvoin, Nathan Wang, Johnny Mandel, Roy Richardson, Scott Bonelli, Paul Aranoff

Finally, there are no words to express my gratitude and love for my children who I hold very dear to my heart: Bruce

Balestier, our firstborn, contributed to various notable sessions at Group IV Recording as first and second engineer. Denise Nicole Balestier was one of my first receptionists handling all aspects of the of the studio.

Grandchildren: Brittnee Balestier, Kyle Jones; Tiffani Jones; Carmen Arrieta; R J Arrieta. Great Grandson: Cameron Lloyd Balestier

ABOUT ATMOSPHERE PRESS

Founded in 2015, Atmosphere Press was built on the principles of Honesty, Transparency, Professionalism, Kindness, and Making Your Book Awesome. As an ethical and author-friendly hybrid press, we stay true to that founding mission today.

If you're a reader, enter our giveaway for a free book here:

SCAN TO ENTER
BOOK GIVEAWAY

If you're a writer, submit your manuscript for consideration here:

SCAN TO SUBMIT
MANUSCRIPT

And always feel free to visit Atmosphere Press and our authors online at atmospherepress.com. See you there soon!

ABOUT THE AUTHOR

Angel Balestier is a renowned sound recording engineer. He started his career working for Phil Ramone at A&R Recording, at the time one of New York's most popular recording studios.

In 1966 Angel made the move out West and joined former A&R employees Ami Hadani and Tom Hidley at TTG Recording, another popular recording studio that had the first 2"-16-track recorder, which was custom built by Tom Hidley.

Angel is currently working in the motion Picture and TV industry and resides with his new wife Li Shan Ping in West Hills, California

www.ingramcontent.com/pod-product-compliance
Lightning Source LLC
Chambersburg PA
CBHW031954150726
47990CB00005B/1701

* 9 7 9 8 8 9 1 3 2 1 8 7 8 *